ARKANA

Dynamics of the Unconscious

Liz Greene and Howard Sasportas are co-founders of the Centre for Psychological Astrology, which offers courses and training in psychological astrology in London and Zurich.

Liz Greene holds a PhD in psychology and is a qualified Jungian analyst and a member of the Association of Jungian Analysts in London. She is the author of a number of books on astrology, including *Saturn: A New Look at an Old Devil* and *Relating: An Astrological Guide to Living with Others*.

Howard Sasportas has an MA in humanistic psychology and in 1979 was awarded the Gold Medal for the Faculty of Astrological Studies Diploma Exam. He is also a graduate of the Psychosynthesis and Education Trust and of the Centre for Transpersonal Psychology and the author of *The Twelve Houses: An Introduction to the Houses in Astrological Interpretation* and *The Gods of Change: Pain, Crisis and the Transits of Uranus, Neptune and Pluto*.

Liz Greene and Howard Sasportas are also co-authors of *The Development of the Personality* (Arkana 1989). Both work as professional astrologers and lecture extensively in Europe and America.

D1428671

DYNAMICS of the UNCONSCIOUS

Seminars in Psychological Astrology

LIZ GREENE & HOWARD SASPORTAS

ARKANA

ARKANA

Published by the Penguin Group
Penguin Books Ltd, 27 Wrights Lane, London W8 5TZ, England
Viking Penguin, a division of Penguin Books USA Inc.
375 Hudson Street, New York, New York 10014, USA
Penguin Books Australia Ltd, Ringwood, Victoria, Australia
Penguin Books Canada Ltd, 2801 John Street, Markham, Ontario, Canada L3R 1B4
Penguin Books (NZ) Ltd, 182–190 Wairau Road, Auckland 10, New Zealand

Penguin Books Ltd, Registered Offices: Harmondsworth, Middlesex, England

First published in the USA by Samuel Weiser, Inc. 1988
Published by Arkana 1989
3 5 7 9 10 8 6 4 2

Printed in England by Clays Ltd, St Ives plc

CONTENTS

INTRODUCTION

Among all the proliferating maps and models of the human psyche
which are now available to us, there is one which dominates the
rest in depth, subtlety and importance: the duality of conscious
and unconscious. This view of the psyche is called "dynamic"
because of the tension, movement and exchange implicit in such a
duality; and its official history begins in 1775 with the Viennese
physician Franz Anton Mesmer's discovery of what he called the
"universal fluid." Of course human duality is a much older concept
than Mesmer's, although known in antiquity under other, more
mythic names. But in the two centuries following Mesmer have
come the giants of modern depth psychology—Charcot, Janet,
Freud, Klein, Adler, Jung—and a growing body of knowledge and
skill has become available to those who wish to, or must, traverse
the strange byways of the unconscious.

Viewed through the flattening lens of behavioural observation,
the astrological chart is static: no more than a listing of fixed character traits, or a map of potentials many of which, for inexplicable
reasons, the individual cannot seem to fulfil. But viewed through
the three-dimensional lens of a conscious-unconscious duality, an
entire play emerges—full of the twists and turns of a surprising
plot, teeming with tragic and comic Shakespearean characters,
ornamented with ingeniously changing stage sets and costumes,
punctuated by perfectly timed cues, the opening and closing of the
curtain, and intervals where everyone goes out for a cup of tea.
The astrological chart is indeed a map of potentials and character
traits, and reveals a rich portrait of a complete individual personality. But, like the characters in a play, the planets do not all come out
at once; the parts may be played differently according to interpretation and the skill of the actors; the timing may be mucked up by a
stage manager too preoccupied with what the audience will think.
And some characters are unable to come out at all, locked back-
stage by the imperious will of the ego or the dictates of parental

voices, numbed or bound, unable to speak save through moods, dreams, illnesses, and compulsions, and capable only of covert sabotage to communicate the fact that they are still, despite one's best efforts at becoming what one is not, alive and waiting to be heard. There are dimensions of every horoscope which are conscious—qualities and values with which the person identifies—and dimensions which are unconscious, partly through childhood repression, partly through social expectations and pressures, partly through sometimes misguided moral conviction, and partly through sheer ignorance of just who these characters really are.

It would seem that the unconscious, whatever it is, possesses its own wisdom and intentions, and its own plan for the proper direction of the play; and this hidden intelligence may or may not coincide with what we believe we are and what we think we want from life. It also seems to possess a drive toward completeness—that is, all the characters seem to want to have their time onstage and their appropriate interaction, so that the innate integrity of the play can be achieved. An unconscious drive or compulsion, be it interpreted as creative or destructive by the ego, is capable of thwarting the achievement of our conscious aims, often creating the feeling that "something" is "working against" us. For example, a man born with Moon conjunct Venus in Cancer in the 1st house might be acutely aware of his need to be involved with another person in an intimate and enduring relationship. He may see himself as a warm, loving person, eager to accommodate the needs of others and frightened of loneliness and solitude. But if this man also has Uranus in Gemini in the 12th house, he will also possess a powerful unconscious drive toward independence and absolute autonomy—a part of him, a character in his play, who furiously resists commitment because it means losing both space and alternatives. The more the man identifies with his Moon-Venus conjunction, and the more he attempts to repress the Uranian voice, the more he guarantees that Uranus will defeat him; for in any contest between conscious and unconscious, it is the unconscious which wins—not because it is inimical, but because it is wiser. The man may be habitually attracted to those partners who are not free to be with him, or who, for whatever reason, cannot reciprocate his advances. Or he may offer love generously with the right hand and unconsciously sabotage it with the left, gradually driving a partner into that separation which he himself covertly desires, although he seems to be a blameless victim of someone else's coldness. And he may, sooner or later, turn up on the astrologer's doorstep asking why, despite his longing for closeness and commitment, fate seems to keep dealing him the wrong cards.

We can, to some degree, educate and manage, or at the very least, provide constructive outlets for, what we are conscious of in ourselves. But if we are unconscious of something, it will sooner or later find a way to dominate and control us. Those characters whom we believe have been removed from the cast list have a way of bursting onstage and disrupting our lives at the worst possible moments. Even more mysterious, what we are unconscious of has a way of not only of erupting from within, but of materialising from without–so we cyclically and inevitably meet those circumstances and people in life who are, in a strange and inexplicable way, distillations of our own unknown selves. Ian Fleming once wrote that once is chance, twice is coincidence, and three times is enemy action. If an individual has a repeating pattern of conscious goals which are blocked or frustrated, then it is wise to look to the unconscious for the reason why.

The astrological chart is a superb map for navigating this mysterious terrain, for it is not only a portrait of those parts of us which we are willing to acknowledge or are happy for the world to see. It tells the whole story, revealing all the characters, and exposing aspects of our natures we may try to conceal not only from others, but from ourselves as well. People, without meaning to, lie; but the birth chart does not. Nor do astrological symbols moralise as we are wont to do, by pronouncing judgement on what is higher or lower, good or bad within us. Every astrological symbol contains a spectrum of positive and negative qualities, and a teleology or inherent meaning. Like a prism, the view depends upon where the source of light is located. Interpreted and understood with some insight into the complex workings of the unconscious, the chart can help put us in touch with all the characters, and offer a possibility of developing a different and more compassionate attitude toward those aspects of ourselves which we may have misinterpreted, feared, or simply never met.

A great body of psychoanalytic literature has accrued in the years since Mesmer's discovery of the "universal fluid," and all of it addresses the question of just what is "down" there. Freud, in his great pioneering work, revealed that whatever else might be down there, all of the more primitive "anti-social" drives—aggressive and sexual—were to be found in abundance, locked in the darkness where we think they cannot harm us. As children, our survival depends upon winning the love of a caretaker. Certain impulses are not very acceptable to the environment; and therefore, for the sake of winning love and securing our survival, we deny or repress them. In other words, they are relegated to the unconscious. But it is also possible that our caretakers might not wholly approve of other, more positive traits we exhibit—innate spontaneity, curiosity, even creativity. Envy has always been a profound human problem, and never more destructive than when a parent envies the creative potentials of his or her child. Once we sense that the environment does not validate such qualities in us, these too will be banished to the unconscious.

It would seem, therefore, that the unconscious is not merely a repository for evil, but a limbo in which dwell many of our best potentials. Even the "bad" impulses are, like every character in the play, essential to the plot—and sometimes they are "bad" not because of any intrinsic evil, but because of the treatment they receive at the hands of a more self-righteous ego. Jung, building upon the edifice that Freud had laid, found that, alongside the more primitive dimensions of human nature rendered outcast by civilised society, the unconscious contains an equally potent urge to transform itself, to become integrated into life, to be transmuted from alchemical dross into alchemical gold. In other words, in each individual lies a motivation toward individuality. This word "individuality" is used a great deal these days, often to describe behaviour which runs against the collective norm. But we are using it here to describe a loyalty to one's own unique nature—an embrace of all the characters in the play. Individuality costs, as T. S. Eliot once wrote, nothing less than everything, and many are understandably not prepared to pay the price of the internal freedom they claim they want. It is much easier to identify with one group against another, or to adopt an "ism" as a surrogate parent. But the astrologer who can respond to the unconscious needs as well as the conscious strivings of the client is in a unique position to offer help to the person who, somewhere along the line, has lost the understanding that it is really all right to be oneself.

The four seminars which comprise this book deal with different aspects of unconscious dynamics—what might be hidden in us, and how we might work with what we discover. Inevitably, because it is what seems unacceptable to conscious eyes that remains hidden in the unconscious, much of the material in these seminars concerns the darker dimensions of the personality. But there is a great paradox in this apparent darkness, because an honest confrontation with it can often yield a profound inner experience of some wiser Other at work within—and such an experience, because it is direct and one's own, is worth more, in the testing-ground of ordinary life, than the most exquisite edifice of philosophical tenets and teachings. When searching for the numinous, one can be very surprised about where God may be found. This is put most beautifully by William Blake:

> God appears, and God is Light
> To those poor souls who dwell in Night;
> But does a Human Form display
> To those who dwell in Realms of Day.

Liz Greene
Howard Sasportas
London, August 1987

PART 1

THE ASTROLOGY AND PSYCHOLOGY OF AGGRESSION

At origin, aggressiveness is almost synonymous with activity.

D.W. Winnicott

THE TWO FACES OF AGGRESSION

One of my first astrology teachers, Isabel Hickey in Boston, compared the energy of Mars to a burning fire. If employed in the right way and in the right places, it is wonderful and helpful, giving light, heat, warmth and power; but if used in the wrong places or in the wrong way, it means disaster. It's the difference between fire burning the floor boards in the middle of your sitting room floor, as opposed to where it is better contained—in the fireplace. The fire itself isn't good or evil. Likewise, Mars in itself is not good or evil, *but* it may become evil if it is misused.

Isabel was bringing out an important point: that all natural energies are neutral. Piero Ferrucci, in his book *What We May Be*,[1] makes a similar point. The natural energies of the wind, the sun, of an atom or a river—these can either bring about disasters or prevent them. A river provides water, power and irrigation and yet it can flood and drown. Natural energies can either kill *or* they can sustain. If you take an atom and split it, the power unleashed could be used to blow us all up or could be directed productively and creatively.

Similarly, aggressive energy is a natural energy. Mars is the most obvious astrological significator for aggression and everyone is born with Mars in his or her chart. We are all born with Mars somewhere—we are all born with innate aggressive urges. In today's seminar, I want to explore both the positive and negative faces of aggression as they relate to the astrological chart.

Aggression is an inborn component of our biological make-up, just as the sexual drive is an essential part of our human instinctive equipment. Sex serves a very obvious positive purpose to humanity: we wouldn't be here without it. So why shouldn't aggression, which is also a natural part of our biological inheritance, likewise

---

[1]Piero Ferrucci, *What We May Be* (Wellingborough, England: The Thorsons Publishing Group, 1982), p. 86.

serve an important evolutionary purpose? It's interesting that Mars has traditionally been associated with both sex and aggression. Astrologers have always known this, but it was only more recently that science showed the close connection between sex and aggression. Do you remember the famous Kinsey Report that was published in the 1950's? Kinsey found a close physiological correlation between a person in an angry state and a person in a state of sexual arousal. In fact, his study found fourteen physiological changes which were common to both sexual arousal and aggression, and only four which were different.[2] It's fairly common that a fight with your lover can end up in an orgasm; or you can be in the middle of sex and it turns into a fight. American psychologist Clara Thompson sums up aggression nicely:

> Aggression is not necessarily destructive at all. It springs from an innate tendency to grow and master life which seems to be characteristic of all living matter. Only when this life force is obstructed in its development do ingredients of anger, rage or hate become connected with it.[3]

While we should try to reduce negative expressions of aggressive energy, it seems ridiculous and even unwise to try to rid ourselves entirely of a part of our nature which is innate and wants to master life. It's true, we see the uglier forms of aggression all around us in everyday life — people are murdered, tortured and subjected to various forms of psychological cruelty. Mars can really get out of hand. Or aggression is turned inward, attacking the self and the body, and becomes a contributing factor in heart disease, skin problems, stomach ailments, or sexual dysfunctions. While we detest these negative forms of aggression, we must bear in mind and honour the other face of aggression — our healthy, natural root aggression — which is laudable, and which we must not disown if we are to survive.

So what does Mars give us? It endows us with the will to unfold more of what we are or can become. When this desire to

---

[2] Alfred Kinsey et al., *Sexual Behavior in the Human Female* (Philadelphia: Saunders, 1953), p. 704.
[3] Clara Thompson, *Interpersonal Psychoanalysis* (New York: Basic Books, 1964), p. 179.

grow, progress, and move forward is blocked (either by other parts of our own nature or by other people) it turns angry. We want to move forward and we are frustrated if this is prevented. Anger can be understood as blocked movement.

Healthy aggression is also the positive impulse to comprehend and master the external world; it is a force deep down inside which provides the impetus to learn new skills. Because of aggression in you, you can choose to attend a class, read a book, or say "no" or "yes." If you didn't have Mars in your chart you wouldn't be able to learn a new language, master a complicated recipe or solve a tricky mathematical problem. Even our language indicates this: we *attack* a problem, we *master* a difficulty, we *grapple* with an issue, and we are awarded a *master's* degree. You could have a very inspired artistic imagination, but if you didn't have Mars in your chart you wouldn't be able to do anything about ordering the canvases or get around to picking up the paintbrushes. Mars gets you going—or as Dane Rudhyar once expressed it, "Mars is the force which propels the seed to germinate."[4] Wherever Mars is operating in your chart is where this form of healthy aggression can exert itself.

Early in my study of astrology, I remember watching the transits of Mars in my chart. Sometimes Mars would bring up wild behaviour, frustration, anger, bad "spots," or headaches. But at other times, Mars transits would correspond with those days when I felt the most alive and vital, a kind of "juicy" ready-for-anything feeling. I remember sitting on the subway or MTA in Boston the day Mars was passing over my MC, and having a kind of peak experience—everything was amplified, vivid, toned up and vibrant. I felt like Mars incarnate. My body was rippling with pleasurable rushes of sensation—what in bioenergetics is called "streaming." I was pulsing; I was excited about being and doing, ready for what could happen next.

So you see, the whole principle of Mars is highly paradoxical. Mars impels us to act in ways which affirm our identity and purpose and yet may give rise to ugly forms of behaviour. This contrasting expression of aggressive energy is shown quite clearly in

---

[4]Dane Rudhyar, *The Astrology of Personality* (Katwijk van Zee, Netherlands: Sevire/Wassenaar, 1963), p. 254.

mythology when you analyse how differently the god Mars was portrayed in Greek and Roman myth.

THE GREEK ARES

In Greek mythology, the god of war is called Ares. The Greeks thought very little of the mighty Ares. In fact, they hated him. Looked upon with a mixture of pity, terror and scorn, his role was very limited—he was simply the god of war and not much else. Equated with blind courage, bloody rage and carnage, he was considered a bully and very brutish. And yet for all his blood-thirsty violence, he was generally depicted as losing most of the battles he fought, and shown limping away defeated and humiliated from the battlefield. Poor Ares, he is constantly tripping over his own feet and getting in his own way. Had the Greeks spoken Yiddish, they would have called Ares a *klutz*. I'm not exactly sure how to define klutz: it means a kind of clumsy twit who knocks things over a lot, or spills soup down his shirt . . . a little like John Cleese's portrayal of Basil Fawlty in the popular BBC television series *Fawlty Towers*.

Zeus, who is the most honoured of the gods in Greece, hated Ares. In the *Iliad*, Homer quotes Zeus berating the god of war:

> Of all the gods who live on Olympus, thou art the most odious to me; for thou enjoyest nothing but strife, war and battles. Thou has the obstinate and unmanageable disposition of thy Mother Hera, whom I can scarcely control with my words.[5]

Zeus is the equivalent to the Roman Jupiter, and this quote can be understood as the Jupiterian principle speaking to the Mars principle. Normally we think of Jupiter and Mars as being quite compatible: Jupiter rules Sagittarius and Mars rules Aries, and both belong to the fire trinity. And yet, on one level Jupiter scorns and looks down upon the rash, impulsive nature of Ares/Mars. Jupiter

---

[5]From the *Iliad* in the *New Larousse Encyclopedia of Mythology* (London: Hamlyn, 1982), p. 124.

stands for the principle of logos or mind—he is a bringer-of-light. Jupiter sees a bigger picture and then acts according to this expanded vision. Self-centred Mars, however, rushes in and acts on impulse, rather than from a place of broadened awareness. Jupiter has a vision or ideal about how one should be or act and then tries to behave according to that vision. Ares acts spontaneously and without much forethought.

In Greek mythology, Ares had two squires who accompanied him in battle or wherever he went. One was Deimos (Fear) and the other Phobos (Fright). The moons of Mars have been given these names. Ares was also accompanied by Eris (Strife) and Enyo (the destroyer of cities), and a group called the Keres, who enjoyed drinking the black blood of the dying—a very jolly band of cohorts indeed! These are the Greek associations with the Mars principle.

It is worth comparing Ares with his sister Athene. They are caught up in a kind of archetypal sibling rivalry. Athene is more a Libran principle and represents cool intelligence. She is probably Zeus' favourite child. According to legend, she is born fully grown from the head of Zeus. Hera (Zeus' wife) is so enraged by the fact that Zeus had borne a child without her, that she contrives to give birth to Ares without recourse to Zeus. So Ares is born of revenge and retaliation. He is the product of the rage stored up in Hera's body. Ares or Mars can be equated to the rage we store up in our bodies and which bursts forth uncontrollably from time to time. I've noticed this dynamic in the charts of people born with Mars in hard aspect to the Moon. The body instinctively reacts to a threat and mobilizes itself into an angry and defencive response. An angry reaction just blurts itself out, and springs out of them before they can even catch it. In another story, Ares is captured by two mortals and trapped in a bottle for thirteen months. In a similar fashion, we sometimes bottle up our Martian energy. You can imagine how Ares felt when he was finally released.

Ares and Athene fought a lot. In one tale the passionate and violent Ares blazes forth into battle with her. Meanwhile, Athene is reclining leisurely reading a book or doing her nails. While Ares hurtles towards her, she simply glances at him, coolly picks up a large stone and hits him with it. Then she finishes her manicure. The dumbfounded Ares crashes to the ground, filling an expanse of seven acres and screaming like ten thousand men—flat on his back, arms and legs flailing in the air, and bawling like a big baby. All in all, the kind of anger the Greeks associated with Ares is very "uncool" and you hardly ever score your point with such unruly rage. It is the kind of anger you feel when you are just so mad you could almost vibrate totally out of existence—you shout and scream and explode, making a fool of yourself and invariably you lose.

Besides these misadventures, Ares didn't fare very well in love. You're probably familiar with the story of Ares and Aphrodite. Aphrodite, the most beautiful of all the goddesses, was married to Hephaestos, the most ugly of the gods. Whenever he had the chance, Ares would proposition and try to seduce Aphrodite. The sun god, Helios, who sees all, warned Hephaestos that Ares and Aphrodite were thinking of getting up to something. So Hephaestos devised a plan to trap them. First he made this net of fine, nearly invisible metal thread which he hung over Aphrodite's couch. Then he pretended he was leaving town on a business trip. No sooner was Hephaestos supposedly out of the door, when Ares came over to take advantage of the opportunity. Ares joins Aphrodite on her couch and they are just beginning to get down to the "Big It" when Hephaestos lowers the net and the two of them are literally caught in the act. Meanwhile, Hephaestos has invited all the other gods to come and watch. They all have a good laugh at Ares' expense. Once again, the mighty god of war ends up looking very silly. The Greek Ares is really easily outwitted. He just isn't very subtle. It is so easy to see what he is up to, that anyone with a bit of subtlety can figure out a way to get around him.

The Greek root of the name Ares stems from a word which means "to be carried away" or "to destroy." And this is what Ares is about—he gets carried away and is very destructive. Roberto Assagioli, the founder of Psychosynthesis, once defined aggression in a similar way to this side of Ares' nature:

> Aggression is a blind impulse to self-affirmation, to the expression of all elements of one's being, without any discrimination of choice, without any concern for consequences, without any consideration for others.[6]

---

[6]Roberto Assagioli, *Per L'Armonia Della Vita—La Psicosintesi* (Florence: Instituto di Psicosintesi, 1966), p. 152; quoted from Piero Ferrucci, *What We May Be*, p. 86.

Because Mars can express itself in Ares fashion, let's look more closely at this definition. Assagioli says aggression is a "blind impulse to self-affirmation." So even though it is blind, there is an element of affirming yourself through aggression. He says that it is "the expression of all elements of one's being": in other words, it is non-differentiated and uncontrolled, involving the body, feelings and mind simultaneously. It is "without discrimination or choice"—there is no sense of the right time or place or degree. It can happen at a restaurant or while seeing a play, whether or not the time or setting is appropriate. It happens "without any concern for consequences": there is no sense of proportion and no concern for the damage it might do to others when this anger comes up. It is "without any consideration for others": it can be unleashed on friends or loved ones or people who at other times have been very kind, loyal and helpful.

THE ROMAN MARS

Now let's compare the nature of the Greek Ares with the Roman equivalent, Mars. Interestingly, the cult of Mars in Roman mythology was more important than that of Jupiter. In other words, Mars commanded a higher position in the Roman pantheon than that of Jupiter, quite the reverse of the Ares/Zeus relationship in Greek mythology. Mars was also believed to be the father of Romulus and Remus, the founders of Rome. In this sense, he represents one of the principles upon which the whole Republic was founded.

The Romans thought there was something more positive about Mars than just the expression of blind, explosive, indiscriminate rage. In their myth, Mars' role as the god of war was secondary to other functions. Not just the god of war, he was also worshipped as a god of agriculture and often pictured quite contented with his cows in the field. He was also the god of spring and the god of vegetation. To the Romans, Mars was associated with fertility, with growth and growing, and with becoming.

The origin of the name Mars is disputed, but it may come from the root *mas*, which means "the generative force," or from the root *mar*, which means "to shine." He was also called Mars Gradivus from the word *grandiri*, which means "to become big" and "to grow." Compare these connotations with the Greek root for Ares, which simply meant "to be carried away" or "to destroy."

Fear and Fright were the Greek squires to Ares, but the Roman Mars had two very different escorts: Honos (honour) and Virtus (virtue). The Roman Mars was accompanied by honour and virtue. It is honourable to stand your ground, to value who you are, to grow into that which you are meant to become. It is virtuous to realise your destiny. The Romans believed it was their destiny and true purpose to rule the world and bring their law to bear on it. For them, asserting themselves was honourable and virtuous: it meant being true to what they believed was their destiny. Negatively, of course, the Roman Mars could be used to validate chopping an enemy's head off if he stood in the way of their purpose. But more positively, for the Romans, the Mars principle meant standing up for who you are and having the courage to unfold and honour your true nature.

So you see the different understanding of the nature of Mars, the paradoxical quality of this planet. It can mean destructive, blind aggression (the Greek Ares) or it can be a way of affirming your individual existence and following the truth of your own innate being (the Roman Mars). Sometimes the two factors can be mixed. For example, the adolescent boy who is rebelling against his parents may do it in a very obnoxious and distasteful way. He is manifesting a positive drive towards independence and autonomy and yet he may do it in a ruthless or destructive fashion.

MARS IN THE HOUSES: GREEK OR ROMAN?

Let's apply this concept more directly to the astrological chart. Look at the house position of your Mars. Is it operating like the Greek Ares or the Roman Mars in that domain of life—or alternating between the two, or some sort of combination of them both? Take the 2nd house: if Mars is placed in the 2nd and he were acting like the Greek Ares, what would he be like there?

Audience: Armed robbery with violence . . . trampling others to get what he wants.

Howard: Yes, the 2nd house is commonly labelled the house of money, possessions, values and resources. So the Greek Ares might go after money and possessions with an avarice or quite impulsively. Picture him at the first day of the Harrods' sale: "I want what I want when I want it!"

Audience: Could this also be the case if Aries were on the cusp of the 2nd house?

Howard: Yes, Aries on the cusp of the 2nd, or contained within that house, could behave that way as well. But what if a 2nd house Mars or the sign of Aries there were acting like the Roman Mars instead of the Greek Ares? How might you interpret this if someone came to you for a reading with such a placement? What is a positive understanding of Mars in this house?

Audience: A lot of energy and enthusiasm for going out and making money, a business drive.

Howard: Right. But what would making money do for the Roman Mars?

Audience: It would give him confidence.

Howard: Yes, you are getting warmer. People with Mars in the 2nd could build up their confidence by earning money. But even more basic than this, earning money could be the way they affirm their individual existence, the way they gain a sense of their power, and even the way they fulfil their purpose and true nature. You see, if you have the Moon in the 2nd, then money might mean security and comfort to you, because wherever the Moon is in the chart is where you are seeking "mother." But when Mars is in a house, we can gain a sense of our power, purpose and identity through the affairs of that sphere. It's different than just gaining comfort or security. Dane Rudhyar believes that the planets in the houses are like celestial instructions which tell us the best way we should meet that area of life in order to unfold who we are. So, if Mars is in the 2nd, being who you are means asserting yourself in that domain, not just hanging around and waiting for something to happen.

Audience: Could Mars in the 2nd give a little bit of both—a little bit of the Greek Ares and the Roman Mars?

Howard: Yes. You might see earning money and acquiring possessions as a way of affirming your identity, and even though this is true to your nature and purpose, you could still go about it in a Greek Ares way.

Audience: What does it mean in the 3rd?

Howard: You should be telling me, but I'll help. If the Roman Mars were operating in the 3rd, then gaining knowledge and being able to communicate would be a way of affirming your identity and fulfiling your innate nature. However, the Greek Ares in the 3rd might use his tongue to lash out and destroy, or use knowledge for the purpose of gaining power over others or fighting with others. Now, *you* tell me about the Greek Ares or the Roman Mars in another house, let's say the 6th. The 6th house describes something about the way we work and the manner in which we approach a job or the daily rituals of life. How would the Greek Ares approach a job to be done? How would the Roman Mars approach his work?

Audience: The Greek Ares would rush into things and do the housework in a big hurry and probably knock things over and explode if the vacuum cleaner didn't work.

Howard: Yes, right. And what would the Greek Ares be like at the office?

Audience: A bully with co-workers.

Howard: Yes, I'm sure he would be a big hit at work. What would he be like with pets—the 6th house has to do with pets?

Audience: He might have a German Shephard or a Doberman.

Howard: The 6th house has to do with our relationship to our bodies and health. How would the Greek Ares treat his body?

Audience: He would be very hard on it, jogging till he dropped dead.

Howard: Yes. Now what if we are considering the Roman Mars in the 6th? What might work mean to people using Mars in the 6th in the Roman way?

Audience: They would take pleasure in doing their work because it would be a way of expressing their identity.

Howard: Yes, remember the root of the Latin name Mars (*mar*) means "to shine." They would want to shine in their work. For the Roman Mars, work is primarily seen as a way of defining or expressing the self. The Roman Mars would take pride in the details of his work, because he would feel that every little thing he did was a reflection of his identity and a way of affirming his nature and existence. Honour and virtue accompany the Roman Mars. He would get a sense of pride and honour from his work. He would also see the body as his vehicle for self-expression so he wouldn't want to abuse it like his Greek counterpart.

Audience: Maybe he would be a health food fanatic or a body-builder.

Audience: Couldn't the Roman Mars in the 6th be very hard on himself?

Howard: Yes. He might be very meticulous because he sees all he does as a reflection of himself. So if an "i" wasn't dotted or a "t" crossed, it would bother him immensely, as if it reflected something askew in his nature. The 6th house has a lot to do with trying to get the outer forms of your life as close a representation of what you are inside as possible. Doing that would give the Roman Mars in the 6th a sense of power and purpose.

Audience: How about the Greek Ares in the 7th? He might rush impulsively into partnerships and frighten the other person away. Or he might want to murder a partner. It would be very stormy, with lots of battles.

Howard: What about the Roman Mars in the 7th?

Audience: The Roman Mars could affirm his sense of identity through relationship. Working or relating closely to another person could give him a greater sense of his identity or purpose in life.

Howard: Yes, we could say a lot about this placement. Those with Mars in the 7th might also try to import another person to be big and strong for them, to make decisions for them, to tell them what to do. But I think you are definitely getting the idea of the Greek Ares or the Roman Mars in the houses. You can work out the others on your own or in groups later.

HEALTHY AGGRESSION

I've put a list on the board of some of the manifestations of healthy aggression, our natural root aggression. Let's go through these. Remember, wherever Mars is operating in the chart is where these factors can be seen.

HEALTHY AGGRESSION SERVES AS PROTECTION AGAINST PREDATORY ATTACK

In the Vedas, there's a story about a snake who is terrifying a village. The snake is biting and killing people. A sage comes to town preaching his philosophy of love and spiritual understanding. The snake happens to hear one of the sage's lectures and is so moved that it decides to put the sage's teaching into practice. The snake has a kind of breakthrough, and overnight, vows not to bite people or be nasty anymore. For the next month or so, the transformed snake has the manners of a saint. Meanwhile, the sage has moved on to another village (he's doing a tour). Eventually, the sage comes back to the snake's town. He meets the snake again, but the once mighty snake is now a mess—downtrodden, beaten, kicked around and taken advantage of. The snake comes up to the sage and says, "I want my money back. I tried your philosophy of love and spiritual understanding and see where it got me. I'm supposed to be enlightened now, but look at me, I'm half dead." The sage succinctly replies, "I never told you not to hiss."

Some of us might think that being spiritual, enlightened or mystical means not getting angry: "I meditate twice a day, therefore I shouldn't be an angry person." But remember, you can still hiss. It's healthy to hiss if something is encroaching on your boundaries or standing in the way of your unfolding or moving forward. Otherwise you might end up like the battered snake.

Audience: I'm confused about the difference between anger and healthy aggression.

Howard: Remember that quote by Clara Thompson. She writes that aggression "springs from an innate tendency to master life." Healthy aggression is the desire to grow into what you can become. But when this life force is blocked, it turns into anger, rage or hate. Inevitably, your ability to move forward will be blocked from time to time. And when that happens, you will get angry or depressed (depression is anger's close cousin). It's impossible to live and not get angry. We all need ways of expressing anger directly and cleanly. If you hold back your legitimate anger at being blocked for too long, then it accumulates, festers and explodes. There is a kind of storage tank in any house containing Mars. The storage tank can only hold so much before it blows. The longer you hold the anger back, the more potentially destructive it becomes.

Bear in mind also, that some charts indicate people with shorter fuses than others. If you have Mars conjunct Pluto in Leo, then when you want something (Mars), you are apt to feel it very deeply and intensely (Pluto). Mars conjunct Pluto in Leo will have a much stronger and burning desire nature than, let's say, someone with Mars in Gemini trine Neptune in Libra. Mars conjunct Pluto will be more easily frustrated. People with this placement might hold back their drives or anger because they are afraid of the intensity of what they feel. If they deny the energy of that aspect too long, it could turn in on itself and attack the body in the form of an illness. Or it could give rise to depression: all their energy is being used in holding back the Mars-Pluto conjunction and this leaves them short of energy with which to live their lives. Or sooner or later the storage tank will explode—perhaps some minor obstacle will trigger a huge eruption. What comes out is not just the annoyance at the immediate block or frustration, but all the unexpressed anger from the earlier blocks which have never been properly dealt with. I'll be talking more about the consequences of suppressing anger or aggression later, but anyone with such an aspect would be wise to learn how to catch that anger and deal with it sooner rather than later. They need to learn to recognise the signs that they are angry and clear it up as they go along.

It's fair to say that some charts are innately more prone to anger than others. Some people have a lower boiling point. Someone with six planets in Pisces and the Moon in Taurus is going to be a lot more placid than someone with four planets in Aries and two in Scorpio square Pluto in Leo. And I might add that those same configurations which connote a hot-headed temper and brimming intensity also suggest the kind of person who can get a great deal done in life. Those charts which are potentially the most aggressive or the most angry indicate people who are 150 watt light bulbs as opposed to 60 watt light bulbs. They have a higher wattage because they have something to do or accomplish which requires a greater degree of personality or "oomph!" than someone who has something else to do in life which doesn't need that degree of energy to make it happen.

HEALTHY AGGRESSION IS A POSITIVE IMPULSE TO
COMPREHEND AND MASTER THE EXTERNAL WORLD.
IT IS A FORCE DEEP INSIDE US WHICH PROVIDES
THE IMPETUS TO LEARN NEW SKILLS.

I spoke about this earlier. Because of aggression in you, you can choose to take a class, go on a diet, learn to drive, etc. We need Mars to demonstrate to the world that we can fend for ourselves. If your healthy aggression to master or comprehend the world isn't being channeled and used, then it builds up and you walk around spoiling for a fight. In this respect, it is not unlike the sexual drive, which also accumulates if you are not giving expression to it.

In his book *Human Aggression*, Dr. Anthony Storr relates an experiment done by Lorenz on a kind of fish called a cichlid.[7] These fish are born particularly aggressive. They need hostile neighbours to vent their aggression on. If they don't have neighbours who frustrate them or with whom they can be hostile, they don't stop being aggressive. Instead they look around for something else to be aggressive toward. The researchers took a family of cichlid fish and isolated them from a tank filled with hostile neighbours. So there was a tank of just Mr. & Mrs. Cichlid and their two little babies. What happened was that when Mr. Cichlid didn't have any more neighbours to fight with, he turned his aggression on his wife and children. And if his wife and children were taken away, then the male cichlid would start attacking the tank itself. Funnily enough, the name given to attacking the substrata of the tank was "digging."

It's a bit like a man who goes out to dig in the garden, rather than expressing his anger toward his wife. Mars in the 4th might be a bit like this Mr. Cichlid. Normally after a long day out in the world or at your job, when you come home (4th house) you just want to relax and take it easy. You know, put your feet up, have a beer, watch television, meditate, or do whatever it is you do to unwind. But for people with Mars in the 4th, when they come home from work they meet their Mars in the home situation. If there are people out there in the world toward whom they haven't expressed their aggression, they will bring it home with them and vent it in the domestic sphere.

We all need to find positive, constructive outlets for our aggressive instincts, and for our need to master something in life or learn various skills. The house containing Mars will point to the sphere of life where this can most naturally be realised. Aspects to Mars also suggest the kinds of outlets a person might choose through which to affirm the need to master life. For instance, if

---

[7]Anthony Storr, *Human Aggression* (Harmondsworth, England: Penguin Books, 1982), p. 56.

Mars is in aspect to Neptune, then you can find an outlet for your desire to assert and master life through Neptunian things: playing music, doing something artistic, dancing, healing, etc. Mars in aspect to Mercury could express the drive of Mars through developing the mental prowess, communication skills, or study. Later, we'll talk more about the connotations of the different planets aspecting Mars.

HEALTHY AGGRESSION IS THE BASIS FOR ACHIEVING INDEPENDENCE AND BREAKING AWAY FROM THOSE WHO WOULD DOMINATE OR OVER-PROTECT US[8]

You are probably familiar with the story of Hansel and Gretel, but have you thought what it might mean psychologically? In the fairy tale, the mother sends Hansel and Gretel away because she cannot provide for them—she cannot adequately meet all their needs. Then they find the witch with the house of gingerbread. The witch is the one who has everything; she is the one with all the goodies. And yet she is the one who threatens most to destroy them. The mother who forces them to fend for themselves in the world is not the witch. The one who can provide everything they need is the witch—the really dangerous one. What does this mean? It means that if someone is always looking after you, providing you with everything, making decisions for you and telling you what to do all the time, then they keep you small. You never become a person in your own right. You need Mars to combat this and assert your own individuality.

Myths and fairy tales from various cultures describe different versions of the figure of the witch who eats children. As infants, we have all been at the mercy of a female figure who has absolute power over us. At times she may take on a very destructive and negative face. For instance, in *Little Red Riding Hood*, the kind and loving grandmother transforms into the devouring wolf. The person who is the most over-solicitous toward you is the one who can

---

[8]Many of the psychological ideas in this section are abstracted from Storr, *Human Aggression*, Chapter 5.

most threaten your development, and therefore the one who could eat you up.

In the beginning mother is the whole world to us—we are totally identified with her. We are originally one with her body, and even after birth, we are dependent on her for our survival. (Human beings are born very unfinished and must stay under the jurisdiction of the mother and family for a longer time compared to other mammals—some of us never break away at all.) The mother (or father) who for too long possesses and over-protects the child, keeps the child from developing into a separate person. The parent takes care of the child so much that the child never develops an individual strength or identity of its own.

But it is not just parents who are at fault here. There is an inner urge to remain under the protection of mother or father and never grow up. We, ourselves, may not want to be born out of the womb of parentage or cut the psychological umbilical cord. Some part of our own nature may want someone else to be big and strong for us. The Moon, Venus, and Neptune suggest parts of us which want to lose ourselves in another person, to reflect, to blend, to merge and be swallowed up by somebody else or something greater than ourselves. We need Mars to counter-effect these more Moon-like, Venusian and Neptunian urges. If Mars is in a difficult aspect to the Moon, Venus or Neptune, then we have a dilemma between these contrasting urges—between parts which want to be independent and parts that don't.

We'll be discussing the various aspects to Mars later, but think about it for a minute. The Moon is the urge to stay regressed and fused within mother's womb-like structure. The Sun and Mars, however, are more assertive principles: they represent the urge to distinguish the self as a separate independent being in one's own right. Mars is a kind of henchman to the Sun. The Sun principle defines us as a discrete, conscious entity and then Mars does things to affirm the point—to punctuate and demonstrate one's individuality. With Mars in conflict with the Moon, you have a dilemma between those parts of you which want to grow, push forward and be independent (Mars), and those parts of you which want to stay fused and merged with another or what is already known (the Moon). There is a tension between the need to explore and grow versus the need for safety and security.

Aggression between mother and child is inevitable. We are born potential victims. We are born helpless—unless someone is there to look after us we will die. We need mother to survive. Whether we are happy or sad, fed or hungry, comfortable or uncomfortable, depends on the mother or mother-substitute. Being at the mercy of the mother for our well-being and survival makes us both love and hate her. We love her when she reads our needs right and meets them; we hate her when she messes up, which invariably she will do from time to time.

Aggression between mother and child does not just arise, however, because our needs are frustrated at feeding time or because she doesn't hold us when we want. Aggression is not just the result of frustration—it also serves a positive purpose. Aggression in childhood development serves as a positive drive toward separation and independence. Mars makes us want to break free of mother's dominance so we can develop in our own right. The child psychologist Winnicott once wrote that "at origin, aggressiveness is almost synonymous with activity."[9] Learning to crawl and then walk is a kind of germinal assertion and the first big step we take in separating from mother. For a while we still run back to her at any sign of trouble. But if we are to become adults in our own right, we do this by gradually overcoming our dependency on the caretaker. This is achieved by demonstrating to the world that we can sufficiently master the environment to satisfy our own needs. Mars is the keynote to this; Mars is the force inside us which compels us to master things.

Obviously, it is not just mothers we have to separate and distinguish ourselves from, but fathers as well. In myths and fairy tales we see giant authoritarian father figures who frighten children into submission. In order to retrieve his or her individuality, a child has to do battle with the father as well. Siegfried has to break Wotan's sword in order to become the hero. In the film *Return of the Jedi*, Luke Skywalker has to destroy the dark side of the father to become the hero. There is a typical theme in hero myths: the hero is the child who at first is the most deprived member of the family, or the most ridiculed. In a sense, we all start out in life as the most helpless person in the family and thereby the most potentially

---

9D.W. Winnicott, *Collected Papers* (London: Tavistock, 1958), p. 204.

aggressive, because as the smallest and most helpless ones, we are the ones who most need to prove the self. The hero must slay monsters (the parents), take up dangerous tasks, and venture from home on a quest in order to prove his or her individual strength and worth. Hard aspects between the Sun and Mars (also the Sun and Uranus) may describe battling with the father in order to become a person in one's own right.

Audience: So the hero or the child needs someone to kick against, someone to fight against, in order to learn to assert his or her individuality?

Howard: Yes, but if the parents are too harsh or too authoritarian then the child could grow up thinking that self-assertion is a crime. It is as if the child is being told: "You are not capable of doing things yourself, you need us to tell you what to do." So the child grows up feeling helpless and hopeless, and underneath that, very hostile toward those who have kept him or her down.

Audience: But parents can be too liberal as well.

Howard: Right. If the parents are too liberal and grant everything the child wishes, then the child may grow up believing that he or she is omnipotent. The child thinks every whim must be satisfied. This is not realistic. Or the child grows up thinking that self-assertion must be wrong. If the parents weren't assertive, then there is no model for assertion. Or the child may grow up highly insecure thinking, "How can these wimpy people look after me?" Children of overly liberal parents have nothing to rebel against, no authority to come up against and, therefore, no justification for their innate urges toward independence. Such children are never able to test out their own strength. If no one opposes the child, then the child's aggression may be turned inward against the self. This could result in children who bite their nails, pull out their hair or become depressed and unapproachable.

The psychologist Alfred Adler, whose name is linked to Freud and Jung, was born with Sun conjunct Mars in Aquarius both square Pluto in Taurus. Freud believed that the sexual component of our nature had the most influence on our development. Adler, however, argued that the aggressive component of the personality was a more important factor in determining how we lived our lives. He theorised that as children we feel inferior and inadequate because of our smallness and ineptness, and this leaves us with a desire to prove our worth and with a strong pressure to achieve. Adler felt that we are motivated by something he called the "striving for superiority," or the "will to power."[10] As he saw it, the fundamental law of life is that of overcoming. His Sun-Mars conjunction fell in Aquarius and he balanced this emphasis on proving one's worth by saying that what satisfied us most was to achieve and assert for the sake of others—for the sake of society or the collective. So he believed that we are primarily motivated by a need to assert and prove the self, but that this is done best by contributing to society or to the development of humanity. A person has to learn to direct his or her urge to be superior into useful activity or work for the group. This fits well with the Sun conjunct Mars in Aquarius, doesn't it?

There is an intimate relationship between closeness, dependency and anger. Someone once told me about a study which showed that the person who is most likely to murder you is the person to whom you are closest; and the place where this is most likely to happen is the bedroom. A close, intimate relationship may act as a catalyst to bring up unfinished business around our earliest and most intimate relationship—the early bonding relationship with mother. Our very survival depended on her—if she didn't meet our needs, then we might not make it, we might die. So, if we were hungry and she didn't come, it would have felt that our lives were threatened and this would naturally produce a great rage and frustration. Because it is so uncomfortable to feel that rage and anger, we suppress it or cut off from it. As children, we fear our destructive rage because it could lead us to destroying the very person whom we need for our survival. This is what I mean by "unfinished business" from childhood. We all have some degree of unexpressed rage at mother or father from those times they blocked us or didn't give us what we wanted. This deep early rage is sometimes called primal rage or id anger.

---

[10]Alfred Adler, *Superiority and Social Interest* (New York: Norton, 1979; and London: Routledge & Kegan Paul, 1965).

A present relationship may trigger or excavate earlier forgotten id anger. We are frustrated by a partner, and up comes the screaming infant in us. Of course, as a baby we didn't have the muscular co-ordination or development to actually act on that rage very much. A little baby can't hop on a bus and go downtown to the gun shop, or connive to slip weed killer into mother's afternoon tea. But, if the "screaming infant" part of us is re-activated when we are adults, then we do have the power to act out those destructive feelings. It's not surprising, then, that the person who is most likely to murder you is the person to whom you are closest.

Closeness can lead to aggression for another reason: being close to others brings up the danger of being smothered by them. Also, the more in love with someone you are, the more dependent you are on that person for your happiness and well-being. As with mother, you are under that person's power—whether you are happy or sad, loved or unloved depends on him or her. The Mars part of you will resent someone having such power over you, and you may want to break out and destroy that closeness in order to take back your power. So you fight for your space—you carry on and bitch and make power struggles, a bit like an animal defending its territory. If Mars is in hard aspect to Venus, for instance, there could be such love/hate relationships. On the one hand we have Mars—the will to assert the individuality. On the other hand, we have Venus—the urge for union. One part of the person wants to blend and merge with the partner (to die as "I" and be reborn "We") and another part is frightened of losing the separate-self sense and individual space. Mars square Venus is found in the chart of the Marquis de Sade, whose name gives us the word *sadism*. For him love (Venus) was directly associated with aggression and violence (Mars). He formed unions based on Mars. But, even if we don't have Mars in hard aspect to Venus, we are all prone to relationships which are a mixture of love and hate, because closeness and dependency often trigger anger. The Marquis de Sade played it out literally, but love and hate are inextricably bound in all of us. We just deal with it differently. The best relationships are the ones which can contain (or make room for) not just the love we feel, but also the hate and anger which will also come up toward the partner. In the same way, a mother needs to be able to make room for the anger and rage which the child will inevitably feel from time to time against her.

The conflict between the urge to be close and unite with another, versus the urge to be autonomous and free applies not just to one-to-one relationships, but also to how we relate to groups and organisations as well. This can be better understood if you think about a placement like Mars in the 11th house. Mars in the 11th represents a dilemma which is inherent in all of us to some degree. By nature we are social beings (11th house of friends and groups) and yet we all strongly feel the urge to assert our identity as a separate person (Mars). We form groups on the basis of common interests, ideals and aims, but it is precisely in those groups where there is a close identification among members that the most bitter disputes arise. As soon as we grow too closely identified, our autonomy is threatened and the urge to split, differentiate, and disrupt naturally makes itself felt. The challenge for Mars in the 11th is to somehow be in the group—work for the group and promote the cause of the group—and yet not lose one's own personal identity, *nor* let it get out of hand in the name of affirming one's separate existence.

HEALTHY AGGRESSION ENDOWS US WITH THE WILL TO UNFOLD MORE OF WHO WE ARE, AND GROW INTO WHAT WE ARE MEANT TO BECOME

The philosopher Paul Tillich once wrote: "Man's being is not only given to him but also demanded of him. He is responsible for it. . . . Man is asked to make of himself what he is supposed to become, to fulfil his destiny."[11]

Healthy aggression as symbolised by Mars is the way we make of ourselves what we are supposed to become. If we deny Mars because we are afraid of its more negative side, then we are in danger of losing touch with that bit of us that wants to grow into what we are. And when the desire to grow is blocked (either by

---

[11]Paul Tillich, *The Courage to Be* (New Haven, CT: Yale University Press, 1952), p. 52.

other people, external events, or other parts of our own selves) then that energy turns into anger.

We must look at this a little more deeply. Mars is the will of the heroic ego: the ability to assert what you want—to go out and get what you want. However, as Jung pointed out, "there are higher things than the ego's will and to these we must bow." This suggests that our individual or personal will can either act in accordance with a higher will, or fight against it.

Now I have to get philosophical. I believe that we all have a deeper core Self (with a capital "S") which guides, unfolds, regulates and oversees our development. Just as an apple seed "knows" that it is meant to grow into an apple and not a pear, there is a part of us which knows what we are meant to become. This is what is meant by individuation, self-realisation, and self-fulfilment—growing into what we are meant to become.

One of the problems with Mars is that our personal ego-will may or may not be aligned with what our deeper core Self wants. Mars makes choices to assert who we are, but the big question is whether or not the choices Mars makes are in tune with the innate identity and purpose we are meant to unfold.

St. Augustine once wrote that "there is one inside me who is more myself than my self."[12] Eastern philosophy uses the term *dharma* to denote the intrinsic identity present from birth that one has to fulfil. It is the dharma of a fly to buzz, a lion to roar, and fire to burn. Mars is the active agent of the psyche which gives us the energy and will to fulfil our dharma: to act it out, express it and achieve it. But there is the possibility that Mars may try to run the show himself: that our individual or personal ego may want something which is out of synch, or out of line, with what the deeper Self wants for us. In other words, instead of buzzing, the fly may try to roar. Or instead of roaring, the lion may just buzz.

This conflict between what you want for yourself versus what the deeper Self has in mind for you will show up most clearly with Mars in hard aspect to the outer planets. We are going to talk more about aspects to Mars later, but I'll say a little now on this point. The power of the outer planets supersedes the power of Mars: they

---

12St. Augustine cited in Irvin Yalom, *Existential Psychotherapy* (New York: Basic Books, 1980), p. 280.

suggest there are forces at work which, in the end, want to bring Mars into line, to bend Mars to what they require, to force Mars to his knees. Let's examine more closely what I mean by this.

Take Mars-Pluto aspects. Mars may have to bow to the will of Pluto. We could talk for weeks about the implications of Pluto, but Pluto, in one sense, can be understood as the inexorable force which propels history. Pluto is a force which compels us to die as a child and be reborn an adolescent, to die as an adolescent to emerge as an adult. Pluto represents the inexorable wending on of life: the death of one phase and the birth of a new one, whether we want it or not. You may not want to go through puberty, but there is no way you can stop it happening short of killing yourself.

Mars may keenly want a particular job or relationship, but Pluto may have something else in mind for you. Pluto might say: "I think *not* getting that job or relationship offers more of what you need, is more in line with making you develop certain traits you are meant to develop, which you wouldn't develop if you just readily landed what you think you want." Mars cries: "What is going on — I've done my assertiveness training, I've done the *est* course, and I'm still not getting what I want!" Your ego can choose something it wants, but if it is not in line with the will of the deeper Self, you just won't get it. Or if you do, you discover it is not all you thought it would be.

Do you recognise this issue? I've seen it operating most clearly in charts with Mars in hard aspect to Pluto, and also in charts with Mars in aspect to Neptune as well. If Neptune is in aspect to Mars, it may ask that we sacrifice or give up something to do with Mars — that our personal will adjust to something higher. Mars may react by pushing harder and harder to get what it wants — pulling out all the stops, being ruthless to win at any odds. Mars can try to turn its will into law. Have you ever tried to fight against cosmic law? Isabel Hickey used to say that you could try to break a cosmic law, but you would break your neck in the process. Have you ever tried to jump out of a 10th floor window because you thought you could defy gravity? Good luck.

The same dilemma may be there for someone with Mars trine or sextile Pluto or Neptune, but these people seem to more quickly or more easily align their personal will with the will of the outer planets. In the case of the trine or sextile, the deeper will of the Self

(Neptune or Pluto) is saying, "You can't have a relationship at present, because you need to grow in other ways." While the personal will (Mars) is thinking, "Gee, it would feel good to go solo for a while and see what that is like." In others words, with more flowing aspects between Mars and the outer planets, there is more likelihood that you will naturally flow in the direction your core Self wants you to go. To paraphrase the Jungian analyst James Hillman, your feeling flows into your fate and you are reconciled with events.[13] Jung himself once wrote that "free will is the ability to do gladly that which I must do."

Mars is needed to fulfil our dharma, to realise our intrinsic identity. Mars may try to buck against what we are meant to become, but in the end we need Mars to grow into what we are meant to become. Mars enables us to make choices to grow into the self which we really are. The Danish philosopher Kierkegaard believed that the most common form of despair is not being who you are. He added that an even deeper form of despair is trying to be someone other than who you are.[14] If you deny or repress Mars altogether, because you are afraid of what might be bullying, self-centred or demanding in you, then you could also throw away your healthy aggression in the process. If you do that, you lose the ability to stand up for the self, to defend yourself, to choose what you want. And you lose the ability to make choices to support your own life and destiny.

Audience: I'm interested in the relationship between aggression and depression. Aggression turned inward can cause depression?

Howard: Yes, it is generally believed that if you persistently hold back your natural aggression or repress your anger, the energy turns inward crystallising into a hard knot deep inside you. When aggression turns in on itself, it can become self-destructive and contribute to illness and depression. All your energy is tied up

---

[13]James Hillman, in his chapter on "Betrayal" from *Loose Ends: Primary Papers in Archetypal Psychology* (Dallas: Spring Publications, 1975), pp. 63–81.
[14]Carl Rogers quoting Kierkegaard cited in Rowan, *The Reality Game* (London: Routledge & Kegan Paul, 1983), p. 62.

holding things back and you have nothing left with which to meet life.

An unexpressed Mars may be one of the keys to depression. The Gestalt therapist Fritz Perls worked with depressed people. He used to ask them: "Who are you depressed at?" He believed that under depression, lurked anger: anger at someone blocking you or anger at yourself for blocking you.[15] If a depressed person can get in touch with that anger, he or she will gain the energy needed to shift the depression and meet life more positively. Various psychologists talk about the three H's: hopelessness, helplessness and hostility. The depressive formula is that if you are feeling hopeless and helpless, then underneath you are normally hostile as well.[16] If you could just get a grip on the energy locked up in the often unconscious hostility and turn it into positive action, then you have the possibility of coming out of your depression.

Audience: What if Mars is very weak in the chart?

Howard: First of all, don't fall into the trap of thinking that if your Mars is in Pisces or the 12th house, it is weaker than a Mars in Aries or the 1st. Mars in Pisces can be just as strong and powerful as Mars in Aries, but in a different way. And Mars in the 12th, as the Gauquelin studies have shown, is no pussycat. But if by weak, you mean not strongly aspected or configured with the rest of the chart, then I would encourage you to strengthen your ability to assert and stand up for yourself. You might enroll in an assertivenes training course. Or you could try practising a meditation to develop willpower. For instance, meditating on or visualising a diamond, which is a symbol of invincibility, can strengthen the will. Or you can meditate on the nature of fire, or the Sun itself.

But to be honest with you, I might also argue with myself about this. If Mars isn't aspected very strongly, then would the person ever get around to even signing up for the assertiveness training course, or would there be enough willpower to undertake doing a meditation on the will? I don't know. Ultimately, I'm reluc-

---

[15]For more on Fritz Perls' gestalt approach see *The Gestalt Approach and Eye Witness to Therapy* (Palo Alto: Bantam Books, 1978).

[16]Anthony Storr, *The Art of Psychotherapy* (London: Heinemann, 1979), pp. 93–112.

tant to deny that we have some element or margin of choice in our lives, no matter what our charts look like. I would encourage clients to work with the chart and try to balance out what is missing. Perhaps the impetus to actually join an assertiveness training group might only come with something like Jupiter transiting Mars. You may have to wait for certain transits or progressions to help you get a grip on your Mars. Or maybe you can find a friend whose Sun, Jupiter, or Uranus (or whatever) conjuncts or aspects your Mars and that person is the one who drags you along to a seminar on assertiveness. So I am not prepared to say you shouldn't bother to develop your Mars, no matter how "weak" it looks by sign or aspect. You shouldn't just grin and bear it when people trample over you. Nor should you just resign yourself to a directionless life.

Audience: Doesn't the house position give you some clue about where to begin to contact your Martian energy?

Howard: Yes, that's a good point. If you are feeling stuck, or down, and unable to get things moving, then you might try looking to the house where Mars is placed in your chart (or the house with Aries on the cusp) as a way of getting things started again. So, if you are sitting home depressed and you have Aries on the cusp of the 6th, then maybe by doing some housecleaning (6th house activity), you can get yourself going again and re-vitalize your energy. Or, if Aries is on the cusp of the 3rd and you are feeling depressed, then try engaging in a 3rd house activity to get moving again. Go visit a neighbour, ring a friend on the phone, take a short weekend break or write a letter—any of those 3rd house things. Or, if Mars is in the 2nd and you are feeling depressed, perhaps you should go shopping and that might enliven you. It's quite common to try to *buy* oneself out of a depression.

However, you might equally argue that if you are down, depressed or stuck, then maybe you need to go into that depression—explore it, be it, and don't fight it. Some people need to more fully go into their pain and be with it for some time before they can shift it. But if you have spent eons of time down "in the pit" and there is really nothing more to gain from being down there, then look to your Mars house (or the house with Aries in it) to get going again.

THE PHYSIOLOGY OF
AGGRESSION AND ANGER[17]

I thought it would be interesting to say something about the actual physiological changes associated with anger or aggression—how Mars manifests in the body. There exists in all of us a physiological mechanism which, when stimulated, gives rise to feelings of anger and to physical changes which prepare our bodies for fighting. This mechanism is stereotyped and easily set off. In other words, on a physiological level, one angry person is very much like another angry person. However, what triggers anger for one person may not trigger it for another. We also differ in the ways we try to adapt or control the anger response. In other words, everyone has Mars in the chart—we all get angry; but the sign, house and aspects to Mars specify the situation that might trigger the anger and how we adapt and control it. By the way, let me clarify something. There are other significators for anger and aggression in the chart besides Mars—both Uranus and Pluto can be highly explosive. I'll talk more about those later—right now I'm focusing on Mars.

Stay with me as I discuss the specific physiological changes associated with anger. We have what is known as the "flight or fight response" in the body. First there is an increase in the pulse rate and blood pressure. Do that now—imagine your pulse rate and your blood pressure starting to increase. Then there is an increase in the peripheral circulation of the blood—the blood is sent out to the external organs. Feel that now; feel the blood flowing out into your arms and hands, into your extremities. You are ready to hit and kick things. The next thing is a rise in blood glucose, a rise in blood sugar. You experience a sugar rush, as if you've just

---

[17]My reference for the physiology of anger is Anthony Storr, *Human Aggression*, pp. 28–9.

come off a two week fast by eating a hot fudge sundae. Whoosh! Your rate of breathing is accelerated. Your muscles tensely contract. Energy comes to your legs and arms and then hardens and contracts, as if there is steel there. Another thing that happens in animals and sometimes in humans is that your hair stands on edge. And there is often a baring of the teeth and the emission of involuntary noises. These are some of the changes that take place when your body is mobilised into an angry response or when your body is prepared for action. This is the physiology of an aroused Mars. Feel how the room has filled up with energy as I led you through these changes. I think I'll hide under the table now!

Let's take this a little further. Anger originates in a part of the brain which is called the hypothalamus, a small area at the base of the brain. The hypothalamus co-ordinates emotional responses such as anger. When it is stimulated, all the signs of rage can be seen in your body. Now, the hypothalamus is actually under the inhibitory control of another part of the brain known as the cerebral cortex. When the cerebral cortex interprets something as threatening, it will release its inhibitory control and notify the hypothalamus to get going. In this sense, it is the cerebral cortex which decides whether to allow the hypothalamus to do its job or not.

Human beings have a very highly developed cerebral cortex. Because of our evolved cortex, humans can examine a situation and imagine various ways of handling it. So the cerebral cortex might think about a situation and decide on some other way of dealing with it rather than getting angry. Animals with a less evolved cerebral cortex just don't have that much choice about releasing aggression. Humans have more choice. We can examine a situation and consider whether it's worth it to get angry, or whether other people would approve, or if it's at all appropriate to respond that way. The cerebral cortex enables us to be reasonable, just, and fair, but often at the expense of a more basic, instinctive and primitive response.

I tend to associate the function of the cerebral cortex with the element of air. Examine the symbols associated with air signs and you'll observe that they are represented by inanimate or human symbolism: the twins, the balance and the water-bearer. Earth, water, and fire signs are symbolised by things like bulls, goats, crabs and rams—instinctive and primitive animals. Air signs are more cerebral and self-reflective than the other signs. Because of this, air signs may have the most difficulty with anger. They think more about what is going on and try to understand things, rather than just coming from an instinctive response. In some ways this is a mixed blessing. People with a lot of air may be sitting on a great deal of anger and rage which they have attempted to rationalise out of existence, or which they have not expressed because they felt it wasn't the refined or fair thing to do. Saturn might inhibit anger out of a sense of propriety, or because it believes society does not approve; but people with an emphasis in air inhibit anger because they *think* they should be more understanding. Oddly enough, they often become the most angry when they feel other people aren't being fair. This is a projection: they, themselves, are worried about being unfair.

Audience: Don't water signs try to be understanding?

Howard: Yes, but it is in a different way than air signs. Water signs are quite sophisticated about feelings. At the end of the day they are capable of accepting all kinds of emotions, including anger, as part of the great round of life, and therefore are more understanding of it in other people. Air signs are more likely to see anger as coarse and unrefined, and desperately try to find some different frame of reference other than the feelings upon which to base their responses. Water accepts another person's anger; but air tries to understand it and respond fairly. Fire will innately fight back or leave the scene; earth will stubbornly defend itself against another or just wait for the other person to calm down so he or she can get on with other things.

Once anger is aroused, it will take a long time to subside. What's more, in modern civilisation we don't have the chance to express the aggressive response that fully—we are not out there hunting prey for dinner or fighting off wild beasts. We are instinctively equipped for the jungle and yet we don't live that kind of life anymore.

People are aroused into anger when their boundaries are invaded, and this happens frequently in the city (the modern jungle). Our primitive anger is aroused over and over again, and yet because of the restrictions of contemporary society, most of us never have a chance to fully release these feelings. For instance, you are driving in traffic and someone nearly bangs into your car and starts blowing the horn aggressively at you. You normally don't get out of the car and punch the other driver—even though your own aggressive response has been alerted. So the adrenalin and aggressive energy stay stored in your system. Then you arrive home and go to the supermarket to buy something for dinner. You have to wait a long time in the queue and somebody cuts in front of you. Up comes more aggressive responses which probably don't get fully expressed. The end result is that we are all walking around with the physiology of an angry body—running on a kind of emergency energy and viewing life from this angry, aggressive stance.

If my body is in an angry state, then I will interpret life through my angry body. Someone may do something nice for me and yet because there is this angry energy festering inside me, I'll probably interpret this behaviour as threatening and harmful. It's like a cat who has just been hurt by someone. Another person comes along a little later to stroke "the nice pussy" and the cat still responds to the second person as if he or she is trying to hurt it, even when that isn't the case.

Even sleep is not deep enough to neutralise the amount of aggression stored up in us. Some studies have shown that the rest gained in meditation is deeper than that of deep sleep, so meditation could help to dissolve some of these deeper levels of stress and anger. Exercising and playing sports also serve to release some of this chronic anger, as well as digging in the garden or pounding a mattress from time to time. Later in the day, we will talk more about ways of dealing with and transforming aggression.

OTHER SIGNIFICATORS OF AGGRESSION IN THE CHART

Audience: Can you say something more about Uranus in terms of aggression? I've seen it strongly placed in the charts of some very violent people.

Howard: Yes, Uranus gets impatient and angry with injustice, or when something is not clear and truthful, or living up to its ideals. Uranus can't go along with something it disagrees with. I notice this over and over again in the charts of people with Sun in hard aspect to Uranus—they are full of principles. They won't or can't do something if it offends their principles. Uranus, for all its associations with egalitarian Aquarius, is rather self-centred and very definite: "I see the Truth and that's the way it is." There is almost something doctrinaire about it. There is a clarity and laser-beam quality to its energy. Uranus can't stand "bullshit." It wants to cut through anything murky, irrational or vague. Uranus breaks away from things it doesn't believe in. I had a client with Sun in Aquarius inconjunct Uranus in Cancer: she keeps breaking away from people, friends, and groups because she doesn't agree with the way they are handling things. In other words, they offend her principles. She doesn't exactly get angry with them—well, maybe she does. She gives them a lecture and then says goodbye. When she does this, she is asserting herself in a Uranian way. She draws a very definite boundary and acts in the name of "truth"—her truth.

In mythology, when Saturn castrates Uranus, some of the blood from the dismembered phallus drips back onto the ground (Gaia's womb) and gives birth to the Furies. So, if we inhibit or suppress (Saturn) some part of us that wants variety and change (Uranus), then the Furies are born inside us. The Furies have names which roughly translate into envious anger, retaliation and never-endingness. If we need to change something or to undertake a certain clear action and we hold back, then the energy which would go into that action turns back on itself and festers in the psyche—giving rise to a deep inner frustration and disease. So much energy is invested in holding back what the Uranian part of us craves to do, that we become tired and depressed. There is no energy left to do anything else. Or we become angry at and envious of other people who are doing what we are not letting ourselves do. If we don't assert our true individuality, we give birth to the Furies.

Let's say, however, that you assert your Uranian side, and do something which transgresses the existing authority or the *status quo*. Then the Furies are hurled at you from the outside! Those you are threatening or disrupting with your changes unleash the Furies on you. It almost seems as if you can't win with this Saturn/Uranus conflict. Hold back Uranus, and the Furies well up inside; express Uranus and other people become furious.

But there is more to the story. In the myth, Saturn throws the dismembered phallus into the sea. Merging with the foam, it gives birth to Aphrodite. You might have seen Botticelli's painting of Venus rising out of the sea. So Venus, the goddess of love and beauty, is born out of this mess. What does this mean? The conflict between Saturn (maintenance) and Uranus (change) gives birth to Venus. I imagine it means that we should try to be diplomatic about change. Diplomatically make room within the old structure for new things to happen. Keep the best of the old but make space for whatever new needs to come. Of course, this may be easier said than done.

Venus/Aphrodite is also the goddess who redresses imbalances. There are times when conflict and disruption are needed in order to restore a greater balance and harmony into the life. A good fight might clear the air and bring two lovers closer again. Also, we may have to challenge and disrupt the existing structure in the name of making our lives more harmonious (Venus) or more in tune with what we are meant to be doing. If we have grown lopsided, then there is the need for some sort of disruptive coup to restore balance again.

IS SATURN AGGRESSIVE?

Audience: You were just talking about Saturn castrating Uranus. Well, that is also an aggressive act and I've always felt that Saturn is where we are aggressive to ourselves—where we castrate or limit ourselves.

Howard: Yes, I take your point. Saturn also eats his own children—he doesn't let his creations exist. Saturn can be associated with the superego, that bit of the psyche which judges us according to certain rules and standards. Reminiscent of a teacher getting angry with a pupil who is not behaving, the superego gets angry if we don't live up to its standards.

Besides the standards set by the superego, I believe there is a part of us which "knows" what we are meant to become. If we persistently fall short of that, then we suffer a kind of existential guilt and pain—the pain of not being all that we could be. Every time we don't act in accord with our true nature, it registers somewhere in us and we start to despise ourselves. Wherever Saturn is placed in the chart is where we need to work hard on ourselves, face our weaknesses, and develop more strength or wisdom in that area. We will be angry with ourselves in that area if we fail to learn what we need to learn. Or it may seem as if God gets angry at us for not learning our lessons or accepting our limits.

I just thought of another way Saturn is aggressive. By house, Saturn indicates where we are frightened or fearful of trouble. As a consequence, we might feel the need to be aggressive or defensive in that sphere. I'll explain what I mean more carefully. Take Saturn in the 7th house of partnerships. If you have that placement, you are vulnerable and sensitive to being hurt in that area. Because of your vulnerability, you may want to control others so that they don't do the thing you are afraid of them doing. You will get angry with them if they over-step these limits because then they threaten to bring up your pain and weakness. So, if you have Saturn in the 7th and you are afraid that your partner might run off with somebody else, you will try to stop them from flirting with others. If the partner does flirt, you will get angry and bolshy because he or she has overstepped the limit of what you can take. But your anger is really masking your fear and pain. Bitter words can be a cry for help. The Greek God of war, our friend Ares, had Fear and Fright for his squires. There is a definite link between fear and anger in this respect. Also Pan—a Saturnine or Capricornian figure—gives us the word panic. We control out of fear and get angry if others won't co-operate.

The same dynamic could apply to the house Pluto is in. Pluto symbolises where we fear being destroyed and overwhelmed. Therefore to compensate for this fear, we can be extremely tough, controlling and aggressively defensive.

COMPARING THE AGGRESSION OF MARS AND PLUTO

As long as we are talking about other significators of aggression besides Mars, let's examine Pluto in this respect a little more closely. First, let's compare Mars and Pluto. Mars has long been linked with both sex and aggression. But when we start talking either about *repressing* the sexual or aggressive drive, or *transcending* sex or aggression, then we enter the realm of Pluto. If you repress your sexual or aggressive urges, they go underground to Pluto's domain. Transcending these basic drives takes a Plutonic act of will and utterly transforms the whole personality.

Mars and Pluto differ in other ways. In the past, it was common to talk about the masculine side of Mars ruling Aries and the feminine side of Mars ruling Scorpio. Most astrologers today still consider Mars as the co-ruler of Scorpio along with Pluto. The masculine side of Mars ruling Aries wants to conquer the outer world. The feminine side of Mars (ruling Scorpio) has to do battle with one's own inner world, and master the intense and powerful feelings inside oneself.

The feminine side of Mars is a bit more like Pluto. You can see the difference between the masculine and feminine Mars in the myth of Jason and Medea. Jason is the Aries type, while Medea is the Scorpio type. In the beginning, Jason's uncle has the sovereignty and Jason is still a minor. But the young Jason is soon to come of age and must take over the crown, which is rightfully his. The power is "out there"—his uncle has it; and the time has come for Jason to reclaim it. The story is about taking power back from something external to the self and finding *one's own* power to direct *one's own* life—it is about gaining an "internal locus of control." Jason has to become the predominant creative force in his own life, rather than letting something out there determine his life for him.

This is an Aries myth, because those born with an emphasis in Aries need (like Jason) to find the power to direct their lives from inside themselves rather than letting the power be in someone else's hands. In order to prove his power, Jason has to go on a quest to retrieve the golden fleece from far-away Colchis. In order to find their own power, Aries people must take up a quest, or do something to challenge themselves.

Jason embarks on his quest in the manner you would expect the masculine side of Mars to behave. He has the gall or *chutzpah* to order the biggest boat ever to be built. He inspires Orpheus, Hercules, Castor, and Pollux to come with him: people who later on become heroes in their own right. Jason, like Mars and Aries, is an initiator.

He is also bolshy and impulsive. When the *Argo* arrives at the clashing rocks of the Symplegades, Jason is ready to chance his luck and drive the boat through. He doesn't really stop to think about the best way to deal with the problem—he will impetuously push himself headlong into things relying on the sheer force of his will. Fortunately, at this point, he meets the old sage, Phineus, who's been hanging around studying these rocks for a long time. Phineus advises him to first send a dove through the clashing rocks. When they see that the dove's tail feathers have been caught, then the rocks will be just about to open again, and Jason can steer the boat safely through. The impulsive Jason needs to be tempered by forethought and practical experience. The impetuous, rushing energy of Aries and Mars needs a little of the common sense and wisdom of Capricorn and Saturn.

When Jason arrives at Colchis, the land which guards the golden fleece, he meets Medea. She represents the more feminine side of Mars, and is reminiscent of Scorpio and Pluto. In fact, she is very Scorpionic. Jason needs Medea to complete his task, although at the beginning he doesn't know this. In order to obtain the fleece, he has to yoke two fire-breathing bulls, sow the teeth of a dragon and fight a crop of armed men who will spring up when the dragon's teeth are planted. A busy day. Jason is all set to rush to these tasks with sheer Aries and Mars bravado. At this point Medea steps in and says: "Hold on Jason, just relax for a moment. You don't stand a chance if you just rush in and try to do all those things relying only on your manly force. Take a tip from me. I'll mix you up a little potion which will lull your opponents to sleep and then you'll have no problem." Medea is a seductress. She exemplifies the feminine side of Mars, not bold force, but cunning, which can examine a situation and "suss out" the best way to deal with it. She doesn't just rush in like Jason; she plans and plots and mixes up magic charms.

I see Medea-type energy as necessary in helping the Aries/Mars type achieve his ends. Aries is so busy giving out and exerting energy that there is no time to take something in, to reflect and evaluate. Medea—acting like a Scorpio—has taken the time to fully evaluate and consider the situation before executing a plan. She is more secretive and plotting than the forthright Jason. The pure Aries/Mars type is so obvious. It's easy for others with a bit more subtlety to come along and outwit them. On the whole, it is fairly easy to see what Aries is up to. They usually are not all that good at keeping surprises.

ID-ANGER VERSUS EGO-ANGER

Now think back to that early, primal rage I was speaking about earlier. It was the rage the infant felt when survival was threatened. I called it id-anger. Id-anger is *global*. When the little baby is angry, the whole world is angry.

This takes a little explaining, but I want to draw a distinction between Plutonic anger and Mars anger. When we are in the womb, we think that everything is us. Even after birth, for a while we still think we are everything. There is no sense of a separate "I." So who and what we are is not differentiated or distinguished from anything else. This is called *primary narcissism*. Imagine you are a little baby and you get angry at mother for not feeding you when you are hungry. You feel tremendous rage at not being fed; or when she lets you down, you may even fear that you are going to die as a result. This anger and rage is directed at mother, but since you have not differentiated yourself very much from the environment, that negativity is also experienced as directed back towards the self. Hanna Segal, in a book about the work of Melanie Klein, expresses it this way:

> A hungry, raging infant, screaming and kicking, fantasizes that he is actually attacking the breast, tearing and destroying it, and experiences his own screams which tear him and hurt him as the torn breast attacking him in his own inside.[18]

So you are screaming at the "out there" but since you have not distinguished yourself from what is out there, you are also screaming and attacking your own self. Pretty gruelling stuff.

What happens is that it becomes too painful and unbearable to feel that hurt and rage, so you cut off from it. You repress and deny the pain and develop a more compliant side. The unfinished infan-

---

[18]Hanna Segal, *Introduction to the Work of Melanie Klein* (New York: Basic Books, 1980; and London: Hogarth Press, 1973), p. 2.

tile rage and destructiveness may resurface later, often triggered by a present close relationship. But we covered that ground earlier.

Time passes, you grow older and begin to acknowledge that you exist as a separate person. You start to recognise your boundaries, where you end and others begin. It gradually becomes clearer that you and mother are not the same person. This is a big step: it means you now have a sense of the self as a distinct entity. What's more, you want to assert your newly found individuality. This is ego-assertion, because you have a separate identity to assert—as opposed to earlier id-assertion, when you didn't have a sense of your individual boundaries.

The energy of Mars can be equated with the ego asserting itself. It is the ego flexing its muscles and fighting for what it wants and defending its identity. I would associate Pluto with the more primitive, wild, and undifferentiated early id-assertion, which exists prior to the formation of an ego or separate-self identity.

While attending a weekend course in neo-Reichian therapy recently,[19] I observed the difference between Plutonic id-anger and Mars ego-anger. The woman who was in the hot seat being worked on had Sun in Aquarius opposite Pluto, and both Moon and Ascendant in Aries. So we have the combination of Pluto energy and Mars energy strongly configurated.

She was having a session with the therapist while the rest of us observed. The session started with her lying flat on her back on the floor. In a regressive state, she was expressing and releasing the anger she felt when she was a baby and her mother didn't come to pick her up. She is not a large woman, but when she started to act out her rage, the whole house was shaking. Her screams were coming from a place of such deep distress that it was painful just to listen. It stirred one's own deep primal pain.

Eventually, with the help of a therapist, she released a great deal of the pain associated with this early experience of being let down by mother. She looked much more relaxed and at peace. Underneath all that distress was peace. The session could have

[19]This weekend course was part of the "Self-Formation" course given under the auspices of The Minster Centre, 57 Minster Road, London NW2, England. The course leader of this particular weekend was David Boadella, a leading neo-Reichian therapist.

ended there, but the therapist encouraged it to continue. It was a kind of demonstration session for us and it was just too soon to end it.

She was done (for the time being) with her Plutonic rage with her mother. She was still lying on the floor and she began to recall an experience that happened with her father when she was eight years old. In a fit of anger, her father had thrown her across the room. She was still lying on the floor as she reconnected to this experience. She began to scream and kick, her feet and arms banging the floor.

At this point, the therapist cleverly intervened with something that I didn't understand at the time. He asked her to get up from the floor and told her to kneel on the floor instead, but to keep her spine erect. He also instructed her to keep her eyes open (they had been closed before) and to shout at her father. So she was kneeling with her back straight and eyes wide open and shouting directly at the therapist/father, "I hate you, why did you do that?" In this way, she was able to free some of the stored-up feelings left over from the experience of having been thrown across the room by him.

Do you see why the therapist made her kneel with her spine erect to work through that experience? The issue with the mother happened when she was a baby lying in the cot with no real sense of her separate identity. The issue with the father happened when she was eight and had already developed an ego-identity. By the age of eight, she could say, "don't do that to *me*, it is *my* body, leave *me* alone." By the age of eight, she could stand up for herself, *because she had a sense of self to stand up for*. That's why he wanted her to make her spine erect when she worked on that experience. Plutonic id-anger is more the helpless, defenceless, flat-on-the-back type rage. It is diffused and global. Mars is your standing-up-anger, when you have an ego to assert and defend.

ASPECTS TO MARS

Before we take a more systematic look at various aspects to Mars and what these suggest, I'd like to say a word or two about the sign placement of Mars. The sign Mars is in tells us something about the way in which a person asserts. Mars in Taurus may be slow to get started, but once it asserts, it does so in a determined and steady way. Mars in Gemini may have trouble deciding what to do; it starts in one direction and is lured off in another. Mars in watery Cancer asserts more indirectly than the demonstrative and dramatic Mars in Leo. You can figure out the rest.

Aspects to Mars tell us more about the way in which a person asserts, and what "comes up" when he or she starts giving expression to the will. Aspects are like table legs; you pull one leg and you get the other ones coming along with it. For instance, if you have Mars in aspect to Neptune, when you "do your Mars" (when you assert) then you will also invoke Neptune in one form or another.

Aspects to Mars also suggest the particular outlets a person might choose through which to affirm his or her sense of identity, power or purpose. So with Mars in aspect to Neptune, one might express the self and affirm the identity through dance, music, poetry or healing.

In general, those with hard aspects to Mars probably have more to learn about the right use of power, and could experience greater excesses, frustration and difficulty with expression of the Mars principle. Even so, it is too simplistic to assume that hard aspects to Mars come out like the Greek Ares and flowing aspects come out like the Roman Mars. It's more complicated than that; the overall chart, the general level of consciousness, and the degree of awareness of the person in question would have to be assessed to determine whether the Roman Mars or Greek Ares, or both, would come through the aspect.

SUN-MARS ASPECTS

The Sun and Mars are both masculine principles—assertive, expressive and outgoing. If they form an aspect to one another then you have a double hit of assertion, an intensification of the masculine principle. The hard aspects may indicate what is known as a "negative animus," someone who is overbearing, tyrannical, even violent. These are extremes of the masculine principle.

Take the conjunction or the square of Sun and Mars. The Sun needs to shine and affirm its individuality, and Mars in aspect to it will heighten this drive. So there is a very pressing drive to assert the self. No matter how shy, quiet, passive, or withdrawn the Sun square or conjunct Mars might look, I know that somewhere inside these people are strong and tough. I wouldn't want to mess with them—they are fighters. I'd sooner have them on my side.

I'm particularly worried by people with Sun square or conjunct Mars who appear docile. Where is all that energy going? If they are not in touch with it, they may find themselves tired, alienated and depressed. Or do they find subtle ways of manipulating others to do what they want? Perhaps they passively control others: "Oh, I am so weak and delicate, you must do this for me" or, "How can you do that to me, when you know how sensitive I am?" One way or another, they get their way.

The conjunction or square is prone to over-excitement or over-stimulation. They may become so angry or excited that they almost vibrate out of existence. They may rush into something so quickly they botch it up or cause an accident. But I don't want to sound negative here, even about the square. There is a powerful spirit and will in operation with these aspects, manifesting in courage bordering on audacity.

The sextile and trine generally indicate the courage, strength and directness to express who you are and success in achieving what you want. While Mars in hard aspect to the Sun may be too brusque and put people off with their way of pouncing, Mars in flowing aspect to the Sun will generally express the self strongly but not go too over-the-top (with the possible exception of the trine in fire, such as Sun in Aries trine Mars in Leo, or Sun in Leo trine Mars in Sagittarius, or Sun in Sagittarius trine Mars in Aries—these fiery trines could be overly enthusiastic or too eager).

With the opposition between Sun and Mars, there is a tendency to project Mars onto others. You feel that you have a strong desire to express who you are, but another person's willfulness (the Mars opposition) apparently blocks or confronts you. You may have the feeling that someone out there is trying to stop you being you. It feels as if your will-to-be is in direct opposition to somebody else's will-to-be. The conflict may be experienced through a parent, often the father. Now, if you feel that someone else is opposing you, then you will have to fight harder to assert yourself. So, those with Sun opposing Mars end up being very Martian. They experience someone else as challenging them or they provoke conflict as a way to justify bringing out their own will and power.

Those with the Sun opposing Mars will sometimes attract people who serve to rouse them into action. Somebody ignites them and the two are off on an exciting adventure or project. Again, rather than this energy just stemming from the self, it appears that someone has triggered it off.

MOON-MARS ASPECTS

Any contact between the Moon and Mars will heat up the emotions. The flowing aspects will enliven and warm up the feelings, but the more difficult aspects are akin to boiling water or scalding emotions. In either case, you have a quick reaction to life.

Whereas the Sun in difficult aspect to Mars often indicates trouble with the father or the male principle, Moon-Mars contacts suggest anger with the mother or trouble with the feminine principle. Those with the hard aspects could literally make war with the mother, or women in general, or experience the mother (or certain women) as warlike, intrusive, pushy and gorgon-like.

A keyword for Mars is action and a keyword for the Moon is sensitivity. Put these together and you have someone who asserts in a sensitive manner and in tune with the environment. With the hard aspects, however, you get someone who is overly sensitive or touchy about things.

Mars in hard angle to the Moon indicates what I call territorial problems. The Moon has a lot to do with making a nest or a home. In aspect to Mars, you have fights in the home or battles over territory and space. I've observed people with a Moon/Mars square or opposition who continually fight with flatmates, landlords, or with other people, over issues such as who has the rights to a house. One person I know with Moon square Mars will let all sorts of people come and stay in her house and then gets angry with them because they are in her way. Her "mothering" side comes into conflict with her need to do her own thing (Mars).

Audience: I have Moon square Mars and I have this conflict you mention between mothering others, versus being tough and assertive. I want to get angry at someone for being a pain and then I start to think, "Oh, he must have had a hard childhood," or I start to reflect on his problems and I feel sympathetic.

Howard: Yes, that sums it up well. Another thing I've noticed about difficult Moon-Mars aspects is that a person may need to act and do something (Mars) but this is in conflict with what they are feeling inside at the time (the Moon). The person may want to go out and find a new job for instance, but inside is feeling insecure or frightened at the prospect. Emotions (Moon) are out of synch with actions (Mars). When Mars is in flowing aspect to the Moon, then what a person wants to do and how he feels inside will harmonize and support one another. If that is the case, he can act with greater surety and confidence.

Audience: I have Moon opposing Mars and what you say fits. I often have the experience of other people trying to push me into something that I don't feel like doing. Am I projecting something?

Howard: With any opposition aspect, a person may identify with one end and see the other as coming from the outside. I don't think we would strongly react to something coming at us from the outside unless it touched something in us. Let's say that inside you there is a conflict between wanting to assert yourself in a certain way (Mars) and other emotions (the Moon) which don't support such action. If you identify with the emotions which are against doing something, then you could project that bit of you which feels pressurized to do that thing onto others: you see them as pushing you, when in actual fact it is a part *inside you* which is pushing at another part *in you* which is more resistant.

MARS-MERCURY ASPECTS

Mars in aspect to Mercury energises the mind. People with this aspect will try to affirm and assert their individuality and master the environment through speech, thinking and intellect. They try to master, dominate and distinguish themselves through anything Mercurial: writing, being clever, making deals with others, distributing goods and information, labelling things, or figuring things out. A negative Mars-Mercury connection can sometimes indicate a vicious tongue, or a mind brimming with destructive thoughts. Or someone who blurts out what he is thinking before he really knows what he is saying. Words spew out faster than the brain can organise them.

People with Mars in aspect to Mercury (regardless of the nature of the aspect) can justify their actions (Mars) on the basis of some rational or intellectual explanation (Mercury). They can defend most anything they do or say with some sort of rationale. They might even be engaged in something destructive or hurtful and yet find arguments to justify their actions. Mars-Mercury fights with the head. More positively, Mars-Mercury aspects give the courage to stand up for one's beliefs and the ability to communicate one's ideas to others in a way which is stimulating. Mars-Mercury aspects can be used positively by taking up a study or pursuing anything which sharpens the mind or enhances verbal or mental ability.

Mars—the archetype of fighting and asserting the individuality—is linked up with Mercury, which is traditionally associated with brothers, sisters, relatives and neighbours. Again and again when I have seen charts with hard Mars-Mercury contacts, I have found problems with siblings.

MARS-VENUS ASPECTS

I already touched quite a bit on these aspects before. On the one hand we have Mars—the need to assert the individuality—and on the other we have Venus—the urge for union and relatedness. The tension is paramount in the hard aspects. The closer we get to others and the more we merge and compromise with them (Venus), the more our individuality feels threatened and we must fight back to distinguish ourselves again (Mars).

Let's take Mars square Venus and look at this dynamic more closely. Remember the table legs: you "do" Venus and you bring

Mars along too. As with the opposition, in the square there is also the tendency to side with one end and deny or repress the other.

Let's say you have Mars square Venus and you side with Venus. You are all loving, adjusting, and compromising and you deny your Mars. Mars will eventually erupt and you will flare up at the other person. A lot of resentment and rage will come out, much of which has been unconsciously brewing from all the other times you have been too compromising. So you start out all nice and Venusian and end up overtaken by Mars because you haven't given enough space to your Mars all along.

Now, let's play it the other way. You have Mars square Venus, but you emphasise Mars. You continually demand that the other person adjust to you. You run the show and must be in charge. You are not being loving or balancing enough. Would you stay with yourself? Probably not. In the end you drive the other person away because of your selfish behaviour. But you love and need the person, so you beg her to come back to you, promising that you'll be good and caring and co-operative and give her everything she wants. What happens? You end up being overly Venusian. But for how long?

Those with Mars in hard aspect to Venus often vacillate between loving and hating, adjusting and then demanding. Passion and power conflicts (Mars) will be met through love (Venus). Rabbi Hillel summed up the Mars-Venus dilemma very nicely: "If I am not for myself, who will be? And if I am only for myself, what am I?"

With Mars in flowing aspect to Venus, there is often a healthy blend of being able to assert and stand up for the self along with a sensitivity to the needs of others. You assert (Mars), but in a charming and diplomatic manner (Venus). You assert with style. You can act (Mars) in accord with your values (Venus).

Audience: I have Mars in Gemini square Venus in Pisces and I have difficulty in relationships with men. At first I am all loving and accepting, but then Mars comes in later. Or I am so critical or argumentative in the beginning that Venus never gets a look in.

Audience: I have Venus conjunct Mars opposing Saturn. When I was younger, I went for people with a streak of violence in them. I was attracted by that in them.

Howard: The aspects to Venus indicate what we tend to find or look for in love. So if Venus aspects Mars then you are looking for Mars through love. Think about it—if you meet someone with violence in them, then you can easily maneuver that person into living out your own unexpressed anger. Or you can make the other person so angry you have no choice but to defend yourself, and eventually you discover your own power in that way.

Audience: Isn't Mars in aspect to Venus meant to be artistic?

Howard: Any planet that touches Mars is a clue to the way you can affirm and assert your individuality. With Venus aspecting Mars, artistic self-expression can be the way you find your power or distinguish yourself. You may also find your power (Mars) by being seductive and using charm (Venus) as a way of getting what you want. Mars-Venus aspects can heighten sex appeal.

MARS-JUPITER ASPECTS

Jupiter tends to inflate or expand whatever it touches, so in aspect to Mars, it can expand the need to assert the self and master things—there is an enthusiasm to assert and to grow. If Mars makes flowing aspects to Jupiter, you can generally express yourself in a way which reaches other people or which furthers your own ends—you spark, expand and enliven others with your enthusiasm. But with hard aspects between Mars and Jupiter, there are problems with proportion. You get excited and want to assert something, but you do it in a way which is over-the-top or excessive. You go too far with it. Enthusiasm is distorted into fanaticism or over-zealous behaviour. You get so excited about what turns you on that you think it's the answer to everything for everyone. What you believe may be true and beautiful, but you can drive others away because of the manner in which you pursue or express yourself. You over-kill or over-promote.

Some people with Mars-Jupiter aspects believe that a higher authority or truth (as symbolised by Jupiter, the head of the Olympians) speaks through them, justifying their actions. They feel as if they have glimpsed some higher truth and therefore they *know*

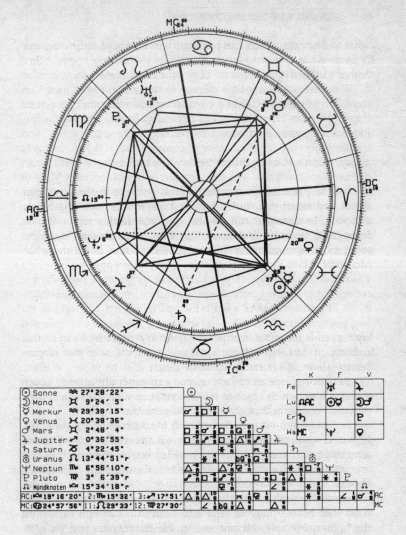

	Sonne	≈ 27°28'22"
☽	Mond	♓ 9°24' 5"
☿	Merkur	≈ 29°38'15"
♀	Venus	♓ 20°38'36"
♂	Mars	♓ 2°48' 4"
♃	Jupiter	♐ 0°36'55"
♄	Saturn	♑ 4°22'45"
♅	Uranus	♌ 13°44'51"r
♆	Neptun	♏ 6°56'10"r
♇	Pluto	♍ 3° 6'39"r
☊	Mondknoten	♎ 15°34'18"r

AC:	♎ 19°16'20"	2: ♏ 15°32'	3: ♐ 17°51'
MC:	♋ 24°57'56"	11: ♌ 29°33'	12: ♍ 27°30'

	K	F	V
Fe	☉	♅	♃
Lu	☊ AC	☉ ☿	☽ ♂
Er		♄	♇
Wa	MC	♆	♀

Chart 1. John McEnroe, born February 16, 1959, in Wiesbaden, West Germany, at 10:30 PM. Chart calculated by Astrodienst, Postfach, CH-8033, Zurich, Switzerland, using the Placidus house system. Birth data from Harmonic Charts *by David Hamblin (Wellingborough, Eng.: Thorsons Publishing Group, 1983).*

what to do or say. There can be more than a tinge of righteousness: "I know what to do and what you should do because I have it on a higher authority." It is a kind of cosmic one-up-man-ship.

Take the chart of John McEnroe for example. (See Chart 1 on page 49.) Mars is the focus for many aspects and part of a Grand Cross. He has Mars in Gemini opposing Jupiter in Sagittarius. Part of the way he affirms his identity is through tennis, and traditionally Jupiter has sporty connotations. When he gets angry, it is overblown and he believes he has seen the truth when the umpires have not. The conjunction of the Moon with Mars in the 8th in Gemini (both square Pluto) suggests that the rage which comes up for him is not just relevant to the immediate situation, but carries with it some deeper infantile rage left over from childhood. Pluto shows what is buried in us, and in aspect to Mars, it suggests some deep rooted id-rage from the past. McEnroe may have a very genuine complaint about an umpire's vision or the Wimbledon establishment in general, but when it comes out in an exaggerated way tinged by the intensity of unfinished childhood issues, then other people react by backing off and putting him down. We all have some degree of unexpressed rage at parents left over from infancy. We don't like to see this coming out in other people because it reminds us of part of ourselves we would rather keep buried.

Remember, we affirm our identity through any planet which touches Mars. In the case of Jupiter, you can do it through sports, religion, gambling, travelling or philosophising.

For example, Werner Erhard, the founder of *est*, has a Mars-Jupiter conjunction in Scorpio. He has built a philosophy (Jupiter) around Mars. Paramount to his belief system is the idea that you are responsible for your own life and that everything you do is a choice.

Consider also the chart of Gandhi, the Indian liberator. He was born with Mars opposing Jupiter. He based his actions (Mars) on the higher principles he believed in. He fought, not just for himself, but for millions of people. His actions (Mars) took on a very broad significance (Jupiter). He asserted himself against the whole way of life and world view of the colonial English in India.

I have often noticed that those with Mars in hard aspect to Jupiter become embroiled in philosophical battles with other people.

MARS-SATURN ASPECTS

Compare Mars-Jupiter contacts with Mars-Saturn ties. While Jupiter indicates a problem with over-expanding, Saturn brings in the idea of limitation, hesitation, and holding back. When Mars wants to assert, Jupiter says, "Yes, do it in a big way." In the case of Saturn, when Mars wants to assert, Saturn says: "Hold on, take it easy, are you sure, are you good enough, is it allowed, what would your mother say?" Saturn sits on Mars' shoulder, judging, inhibiting, censoring and checking out. Mars is action and Saturn is hesitation, so you may literally act hesitantly or at least very carefully. Or you hold back so long that when you do act, a kind of pressure has built up which makes everything blurt out.

Alan Oken once described the hard aspects between Mars and Saturn as "driving a car with the brakes on."[20] Mars is the accelerator and Saturn the brakes. Mars is a green light, Saturn is red. Some people with the hard aspects between these two planets perpetually make excuses for their existence. They apologise for their actions: "I'm sorry to apply for the job—I know I'm not right, but I thought I might try for it—of course, I'll understand if you don't hire me because. . . ." Approaching things this way does not inspire much confidence. And yet, ironically, there is often a tenacity about Mars-Saturn. Once they do start to proceed they will usually persist with noteworthy stamina.

Zipporah Dobyns has referred to Mars-Saturn problems as an overdrive-underdrive dilemma.[21] You might come too much from the Mars side and try to turn your will into law; even if there is an obstruction (Saturn), you will push headlong into it. So these people often hit their heads against brick walls. This is the overdrive side. The underdrive side gives in to obstacles too easily. Because you perceive a block (Saturn) you don't do anything at all. One resolution to this dilemma is to try to do as much as you can within the limits and then see what happens.

---

[20]Alan Okan, *The Horoscope, The Road and Its Travelers* (New York: Bantam, 1974), p. 248.
[21]Zipporah Dobyns and Nancy Roof, *The Astrologer's Casebook* (Los Angeles: TIA Publications, 1973).

With Mars-Saturn in conjunction or square, you may feel the urge to assert and then stop yourself. I have Mars conjunct Saturn in my own chart, and Pluto is there to boot. I catch myself at it all the time. Mars gives me the impulse to do something and rather than just going ahead and executing the action cleanly, I start to dither and wait and worry if it is the right thing to do. So I might think, "I want to ring this person up." I start to do it and then I think, "Wait a minute, is the right time? Maybe I shouldn't ring at all."

Perhaps because Pluto is there, sometimes the decision is turned into a life-death issue. For example, I might think "Should I go to this party or not?" Mars perks up, "Yes, go." Saturn then has his say: "No, you've got other things you should be doing, like preparing this seminar." Then I am stuck in indecision and I don't know until two minutes before I'm meant to be at the party whether I'm going or not. At this point, Pluto turns it into a matter of life or death. If I decide I'm not going to the party, I stay at home and end up thinking: "I've ruined my whole life now by not going." Or I go to the party and as I'm ringing the doorbell, I'm thinking, "I know I should have stayed home—now I've really messed up my life." Sometimes Mars-Saturn can give crippling indecision.

With flowing aspects between Mars and Saturn, you tend to know just the right amount of energy to put into something. Let's say you have a test coming up in a month. Mars trine or sextile Saturn might think, "I'll go to the library two hours a day for the next month to prepare for the test." This is reasonable. Mars in good relation to Saturn can plan, work well within limits, is disciplined and able to adhere to a procedure. What might Mars square or inconjunct Saturn do about the upcoming test? On the one hand, if you have the hard aspect, you might be so afraid of failing the test that six months before it is scheduled you go and live in the library. So you apply more action than needed. On the other hand, the other type with this aspect puts off going to the library until the night before the exam and then hysterically crams till morning.

Some people with Mars in aspect to Saturn may worry so much about their ability to assert, that they compensate and work hard at becoming good at asserting. A man with Mars-Saturn may be so concerned about his masculinity, that he goes out and learns to box, or becomes a body-builder and ends up looking extra macho. The German poet Goethe, born with Saturn rising and Mars in Capricorn, once wrote, "It is in limitation that the master first shows himself."

Those with Mars opposing Saturn may see someone or something out there stopping them. Mars wants to assert and perceives others as blocking (the Saturn opposition). If you have this aspect, there is probably a part of *you* that is blocking you, which is then projected onto the environment and seen as coming from the outside. I've seen more than a few cases of women with this aspect blaming their husbands for stopping them doing something. Then (for whatever reason) the husband isn't around anymore, and they still don't do what they said they wanted to do. It looks like someone else is opposing them, but the battle is an internal one, raging between the two very contrasting archetypal energies of Mars and Saturn.

Try the reverse situation. Some people with Mars opposing Saturn actually side with Saturn and see others as pushing them. So they wish to go slow, hold back, or stay where they are (Saturn), and they feel that others are pushing or forcing them into action (Mars). More likely than not, the tension of whether to act or not is actually an inner one. Everything that has an outside also has an inside.

MARS-URANUS ASPECTS

Both Mars and Uranus are animus or masculine type energies. The animus is associated with assertion, self-expression and creating from inside oneself. With Mars-Uranus there are strong individualistic tendencies—not only do these types have to establish themselves as separate entities, but they have to do it in their own way. There is a need to produce or express (Mars) something which is original or unique (Uranus).

If those with this aspect don't have outlets for creative energies, they stay highly strung: there is too much energy and nowhere for it to go. Also, I've noticed a similarity with Mars-Jupiter aspects in that Mars-Uranus may also justify action on the basis that it is "the Truth." Dane Rudhyar associated Uranus with the cosmic, divine, or universal Mind—the mind of God. People with Mars in aspect to Uranus may act as if they have an insight into what God is intending to make happen. Obviously this adds greater force or power to their way of acting. Very often, they seem in tune with new ideas or opinions or trends which are just beginning to filter into the collective.

Even in very earthy charts, Mars-Uranus aspects speed up and excite the nervous system. Physical outlets such as exercise and sport are useful to discharge the energy of the combined effect of these planets.

Audience: My brother has Mars in hard aspect to Uranus as part of a Grand Cross. He has frightening explosions of temper. Only in the last couple of years has he realised that if he runs around the block or takes up body-building he feels better.

Howard: People with Mars-Uranus contacts seem to vibrate at a high speed. They may wake up in the middle of the night with a jolt of energy and bolt up in bed, eyes wide open. It feels like electricity running through the body. In some instances, when Mercury is configured with the Mars-Uranus contact, the person has suffered from epilepsy or convulsions.

Audience: I had a girlfriend who was epileptic—she has Mercury square Mars conjunct Uranus.

Audience: My friend with Mars square Uranus has such an awful temper that it is almost like a fit. It is really frightening because he can't control it.

Howard: Yes, imagine the suddenness and strength of bolting Uranus combined with the principle of Mars. An explosive temper is the impulse to self-affirmation gone wild.

If people with Mars-Uranus contacts can't find an outlet for their power and creativity, then that energy has nowhere to go and may turn in on itself in the form of illness or depression. If a hard Mars-Uranus aspect appears in the charts of those who are predominantly Piscean, Libran, Cancerian or even Taurean, they may have difficulty integrating the aspect into their lives. They may be placid and easy-going much of the time and then suddenly break out and go berserk. If a Mars-Uranus contact is found in charts that are predominantly fire and air, those people will probably have an easier time integrating this force into their lives—they will be hell to live with, but at least the energy won't be turning in on itself. It may land on everybody and anything else, but at least it's not turning in on the self so much.

I have done many charts for people with Mars conjunct, square or opposing Uranus who have not felt comfortable with their own power. At the risk of being a Dr. Frankenstein, I sometimes encourage these people to take greater free-range and give themselves permission to be disruptive: rather than always adjusting to others, let others adjust to them once in a while. You wouldn't be born with a Mars-Uranus contact unless you were meant to be a little shocking and disruptive now and again. People who don't consciously "own" or give space to a Mars-Uranus aspect and the need for self-assertion it suggests are probably finding devious ways to manipulate and control and get what they want in any case. So why not be more overt about it?

Both Charles Carter and Isabel Hickey observed that the hard aspects between Mars and Uranus give rise to those who are accident prone. Isabel believed that if you carry around a lot of discordant and disruptive energy bottled up inside, you would attract accidents and discord toward the self. I've noticed this as well with these aspects.

More than a few times people with close hard aspects between Mars and Uranus bring an unusual amount of disruption before or during a session with me. One woman with Sun conjunct Mars and Uranus came for her reading just a few minutes after my landlord unexpectedly knocked at my door and told me I would have to move. It seems that whenever I do a reading for someone with these kinds of contacts, out of the blue the doorbell rings and it is something I must attend to. So the reading gets disrupted. Things happen which I haven't planned for which upset the normal pattern of events. For example, I never do readings on Sundays. Someone rings up for a chart and for some reason I agree to break my pattern and do it on Sunday because that is more convenient for the client. I set up the chart and discover Mars conjunct Uranus on the Ascendant!

There is often something quite magnetic and exciting about people with Mars in aspect to Uranus. They may have a kind of healing power. You can feel them buzzing with energy. People with Mars trine or sextile Uranus seem to have less difficulty handling the power and energy of the combined effects of these two planets. I've seen the trine or sextile in the charts of people who are highly original, inventive and individualistic, and yet they seem to get away with it. They usually have remarkable powers of resilience. Mars sextile or trine Uranus suggests a deep underlying strength.

Audience: I've heard it said that people with Uranus in Aries *do* what they like; people with Uranus in Gemini *think* what they like; and people with Uranus in Cancer *feel* what they like.

Audience: People I've met with Mars-Uranus conjunctions sometimes have unusual sexual tastes. They are conventional in other ways, but express their individuality through sex.

Howard: That's nice. Others I know with Mars-Uranus aspects find outlets for their Mars through playing with computers, inventing better mousetraps, and being astrologers.

Audience: Can you say something about the opposition?

Howard: Mars opposite Uranus is a curious aspect. These people have a powerful need to assert themselves. Now you might think that it makes sense to assert yourself against others who are compliant, but Mars opposing Uranus don't get off on this. They have to find other people who are bossy and bullying and then try to assert themselves against them. It's no big deal asserting yourself to a wimpy person! But to lock horns with someone who is equally obstinate and powerful—that is the real test. The more assertive the other person is, the more assertive Mars opposing Uranus will become. Fighting with others is the way they find their power and affirm their identity. I'm sure they secretly relish a fight: it makes them feel more alive and brings them closer to who they are. As in politics, the opposition party helps to define the party in power, and vice versa.

Audience: Yes, I agree with that. I have Mars square Uranus but even with the square I notice that I am attracted to Uranian types—people whose Uranus comes on my Sun or Moon or opposes my Sun or Moon. I need to be involved with people who are like that, who are strong and alive.

Howard: Yes, people with strong opinions help us to define our own opinions. But you know something else I've noticed. Sometimes I meet people with Mars conjunct, square or opposing Uranus and I have a distinct feeling that I don't know what they are going to do next. To me, they seem unpredictable, as if they could change at any moment—which probably says something about the relationship I have to my own Mars sextile Uranus. But sometimes my Capricorn Ascendant and Mars-Saturn conjunction feel uncomfortable with Mars-Uranus types. They too often surprise me just when I think I know where I am with them. In a funny kind of way they almost make me feel quite staid and conventional. Don't laugh!

MARS-NEPTUNE ASPECTS

There are many different ways of looking at these aspects. Neptune sometimes nudges us to make sacrifices around the principle or planet it is aspecting. So if Neptune contacts Mars, there may be an urge to sacrifice, transcend and dissolve Mars. In other words, Neptune can have a transcending, dissolving or eroding effect on Mars. Mars favours the physical and instinctive, while Neptune yearns for the etheric and refined. Rather than letting Mars be gross and corporeal, Neptune encourages Mars to rise above physical and animal desires. Rather than letting Mars explode into anger, Neptune nudges Mars to be more compassionate, understanding and sensitive to others. Neptune wants Mars to transcend selfishness, to give up being purely self-assertive and go beyond just wanting to achieve something for its own ends. Mars wants to assert and stand up for the self and Neptune universalizes this: "Be more sympathetic, more evolved, don't just live for yourself but give yourself to higher causes or things greater than you."

There is a basic archetypal dilemma between Mars and Neptune. Mars is the desire to affirm the individuality while, by contrast, Neptune is the urge to dissolve boundaries and merge back again into unity. If these planets are in aspect, then these two urges come up against one another and creative solutions to this dilemma need to be found. One way around this is to assert yourself (Mars), but do it for the sake of others or for the sake of the larger whole of which you are a part (Neptune). In this way, you are affirming your identity but also taking something other or greater than yourself into account. Or you can be the artist who serves as the medium through which universal, mythic and larger-than-life archetypal images and ideas can flow.

The person can assert and affirm his or her identity (Mars) by doing something Neptunian: this can mean being an artist, musician, healer, mystic, psychic, meditation teacher, a dancer, a model, poet, actress, nurse, a chemist or, in some cases, a drug dealer!

With Mars in aspect to Neptune, Neptune wants to come through Mars. So when people with these aspects do assert themselves, they should do it with sensitivity, refinement, and artistic flair. In some cases, those with difficult Mars-Neptune aspects appear to be taken over by external forces which compel them to act in a certain way. For instance, if there is a lot of anger in the atmosphere that is not being expressed, it may be a person with Mars in aspect to Neptune who ends up acting it out. Neptune acts as a psychic vacuum cleaner, picking up the nature of whatever planet it aspects from the atmosphere. I know people with Mars conjunct or square Neptune who occasionally act strangely out of character, or even "whacky," as if something has overtaken them. More positively, they can be a vehicle through which artistic or spiritual inspiration flows.

I do worry about people with strong Mars-Neptune contacts (good or bad) abnegating personal responsibility. I'm thinking of the Nazi war criminals who proclaimed their innocence because a higher authority made them do it. Sometimes people with Mars-Neptune aspects seduce other people to seduce them. They want to do something but are guilty about it and afraid to admit it to themselves. Accordingly, they set up a situation in which someone else then coerces, forces or pleads with them to do that thing they are afraid to admit they are wanting to do. You know what I mean — it's the "I did it because I was drunk" syndrome; or "I did it because the other person needed me to do it" or "I did it for Jesus." Because someone else has coerced them or because someone else needed them to do it, they feel they are not responsible and they are exonerated from guilt. I am also thinking of the suicide squads in Iran — the kamikaze brigades. Mars in aspect to Neptune may do anything in the name of a cause. They can justify any action on the basis of emotional or religious ideals, believing that dying for something higher will win them a place in heaven, even if they have murdered hundreds of people in the process.

There is a common thread or pattern I've noticed with some people who have Mars square or opposing Neptune. As children, many of them were frustrated because they didn't feel heard. Somehow they have grown up with the feeling that their will is impotent or that they are ineffective. In a few cases, they were actually harbouring a fantasy that something they wished for (or did) created a mishap or tragedy. Perhaps they had the thought of killing a brother and the next day something bad actually happened to the brother. They may then walk around thinking that their wicked will has made this happen and they wind up feeling guilty about ever again freely asserting themselves.

If you grow up thinking that you are a failure at asserting then you may never bother to assert yourself at all. Or you keep setting up unrealistic projects and aims which are bound to fail, as if you are determined to prove again and again that you are not effective. In order to start changing the pattern, you first have to acknowledge your underlying belief that you are inept. It helps to explore what might be the childhood sources of that expectation and then do something to replace that belief with a different one. You need to gradually build up your confidence by taking small steps, undertaking something which is manageable, and then move on from there.

Neptune has a slippery grip on Mars. I want people with Mars in aspect to Neptune to grip Mars better. Anne Dickson, in her book *A Woman in Your Own Right*[22] gives advice on how to

---

[22]Anne Dickson, *A Woman in Your Own Right* (New York and London: Quartet, 1982), Chapter 8.

be assertive without being pushy and how not to fall into what she calls "the compassion trap." By the compassion trap, she means those times that you don't assert yourself because you are afraid of hurting or upsetting others—a typical Mars-Neptune issue.

In actual fact, I haven't noticed a great deal of difference between the harmonious Mars-Neptune aspects and the more difficult ones. Much of what I have discussed can apply to the sextile, trine, square or opposition. The more harmonious aspects probably have an easier time taking inspiration and applying it practically and making it happen. Isabel Hickey called Mars trine or sextile Neptune "the practical idealist." However, people with the square and opposition, or difficultly aspected Mars-Neptune conjunctions, might be more confused about their direction in life or what action to take. They may have problems with an over-sensitive or delicate nervous system.

This is sometimes the case with the trine as well. Neptune can put whatever planet it touches in a fog. Those with the opposition may feel the most victimized by others when very often it is the Neptunian part of themselves—that part which is anti-structure and form—that keeps landing them in situations where everything dissolves and falls apart. They attract circumstances which compel them to make sacrifices.

MARS-PLUTO ASPECTS

We discussed some of the effects of Mars-Pluto aspects earlier but there are a few more points worth noting. Pluto wants to tear down and rebuild whatever planet it touches, so people with Mars linked to Pluto by aspect may find it necessary, at certain times in their lives, to re-think and rework the way they are using or expressing the Mars principle. If they have been out of touch with their anger or assertive energy, then a transit or progression involving the natal Mars-Pluto aspect could trigger anger they didn't even know was there, or create a situation which arouses a hitherto latent, but powerful urge to forcefully assert their will. Conversely, for those with Mars-Pluto aspects who have tended to over-do Mars—that is, their pattern has been to be too dominant, willful or even violent—then a transit or progression to the natal aspect may ask that they find ways to redirect their Mars into more constructive outlets or forms of expression. For example, a man came to see me who had Mars in Scorpio square Pluto in Leo. Transiting Pluto was going over his Mars and bringing out the natal square. He was in a situation where he felt incredibly angry and vindictive toward someone, but because of certain circumstances, it was not at all possible for him to directly express that rage. Transiting Pluto, touching off the Mars-Pluto square, had brought up all his rage and anger and he had to "sit" on it and find ways to re-channel or redirect those feelings.

If you have an aspect between Mars and Pluto, there is a good chance that whenever you assert yourself, you also bring Pluto along. You "do" your Mars in a Pluto way. This could give rise to covert and secretive action, and you would make a good detective or undercover agent. An ulterior motive may lurk behind many of your actions. Or you assert your will (Mars) in order to tear down or transform (Pluto) those things in society or in other people that you don't like or want to eliminate. Using your power to change what you consider a social ill could be a constructive expression of a Mars-Pluto contact.

In the process of rightly standing up for themselves or expressing even a justifiable anger, people with Mars conjunct, square or opposing Pluto may find that they are inadvertently taken over by a more deeply seated infantile rage leftover from childhood. For instance, take the case of a woman I know with Mars conjunct Pluto. She may start out by having a small argument with a shopkeeper over whether or not the dress she bought can be returned. The argument begins quite civilly, but then something happens: as they are arguing (and especially if the shopkeeper offers any resistance), this woman grows more and more angry until she could nearly murder the shop assistant. Her immediate here-and-now anger snowballs into something much more intense, hooking into that deeper id-rage I spoke about earlier. The shopkeeper turns into an image of "the depriving mother" and up comes her infantile rage. John McEnroe has Mars square Pluto and he takes it out on umpires.

Audience: That reminds me of something I read in the paper recently about a man who murdered a salesman at an Oxford Street shoe store because the salesman wouldn't let him return a pair of shoes he had just bought. I have Mars conjunct Pluto square the Moon and I could actually understand how that could happen.

Howard: Yes, I read about it too—with glee. Don't get me started on British shop assistants.

Audience: Not long ago there was a story on the news about a man in Croydon who shot someone who snuck into the parking space he wanted.

Howard: Look how interested we are in these stories. I must have struck a nerve.

Audience: Does the opposition work in the same way?

Howard: With the opposition between Mars and Pluto, you might start arguing with someone and inadvertently (or maybe not so inadvertently) trigger off the other person's infantile rage. There you are, fresh off your assertiveness training course, nobly standing up for your rights, and the other person goes berserk.

Those with Mars opposing Pluto have a knack of winding people up—they meet their own Plutos through others, or they manage to get another person to live out Pluto for them.

Obviously the trine or sextile between Mars and Pluto is going to be easier to handle and yet Pluto may still ask that Mars is periodically rechanneled or sublimated rather than expressed in a primitive or explosive form.

Audience: I've noticed that some people with Mars in aspect to Pluto will drive themselves very hard, as if they have to test the limits of their strength and will-power.

Howard: Yes, I've seen this as well—especially with the square. I'm thinking of a few people with this aspect who constantly challenge themselves by undertaking feats of endurance and pitting themselves against very tough odds—such as looking for the highest mountain to climb in the worst weather conditions, barefoot. I've only done two charts for people who admitted some past involvement with the SAS, but one had Mars trine Pluto and the other Mars square Pluto

Pluto brings out the extremes of whatever planet it touches—in this case, the best or worst of what Mars has to offer. The best of Mars is pretty obvious; I'll leave the worst of Mars to your imagination. If you are short of ideas, just watch the 9 o'clock news.

How Do You Express Aggression in Your Life?

We are going to do an exercise to look at ways you express aggression in your life. In preparation, I want you to study this list on the board, which is taken in part from Piero Ferrucci's book, *What We May Be*.[23] This is from a chapter entitled "The Tigers of Wrath," and the list shows the various attitudes through which aggression expresses or disguises itself. You may think you are not an angry or aggressive person, but if you are prone to any of the attitudes listed here, then you are very likely masking it. Aggression shows through:

1) cold, silent hatred

2) criticalness

3) self-destructiveness

4) sarcasm

5) irritation

6) pique

7) grumbling

8) brooding

---

[23]Ferrucci, *What We May Be*, p. 86.

9) vicarious enjoyment of violence

10) sneering

11) aggressive fantasies

12) passive sabotage

13) cruelty

14) bitterness

15) unreasoning dissent

16) sulkiness

17) vengefulness

18) bitchiness

So, if you sulk a lot then you are masking aggression. Just look at the body posture of the sulker: often he will have his arms folded tightly pressed in front of the chest or solar plexus and is bent over with a broody look on his face. His arms are wrapped into each other as if they are being held back from hitting out. (Remember that physiologically when you are in an angered state, the blood circulates to the extremities of the body. Folding the arms across the chest is a way of restraining the force building up in the forearms and hands. You are stopping yourself from hitting and instead feeling sulky.) Or sometimes the sulker's arms and hands just dangle lifelessly, hanging down from drooping shoulders like useless appendages.

Criticalness can be aggressive. Bitchiness can mask both anger and pain. Sarcasm can mask anger and resentment. Self-destructive behaviour can be anger turned inward.

You can detect aggression or anger in yourself when you start taking "swipes" at other people. If you are holding onto negativity and hate, you will find it difficult to be loving. You send out little poison barbs directed their way. A wife may be angry at her husband at breakfast but instead of being up front about her anger, she complains irritably about the way he leaves bits of his toast on the butter.

I'm thinking of a woman I know who has the Sun square Mars who was in therapy with me. Before one session, she arrived early to the part of town where I lived so she went to a local tea shop. She wanted Horlicks and they didn't have any. She spent the first half hour of our session bitching about how this shop didn't serve Horlicks and how angry it made her. She was really in a state about it. Finally, it dawned on me to ask her if something had happened to her in the last week that upset her. She then told me that her boyfriend had moved out and was living with another woman. She hadn't connected her anger about the Horlicks with the unexpressed rage she felt about her boyfriend's departure.

Time for the exercise. Pick a partner. One of you will be A and the other person will be B. Person A is going to talk for several minutes and person B is going to write down what person A is saying. So A's get your mouth ready and B's have some paper ready.

1) Person A, I want you to tell person B how you express aggression in your life. Any way, any situation, large or small. You can refer to this list on the board.

2) Person B, you just listen and write down what person A is saying. If person A stops, then person B should ask, "How else do you express aggression in your life?" You have five minutes to do this.

Ready for the next phase?

3) Person A, I want you to tell person B all the ways in which you *don't* express aggression in your life: the situations and circumstances, large or small, in which you *don't* express aggression or assert yourself.

4) Person B, you just listen again and write down what person A is saying. If person A stops, then person B should ask A, "How else do you *not* express aggression in your life?" You have five minutes for this phase.

Wind up that bit of the exercise now. Next phase:

5) Person B reads the list back to person A: all the ways that person A expresses aggression and all the ways that person A doesn't express aggression.

6) Person A just listens. Listen to what kind of person you are in this respect. After that, person A should come up with a statement about how he or she relate to aggression in life: just one statement which summarizes the way you (person A) relate to aggression. When you have your statement look at your chart and see what kinds of correlations you can find. How do your statements and patterns around aggression correspond to chart placements— especially look at the house, sign and aspects of Mars, Uranus and Pluto. I'll give you enough time to do this.

When you have finished, I want you to switch roles. Person B talks and person A writes down. Go through the same procedure we have already done, but person B is talking now and person A is writing.

Is anybody willing to share their statement and discuss it in relationship to the chart?

Linda: My statement is, "I'm a self-destructive victim in order to make other people feel guilty."

Howard: Your statement is that you put yourself into the victim position as a way of making other people feel guilty. That's somewhat complex. Let's put your chart on the board and discuss this. (See Chart 2 on page 67.)

Audience: She has Mars conjunct the Sun in Pisces, inconjunct both Neptune and Pluto.

Howard: Yes, well spotted. The Sun-Mars conjunction is part of a Yod or Finger of Fate configuration. The Sun and Mars are at the apex, approximately 150 degrees from both Neptune and Pluto, which are sextile to one another.

We had better start by analysing these aspects step-by-step and then I'll say more about the Finger of Fate. The Sun-Mars conjunc-

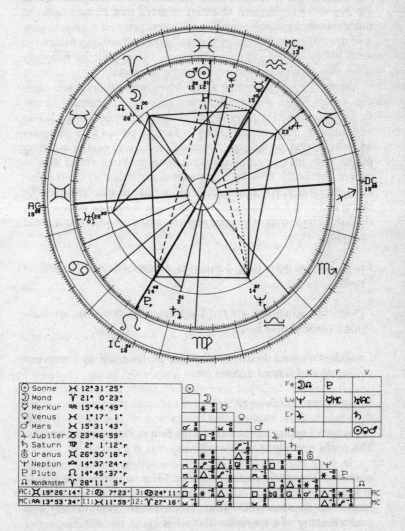

	Sonne	♓ 12°31′25″
☽	Mond	♈ 21° 0′23″
☿	Merkur	♒ 15°44′49″
♀	Venus	♓ 1°17′ 1″
♂	Mars	♓ 15°31′43″
♃	Jupiter	♉ 23°46′59″ r
♄	Saturn	♍ 2° 1′12″ r
♅	Uranus	♓ 26°30′18″ r
♆	Neptun	♎ 14°37′24″ r
♇	Pluto	♌ 14°45′37″ r
☊	Mondknoten	♈ 28°11′ 9″ r

AC: ♓ 19°26′14″ 2: ♋ 7°23′ 3: ♋ 24°11′
MC: ♒ 13°53′34″ 11: ♓ 11°59′ 12: ♈ 27°16′

	K	F	V
Fe	☽♌	♇	
Lu	♆	☿MC	♅AC
Er	♃		♄
Wa			☉♀♂

Chart 2. Linda. The birth data has been withheld for confidentiality. Chart calculated by Astrodienst, using the Placidus house system.

tion suggests a strong need to assert your individuality. But it is in Pisces—so you will need to assert yourself in a Piscean way. In other words, by doing something Piscean you will derive, bolster and strengthen your sense of "I-ness." One of the things associated with Pisces is "the victim." Therefore, being a victim ironically gives you an identity and even a sense of power.

Now, it is less likely that a Sun-Mars conjunction in any other sign except Pisces would choose to define itself by being a victim. Sun conjunct Mars in Aries would get its identity by being a leader and initiator, Sun conjunct Mars in Gemini would find its power by being clever or through communicating well and stimulating others with ideas; or Sun conjunct Mars in Virgo could find its power and define itself by being technically efficient. But the Sun conjunct Mars in Pisces will get its kicks and sense of "me-ness" by doing or being something related to the principle of Pisces. Now that could be a sympathetic server who cares for others or it could be a victim type.

Linda: They're both true. I work as a therapist in a hospital in London.

Howard: So, when you are not busy being a victim, you are busy being someone who helps others.

Linda: Sometimes I do them both together. Recently my supervisor at the hospital turned against me.

Howard: So you became the victim at the same place where you are the saviour. How efficient and economical of you! The Sun-Mars conjunction appears to be in the 11th house, the house of groups. You could even do that here with us—this is a group.

In your statement you said, "I'm a self-destructive victim in order to make other people feel guilty." The Sun-Mars conjunction in Pisces is helped in achieving those ends by the Neptune inconjunct. The Sun-Mars inconjunct Neptune in Libra also suggests your empathy as a therapist. But what about the self-destructive side and your need to make other people guilty? Say more about that.

Linda: I can be quite direct about helping other people get what they want, but I tend to be indirect, subtle or confused about my own needs. I guess I try to put other people's needs first in order to win acceptance. That fits with what you said about Mars inconjunct Neptune: sacrificing or giving up Mars for the sake of others. But I think that my Sun-Mars inconjunct Pluto in Leo wants to control others so that they don't manipulate me. I can control others best if I make them feel guilty—it's a non-direct way to assert my will.

Howard: You'd make a good "Jewish Mother." I'll introduce you to one or two I know and you can swap ideas. (How does the Jewish Mother motto go?—"Control guilt and you control the child.") More seriously though, what you just said about putting other people's needs first in order to win acceptance is very revealing. Ideally, when we are children, mother is meant to be adapting herself to our needs. But the reverse often happens. Rather than her adapting to us, we adjust ourselves to fit her needs, beliefs, and desires. We do it to win her love and ensure our survival. This can set up a pattern which remains with us our whole life. Your Moon is opposite Neptune, which suggests you would have been very sensitive to her needs.

Linda: I really feel what you said earlier about the personal will of Mars having to acknowledge a higher will. I may want something badly but often I feel forced to give it up or let it go because of circumstances beyond my control. That feels like Mars caught between Neptune and Pluto.

Howard: Yes, the picture I have of that Yod configuration is also that Mars is caught between Neptune and Pluto—or better still, Mars is caught by *both* Neptune and Pluto. Neptune and Pluto have separate lassos and each has roped Mars, like in the Westerns. Two cowboys standing some distance apart have both lassoed the same steer, in this case Mars. Neptune and Pluto will be pulling Mars' strings. Unconscious factors will be controlling your actions. Mars may want to act according to its own whims, but Neptune and Pluto tug Mars the way they want. Mars is not free of Neptune or Pluto and will somehow have to act in accordance with those planets. By the way, Neptune in Libra was sextile Pluto in Leo from roughly 1943 to 1956. So there was a good chance that planets in Pisces—be it Mars, the Sun, Moon, Venus or whatever—could be entangled in Yod configurations during that time. Then we have Neptune in Scorpio sextile Pluto in Virgo until the early 1970's, so planets in Aries could be caught in this aspect. Then Neptune moved into Sagittarius sextiling Pluto in Libra and Taurus comes under fire. Now Neptune in Capricorn is sextile Pluto in Scorpio and Gemini planets will be the apex of the Yod.

Linda: I feel self-destructive in the sense that part of me feels as if it didn't want to be born at all. I long to dissolve back into unboundedness—that is one of the pulls of Neptune. But I would rather use my Neptune in a more productive way, such as in a creative outlet or by being a more empathetic person who can bring other people to a healthier state of being.

Howard: The inconjunct has been called a "neurotic" aspect, because sometimes the two principles brought together can work well with one another and sometimes they don't work so well together. Sometimes the Mars will be swallowed up and confused by the Neptune, but at other times Neptune helps Mars assert in a sensitive or healing way.

The same rationale would apply to your Mars inconjunct Pluto. On the one hand, Pluto could sit on the Mars and turn the energy inward in a destructive fashion. On the other hand, you could learn to assert in a strong, courageous and powerful way when the Mars and Pluto co-operated together. Your self-destructiveness could also be your anger at not getting what you want, turning in on the self.

Linda: In my own therapy, I am learning to look more closely at my own needs first and then at other people's needs. Before that I was defining myself too much by what others needed me to be. I became what others needed or expected and I didn't have a clue who *I* was or what *I* wanted.

Howard: Good, so you are finding the power of Sun and Mars. I would venture to say, however, that because the Sun and Mars are in Pisces and inconjunct Neptune, that even when you have learned who you are and what you want in any situation, you may be asked to sacrifice this or adjust it to fit with what others, or the situation, require. But at least then you would know what you are sacrificing. Before you were deriving your identity from what others wanted and you didn't acknowledge what you, yourself, needed or wanted. Now you know more who you are and part of that is someone who can adapt, adjust or give to others. Do you see what I mean? You are shifting from being someone who has previously derived her identity from being what others need into someone who can more freely *choose*, when appropriate, to make some sacrifices, compromises and adjustments for the sake of others.

With the Sun and Mars in Pisces, you need to be able to choose the extent to which you want to be adaptive and open to others rather than merely reflecting whoever you are around. Because the Sun-Mars conjunction is in a Finger of Fate, you may have no choice but to adapt at times. It is a kind of *karma* and does limit your freedom to be, do, or have just anything you might want. Thanks, Linda. We could discuss your chart a long time, but we had better move on.

THE PSYCHOPATHOLOGY OF AGGRESSION

I wanted to clarify what happens if we are unable to come to terms with our own aggressive drives. There are three broad repercussions:

a) We repress our aggression and turn it inward against the self.

b) We express the aggression in explosive and childish forms.

c) We disown our aggression and attribute it to others.

We have already discussed how, if we hold back our natural aggression or repress our anger, the energy turns inward and can be a contributing factor to illness and depression. I would watch for this in the charts of people with Mars in aspect to Saturn, Uranus, Neptune or Pluto.

If you hold aggression in for too long then it will explode. When it does, it may come out in the form of temper tantrums or in ways which are inappropriate to the immediate situation.

If you disown aggression, then you may attribute it to others and fear that they are going to destroy or attack you. A man who denies his anger ends up feeling that there is nothing bad in him, but there is something "out there" which is bad, or out to get him. The nature of life is wholeness. If you are not living your wholeness then the outside brings the parts you are denying to you. What we deny in ourselves we attract from the outside and call it fate.

Paranoid people deny their hostility and attribute it to others. People who have strong placements of Mars, Uranus and Pluto, who have not acknowledged and worked with these energies, will fear that others are potentially violent or destructive. They could even subtly coerce others to act out their own anger and destructiveness for them. Oppositions to Mars, Uranus and Pluto would make it look as if the anger or assertiveness is coming at you from another. It may well be, but what part have you played in setting that up?

WAYS OF EXPRESSING AND TRANSFORMING AGGRESSION

Invariably there are times when our natural root aggression will be blocked and anger and rage will ensue. While it is not healthy to hold these feelings in, it is not always appropriate or even lawful to let them out. So what do we do with the more negative forms of aggression which come up in us?

If aggression is stored up, it needs releasing—it needs some sort of muscular discharge. Rather than just unloading your anger on someone indiscriminately, it can be expressed by pounding a mattress, hitting a cushion, through sports, or digging in the garden. This is a kind of emotional hygiene. Having discharged some of the physical build-up, it may be possible to then approach the person or situation which has angered you and express your feelings in a more steady or clean way.

You can write an angry letter and not mail it. You can pick up some crayons and draw your feelings. Such things help to bring the aggression to the surface and get it moving. If you deny some-thing in you, or shove it down, it doesn't go away, it just reappears with more force. But, if you can look at something and bring it to the surface, it eventually finds a way of shifting or flowing into something else.

Audience: I have tried drawing my feelings and my anger. It works well. I may start using a lot of black crayons and dark colours. In the beginning I am drawing furiously, letting the feelings come down through my arms and hands onto the paper. After a while doing this something starts to change—my feelings start to change. They are no longer just angry ones. I find myself reaching for lighter colour crayons to express these new feelings.

Howard: Yes, by drawing out your anger you are mobilising it, and it will begin to move and shift.

Whether you are in therapy or not, you can use your anger to work more deeply on yourself. Rather than just expressing the anger or finding ways to let go of it, you can ask, "Why do I feel that way?" or "What is this reminding me of or touching off in me?" Feeling angry gives you more "stuff" to work on. If your anger is very intense, then it may be connected to unfinished busi-ness from childhood.

Someone with a Buddhist inclination might advise you to deal with the anger by cultivating the opposite principle. Acknowledge that you feel hateful but choose to come from the opposite princi-ple of love and understanding. I'm a little wary of this because it smacks of denying or repressing your rage and trying to be too good. It is wrong to assume that if you become a mystic your anger will just go away. Nonetheless, if you can really accept you are angry, but see that it is inappropriate to express it, then perhaps this method of choosing to be the opposite will be helpful. Please remember that you can't transform anything you are condemning. If you judge your anger as bad, it will be more difficult to trans-form.

Even though anger is part of life, there may still be times when it's better to handle a situation in another way. Piero Ferrucci writes that when Florence Nightingale was asked what motivated her productive hospital work, she answered in one word, "Rage."[24] She took her anger at the conditions of medical help and channelled this into a creative and constructive outlet. If you are feeling very angry, it may be possible to channel that anger into a project you would like to be doing. You are not changing the intensity of the feelings, but you are altering the target from being angry at someone or something to putting the energy contained in anger toward constructive ends.

CONCLUSION

If you deny Mars in yourself because you are afraid of its more negative sides, then you are in danger of losing touch with that bit of you which wants to grow into what you are. If you deny Mars and the other aggressive type planets, you not only become depressed, ill or bottled up, but you also commit the fourth cardinal sin, known as *accidie* or sloth—which has been interpreted as the sin of failing to do with your life all that you know you could do. You are left with a guilt at failing to fulfil your possibilities.

I want to end today with a quote from Abraham Maslow, one of the first humanistic psychologists. He summed up the consequences of losing touch with yourself:

> If this essential core of the person is denied or suppressed, he gets sick, sometimes in obvious ways, sometimes in subtle ways, sometimes immediately, sometimes later. . . . Every falling away [from our core], every crime against one's own nature . . . records itself in our unconscious and makes us despise ourselves.[25]

Ultimately, it's up to you to make good use of Mars and the other planets that symbolise aggression in the chart.

---

[24]Ferrucci, *What We May Be*, p. 91.
[25]Abraham Maslow, *Toward a Psychology of Being* (New York: Van Nostrand, 1968), pp. 4–5.

PART 2

DEPRESSION

*. . . The descent to Avernus is easy; night and day
the door of Dis stands open; but to recall your steps
and escape into the upper air, that is the task,
that is the labour!*

Virgil

THE PSYCHOLOGICAL DYNAMICS OF DEPRESSION

Given the theme of today's seminar, I hope all of you are looking forward to a truly depressing day. Perhaps it might be interesting to begin by asking if there is anyone in the group who believes that he or she has never experienced depression. No one? If anyone had claimed such a state of perpetual good spirits, I would have been profoundly suspicious. I would like to start our discussion of depression with what we have just observed—that depression is a universal experience. We might even say that it is an archetypal experience. In its most severe forms it is crippling, and there are many people who are unable to function in life because of it and can only cope because of the antidepressants which are prescribed for them by their doctors or psychiatrists. In fact the "pill-popping" depressed housewife has become a kind of caricature—the Rolling Stones' song "Mother's Little Helper" is testimony to this. A perusal through women's magazines each month will reveal that there is almost always an article on depression in one or another of them—usually from the perspective of how to overcome or get rid of depression. There seems to be a general collective attitude which believes that, unless depression is truly severe (in which case one is "ill" and must seek help), it is best ignored. One closes one's eyes, thinks of England, and gets on with whatever one is supposed to be doing. Making sure that you are busy is generally considered a suitable antidote, and paying too much attention to it is generally considered "wallowing." Depression is not dealt with seriously unless it is serious depression; it is instead, for many people, an irritating and self-indulgent mood which is believed to arise from a concrete situation such as a relationship breakup or a bereavement, and which will pass if one does not pander to it.

Whether depression is considered a state worth exploring seriously seems, therefore, to depend upon how debilitating it is. If the individual is strong-willed and strong-minded, he or she can often get on with life. What is not generally recognised is that the depression does not go away in such a case; it merely becomes more or less unconscious, or expresses itself through the body. For those people who have become overwhelmed by depression, it is simply not possible to get on with it, and this is not necessarily a reflection of a weak will, or a tendency toward self-indulgence, as some might imagine. It may be that such an apparently unfortunate individual is in better touch with his or her feelings than the more rigidly controlled type; or it may be that however strong one is, the unconscious is stronger.

I think it would be worthwhile to first look at the clinical picture of depression. There are certain typical symptoms by which depression is identified, and one or another of them will be present to a greater or lesser extent. The most characteristic symptom is loss of libido—that is, a state of apathy and listlessness which coincides with the withdrawal of interest and energy from people, objects, and activities in the outer environment. One simply cannot get it together to do anything, or see anybody, or go anywhere. Chronic tiredness is usually the physical correspondence to this loss of libido, and sometimes it is the tiredness alone, rather than conscious awareness of apathy, that registers on the person as a symptom. The life-force has dissociated itself from life, and seems to have dropped into a hole somewhere. There is also often a kind of absent-mindedness which accompanies the loss of libido; one's threshold of consciousness is lowered, one cannot concentrate, and ordinary mundane responsibilities and tasks are forgotten or neglected. The body is one of the first things to become neglected in such a state; one cannot be bothered to wash one's hair, iron one's clothes, and so on. So a kind of mess begins to accumulate, full of unwashed dishes, unlaundered sheets and smelly shirts, overflowing rubbish bags, sour two-week-old milk in the refrigerator—I think you get the picture. Lack of interest in personal hygiene is one of the most frequent external expressions of depression.

Around all of these surface manifestations of depression one gets a very clear portrait of a kind of process of decay occurring in the individual's relationship with external reality. The sleeping pattern is often disturbed, so that one wakes up very early in the morning and has difficulty in getting to sleep the night before. Eating habits can also undergo changes—compulsive eating or ignoring food, and reaching for the alcohol more and more frequently. I think that most people experience this level of depression at some time in their lives. Sometimes the symptoms of depression are more severe and more frightening. The individual may feel his or her body to be ugly, an object of disgust; and there is a kind of vicious circle in this, because the tendency to neglect the body increases the feeling that it is dirty and disgusting. Sometimes there are deeply disturbing fantasies that one is rotting, or has a bad smell, or is full of worms or disease. Because it is so embarrassing for people to talk about such fantasies and feelings, the deeply depressed person often does not realise that these are not uncommon experiences, and that they may be more meaningful than they at first seem.

You will see by this charming description of the classic symptoms of depression that much of this mysterious psychic state seems to be linked up with one's relationship to one's body. The body is often the first part of us to act out the depression, sometimes long before the individual even realises any of the feelings which are inherent in it; and it is also the body which is experienced as bad, ugly, or rotten. The negation of life which is part of depression is experienced first through one's feelings about one's body. If the depression becomes very severe, then the individual may simply sit and do nothing at all; and then we can begin to talk about what psychiatry calls depressive breakdown, where there is no longer any capability of functioning in ordinary life. One cannot get up in the morning, one cannot go to work, one cannot communicate. There is a kind of numbness or paralysis. The queer thing about this numbness, especially when it occurs without the more florid symptoms of depressive breakdown, is that often the individual is not aware of feeling anything at all. We usually think of depression as a state where we feel terrible or hopeless or in despair. But it would seem that if you are actually in a position to experience and express such feelings, you are a good deal more related to yourself—and perhaps much healthier—than the individual who has simply blanked out and feels nothing but apathy.

Perhaps we should not even call the more emotionally expressive state depression, but rather, immersion in negative or dark feelings. I think that what we call clinical depression is very bound up with despair which is not felt. There is no sense of being depressed, for the depression has the person, rather than the person having the depression. The deadness and the apathy, and the mess building up in the cupboard, express to the outside observer what the individual cannot express because he or she does not experience any feelings. The fantasies of the rotten or ugly body are not feelings; they are obsessive thoughts, like the conviction that life is worthless, or that one is a failure. There is no feeling attached to such obsessive convictions and fantasies. One does nothing because it is all hopeless anyway. Any of you who have ever actually experienced such a state will know that the last thing a person in the grip of this kind of depression can do is say, "I feel terrible." He or she feels nothing at all.

Now there seems to be a dichotomy on the part of orthodox psychiatry when dealing with severe depressive states. On the one hand, there is reputedly one kind of depression which is caused by circumstances, and another kind which is endogenous, that is, organic and unconnected with external events. In other words, if someone becomes very depressed and it can be determined that his or her mother died six months before, then it is assumed that the depression has been caused by the death of the mother and that therefore the individual will get over it. But this is much trickier than it seems. Obviously here is a concrete factor which can be linked directly to the depression. I remember once reading an article in the British Journal of Psychiatry, in which careful statistical research over a period of years demonstrated incontrovertible proof that most people who lose a loved one become depressed. Thank God for statistics; we would never have been able to work that one out ourselves! Anyway, we cannot argue that certain typical life situations trigger depression. I am using the word "trigger" rather than "cause" very deliberately. Grief is one of these triggers, particularly grief which has not been expressed or acknowledged at the time of the triggering event. If a loved one dies or leaves, and the individual represses all emotional reactions and does not acknowledge the terrible sense of loss and rage and hopelessness, then often that person will become very depressed some time later—often a considerable time later—when there is no longer any apparent reason for the depression. A little judicious counselling, even from a friend rather than from a professional, will often reveal that the process of mourning, which is natural and inevitable, has not been worked through; and so depression seems to follow as a kind of substitute for mourning, a way in which the repressed feelings can express themselves.

This is often the case when a relationship ends—particularly with the more reasonable type who thinks he or she understands all about why it went wrong and why it was necessary to part. Everyone stays friends and it is all very civilised, and the feelings which would be natural to this situation—which is, after all, a kind of death that merits grief and mourning—are not acknowledged. Then depression follows later. I think this causal aspect of depression, even when it is delayed long past the actual event, is understandable enough. The astrologer may not necessarily be concerned with this causal kind of depression, except insofar as the horoscope will often suggest a personality which is prone to repressing the natural feelings of grief, rage, and despair after a loss. The psychiatrist must concern himself or herself with this type of depression because it is commonly met in the hospital wards. Psychotherapy can be of enormous value here, because the individual can begin to grieve openly, and then the depression may leave. There is, of course, a much subtler and more complicated aspect to causal depression, which I will talk about in a little while. This aspect concerns the reasons why the same experience of bereavement or separation causes a brief period of depression in one person, and a severe depressive breakdown in another. But we will come to that later.

The second type of depression, which psychiatry calls endogenous, is more baffling. There appears to be no external cause. There may be a very minor trigger, but it is obviously minor, and utterly out of proportion to the severity of the depression. Here the event, if there is one, is very obviously a catalyst, rather than a cause. Other individuals might bounce back quickly from such a trigger situation, while the depressed person simply cannot seem to recover. It is fashionable in some psychiatric circles to attribute endogenous depression in women to the menopause, because this kind of depression occurs very frequently in women at this time in life. But unfortunately for this theory, men are also afflicted by endogenous depression; and there is not such a handy hormonal culprit to blame. Then one may hear the equally specious explanation that there really is a cause—the problem of ageing, and facing the dilemmas of growing old. One reaches middle age, the body is not as attractive as it used to be, wrinkles are forming, arthritis appears in the joints, and lo and behold, the person becomes depressed. It seems that many people—particularly in the medical and psychiatric fields—cannot relinquish the idea that there must be a sole and specific external cause or reason for depression.

Another baffling aspect of endogenous depression is that it tends to be cyclical in many people. The out-patient facilities at psychiatric hospitals are full of people who come and go with regular cyclical depressive states. Usually the bouts of depression last for roughly a two-year period. Now you all know how long Saturn spends in one sign of the zodiac. I will slip that in as an aside. There has been some interesting research done with people afflicted by such cyclical depressions, and it seems that whether or not the individual is given treatment—antidepressants or ECT or whatever—he or she tends to get better anyway after that malevolent two-year bout. There is a peculiar timing with many cases of endogenous depression. What all this really says is that, unless there is an intelligible external cause for depression, its meaning and its workings remain a mystery to organic psychiatry.

Audience: But don't you think that there are many justifiable causes for depression given the current state of the world? Perhaps the cause is not so specific as a death, but more to do with the general environment.

Liz: If we wish to consider depression as always having a literal cause, then yes, everything in life could be seen as a potential cause of depression. The fact that we are mortal and one day must die is in itself depressing. There is a kind of "existential *angst*"—I think that is the correct expression—which arises from the sheer absurdity of the human condition. No doubt Jean-Paul Sartre was always depressed. But I feel it is very specious to view depression solely from this perspective. Some people cope with basic life conflicts and challenges; and some don't. Some find the world unutterably depressing, while others find great beauty and meaning in it, even if their personal circumstances are difficult. Why should this be? We are always led back to the individual. If depression were really a reflection of the fact that life is basically rotten, then why doesn't everybody think so? Yet some people who have been through truly terrible experiences do not see life as a horrible place. They find richness and joy in it. Others, who have had it pretty easy from the point of view of circumstances, fall into tremendous depressions for no observable reason, or only a very slight one. To only look outside for the roots of depression is, I feel, extremely naive. Astrology is a tool for great insight into the individual, and I think it will be useful for us today in exploring why people differ in their responses to these apparent external causes for depression. Some people are apparently resilient enough to deal with the vicissitudes of life, while others are not. Something which would push one person into a period of sadness and loneliness for a few months might completely cripple another individual for many years. One person takes as an optimistic challenge an experience which another takes as total defeat. We are always facing the mystery of subjective response, even when we are dealing with an obvious cause like death or separation. There is a unique individual who responds to that situation in his or her own special way; and there are people who seem to be predisposed toward responding with chronic or severe depression. This is one of the main points which I would like to explore today: Is there anything in the birth horoscope, and in the transits and progressions, which might suggest that an individual is predisposed toward depression? And if so, what does this mean? In my experience, just about anything in life can cause depression if the individual is predisposed toward becoming depressed. Sometimes achievement and the attainment of long-sought goals can trigger depression. And ultimately, knowing the trigger does not always help. It may simply make no difference, because it is the individual response which holds the real key.

THE ARCHETYPAL BACKGROUND OF DEPRESSION

Now I would like to leave the clinical picture of depression aside for the moment, and begin to look at ways in which we might approach the experience of depression through amplification. I think it is useful to look first at some of the mythic images which portray the state of depression, and there are a great many of these. This is because, as I suggested earlier, depression is an archetypal experience, just as birth and death are. The imagery of depression which appears in an individual's dreams is filled with this archetypal background, and we need to consider not only mythology but symbolic systems such as alchemy and the tarot to help us focus on the deeper meaning of depression.

I will start with the symbolism of alchemy, because the imagery of alchemy is full of pictures of what we call depression. In alchemy, depression is placed in context as a particular stage of the alchemical process, rather than as an isolated occurrence. I think this is a most important point, for we do not often consider depression as part of a larger cycle of development. Also, I have found that alchemical imagery occurs very frequently in the dreams of people who are deeply depressed. These images seem to revolve around the theme of the decay and death and irrevocable mortality of the body—the fact that it is seeded with its own doom from the moment of birth, and that it carries within it this inexorable fate. Alongside images of the decaying body or rotting corpse—delightful, I should have saved this bit for just before lunch, don't you think?—one finds in alchemical literature many images of filth, shit, mud and black earth. These are, in short, the images which we associate with the experience of the shadow-side of the personality, and the confrontation with one's own inherent evil.

I mentioned in *The Astrology of Fate*[1] a dream which a man told me during the chart interpretation I was giving him, which I would like to mention here because it is very relevant to alchemical symbolism. This man was very depressed when he came to see me about his chart. The transits were hardly surprising; Saturn and Pluto were conjunct in Libra and transiting his natal Sun in the midheaven. Now we will see as we go on today that Saturn and Pluto are key planets for the theme of depression. My client was a successful publisher, who had built up a solid international market for his scientific and technical books. But he was fed up with it all, and had bought some land in Australia which he wanted to farm. It

---

[1] Liz Greene, *The Astrology of Fate* (York Beach, ME: Samuel Weiser, 1984; and London: Unwin Hyman Ltd., 1984).

seemed as though his life should have been opening up, since he was able to sell his company for a large sum and could enjoy the rest of his life on the profits. But he fell into a terrible depression. This is not as surprising as one might think. It is a very common experience for many people who have finally achieved a lifelong dream and then feel perfectly awful. And it is useless to look for an obvious cause, since the cause is the opposite to what it logically ought to be. When I looked at my client's chart, I was particularly interested in the fact that he had a midheaven Sun and a Capricorn ascendant. I began to talk to him about some of the typical experiences of Saturn and Pluto transits—especially the latter planet—and about the alchemical imagery of death, dismemberment, rotting bodies and skulls. The skull, the "dead head" or *caput mortuum* of alchemy, is an image for what is left of the true essence after all the dross has been stripped away. My client told me he dreamed that he had died; and instead of his head, he had a bare skull. In order to converse with his friends, he had to wear this skull; for without it he would have been invisible, as he was no longer alive. In another room were all his technical books lined up in glass cases like the display cases at the British Museum. In yet another room his funeral was taking place. and his mother was weeping wildly over his coffin. She didn't know that he still existed, for she identified him with the body, which had died. He knew that he must wait for his rebirth. His friends were disgusted by the skull which he wore, and left him, so he was alone in the dream with the books in one room and the wailing mother in the other.

My client told me that for some unaccountable reason this dream had made him feel better about being depressed. He couldn't explain why, but he was left with a deep sense that he was waiting for something, and that his depression was a strange kind of transition. Here you can see what alchemical symbolism portrays—that the man's depression is indeed an initiatory stage, between one phase of life and the next. His worldly success was bound up on very deep levels with his relationship to the mother, who was extremely ambitious and tried to live through him. She wanted a brilliant intellectual son, and that was what he became—although he had always wanted to farm. To the extent that his identity, his Sun, was glued to his mother's unconscious need for a vessel who would act out her own redemption, he had never lived his own life. The publishing empire that he had built was a great achievement from a worldly point of view; but from an inner point of view, he had no idea who he was at all. When Saturn and Pluto reached the Sun, this was the beginning of his true separation from the mother. It is the symbolic death of the mother, and the birth of his own identity. The physical act of buying land in Australia and at last fulfilling his own ambition to farm was a reflection of this inner death. Naturally he became depressed, for he had to mourn the loss of the old self, the false self, and also mourn the inner death of the mother. The mother in the dream was grieving over the person who died because that was the identity that belonged to the mother. But the man remains, although his mother cannot see him. The books in glass cases are the fossilised trophies of this completed incarnation. Meanwhile he awaits the new birth—the emergence of the man who is himself rather than an extension of his mother's unconscious ambitions.

In alchemy, the darkness and disintegration which precede and surround the imagery of the skull, or "dead head," are called the *nigredo*. This stage of the alchemical process reflects the breaking down of the old substance into its essential components, which can only be accomplished with a certain amount of stink and decay. Nigredo simply means "blackening." Without the nigredo, there is no possibility of the old base substance being transformed, for it must first be stripped and cleansed and reduced to its essence; and that cannot be accomplished without decay and death. Without the nigredo, there is no possibility of anything new growing. So the imagery of the nigredo, which is also the imagery of depression, is, in alchemical symbolism, necessary and fitting, although ugly and unpleasant. My client had read no alchemy (it was not scientific enough), and at first couldn't understand what I was talking about. His dream formed the basis for his understanding. Yet the image in the dream is an archetypal one, because he is an individual making a passage through an archetypal place—the separation from the mother, and the birth of his masculine identity.

Perhaps I should mention at this point something about the condition which psychiatry calls manic depression. We might understand the manic end of this undulating spectrum of emotional states as a kind of frenzied defence against the depressed end. Some people fly away from the encroaching darkness of deep depression by climbing up into semi-divine heights, where one believes one is gifted, special, capable of achieving anything, and virtually immortal. Naturally a person cannot stay on this high level, because sooner or later reality intrudes, and then the person falls like Icarus down into the sea of the depression. When the mask is stripped away, then what is left is the skull, the *caput mortuum*. Behind the manic flight, where the individual experiences himself or herself as shining and beautiful and omnipotent, lies the darkness of the shadow. I think we should include manic depression under the general topic of depression, because as I have said, the manic phases are really a particular kind of defence against depression. Some people, on the other hand, have no defence against it at all.

So, in summary, the nigredo of alchemy is an image of a particular phase of the alchemical process, which is in its entirety really a description of psychological development and transformation. The nigredo is necessary, and must precede the more advanced stages of the process. It reflects the problem of being plunged into the experience of mortality and the darker world of the shadow. Often this nigredo, when it is experienced by an adult, is a kind of regression back into childhood, where the mature ego breaks down and all the dark and primitive infantile feelings come rushing to the surface. The term "shadow" is a very large one, and can cover a number of dimensions of experience—one's weakness, one's inferiority, one's evil, one's deformity and darkness, one's primitiveness. Who are you without your mask, your acceptable persona? Behind it lies the skull. We might say that the person who has plunged into depression is no longer able to use the persona to hide from the thing beneath, the mortal body with all its sin and darkness. One is not an eternal spirit, one is not going to live forever in youth and beauty and divine grace. One is simply human. The alchemists were very insistent about their nigredo; without it, they declared, you can make no gold, you can never release the divine essence within base matter.

So, in certain instances and with certain experiences of depression, it is possible to see this difficult state as the beginning of something very important. If we look at depression in this context, it is the real end of childhood, the real facing of one's essential self and one's limits. It is the first stage of a process, rather than a nasty illness which must be cured. I do not mean that we should not make the effort to work with and help the state of depression. But one can see its value and its meaning at the same time, rather than viewing it like a dose of the flu, or the mechanical effect of some external cause. I think the amplification of alchemy throws a rather disturbing light on our collective attitudes toward depression. There is something inside depression which is worth seeking and exploring. If one runs away from this, then one has blocked the process of growth which depends upon an understanding and integration of this state; and then, naturally, it will come back again, and again, and again.

Audience: What about the person who has been depressed almost all his or her life? That is an awfully long nigredo.

Liz: Yes, it is rather like the person who is still trying to make it through puberty after fifty years. I don't mean to imply that every depression is a nigredo. But even if we see it in this light, it is possible for a person to get stuck in it, just as it is possible for a baby to encounter difficulties during the process of birth. A depression of many years' standing began someplace, at some time; and it is possible that, had the thing been understood and worked with then, it might indeed have represented a rite of passage. But if nothing at all is understood, then one can get stuck. I don't think we have many collective resources with which to approach depression in a spirit of real comprehension. Most of the time, one starts taking antidepressants, which initially may be very valuable because they help the person to cope again; but they are usually seen as a solution rather than a temporary aid to facilitate the individual arriving in a place where understanding can begin. It is like Theseus in the myth, going down into the underworld and sitting on a rock and then finding that he cannot get up again. Perhaps the best way to view this problem of the depression which does not fulfil its function as a rite of passage, a nigredo, but which becomes fixed and unalterable, is to look at an example. Let's look at Chart 3, a woman with just this problem. This will begin to take us into the astrology of depression, as well as addressing the problem of why some people never seem to come out of it, or spend half their lives in it.

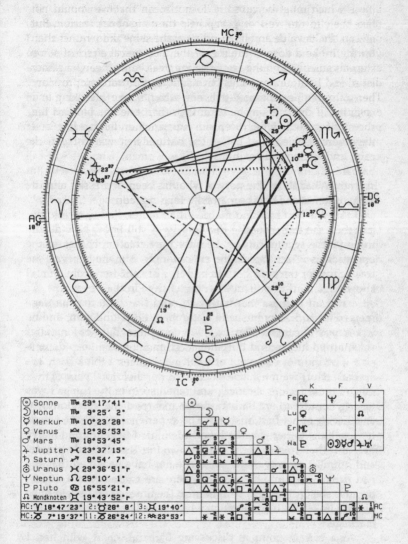

								K	F	V
☉ Sonne	♏ 29°17'41"						Fe	AC	Ψ	♄
☽ Mond	♏ 9°25' 2"						Lu	♀		☊
☿ Merkur	♏ 10°23'28"						Er	MC		
♀ Venus	♎ 12°36'53"						Wa	P	☉☽☿♂	♃♅
♂ Mars	♏ 16°53'45"									
♃ Jupiter	♓ 23°37'15"									
♄ Saturn	♐ 8°54' 7"									
⛢ Uranus	♓ 29°36'51"r									
♆ Neptun	♌ 29°10' 1"									
♇ Pluto	♋ 16°55'21"r									
☊ Mondknoten	♉ 19°43'52"r									

AC: ♈ 18°47'23"	2: ♉ 28° 8'	3: ♓ 19°40'
MC: ♉ 7°19'37"	11: ♉ 26°24'	12: ♒ 23°53'

Chart 3. Barbara. The birth data has been withheld for confidentiality. Chart calculated by Astrodienst, using the Placidus house system.

Let me first give you some case material on this woman. She has been in and out of psychiatric care for about thirty years, always for deep depression and depressive breakdown. She is, I think, the kind of individual to whom you were referring. When she was still quite young, around seventeen or eighteen, she had a lover and became pregnant; but her lover did not want to marry her, although he continued to live with her, so she gave birth to an illegitimate child. Then she became pregnant again, and this time she managed to talk her lover into marrying her. But not long after they were married, and before the birth of her second child, the man left her, and killed himself. This woman, whom I will call Barbara, then raised her two children—daughters—by herself. But she never told them the story of what had happened, nor told the first child that she had been born before the marriage. She simply said that she had met and married their father, had two children, and then the father died. I think many of you know how deadly these family secrets can be, because they create a charge in the unconscious which infects the entire family. But she believed she was acting for the best, both to preserve her children from painful knowledge, and to preserve her own image in their eyes.

Later on Barbara married again, and this time the marriage seemed to work. Her husband was apparently a kind man, and he was happy to care for Barbara's two daughters. But not long after she married her second husband, Barbara fell into a deep depression. She did not come out of it for many years. I think there are several factors we must look at from the psychological perspective. One of these factors is causal, and reminiscent of the things I was talking about earlier: Barbara never mourned the abandonment and suicide of her first husband. This experience must have been a terrible blow to her—she had worked so hard to get him to marry her, and then immediately lost him, and in a particularly painful and humiliating way. How could she not have imagined that she had driven him into suicide? So there are causal factors which, because she did not deal with them at the time, could be said to be directly linked to the depression which came later, after her second marriage.

At a certain point in discussing Barbara's chart with her, I asked her about her relationship with her father. She told me, "Oh, he was a wonderful man. We had no problems at all." I think you all know how inclined I am to question statements like that. If one has had such a wonderful childhood and such a wonderful father, why then does one get oneself into such a mess over men? Ian Fleming once wrote that once is chance, twice is coincidence, and three times is enemy action. This is enemy action—the action of an unconscious complex. Barbara's birthtime is vague, and consequently the Ascendant and house cusps are uncertain. But I think the signs and aspects are rather interesting. There is an apparently causal basis for Barbara's depression—the unexpressed mourning for her first husband, and the burden of carrying what for Barbara constitutes a shameful secret. But there is something else at work here besides the causal issue.

You will see that the Sun and Moon are both in Scorpio, along with two other planets. Although I cannot calculate the Moon's degree precisely, it was at 2 degrees Scorpio at GMT midnight, so it is unquestionably in Scorpio—anywhere from 2 to 14 degrees. My guess is that it's in conjunction with Mars, because of the way in which Barbara has acted out her problem. When she was in one of her very bad states, she had a tendency to stand in front of the window and start yelling that she was going to jump. A powerful and particularly ferocious anger erupted from her, and it is this anger which seems to have underpinned the depression and motivated the suicide attempts. Barbara took overdoses and left the empty bottles lying about. She made small cuts on her wrists, just deep enough to look messy and frightening. The clinical label for this kind of behaviour is "incomplete suicide," which is one of those truly helpful labels which abound in the psychiatric world. An incomplete suicide is a suicide which fails because it is meant to fail. It is not a true attempt at suicide, because if one really wishes to make an end of it, one can find ways where one is not likely to be found. The incomplete suicide is not only a "plea for help," although it is certainly that too. It is a way of punishing others, of making them feel guilty and responsible for the terrible depressed state in which Barbara lived; and it is an expression of deep rage.

Apropos of the wonderful father with whom Barbara had no problems at all, it is perhaps worth mentioning that she feels disappointed and let down by both the first and second husbands. The first one was an obviously hurtful experience, and I have told you how it ended. But her second marriage has not been a success either, despite its promising beginning. She feels great anger toward her husband because, according to her description, he is very cold and does not respond at all to her emotional needs. He has been inclined to treat her depressions and violence in a very detached way: "Oh, well, here she goes again," and so on. He was very competent with her during the worst periods. He bundled her into the car and drove her to the doctor or to the hospital, and did the necessary. But he does not seem to react on any personal level to what she has been trying to say through all her acting out. He never has, through all the years of the marriage. I think we should look at the square in Barbara's chart between Venus and Pluto. Her feelings have a terrific intensity. There is so much water in this chart – the stellium in Scorpio, and Pluto in Cancer, and two more planets in Pisces. That's seven planets in water. She is inundated with passionate feeling, and has chosen a man who does not seem to value or respond to any of it at all. That must have been a truly wonderful father she had.

Audience: Does she have any outlet for her creative imagination?

Liz: She has just begun to find outlets now. She has started to take a university degree, at this late stage in life. That in itself is a kind of miracle, considering how deep the darkness was in which she lived for so many years.

Audience: But now she has begun to work with her feelings.

Liz: Yes, now she has begun. She started analysis some time ago, with someone who was able to handle her depression and her anger, a man who could contain the immensely powerful erotic transference she needed to place on him without recoiling. It is not easy for anyone, therapist or husband or wife or lover or friend, to remain firm but emotionally receptive when confronted with a double Scorpio on the rampage. The dominant note of Barbara's feelings through most of her life has been hatred and anger, and a desire to destroy not only herself but everyone around her. But apart from the suicide attempts, which were usually understood as manipulative pleas for help and nurturing, her depression was not interpreted as an expression of rage. When she was deeply depressed, one would not have immediately said, "Ah, here is an angry woman." Only the suicide attempts revealed the anger beneath. But the doctors who treated her, and her husband as well, understood these as expressions of hopelessness, not of killing fury. Under Barbara's depression something had got stuck, a kind of failed nigredo which somehow could not progress to the next stage. She was simply unable to formulate her feelings, and as long as she could not formulate them, she could not move.

Audience: Does this have something to do with the lack of earth in the chart?

Liz: Yes, I think the lack of earth has something to do with it. Perhaps even more, I think this reflects Barbara's lack of air. There is only one planet in an airy sign. Both earth and air are concerned with detachment and perspective, rationality and realism. Without these, Barbara's feelings constantly threatened to overwhelm her, but she could not express them, or name them, or ground them in any way. Also, she has a tendency to idealise people, which is also related to the lack of earth and air. She could not face her own hatred and destructiveness. I would make an educated guess that Barbara had some rather violently angry feelings toward the first husband, long before he ran off and killed himself. After all, she had to work so very hard to get him to marry her in the first place. I think the murderous rage was there much earlier than the outbreak of the depression. It was cumulative, as it often is with Scorpios. There was probably also the same murderous rage toward the wonderful father, whom I suspect treated her in much the same way as the two husbands, and made it plain that he did not really want her or her passionate feelings. But of course she could not have said to herself when her first husband died, "I'm glad he did that, because if he hadn't I would have done it for him." What sort of nice decent woman can admit to such feelings at the death of a husband? Lack of earth in Barbara's chart suggests to me that she has had little sense of realism about her feelings. She has had to work very hard on this issue. She could not see and accept the human limitations of another person; she was quite without boundaries around her feelings. She could not hold her emotions within her body. They flooded out everywhere and swamped her and the other person as well. I think that she was very frightened that if the full force of her anger erupted, she would kill. Faced with that terror, it becomes more sensible to kill oneself instead, because one is so awful. So she was terrified by her own feelings, and the lack of air in turn has made it very difficult for her to step out of her own dilemma and look at it objectively.

Audience: Can you say more about the possible Moon-Mars conjunction? Why is this a significator of great anger?

Liz: I think Moon-Mars is the significator of a very powerful desire nature which does not like being thwarted. Moon-Mars is not angry if the person gets at least some of what he or she wants. The Moon reflects an individual's instinctual needs, while Mars reflects aggression and desire. If they are found together, then this is the picture of a rather greedy appetite. Do you remember the nickname of the main character in the film *The Return of Martin Guerre*? He was called Pansette, which in French slang means "the Belly," because he had such huge appetites for everything—wine, women, food, fighting, sensual pleasures of all kinds. Moon-Mars is like Pansette. It can be wonderfully vital and sensual, as long as it is satisfied. But when the Moon happens to be in Scorpio, which is not known for its cool detachment, and when the object of all that desire is not able to respond, then I think great anger is the inevitable result. Moon-Mars is not a statement of anger, but rather of wilfulness. It is interesting that Barbara attacked her own body during her acting out periods—threatening to throw herself from windows, and cutting her wrists. It is almost as though she were punishing her body for feeling all those powerful desires. By destroying her body, perhaps she believed she could free herself from the body's passions. This is not very far away from the medieval flagellant who viciously punished his body because of its disgusting carnality. But it is sad that, during all the years that Barbara underwent psychiatric treatment with antidepressants, nothing changed. It was not until she began to express her anger, and the intense erotic desire that hid underneath it, that she could move from the nigredo into the next stage. And the danger of real, as opposed to "incomplete," suicide only occurred as she began to come out of the darkness. Depressed people are, statistically, more likely to actually kill themselves at the moment that they start getting better. Perhaps this is because they are finally facing the depth of their own rage, and the picture of themselves is too black and terrifying. When the rage is blanketed by deep depression, they are numb, and feel nothing but hopelessness. But at least in that state they do not have to face the violence and the destructiveness, and can still retain an illusion of being a nice person who has been victimised by life.

I will now make what will probably sound like a sweeping generalisation, but sweeping though it is, I think it is valid. There are two astrological signs which are inherently prone to depression—Scorpio and Capricorn. These signs tend to express their problems through the symbol of depression because depression in a strange way serves their purposes. Capricorn favours depression over other expressions of inner conflict because depression serves Capricorn's inherent sense of guilt. It is a good vindication of what a miserable lot it is to be alive anyway, and what a wretched place the world is, and what a thoroughly appalling person one is oneself. Scorpio favours depression because it is an excellent and effective form of expressing vindictive anger while remaining relatively blameless in the eyes of others; and also, depression keeps others out. One can nurse one's wounds in privacy. There is some of this at work in Barbara. It was easier for her to be poisoned by hate than for her to actually allow another person to give her love, since this would have made her vulnerable. To be vulnerable means that one relinquishes power, and that is often very frightening to Scorpio. It is better to have a grievance which justifies Scorpio's mistrust and withholding, since the mistrust serves as a defence. Like impotence, depression can be a disguised form of aggression, because it forces others to look after the person and puts them to terrible trouble and pain. In Scorpio's hands— and I include under this umbrella the individual who has a strong Pluto as well as the person in whom the sign is dominant—it can be a form of control. Obviously none of this is done consciously. Barbara did not sit down and work out a strategy. But you can see the "secondary gain" factor in Barbara's depression, which is a characteristic Scorpio depression. It is a very successful manipulation of the environment, because depression can dominate an entire family, as well as one's friends and work colleagues, all of whom must make allowances and be attentive.

Audience: Can it be a call for help?

Liz: Certainly it is a call for help, just as "incomplete suicide" is a call for help. But there may be other things at work as well, which is why the therapist or family member or friend who interprets it as solely a plea for help is so often baffled when the proffered help is rejected. Any symptom is a call for help; but the call is ambivalent, and contains many conflicting messages. The person is saying, "Help me!" but at the same time he or she is saying, "If you come near me I will kill you." Also, "You cannot help me, you are powerless and impotent, no matter what you do I am still depressed." And additionally, "I will make all your lives miserable to punish you because you cannot redeem mine." And maybe even, "I am such a disgusting and abhorrent creature that I deserve to be in this state, so do not try to get me out, for I will defeat you." I think all these statements were being made by Barbara's depression. The morass of complicated and conflicting feelings is also very characteristic of Pluto, which is about as simple and easy to read as shaking hands with an octopus. It is very difficult to help a person who is deeply depressed, because at the same time that he or she has come for help, there is a resistance against being helped. And what we call the countertransference when one works with a depressed person can also be very difficult, because the psychotherapist can easily begin to be infected by it and ends up having to carry the unconscious anger of the patient. The anger is directed against the psychotherapist, and the psychotherapist starts thinking, "I am probably not any good at this. I cannot help this patient no matter how hard I try. I am a failure." One can begin to feel deeply undermined and impotent. If one keeps one's wits, one might begin to see from this how much anger is directed at oneself as the therapist. It is as though the depressed patient has brought a Gorgon along to the sessions. You will be familiar with the Gorgon in Greek myth—the hideous creature whose face turned anyone who looked at her to stone. Depression is like a Gorgon. The Gorgon sits there staring evilly at the therapist, and says, "You can try anything you like. I am not going to get better. I will sit here and rot, and you will discover that you have no power at all to help me." So yes, depression is a desperate call for help. There is something underneath the depression which is trying to come out, so that the nigredo can progress. But at the same time, the depressed person may mercilessly punish anyone who tries to come too close with an offer of help and sympathy. Depression of this kind, which I associate with the astrological Scorpio and Pluto, contains a deep ambivalence.

Audience: Is depression different from melancholy?

Liz: I think it is what medieval medicine and philosophy meant by melancholia. The melancholic humour was always associated in medieval astrology with Saturn. There is a very interesting book on the theme of melancholia called *The Occult Philosophy in the Elizabethan Age*, by Frances Yates.[2] This book explores the philosophical attitude of the Renaissance toward what we would now call depression. There seems to have been a belief that in order for a person to be truly creative—that is, inspired by a divine spark—he or she had to be melancholic. A connection was drawn between creative inspiration and the black state into which the true artist or philosopher fell. This is essentially the same thing that alchemical symbolism portrays—that the elixir, the alchemical gold, can only emerge if the black and putrid state of the nigredo is passed through first. It was assumed during the 15th and 16th centuries, when Hermetic philosophy and alchemy were at their peak in Western Europe, that one had to be of a melancholic nature in order to be in touch with any of the deeper mysteries. And this was connected with Saturn, both in the birth horoscope and in transits. When we use the word "melancholy" now, I think we mean something a bit less severe than depression. There is something very profound hinted at in this strange relationship between depression and creativity. Obviously many very depressed people, such as Barbara whose chart we examined earlier, are not able to be creative. They are simply depressed. But despite this, there seems to be a connection. It is one of the secrets hidden beneath depression,

---

[2]Frances Yates, *The Occult Philosophy in the Elizabethan Renaissance* (New York: Methuen, 1983; and London: Routledge & Kegan Paul, 1979).

and one of the reasons why it seems to be so important to explore depression, rather than trying to fly out of it with antidepressants and no insight. Later on, when we go further into the astrological patterns which might be associated with a tendency to depression, you will see that these same configurations could also be viewed as enormously creative ones – at least, in potential. Depression is like a prism. If you turn it one way, you see an illness. If you turn it another, you see a key to a door that leads to a very mysterious and numinous place.

There have been periods when the melancholic temperament was seen as very romantic, and even fashionable. To a certain extent this was the case during the Elizabethan period that Frances Yates has explored so deeply. One can visualise the figure of the magus – someone like Giordano Bruno, perhaps, or John Dee – sitting in a foul black mood surrounded by vials and alembics and parchments, completely depressed and unable to work, brooding and contemplating all sorts of dark things. And then suddenly the light of inspiration strikes, and the magus leaps up and begins furiously writing and experimenting because he has had a great revelation. It is almost a caricature. But the so-called artistic temperament does indeed behave a little like this, and it is not just posturing. There is naturally some posturing in it. The melancholic poet, such as Byron or Shelley, or Keats who was essentially a manic depressive although it would be rude and unromantic to call him that, was expected to behave in such ways because melancholic troughs were felt to be part of the suffering of the creative nature. It isn't very romantic any more. There are too many people suffering from depression which produces no magical bouts of creative inspiration, and manic depressives are now put on lithium. Melancholia has been stripped of all its romantic connotations. It's all very well if one is an artist, but if one isn't, then what is the point? Barbara's depression was in no sense romantic. And yet, and yet . . .

Audience: Liz, can I go back to Barbara's chart? Wouldn't so many planets in Scorpio make her rather paranoid about her depression? She might be particularly ashamed of it, and secretive about it, and therefore unable to work with it creatively.

Liz: I see your point, but I think what you are calling paranoid is actually part of the condition of depression. I would have thought that it is the planets in Scorpio which predispose Barbara toward being what a medieval physician would have called melancholic, and the slightly paranoid flavour of that state is an inevitable dimension of it. I would like to talk a little about this issue of shame and paranoia, because it is an important facet of the psychological dynamics of depression. Melanie Klein is a very interesting person to read on what she called the "depressive position." This stage of development is part of the process of the emerging ego in childhood. If the process is arrested or is not worked through, then particular stages of it will reappear in the adult person's pathology. Klein's language is rather heavy, and terms like "paranoid-schizoid position" and "depressive position" are a mouthful. But I will try to describe these as best I can, because I think Klein's ideas are very valuable in helping us to understand the workings of depression.

The idea of the paranoid-schizoid position is that a very young child is not yet capable of containing ambivalent emotions such as love and hate at the same time. There is not yet an ego which can handle the tension between these states, and no faculty of reason which can render them less primitive. The young child cannot yet cope with the experience of both good and evil in the mother, or in himself or herself. When there is an experience of unity with the mother, and a trust in the eternal presence of the good nourishing breast, then the mother is good. When the mother goes away, she becomes evil, and the child feels terrible rage and destructiveness toward her. Klein suggested that there is enormous tension between the feelings of love and trust on the one hand, and hatred and destructiveness on the other. If the ego cannot yet contain the realisation that it is possible to feel both hate and love about another person without anyone being destroyed, and that it is possible for another person to be both lovable and hateable, then these ambivalent feelings will be split. This is what is meant by the term "splitting." So either the mother becomes a black, rejecting, evil monster while the child experiences himself or herself as good and loving, or the mother is good and beautiful and loving, but the child experiences himself or herself as black and evil because of the destructive feelings. Either the good or the evil will be projected, while the opposite becomes identified with oneself. This is the paranoid-schizoid position—paranoid because paranoia always involves projection of one's own destructive feelings outside onto other people, and schizoid because there is an essential split between emotions which belong to the same person and are felt toward the same person.

To actually experience the mother as someone who can sometimes be good and loving, and sometimes bad and rejecting, requires a certain degree of ego development. The same applies to oneself and one's experience of being someone who is capable of both loving and hateful feelings. The movement from the paranoid-schizoid position to the depressive position means a gradual separation from the mother, so that the child emerges as a separate entity with the beginnings of an individuality, and the mother also emerges as a separate entity who is different from the child. Many people get stuck somewhere between these two stages of development. They never fully enter the depressive position, because it is, quite literally, depressing to realise that life is not as simple as good and bad breasts. Thus depression, viewed through Kleinian eyes, is concerned with an acceptance and internalisation of one's own evil, one's own potential for destructiveness. If an individual has got stuck before reaching this relatively mature point of development, then something of the old paranoid-schizoid attitude will remain beneath that person's behaviour in adult personal relationships. Lovers become either idealised divine objects, or terrible cold rejecting monsters. Usually the lover will start by being idealised while one feels oneself to be inferior and lucky to have found such a wonderful person; and then, when he or she does something hurtful—which is, of course, inevitable sooner or later—then the divine object rapidly deteriorates into the devil, while one emerges as the blameless victim of someone else's callousness. This pattern is extremely common, as I can see some of you realise by the uncomfortable grins on your faces. In its more pathological forms, paranoia is a projection of very powerful destructive feelings onto outside objects and people. Everyone else is murderous, but certainly not me; I am a sweet and loving person who hasn't got a nasty thought in my head, but the world is full of evil, vicious creatures who are out to destroy me personally. Severe depression, on the other hand, looks rather like the reverse. I am a vicious, evil person who doesn't deserve to live, while the world is full of wonderful loving people who wouldn't come near me if they knew what I was really like. These are the extreme forms of a state which, according to Klein, goes back to a blockage of some kind during infancy that has interfered with the difficult process of separating one's feelings from identification with the mother so that one can own one's own complexities.

Klein's description of the paranoid-schizoid position suggests that this is a psychological state which does not permit integration of good and bad feelings. It is a way of perceiving life which is distorted and split; and no one, including oneself, is allowed to be whole. It is a natural state at a certain period in infancy when the child still experiences the mother as an extension of himself or herself; but it is life-destroying as an underlying attitude in adulthood. The movement into the depressive position is a hard and painful one, and it involves the strengthening of the individual ego or sense of self, to the point where one can live with one's own contradictions. Then one can also live with the contradictions of other people without feeling so enormously resentful and betrayed. We could call this depressive position a capacity for realism. I think you can begin to see why I associate Pluto and Saturn with the entire issue. The powerful primitive feelings of the child, which encompass rage, the desire to devour, the desire to destroy, and the desire to merge, certainly seem to belong to that domain of human experience which I associate with the astrological Pluto. Pluto is, in a nutshell, a symbol of primitive instinctual need. One hates the person one loves because that person has the power to hurt and humiliate by withdrawing. Saturn, on the other hand, has much to do with the realistic acceptance of human limits – the capacity to face and tolerate the ambivalent nature of the world and of oneself. Maybe I might even suggest that, when these astrological significators are unusually powerful in a horoscope – as they are in Barbara's – then the person is faced with the challenge of not only working with this particular aspect of human development which alchemy called the nigredo, but of working with it at great depth. And not everyone makes it.

One of the interesting insights in Klein's work is the view of what happens to a person when he or she moves into the depressive position. Naturally that person will become very depressed. It is a frequent phenomenon of psychotherapeutic work. Esoteric and spiritual circles tend to abound in people who have become stuck in what Klein calls the paranoid-schizoid position. That is why many of them have become so strenuously spiritual even if there is little sense of a real spiritual "vocation" in the old sense of the word. They have not yet learned to cope with the ugliness in life because they have not yet integrated the ugliness in themselves. If one works therapeutically with such an individual, one will eventually see him or her becoming extremely depressed, because the whole paranoid-schizoid edifice begins to crumble. Instead of a clear-cut vision of black and white, life starts looking increasingly and confusingly gray. One cannot transcend the filthy old body after all, one has to live in it, and one cannot dispense with the shadow by trying to identify with the light. This depression is in fact healthy, because it marks the movement out of what is essentially an infantile view of reality, where the good guys ride white horses and the bad guys ride black ones.

Paranoia, therefore, is a pre-depressive state. When the destructive feelings which have been projected onto other people are taken back inside and understood and accepted, then the result is a period of depression. But one can get stuck at this stage too. You can begin to see what the alchemical nigredo looks like in psychological terms. This is why the alchemists thought it was so necessary in order to make the gold. The depressive position is necessary in order to make the individuality. Recognising that one is capable of evil and destructiveness is not as simple as it sounds. Integrating such realisations is hard work. It is possible for a person to be so horror-struck by the discovery that he or she becomes frozen, just as though the Gorgon's head had appeared and rendered one paralysed.

Audience: Then splitting is a characteristic of a Pluto-dominated person.

Liz: I would say so, yes. Every sign has its own particular way of responding to life. When faced with the complexity of ambivalent emotion, the Plutonian personality will often divide the package neatly, and either the person or the world becomes good while the other becomes evil. I have met both kinds—those who identify with all the blackness and ugliness in the family and unwittingly carry the family shadow, and those who project all the blackness and ugliness onto other people and then try to fight or convert the evil outside. The religious world is full of the latter kind of Plutonian, busily attempting to exorcise the devil in others through a particular spiritual dogma. Psychiatric hospitals are full of the former kind—like Barbara—carrying everyone else's burden of excrement. But look at the creative potential, if one can embrace both. Now you see what medieval philosophy was trying to say by the connection between melancholia and inspired wisdom.

Oddly enough, splitting is characteristic of Gemini and Sagittarius as well as also being characteristic of Scorpio and Capricorn. These pairs of signs are wildly opposite in nature, and they tend to do their splitting in reverse ways. Usually I have found that Scorpio and Capricorn tend to take on the bad side of the split, although as I have said, there are exceptions, particularly in the religious and esoteric fields in the case of Scorpio, and the sociological and political fields in the case of Capricorn. But usually Scorpio and Capricorn will cheerfully identify with the chap on the black horse, and will sit in deep depression for long periods of time because the good bits are still being projected outside. The exceptions behave very peculiarly, and I sometimes feel that when a Scorpio or a Capricorn projects the darkness outside then I am meeting someone who behaves like a fake Gemini or a fake Sagittarius. More frequently these signs will accept the dark end of the bargain, and look with bitterness and envy at other people who seem to be so much healthier and nicer than they are. But Gemini and Sagittarius will usually project the darkness outside, onto other people, or onto society, or onto the body. All four signs have a propensity for this kind of splitting, perhaps more than the other signs.

Another way of looking at the issue of splitting as I have described it in Scorpio is that the individual identifies himself or herself with the bad, destructive feelings, so that there is no distance at all from them. One is simply a distillation of essential badness, rather than being a person who sometimes experiences destructive feelings. In extreme cases, one can sometimes hear the depressed person expressing the feeling that he or she will contaminate others, or bring bad luck to them, as though the person carried some kind of virus or noxious cloud which will infect and poison others. The individual does not HAVE badness inside; he or she IS badness. This is not the Kleinian "depressive position," this is being stuck in the paranoid-schizoid split, and identifying with one end of it while projecting the other. One of the characteristics of the depressive position is that the individual experiences his or her own destructive feelings, rather than identifying with them. There is an ego which can have feelings, both good and bad. This is why, in analytic circles, there is often great relief when a patient becomes properly depressed, that is, depressed in Klein's sense of the word. That is an important reflection of progress, of an ego which has become strong enough to have its own feelings. The patient has finally sunk into his or her own earth, instead of flapping about all over the ethers avoiding the bad feelings, or wallowing in subterranean darkness and identifying with the world's evil. The manic depressive, if you want to view this problem through a Kleinian lens, is stuck in the paranoid-schizoid position, bouncing back and forth between identification with all-badness and all-goodness alternatively.

Now I am not a Kleinian analyst, and I would not use terms such as "depressive position" and "paranoid-schizoid position" to a person with whom I worked. But I think Klein's model is a very useful and important one, and it would be a mistake to disregard it because of the awkwardness of the language, or because it has no "spiritual" dimension. It is one of the best models in psychology to help us understand the dynamics of depression as a developmental stage. It is strange that an analytic model as clinical as Klein's should bear such close affinities with an apparently esoteric model like alchemy. But they are both describing the same process. You can see from this how subtle and complex the issue of depression actually is. Depression on the one hand may be seen as a particular response to experiences where unpalatable feelings are repressed and then surface in a different form. We can see this facet of depression in the case of Barbara. Rage and grief and destructiveness have been repressed and have reappeared as self-destructiveness, which is also covert destructiveness toward others because of the powerful effect which a severely depressed person has on the family. But the tendency to repress such feelings is related to something deeper—an inability to deal with one's own badness. The depression carries all the angry, black feelings; it is a symbol of them. It can also be a tremendous opportunity to work on issues which have their roots in very early life, unfinished business which pertains to the interrupted development of the ego. But the problem is that the opportunity is often not taken. People simply do not know how to work with such a challenge; no one has ever taught them. Many people working on the therapeutic side—psychiatrists, clinical psychologists, social workers—also do not know how to work with depression, because it is interpreted as an illness rather than as a symbol. The individual is then seen as wallowing in the depression and identifying with it, and it must be treated rather than worked with. And one can get stuck there, and it goes on and on. Depression is like a flag being hoisted by the unconscious, making a statement: Look, there is something inside that needs to be felt and experienced and you are not dealing with it so here is a flag, a depression. Pay attention to it instead of running away from it. Go into it, find out what is inside it. Sit with your fantasies, and try to paint them or write about them. What pictures does the depression make, what colour is it? If one allows fantasy activity into a depression, it comes alive. Otherwise the container is sealed, and nothing can move it. It just remains the same.

Another facet of this problem is that a person can be depressed all the time and not even realise it. It is only when an event occurs, such as a separation or a career failure, that the depression is triggered and rises to the surface and the person suddenly plunges into it. But it is not a new depression, and it is not caused by the external event. The threshold of consciousness is suddenly lowered, and the ego is swamped and its defences broken open. Very often the defences are intellectual ones. This is particularly true with a highly analytical temperament, which can use the mind to create an illusory distance from the depression beneath—rather like flying a plane above the sea. But the sea always threatens, and at any moment the plane might go down. This might tell you something about flying phobias. Something black waits underneath and the individual is afraid. This kind of unconscious depression makes itself known in rather convoluted ways—usually through physical symptoms and behaviour patterns of a compulsively self-destructive kind. There is not yet a connection between the person and the depression, except the symbolic one which the observer can see—the compulsive eating, or the lack of care for the body, or the posture, or the annoying symptoms, or the sleeplessness. If there is no connection with the depression, then the depression is a sealed container within which nothing can grow. If one can let fantasy loose in it, then something begins to happen—usually the realisation that one is terribly depressed. That is a beginning.

Audience: What about the idea suggested by many humanistic therapies—of shouting or hitting pillows? Can that help a depression?

Liz: I wish it were that simple. You cannot just pick up a pillow and start hitting it and release deeply unconscious destructive feelings as if by magic. If a person really feels like shouting or hitting a pillow, then usually he or she is aware of anger, and that is already a sign of movement. If the time is right, then certainly a "safe" outlet for violence is highly desirable and very freeing. But the time cannot be artificially manufactured. There are so many emotional issues around this problem of introjecting one's "badness," and they are too subtle for pillow-punching. Acting out anger can be an effective release after a lot of preliminary work. But think of the Kleinian model. I have the feeling that many therapists who claim to have worked successfully with such techniques have actually done a lot of groundwork with the patient first, sometimes without even realising it—by providing a safe container for the depression and offering a relationship which can be trusted, a "good" parent whose physical reliability and emotional acceptance are quietly healing over a period of time. But nothing has been said and no techniques used, and it is difficult to explain just how one has helped. The only visible thing is that at a certain point one has offered one's pillow.

THE ASTROLOGICAL SIGNIFICATORS OF DEPRESSION

Now I think it might be appropriate to look more closely at some of the astrological factors which seem to turn up regularly in cases of severe or prolonged depression. I would like you to keep in mind the main points which we have covered so far, because I want you to understand what these astrological indicators really mean in human terms, rather than simply memorising a list of things to look for in a chart. We have considered depression as an inverted or indirect statement of unexpressed destructive emotions, and also as a stage of development which is necessary to allow the individual to pass from an infantile and unformed state to one where the ego, the centre of consciousness, is strong and able to cope with and relate to life. Perhaps we should also keep in mind the quality of mourning which inevitably accompanies this passage to a sense of individual self, because it is really a passage from childhood with its parental identification to maturity with its sense of separateness. Depression is concerned not only with destructive feelings, but also with separateness and separation, and therefore with mourning, even though there may be no apparent external cause for grief.

I have already mentioned Scorpio and Capricorn as dominant astrological themes in depression, and under this general umbrella, in addition to charts in which either or both of these two signs dominate, I would also consider aspects such as the Sun or Moon conjunct, square, or opposing Saturn or Pluto, and Mars conjunct, square or opposing Saturn or Pluto. I would also look carefully at Saturn when it is placed in the 4th, 8th, or 12th house. And I would look carefully at Venus conjunct, square, or opposing Saturn. This last one is notorious for its link with depression, and I think the reasons should be apparent to you. Venus in difficult aspect to Saturn is one of the astrological symbols of a lonely and emotionally deprived childhood, and of feelings of being unloved, unlovable and isolated. It is also, if I go back to Klein's model, one of the red flags which suggests that, because there is emotional withholding or deprivation of some kind in the family background early in life, the individual will probably not have been able to make that critical journey of separation from the parents, since any child will find it almost impossible to separate from what he or she has never had. One can only leave the dinner table willingly if one's hunger has been at least moderately satisfied. If one is starving, one can think of nothing but food. So there is a stuck place, before the "depressive position" of a separate individuality can be reached; and consequently one of the characteristics of difficult Venus-Saturn contacts, until they are worked with on a deep level, is to repeatedly seek a kind of perfect and unconditionally loving parent in every adult relationship, and then to feel disappointed, rejected, and bitter when the lover or spouse turns out to be just an ordinary person with ordinary human love to offer. You can see why any rejection or separation, however slight, can throw a person with a difficult Venus-Saturn aspect into depression, since the depression is there underneath all the time—encapsulated in a lonely, emotionally hungry child who cannot let go of the dream of unconditional parental love, and who is full of rage against life because the love has never materialised.

Sometimes one finds curious juxtapositions in the chart of a severely depressed person, such as hard Venus-Saturn or Sun-Pluto contacts alongside something apparently bright and cheerful such as the Moon conjunct Jupiter. One would think that the "nice" qualities of the Moon conjunct the Great Benefic would counteract the depressiveness of a difficult Saturn or Pluto. But remember what I mentioned earlier about Gemini and Sagittarius and their tendency toward splitting, because this also applies to the planet Jupiter. Strong Moon-Jupiter contacts tend to idealise life; the split runs the other way, and the individual projects all the bad outside and identifies with a wonderful mythic world where he or she is the divine child of the gods and is entitled to special exemptions from the usual rubbish which lesser mortals have to put up with in life. This is a rather manic pattern, since Moon-Jupiter or Sun-Jupiter contacts are prone to identifying with the all-good while Sun-Saturn, Moon-Saturn, Venus-Saturn, and Sun- and Moon-Pluto all tend to identify with the all-bad. So if a relationship or worldly goal goes wrong, then the crash is a very big one, because the flight was so high. Something similar might also be said about juxtapositions such as Sun-Saturn or Moon-Saturn aspects with Sun-Neptune, Moon-Neptune and Venus-Neptune. Neptune, even more than Jupiter, seeks an ideal state of existence, and longs to return to the waters of the womb or the eternal spirit where there is no conflict or pain or separateness. The gap is too great between the individual's longing and the inner and outer reality which he or she meets in life; and the abyss in between is the depression, the difficult place of passage among the rocks and thorns.

Audience: Can I ask a question about Barbara's chart? What transit reflected the change which happened in her? You said she began analysis. What was happening at that time?

Liz: Uranus was transiting over her Sun. I would like to spend more time on the issue of transits later. But very briefly, I think a transit like Uranus conjunct the natal Sun can be tremendously creative for a person stuck in a depression, because the transit reflects an inner movement, a breaking open of everything that has been locked up. It is the awakening of the sense of individuality, the light at the end of the tunnel, because the Sun is the symbol of the self—the goal of the alchemical work. Transits and progressions are very important if one wants to get some idea of when something is trying to move in the psyche. Any therapeutic work will be of optimum benefit at such a time, because one is working with the flow of the unconscious.

Audience: I am interested to know what happens after a depression like Barbara's. Where does one go?

Liz: You mean, is there life after depression? Hopefully one of the things that happens is that individual potentials and gifts get integrated into consciousness and into life which were not available before. Usually this includes a capacity to cope with separation and aloneness which the individual may have previously lacked. It strengthens the ego, which means strengthening self-confidence, self-worth and faith in life. One has let go of the parents at last, and can therefore live one's own life without being unconsciously driven from within by a longing to find the perfect parent, and by a terror that without that parent one will not survive. That may not sound like much, in terms of guarantees of happiness. But I think it is what we mean by freedom. If one can get this out of a depression, even a very long depression, then one has received a very great gift, which is well worth the price paid. This is the alchemical gold of Saturn and Pluto, although Saturn and Pluto are also, paradoxically, the planets which particularly seem to reflect an individual's propensity for winding up in such a dark state to begin with. Saturn's gifts are, I think, very apparent in this context. They include a truly serene acceptance of reality, a compassionate recognition of one's limits, and a capacity to contain one's difficult experiences without being torn apart by them. Saturn provides earth, and very often a better relationship with the body emerges out of a depression as well. Pluto's riches seem to be bound up with the capacity to face one's own darkness, to accept fate, to relinquish the attempt to control life, and to trust that invisible inner Other that intelligently unfolds one's path in life despite oneself. It becomes possible to live with a fuller embrace of life, because one no longer fears what it might do. This is the psychological meaning of the symbolism of alchemy—that out of the nigredo comes the elixir, the indestructible gold.

But of course something is lost after a depression as well. If one works with depression, and finds these apparently unromantic but nevertheless priceless experiences, one must give something up too. One sacrifices one's naivete. The uroboric bliss of infancy, where one is merged with the mother and life is devoid of the pains of separateness and self-responsibility and aloneness, is a vision which dies during the process of the nigredo. It may reappear later as a spiritual vision, which is perhaps more appropriate, although I have found that the quality of this kind of spirituality is quite different from the flight into the so-called spirit which is so characteristic of the unformed personality. But in terms of ordinary life, the vision dies. This is the state of mourning which I mentioned earlier. One's faith in life may be restored after the passage is made, and it will be much stronger than before because it is now built on solid rock rather than intellectual defences and intuitive fantasies. But the infant's relentless demand for the perfect caretaker cannot survive depression if the depression is worked through rather than suppressed with antidepressants.

I think that we need to respect the limitations of an individual's character when considering how to work with severe depression. One might be able to heal many of the wounds of childhood through good psychotherapy, and since the predisposition to certain kinds of depression is related to such wounds, one might like to think in terms of a "cure." But a person cannot be cured of his or her character, and it is the character which responds to the childhood wound in a particular way. There are dimensions of the personality in everyone which are not well adapted to certain kinds of life experiences. This may sound unfair when compared with some idealistic Uranian map of human potential, but what astrology implies about human nature is an unfair cosmos—we are not all equal in terms of our strengths and weaknesses. Barbara's chart is an excellent example of this unfairness. There is no earth in her chart, and very little air. Thus two of the four elements are virtually absent. Viewed from a more holistic perspective, that is not a bad thing, because it suggests a richer development of her strong elements, and also it suggests great fulfilment to be found in the practical and intellectual realms later in Barbara's life, when she is ready to explore these undifferentiated dimensions of herself. But viewed from the perspective of ordinary adaptation, Barbara cannot cope with the limits and disappointments of life as well as some people do. That is a fact about her character, and not the product of her childhood. She can improve those weak functions, but they will always be vulnerable. There is no blame of any kind attached to this statement, nor any implication that Barbara has somehow not "done" enough work on herself. But she has never been able to deal gracefully with situations where she cannot immediately have all that she desires. This facet of her character does not mix well with the sort of emotional rejection she experienced in early life—or the sort that she would inevitably encounter later, since the world is not overrun with available heterosexual men free of mother-complexes who have Venus conjunct Moon conjunct Mars conjunct Sun in Scorpio and might therefore appreciate the richness of her passions. Remember her Moon-Mars conjunction, and her Venus-Pluto square, and all the planets she has in Scorpio. Also, consider Barbara's Sun-Neptune square, which suggests that she might resist forming as a defined individual, and would prefer to remain in a state of blissful merging with those she loves. The most positive dimension of Sun-Neptune comes from its openness to the oceanic world of the imagination, and if it is combined with a capacity to actualise this gift in concrete form, it reflects enormous creative potentials. But Barbara is lacking in the ability to formulate and actualise her inner life, and thus the Sun-Neptune contact would, in my view, probably exaggerate her emotional needs beyond any possibility of their being met in real life.

She is a fixed sign, and therefore lacks flexibility and the capacity to bend with the wind. Her vision of life is intensely romantic, and when she wants something she wants it very, very badly; and she will not take kindly to being thwarted. These are descriptions of Barbara's essential character as it is reflected by her chart, or what we have of her chart—which is enough for our present purposes. This essential character is neither good nor bad. It is simply Barbara. But you can see how her depression is the product of a kind of chemical reaction between her circumstances and her character. The qualities which she needs to develop within herself come to meet her from outside in the form of restrictive situations and detached people who frustrate her emotional needs. Life appears to have an irritating way of doing this in those spheres where we are lopsided. That is what Novalis meant when he wrote that fate and character are two names for the same principle.

It is a very big step for Barbara to have reached the point where she could say, "All right, I give up, there is no Santa Claus." No fixed sign likes to give up, particularly not Scorpio, which has Lucifer's pride. It seems like a defeat and a humiliation. To face at last the fact that there will be no handsome prince on a white horse who will give her all the love her father denied her, and who will adore her enough to heal her wound without her having to take responsibility for it, is a very slow and painful business. It is work on basic character as much as it is work on healing childhood wounds. So it is not surprising that Barbara got stuck in her depression for as long as she did.

Audience: What if the Sun-Neptune square had been in cardinal signs? Would she have been able to cope better?

Liz: If the Sun-Neptune square had been in cardinal signs she would have been a different person, with a different path in life. She would then not be a Scorpio, and the entire picture would be different. I don't really think it is possible to answer such a question. That is like saying, "If I could have the same chart except without the Moon conjunct Saturn, would I be happier and less inhibited?" Certainly, but you would be somebody else, with some other dilemma. Every single factor in a chart works with every other single factor, and the whole is reflected in what happens to a person. One cannot speculate like that.

Audience: I would like to ask a question about guilt. You have talked about feelings of loneliness, sickness, ugliness, and badness in relation to depression. But you didn't mention guilt. Isn't that a big part of depression?

Liz: I don't believe it is, except as a mask for all those other difficult feelings. Remorse may be, but remorse is very different. Guilt has always seemed to me to be not a real feeling, but rather, a defence against feelings—of loneliness, ugliness, badness and perhaps remorse. Guilt is a defence against real suffering. That may sound heretical to you, but there is something very manipulative and slippery about guilt. When people go on about how guilty they feel about something, I often have the sense that it is unreal in some way. It requires an audience. Remorse is much deeper, and more painful, and no audience can redeem it, because it is a confrontation with one's own soul. This is very difficult terrain, because I think I am touching on moral issues which are very emotive for many people. Remorse may be related to some deep intrinsic morality which is part of the inner self, while guilt may be related to offences against collective morality. Remorse is often the beginning of a movement into reality, into accepting one's ambivalence—in other words, Klein's depressive position. I will give you an example. I worked with a woman who had been in psychiatric treatment for manic depression. She had the Sun conjunct Saturn and Pluto in Leo. For a long time, she could experience no remorse, in the deep sense that I understand it. She certainly felt guilty. She did some pretty dreadful things to people, and then would say, "Oh, how terrible I am; I shouldn't have done that." But beneath this guilt, there was nothing. There was no real connection with her feelings, or with the feelings of the people she injured. People were not real individuals to her; they were seen as extensions of her, objects existing solely for her gratification. When someone came through with the goodies, she "loved" him or her; when they failed to meet her demands, she ceased to love, always for "justifiable" reasons. This is a very infantile and regressive state. It is a pre-ego state. For a long time she would habitually arrive 20 minutes or half an hour late for sessions, or just not show up at all. She would always apologise the next time, and express guilt, and readily pay for the missed session. But this was a conventional formula. Beneath it she had absolutely no perception of me as a separate entity who might be inconvenienced by these absences. And there was also, of course, considerable aggression in her behaviour. She wanted on some level to inconvenience me, to hurt me, and to prove that she was more powerful than me by keeping me waiting for her, because she felt so desperately helpless and impotent inside. The feelings of guilt protected her from facing her own aggression. For a long time I did not react to these missed sessions, until it became apparent that she was building up steam; and then I asked whether she thought there might be anything lying behind this repeating pattern of lateness and absence. She became very angry, and told me I made her feel like a child being reprimanded. She needed a reason to become angry with me, so that her aggression could be legitimate. Here the badness was projected onto me, so that I became the terrible stern Saturn-Pluto mother who curtailed her freedom. That night she had a dream, in which she missed her session with me. In the dream, she felt very deep remorse, because she realised not only that she was wasting my time, but that she had wanted to hurt me. This is a remarkable dream, because it reflected with total truthfulness all those feelings she would not permit into consciousness. Once she had this dream, a great deal of movement followed in the analysis. One can only feel remorse if one has an ego which can take responsibility for one's actions, and which can be separate enough to be aware of one's effect on others. That is the depressive position. Klein's paranoid-schizoid position, which reflects the split of the very young child, can produce no remorse. But the person can feel guilty, and the guilt serves as a defence. Guilt, to put it crudely, is a species of psychic antidepressant.

Audience: Then depression is connected with the formation of conscience.

Liz: Perhaps. I think we are on rather dangerous ground here. I personally believe it is. But I do not know whether anyone else would agree with me. I don't think conscience is really a rational issue. There is a kind of internalised parent, which Freud called the superego, which most people believe is conscience—a voice which dictates moral rights and wrongs according to the parental and social norm. One can have a very developed superego, and live a very correct life, but lack a real individual conscience. And one can have a very powerful conscience, a deep connection with the voice of the Self, but behave in ways which the superego would consider wrong. There is something extremely mysterious about conscience. It is very bound up with an individual experience of an Other within—a centre which possesses its own intelligence and wisdom. But it does not appear to be the same as the moral dictates of religious dogma and social "normality" which often profess to be identical, but are not individual. Of course we must observe some of these collective dictates, or the fabric of society would utterly fall apart. But this is not the same thing as conscience. And yes, I believe that depression—the kind of depression which is a nigredo, a rite of passage into separateness and "selfness"—is also the archetypal initiation process out of which is forged true individual conscience.

I would like to go back to some of the astrological factors I mentioned earlier, and look at them more closely. We have considered Venus-Saturn, and I think the kind of depression associated with it should be clearer to you. Now I would like to consider difficult Moon-Pluto aspects—the conjunction, square, and opposition—because this is another red flag, but of a different kind. Although I have yet to be convinced by psychiatry that such things as depression are physiologically inherited, I think there is such a thing as a psychologically inherited depression. It is possible for a person to carry the parent's depression. The children of depressed mothers often themselves suffer from depression—especially if the mother does not know she is depressed, and goes around being very forcibly cheerful and efficient. At the beginning of life the unconscious of the mother and the unconscious of the child are fused together, because the child's ego has not yet formed and separated out from the maternal psyche. If the mother is in a state of despair, then the child will be infected by this. To use a rather brutal image, it is like drinking poisoned milk. The personal mother is the mediator of the archetypal mother for her child, and if she is wandering blind and despairing in the dark, then she will inadvertently mediate only the Dark Mother—which means, on a more human level, an experience of life which is negative, hopeless, bitter, and bleak. The mother's depression will come out in the child. But the mother did not put the Moon-Pluto contact into her child's chart, and can hardly be blamed for something of which she herself is the victim. It is as though some archetypal dilemma were present in the family, shared by both mother and child.

Audience: How does one actually separate from such a thing, if it is the mother's depression?

Liz: I think one accepts and works with one's own share of it. But one must first have one's own feelings, which means forming a sense of self that is strong enough to disengage from the mother. I have found that with most people who have difficult Moon-Pluto aspects in the chart, the depression is always present, but it is generally unconscious, except for those occasions when it bursts into conscious life in the form of black moods, or physical symptoms. The person does not know that it lies there underneath, and that there is a predisposition toward experiencing and interpreting life as a bleak and hopeless place where all one's desires will be disappointed and all one's instinctual needs frustrated. This is particularly the case, as I mentioned before, when the Moon-Pluto is juxtaposed with lots of fire and air, or with strong Jupiter and Neptune contacts. I think the first step in trying to achieve a separation from this inherited depression is to discover one's own destructive feelings, to smoke out the depression, because otherwise it will surface in covert ways—particularly as illness. Bringing it out into the light makes a big difference. For one thing, a younger person will usually not have had life experiences which can justify such a bitter stance. Remaining loyal to one's own experiences, really looking to see whether they merit such negativity, is very important. Moon-Pluto has a way of sucking every tiny misfortune into a kind of psychic black hole where all disappointments are used to confirm a single sweeping negative conviction about life. Experiences are not allowed to remain individual; they are reinterpreted monotonously to feed Kali's maw. It can matter a great deal for someone to realise this. And it is also important to allow the more serious and sombre side of the personality to find expression, which is the positive dimension of Moon-Pluto, rather than perpetually trying to reassure oneself that life is really always a wonderful place if only one were evolved enough to see it.

Sometimes it helps to look more honestly at the mother, not in order to blame her, but to see what may have lurked beneath her surface. This can also make a difference. To realise that she may not have been the strong, self-sacrificing person one thought, but that she may have been deeply bitter and despairing, or perhaps even at the edge of a breakdown—that can be a shock, but unless one can perceive this dimension of her life, one will project all kinds of things onto her. I have heard people with Moon-Pluto describe their mothers as "cold," but Pluto is never cold. It can be vindictive, and can make the family suffer because the person has been so humiliated through the denial of emotional needs. But the "cold" mother needs a closer look. Depression is also not mutually exclusive of love, and to recognise that one's mother may have been deeply unhappy during one's childhood does not automatically mean she was unloving. But she may have been emotionally starving, and turned to her child for solace from her unhappiness—which of course means turning the child into the mother, while the mother is secretly the child. All of this is implicit in hard Moon-Pluto aspects. You can see what a subtle combination this is.

Trying to understand the mother more objectively, and recognising the dark and perhaps even poisoned atmosphere of childhood beneath the surface, is only the beginning of it. There is also the problem of the natural anger and outrage and abandonment the child feels because he or she has been powerless in the face of this psychic contagion. One has not been mothered, on some very deep level, and inevitably there will be a hidden pocket of very destructive feelings toward the mother which must come out. And it is likely that the mother herself was full of anger, and therefore frightening in some way. Facing such feelings is also very hard, because we are back again full circle to the problem of accepting one's own destructiveness without identifying exclusively with it. This was, in all probability, the mother's problem too—otherwise she would not have remained passively suffering, but would have erupted with anger and tried to change her situation. So the mother is not able to help the child to internalise bad feelings because she cannot cope with her own bad feelings; that is why she was unconsciously depressed. It may sound rather complicated. But try to think about it, for actually the dynamic is very simple, and very human, and very common. Moon-Pluto is not a "rare" aspect. It represents one of several typical family constellations.

Usually the hard Moon-Pluto contacts keep their dark despairing feelings suppressed, until a transit comes along which triggers the natal configuration and therefore, by implication, triggers the childhood. Then there is an eruption of the poison which has been sitting there all along. Often an event occurs which is a catalyst for these feelings. The event is not the cause, although it may seem so. It is like putting money into one of those one-armed bandits, where all of a sudden all three cherries come up, or lemons, or whatever, and the person is overwhelmed by feelings which are far out of proportion to the actual triggering experience. These are some typical situations which seem to occur when Moon-Pluto is triggered. Nasty conflicts with women are very common—a particular woman enters one's life who seems to be really poisonous or destructive, or a female friend or companion seems to turn treacherous and nasty or betrays one. Men very commonly experience such transits through their wives or lovers, or through their mothers, and women very commonly experience them through another woman, or through the Other Woman. Here the Dark Mother is projected outside, and seems to manifest as an individual. Troubles with the body are also common, and in women, these may be difficulties in becoming pregnant, sexual problems, abortion, or miscarriage. Or the individual may simply slide into a very black depression, for no apparent reason. The despair of the mother now comes to the surface, and one falls into it—even against reason, which can point out that the actual situation may not be so bad. It might not be bad at all, in fact. So Moon-Pluto marks a vulnerable place in the chart, just as Venus-Saturn does, and often it is the triggering of an aspect like this by transit that coincides with the onset of depression. But at the same time, such a transit also suggests that greater insight into the roots of the depression might become available, and a lost part of oneself might be found.

I think that there is a basic predisposition toward the experience of depression in certain signs. I have already talked a little about this in relation to Capricorn, Scorpio, Gemini and Sagittarius. Each sign has its own special way of viewing life, and expresses selective vision—that is, one sees what one sees best oneself, as Jung put it. It is as though we look out at life through lenses tinted by a particular colouration, and therefore we interpret life in very selective ways. Sagittarius, for example, perceives through the lens of Jupiter-Zeus, so that, given the enormous range of experiences available in life, Sagittarius will focus selectively on the meaningfulness of those experiences, the lessons inherent in difficulties, the higher purpose behind why things happen. The event is not as important as what it has to teach. Somewhere in the psychic background is a feeling that life has meaning and is moving somewhere, and that there is a beneficent deity of some kind who infuses things with teleology, with purpose. Therefore if something bad happens, Sagittarius reacts by asking, "What am I supposed to be learning from this? Why has this experience happened to me? How is it connected with other experiences, and for what purpose?" So Sagittarius selectively perceives opportunities for growth, and will often not deal with the immediate negative feelings which a bad experience provokes. The negative feelings would cloud the intuitive perception of the meaning. I have often heard Sagittarians talking about their lives as though it were one long adventure story, with every incident revealing a secret design. One does not commonly hear a typical Sagittarian describing his or her feelings about a past experience. The actual pain, shock, loneliness, anger, betrayal, whatever, has vanished from memory, because the person's perception is focussed almost exclusively on the meaning. The Sagittarian will say, "And then I had an amazing affair with an exiled lama in Katmandu. We separated in the end, but I learned a lot about space and boundaries from it, and then when I was travelling in South America there was this Indian shaman. . . ." Because of this particular way of responding to life, there is often a big backlog of difficult emotions tucked away in the basement of the Sagittarian's psyche. That is why, if one finds aspects such as Venus-Saturn or Moon-Pluto in a Jupiter-dominated chart, they are red flags for depression, because when these configurations are triggered, all the lost feelings come to the surface—or, at least, they will try to come to the surface. Sagittarius, however, is a very good long-distance runner, and can succeed in avoiding depression for many years.

On the other hand, Capricorn's perceptions are just as selective as those of Sagittarius; but the god who stands behind Capricorn is not Zeus; it is Kronos. Capricorn is not predisposed to see a world full of inherent meaning pointing toward some profound spiritual goal. It is the mortality of the world that Capricorn sees—its limitations, its inherent struggle, the very fragile nature of life, and the extreme vulnerability of the human animal. For Capricorn, one cannot expect grace from heaven; life is hard, and one must work doggedly to achieve any foothold in the midst of reality's constrictions. Human beings are always at the mercy of their own bodies, no matter how advanced the technology and how sophisticated the intellect. So Capricorn's selective perception does not register the inner meaning of an experience; it registers the experience as confirmation of the human condition. This is an essentially pragmatic and rather melancholy perspective. It is an embrace of immediate experience rather than an intuition of the implications of the experience; and the sensation function, rather than the intuition, is the primary tool of adaptation and adjustment. Facts are registered, rather than teleology.

Therefore you can see that depression in a Sagittarian will have rather different roots from depression in a Capricorn. Depression of a kind is there all the time in Capricorn; the individual lives with it because it is built into the way he or she experiences life. The Capricorn personality usually comes to terms with this inbuilt melancholy sooner or later, for there are compensations for it: the tenacity and patience to work hard and build something permanent and worthwhile in a world where everyone grows old and dies sooner or later. If Capricorn can architect something that stands after he or she is gone, something which can contribute to the next generation, then a fulfilling life statement has been made, and it arises out of the rather melancholic vision of life which is reflected by this astrological sign. Thus Capricorn copes with his or her inherent predisposition toward depression through certain kinds of actions which we immediately recognise as typical in the textbooks. I think it is more important to understand, to feel into, the selective world-view which produces the characteristic Capricornian ambition and determination, rather than dwelling on the behavioural tendencies of the sign. Capricorn's innate depression is neither pathological nor "curable," because it is part and parcel of the individual's vision of life.

Sagittarius becomes depressed, in contrast, because the individual more often than not has crashed into limits that he or she did not wish to believe were there. The discovery that one is not after all immortal and special and exempt can be quite crushing to Sagittarius. So too is the realisation that one cannot have everything one wants, and that the finished product on the earth plane will always fall short of the brilliant possibilities that were initially envisioned by the intuition. This depression is quite different, because it is not part of Sagittarius' world-view; it arises when the world-view is challenged too harshly by life itself.

Audience: Is it the depression of the puer aeternus?

Liz: Yes, that is one way of looking at it. Capricorn's depression reflects the archetypal background of the senex, the old man who has seen it all and has no illusions left. Sagittarius' depression reflects the pain of the puer who has been flying along happily, marvelling at the lovely cloud formations, and then runs into a brick wall.

Audience: So it's depression arising out of disillusionment.

Liz: Yes, that is a good word for it. But one must work with it differently than one might work with a Capricorn's depression. For Capricorn, it is important to discover some spiritual reality behind the dense world of objects and limits—some glimpse of joy, or the discovery that life can include play. This is not an antidote to depression, but an additional ingredient which makes it purposeful. But it is as useless to try to turn Sagittarius into a senex, by ceaselessly reminding him or her that life is a tough place, as it is to turn Capricorn into a puer by talking about how beautiful it really all is. This would crush the bright spirit which is the most creative facet of Sagittarius. For the Jupiterian person the physical world can be a problem, and the individual needs to strengthen his or her capacity to cope with its limits. Sagittarius needs to get depressed at some point, and it is usually a rite of passage which can eventually lead to the person becoming really productive with his or her imaginative gifts. But I think it is important to remain loyal to the vision, and to help the Sagittarian to see that even the act of making peace with mortal limits is itself meaningful and part of an overall pattern of growth. To destroy the puer's dreams is an act of violence which is not only unnecessary, but very negative. I have known very reductive analysts who try to work in this way—rather like the protagonist in O'Neill's *The Iceman Cometh* who goes about destroying what he calls the "pipedreams" of the tramps and drunks whom he meets—and such people, instead of healing, can deeply damage the Jupiterian individual's capacity to trust in life. This is not an antidote to depression. It is a guarantee that a worse depression will follow. Yet one cannot feed the natural inflation of Jupiter either. It requires a very delicate balance.

If both Jupiter and Saturn are strong in a chart, through the placement of the planets or through emphasis in their signs and houses, then I think a major life-dilemma is described, and there is often a strong up-and-down movement with depression and a kind of manic defence alternating in the cycle of the individual's moods. One way of viewing manic depression is that it is a complex expression of the pain of accommodating a naturally imaginative, intuitive and romantic temperament with the limits of stark reality—inner and outer—and I can think of several cases of this problem where the Jupiter-Saturn polarity appears strongly in the birth chart. Jupiter and Saturn together form two sides of what is essentially a religious problem. That dimension of depression which has its deepest roots in struggling to formulate a viable world-view has its astrological reflection in Jupiter and Saturn, Sagittarius and Capricorn. The meaninglessness and mortality of life versus the meaningfulness and boundlessness of it perform a constant dance in both these signs, which are peculiarly prone to depression; and the personal losses, disappointments and separations which occur from childhood on tend to feed into that basic and essentially archetypal conflict.

In contrast to both of these, the roots of Scorpio's depression are different yet again. Separation, loss, and the dilemmas of human relationship form the core of Scorpio's depression, because the god who stands behind this sign is the Great Mother, who represents the unity and life-preserving drives of all instinctual life. The Scorpio personality always seeks to merge with what he or she loves, while at the same time fearing the loss of power which accompanies such merging. The trigger for Scorpio's depression is loneliness and separation. Obviously no individual is purely Sagittarius, Capricorn, or Scorpio, and the actual roots of depression in a particular case are usually a tangle of all three. You can see how emotional disappointments might feed the innate cynicism of Capricorn, or destroy the romantic dreams of Sagittarius. You can also see how the vision of Sagittarius can cause Scorpio to assume too much in relationship, or how the basic mistrust of Capricorn can lead Scorpio into behaving defencively and therefore creating the very separation the individual fears. But I think it is useful to create these artificial lines of demarcation with the different kinds of depression reflected by different signs and their planetary rulers, even though in practise the individual may be suffering from a combination of all of them. One can get the feeling that there is a core dilemma, an essential life conflict which is the spinal column of the person's life-story, and which acts like a magnet and draws to itself all those hurtful or disappointing experiences which can feed the complex. If one can reach straight into that core, and empathise at least a little with the essential struggle, then often the peripheral tangle of threads can seem a little clearer.

Separation and loss therefore often seem to be at the bottom of Scorpio's depression. I think that, just as Capricorn has a kind of permanent melancholy because of the nature of the sign's world-view, so too does Scorpio, for separations are part of life, beginning with the primal separation from the mother. Scorpio's passionate nature always seeks to merge with the object, whether this object is a person, a job, or whatever. If the beloved object is wrenched away, through rejection or death, then there is a deep rage which arises—the black rage of nature when it has been violated or frustrated. This is why we find those charming mythic images such as the Gorgon, or the furious Demeter when her daughter Persephone is stolen from her. When Demeter loses Persephone, she takes revenge on the earth itself, and the land becomes barren. She scourges the land in her pain and fury. There is famine and darkness, because this primordial earth-goddess who represents the power of nature itself is going to punish anything and everything in her path. Where we might find a religious problem at the core of Capricorn's depression, we will usually find a problem of separation at the core of Scorpio's. I would like you to remember what we examined in Barbara's chart and case history earlier, for she is an excellent example of just this point. The depression in this case masks a deep and enduring rage against life, and the focus of the individual's energy is on the injury, the outrage.

Audience: This seems to be anger rather than sorrow or grief.

Liz: I suspect that Scorpio's healing begins when it becomes possible for the individual to grieve rather than rage. Grief, sorrow, and remorse are feelings which seem to transform the bitter vindictiveness into something more fluid. One can begin to forgive life then. You can see this often during the process of psychotherapy, where rejection or too early and too violent separation from the parent has resulted in a black rage which underlies a bad depression—as is the case with Barbara. When it became possible for Barbara to grieve for what she had lost, rather than hating both the lost object and herself, she began to heal. One might well ask what makes such a transition possible. I believe it has a great deal to do with the rapport with the psychotherapist, and with the sharing of that black rage and pain with another person. The key to working with Scorpionic depression seems to be a containing relationship, where all the infantile feelings can be expressed without fear of reprisal. It is connected in some mysterious and deep way with the issue of emotional honesty. If one can truly be the raging infantile beast who wants to destroy the world, and can face these feelings in front of another, then one has reached the bottom—and one can begin to feel compassion for oneself.

Audience: What is the key to working with Capricornian depression, or Sagittarian?

Liz: I think the individual must also reach the bottom, but this bottom is the experience of total meaninglessness. For Sagittarius particularly, I believe there needs to be a confrontation with the body and with one's baseness—all the issues of sin and corruption which Sagittarius flies up to heaven in order to avoid. One must discover that it is possible to live without spiritual meaning, and to find pleasure on the earth itself. Sometimes such a person needs to stay in a depression for quite some time. If you are always accustomed to walking in bright light, and then suddenly someone turns the lights off, at first it seems totally black, and you cannot find your way. But after a time the eyes become accustomed to the dark, and you begin to notice the faint light of the moon, and the dim light of the stars, and the florescence of nature. These things go unnoticed when the overhead solar or Jupiterian light is very bright. For Capricorn, I believe the key lies in the capacity to at last admit helplessness in the face of life, and to acknowledge the cry for divine help. This is terribly difficult for Capricorn, because there is such a tough, stubborn, wilful and pragmatic character in the sign; and Capricorn must often be broken by life before he or she will concede defeat and the need for salvation. Capricorn fights the experience of redemption through something as invisible as the spirit, because the person cannot accommodate the anxiety of putting faith in something that might turn out to be a fake. This is perhaps one of the deeper meanings of the symbolism of the knees, which Capricorn traditionally rules; one must at last bend one's knee to a will that is greater, and learn the difference between humiliation and humility. It is a hard task for Capricorn, because the pride in the Capricorn individual is at least as great as the pride in Scorpio.

I think it is interesting to consider the ways in which astrologers cope with the issue of a depressed client—not to mention one's own depression. Depression in any person has a way of making others feel useless, because one does not seem to be able to do much to help. We all react to another person's depression by trying to cheer them up or talk them out of it, because the inner images of depression—the experiences of meaninglessness, despair and isolation—are archetypal, and can be threatening if we have not confronted these feelings in ourselves. Every psychotherapist knows how difficult it is to let a client remain depressed, week after week. And the depressed client, or the depressed loved one, has a way of intentionally, although unknowingly, making us feel useless, which is the unconscious aggression making itself felt. Many astrologers learn astrology in the first place in order to cope with the unpleasant feeling that perhaps life is really meaningless after all. If we can find a bad Saturn transit, then we can say, "Ah, well, that's what's causing it, it will be alright in two weeks," and that is not really any different from *Cosmopolitan's* advice to go to wine bars and mix with friends if you are feeling depressed. The kind of approach I am trying to take today in using astrology to explore depression is rather different; but it is not universally popular in astrological circles any more than in other circles. The great danger of blaming Saturn because he is transiting your whatnot is that you don't have to make the kind of deep and often frightening exploration which would lead to the core of the depression—and, ultimately, to the core of yourself. Then astrological language is used not to deepen understanding of an experience, but rather to create a barrier between the person and the experience. All that this does is put the issue off until another transit, and the astrologer remains unable to really grasp the importance of Saturn and Pluto; and it is ultimately the client who is shortchanged. I do not think it is possible to comprehend these two planets and their signs without having had some experience of depression—the hopeless wasteland of emotional and spiritual impoverishment which is one of the dark faces of life. We often use spiritual beliefs and disciplines in order to avoid descending into this realm; and then a depressed client can be extremely uncomfortable to work with.

Audience: But there is truth in spiritual beliefs and disciplines.

Liz: I did not say there wasn't. But there is truth in depression as well. I suspect that we need to perceive both truths. Otherwise depression will always be frightening, whether it is one's own or another's. There is truth in the perception that life is meaningless and that in the end everything is mortal; it is a fact that one day we will all die, and no one has been able to demonstrate in any pragmatic way the existence of an afterlife of the spirit. It is also true in its fashion that we are ultimately alone, imprisoned in our separate bodies and psyches; and the experience of universal oneness is a subjective state, perhaps even a subjective fantasy, rather than a physical reality. Likewise immortality is a subjective experience, not an empiric fact. Depression is the body's truth, just as meaningfulness is the spirit's truth. One does not cancel the other one out. It would seem that life, like Janus, wears a double face.

TRANSITS AND PROGRESSIONS
AS TRIGGERS FOR DEPRESSION

We might look now at how certain transits and progressions can coincide with the onset of depression, or with its healing, or with both. This question came up earlier, when someone asked about what was happening in Barbara's chart when she seemed to begin to emerge out of her darkness. Now it will be obvious that the transits and progressions of Saturn are often involved when a person becomes depressed. I suspect that what psychiatry refers to as endogenous depression is frequently connected with the two-year transit of Saturn over some critical point in the birth chart. Transits have orbs, just as natal placements do, and one begins to feel Saturn when he is 10 degrees away from an important point in the chart; and one continues to feel him when he is 10 degrees past the same point. When the transit is over, the individual seems to come out of it. It does not seem as though psychiatry asks whether anything has changed internally, because in more orthodox medical bastions the decisive issue is whether the person can return to a "normal" way of functioning with job and family—whatever that means. Likewise a Pluto transit often appears coincident with the onset of a depression, and because Pluto spends such a long time passing back and forth over a particular point in the chart, such a depression can go on for a considerable time. Try to remember this issue of orbs; one does not suddenly wake up depressed one morning with Saturn exactly on the Moon. There is a long buildup, and if the natal planet is part of a configuration, then the entire configuration will be triggered by the transit, and the orb may need to be increased even more. For example, if one has a Moon-Saturn square, and the Moon is at 8 degrees Libra and Saturn at 18 degrees Cancer, then the transit of Saturn approaching a conjunction to the Moon will start making itself felt when Saturn is in around 29 degrees Virgo, within orb of the natal Moon, and will not pass until it reaches 28 degrees Libra and finishes the square to its own natal place. And that is a period of roughly two to two-and-a-half years.

One way of understanding why Saturn triggers depression is to look again at Melanie Klein's idea of a "depressive position." In any area of the psyche where there is a split—where feelings or

needs have been disconnected from the ego's perceptions and relegated to the unconscious—Saturn will immediately challenge the
person with the split-off part of himself or herself. So we need to
look at configurations in the birth chart which reflect something
unintegrated—squares and oppositions between inimical planets,
such as Sun and Saturn, or Moon and Uranus, or Venus and Pluto,
and also singletons by element, such as only Mars in earth, or only
the Moon in water. Most importantly, we are looking at issues that
are linked back to childhood and to early separations, losses and
disappointments which have been split off because the emotional
reactions are too powerful to handle. It is important to consider a
birth chart from the perspective of what is likely to be conscious
and what unconscious, as we have been doing in all our seminars;
for once you have a feeling of the hidden pockets of the chart, the
characters in the play who are not allowed out on stage and who
have perhaps been locked up in the unconscious since infancy,
then you can see why an important transit such as that of Saturn or
Pluto, passing over such a hot place, will pitch the individual into a
powerful experience of what has been split off. Saturn and Pluto
both tend to confront an individual with the truth, and if the truth
is an aspect of oneself which has remained infantile, hurt, and
unable to forgive life for its horribleness, then one sinks down into
one's own primitive underworld. Pluto strips things down to their
bare bones, right back to the earliest experiences of childhood and
the parental unconscious, and a kind of global rage is often the
result. Such global rage is natural and characteristic of children's
feelings. But an adult without a solid sense of self is likely to be
terrified by such savage feelings, and depression is frequently the
only option. Saturn forces us to confront our aloneness and the
issue of being responsible for ourselves, and there are areas in
everyone—after all, we all have Neptune somewhere in the chart—
which would much rather return to the amniotic waters, immune
to separation, loneliness, and mortality, and at one with the numinous source of life. This longing is especially strong if one has not
been parented in the deeper sense, and therefore remains hungry
and childlike somewhere inside. If one has not got enough of
something, then one cannot readily let go of it. I think these faces
of Saturn and Pluto should be apparent to you after the various
dimensions of depression which I have talked about. But what is

perhaps more important, and more telling, is the thing in the birth chart which is triggered. You will see what I mean when we look at some examples later.

Transiting Pluto is a particularly difficult planet for the person who has large unconscious pockets of emotional hurt and unhappiness, because under a Pluto transit one's outer persona gets stripped away. One feels the advent of fate, the sense that something unknown and overpowering is coming. Sometimes circumstances coincide with such an internal descent, but often they do not. The loss of a job or of a partner is very commonly the apparent cause of depression under Pluto, but there is always a good deal more going on, and sometimes the trigger is the reverse—one achieves something one has always wanted. It is what the current situation has activated from the past—all the early experiences of loss and powerlessness which have not been dealt with. This is also true of progressed planets moving into strong aspect with the natal Pluto, particularly into conjunctions, squares, and oppositions. Very often this is the significator of a potential reclaiming of emotions and values which were lost in childhood, and buried under a great deal of rage and pain.

Uranus is also an interesting planet to watch as a trigger for both depression and the healing of depression—although in a strange way the two may be the same, if we consider what I said earlier about depression being a necessary stage in a process of development. Uranus has a particular flavour when he approaches by transit; he seems to release energy which has been trapped in the unconscious, or trapped in old structures. Very often the libido which is released is very difficult to integrate into the existing life situation, particularly if it is a transit of say, Uranus over Mars. An outburst of some kind may be badly needed, but the individual often fears disrupting the status quo; so the energy inverts and the person falls into a depression instead. This is true of Uranus-Mars and also of Pluto-Mars transits and progressions. Once again, what is important is what is being triggered in the birth chart. If Uranus touches off, for example, a natal Moon-Saturn square, then the very earliest feelings of loneliness, rejection, and isolation will begin to come into consciousness, along with the anger of the child who has been neglected on some fundamental level. Sometimes the natal placement looks very positive—I have seen depression occur when Uranus hits Jupiter, or Venus. This is often because the individual has not previously been able to express the Jupiter or Venus, and suddenly there is the possibility of bringing a new and more joyful element into life. But if the present situation cannot accommodate this new element without some kind of confrontation or separation, then the individual may try to deny that he or she is changing, and depression may be the result. Uranus is often present also when an individual has been in a depression for a long time and begins to achieve those realisations which may shift the suffering. Uranus frees energy through sight, insight, realisation and sudden comprehension, as well as through outbursts and separations.

Audience: Is Uranus more connected with a mental breakdown?

Liz: I am not sure what you mean by "mental breakdown." If you mean a psychotic episode which is not depression—say, with visual or audial hallucinations, or a messianic identification, or whatever—then I think this is not so much related to the transit of one planet or another as it is to the overall temperament and the predisposition the individual has to reacting to stress in particular ways. That is why I spent so much time talking about depression in connection with certain signs and aspects. An individual with little emphasis in Capricorn or Scorpio, but with, say, a lot of Pisces or a strong Neptune in the chart, might under unendurable stress become an alcoholic, or display hysterical symptoms such as functional blindness, paralysis, and so on. Or there might be an inflated identification with a saviour-figure. And Uranus might equally be the trigger in such a case. The transiting planet is a trigger, and the experiences that take place at the time of the trigger are catalysts which reflect the nature of the transiting planet. But what is triggered is what the birth chart reflects; and this is the more important issue, if we want to understand the deeper meaning of depression or any other symptomatology in an individual. I often feel that psychiatric classifications, which are based on differences between symptoms, miss the fundamental point that the same kind of deep wounding and pain can result in quite opposite clinical pictures depending upon the character of the individual and his or her typical ways of reacting to great emotional stress or anxiety.

Audience: I thought Uranus was uplifting, and had to do with breakthroughs. I cannot seem to relate it to depressed states. I understand what you mean about Saturn and Pluto, but not about Uranus.

Liz: Once again I think you need to keep your eye firmly on what the birth chart reflects. If there is a split—a deep and apparently irreconcilable conflict—between different sides of a person's nature, and the individual has not explored this split and made any effort to come to terms with it, then anything which pushes the split up into consciousness can trigger a depression. Uranus does indeed imply a breakthrough or a change of some kind, but such a breakthrough is not always kindly received by the ego. Change sounds wonderful on paper, but what if the change means a complete alteration not only in one's self-image, but in one's entire environment, which has been built up according to the rules of the old game? If an individual has a lifestyle and a persona and a set of defences which rigidly hold down all the demons and keep at bay unresolved parental complexes, then the awakening of Uranus is not going to be very pleasant. The transit will unleash all those demons which one has just spent the last forty years attempting to silence. Depression is an important movement in this context and can be a very creative stage in the task of integrating the dissociated bits of the personality. We all like to think we want to be free, but Uranus' liberation is not always as nice as it sounds in theory. The ego still wants to be able to control the parts which have been liberated according to its own wishes. This is an impossible situation. We say we want to grow, but only if we can dictate the plan of growth according to the ego's security needs. Uranus of course will not pay the slightest attention to the ego's demands, nor will Neptune or Pluto. I observed quite a lot of this during the time when Uranus transited Scorpio square transiting Saturn in Leo, and began lighting firecrackers underneath clients with Moon-Pluto or Mars-Pluto contacts in the fixed signs. I saw client after client in a state of depression, because the Uranus transit was bringing the deep distress of Plutonian childhood feelings into consciousness. It was indeed a breakthrough, but such a breakthrough is at first not always fun.

We make the mistake of assuming that the source of depression is always a nasty planet such as Saturn or Pluto, and I have spent quite a lot of time talking about difficult Saturn and Pluto contacts in the birth chart. But often it is the transits of Saturn or Pluto which trigger depression in someone whose problem is an unexpressed Mars, or an unlived Jupiter, or a frustrated Moon or Venus. The source of depression seems to me to be a pocket of unlived life, of dammed-up emotion, of stifled imagination, of unresolved pain and anger. Some fundamental piece of the self has not been allowed to live, usually because the parents found it unacceptable; and it makes itself known like an energy vortex which begins to suck all the life-force down into itself. The Moon is a particularly vulnerable point in the birth chart, because it throws one back to infancy and to the mother. Difficult natal aspects to the Moon, particularly from outer planets or from Saturn, suggest unresolved problems in relation to the mother; and this is often what is triggered at the onset of a depression. Neptune is also a sensitive issue here, because an individual who is strongly Neptunian is inclined to idealise others, beginning with the parent, and to resist separating. Contacts such as Moon-Neptune and Venus-Neptune and Sun-Neptune, when they are linked to a secret unconscious union with a vanished parent, are extremely vulnerable when transits such as Saturn, Pluto, or Uranus move over them. The sense of loss, confusion, and anxiety can be very great, and the hopelessness of the child who is not yet ready to leave the mother and come out into life can form the core of a depression. I know that it sounds a bit as though any planet can be a significator for depression. In fact I think any planet can. But we need to really illustrate this with more example material.

DISCUSSION AND EXAMPLE CHARTS

I think we have time for some discussion before we consider charts from the group. Does anyone have a question or a point they wish to comment on?

Audience: My experience of depression certainly accords with the idea that it is linked with repressed feelings. I realised about six months ago that I have been depressed for most of my life. It seems to me now that in my case this has a lot to do with repressed anger. I find that very difficult to work with because I am so afraid of becoming intensely angry. How can one work with this?

Liz: This issue is a central point in many kinds of psychotherapy. I think that, in the end, the issue is not so much to "get your anger out" as to develop sufficient trust in your own capacity to contain such powerful emotions. The process of real healing and forgiveness, it seems to me, depends upon separating oneself from identification with the person or situation who has inflicted the original hurt; and that can only happen if one can have recognition of and compassion for one's own feelings. There is a difference between saying, "You have done this and this to me!" and saying, "I loved you so much that I would have done anything for you, and because of my love I felt terribly rejected and humiliated by your neglect—whatever the reasons for it." The first is an accusation; the second is an acknowledgment of oneself. Also, the first is an expression of powerlessness, while the second is an acceptance of self-responsibility. This process of separating has to do with the development of the ego; and it is the ego which is damaged in difficult parental entanglements. For this reason a therapeutic relationship is extremely important. It is via the discovery that another person can stand your anger and destructiveness that you yourself learn to stand it, and to accept yourself. Some people seem to have more of a propensity for violent anger than others. People are not all born the same, as astrology makes so patently obvious. We saw in the case of Barbara how her nature colluded with her early circumstances, and how her childhood rejection combined in an unfortunate way with an inordinate share of passion and emotional intensity. A person with a Mars-Pluto-Saturn configuration will have more powerful and self-willed emotions than one with Mars in Pisces trine Neptune. The anger is greater because the instinctual power is greater, and thwarting of desire is therefore felt more painfully. I would suggest that you work in psychotherapy on this issue, because I believe the presence and support of another person is critical. It is your fear that you will go off and kill somebody, or destroy all your relationships, or cause everyone around you to recoil in horror, which leads you to repress your feelings. But you may need to remember that this kind of global rage is the natural rage of a child who has strong passions and a very deep capacity for love. You are no longer an infant, and therefore can parent yourself sufficiently to contain these furious feelings until they are able to shift and transform into grief and mourning, and then into acceptance.

I think that perhaps you badly need to talk about these feelings, and find out who it is that you wish to destroy—and allow yourself to experience this wish on an inner level—before you can learn to trust yourself with the knowledge that you do not have to act it out. Feeling is one thing and acting out is another. For a child, there is no difference, but the sense of confidence that derives from a stronger ego makes all the difference. On a very basic psychological level, this issue of the terror of one's own destructiveness is connected with the inability of the parent to cope with the child's natural and healthy anger and aggression. There are many parents who are not frightened of this aspect of the child, because they themselves have been well parented in this area. Others, however, are made anxious and fearful because their own aggression was blocked or unacceptable in childhood. It is through the parent's acceptance of the child's rage that the child learns to trust himself or herself; and the rage itself tends to transform, or mature, into something less global. I was thinking of something a client told me recently—a memory she had of sitting in her high-chair at around two years old. Her mother was trying to get her to eat apple sauce and she didn't like it; so she spat it out and threw her spoon on the floor. Her father, who was an army officer, said to her threateningly, "Are you trying to provoke me?" Here the father's immediate reaction to natural childish anger is, "You're doing this to me on purpose and, by God, I'm going to crush this insubordination." One may well ask what the unconscious aggressive issues are in anyone who becomes an army officer; but never mind.

So there is probably an issue in your own childhood about your anger being threatening to the parent, which will inevitably come out in your relationship to a therapist.

Audience: I would like to comment on this lady's question. I have a client who is forty-one, and who has never allowed her rage out into the open because she has an omnipotent fantasy that it will destroy others. She recently had a dream in which she rushed into a room full of people very angrily, and was trying to kill all of them with her gaze. They just looked back curiously, and nothing happened. My client then began to turn the corner in my work with her. She was also extremely depressed when I began working with her.

Liz: This is not an uncommon issue – the feeling that one is carrying a nuclear bomb which will destroy the world if it ever goes off. Yet at the same time it is a compensation fantasy to balance the feelings of infantile impotence and helplessness. Sometimes I have heard people say, almost proudly, "Well, the reason I won't enter psychotherapy is because I know I'll never find anyone strong enough to handle my anger." This is compensation for a very great fear, an inflationary fantasy which masks deep anxiety that the person will himself or herself not be strong enough to handle it – or that severe punishment will be immediately forthcoming from the all-powerful parent-therapist.

Audience: Are there characteristic astrological significators for this kind of problem?

Liz: There are several which can suggest something like it. But it is hard to describe them out of context of an individual chart. Hard aspects between Moon and Pluto, or between Moon and Neptune, or Moon and Uranus, or even Moon and Mars, can suggest that the mother was herself so unhappy or fragile or anxious that she blocked anger in the child, for fear that she herself might go over the top. Sometimes the father is implicated, by significators such as Mars or Pluto in the 4th house, or Mars square the Sun. But you must look at actual charts to see how these things really fit together. There are often implications of humiliation and impotent rage in childhood, and the child often carries the belief that his or her anger is bad and evil although it may in fact be a healthy response to an unhealthy psychological environment. That is why it is so important to express the anger; it might seem excessive or inappropriate in the adult but it may well have been appropriate and necessary in the child.

Now let's have a look at the chart which I have put up on the board. It belongs to Alan, who is in the seminar today. (See Chart 4.) Alan, do you want to explain to us why you wanted this used as an example?

Alan: I particularly wanted to understand why, when a relationship broke up, I plunged into a terrible depression. It was really a depressive breakdown, and it took me a long time to come out of it. I should also say that, in the same year that my girlfriend and I broke up, my mother died. I didn't seem to react to her death at the time, but there was obviously a delayed reaction of some kind. Then I had the relationship bust-up, only about a month after my mother's death.

Liz: Did you know your mother was dying?

Alan: No. She had been quite ill for many years but I didn't know she was dying.

Liz: Why don't we look at the issue of the mother in the birth chart, since she seems obviously connected with your depression? Here is Uranus in the 10th house, appearing as a mother-significator. There is also a Moon-Jupiter conjunction in Virgo, and the Moon also conjuncts Neptune, which is in the first decanate of Libra. This Moon is also square Saturn. Can any of you interpret this combination of images? The presence of Saturn is not surprising in a case of severe depression, but we need to look at the whole parental picture.

Audience: This is one of those double message mothers you keep talking about.

Liz: Yes, quite. There are a lot of them about. The presence of Uranus in the 10th makes one statement about the experience of the mother, and the Moon-Jupiter-Neptune square Saturn makes another. Moon with Jupiter suggests a woman of high intellectual calibre, perhaps with a lot of spirit and independence; and the 10th

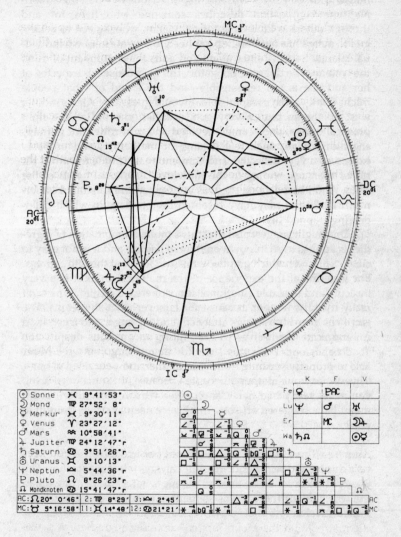

⊙ Sonne	♓ 9°41′53″
☽ Mond	♍ 27°52′ 8″
☿ Merkur	♓ 9°30′11″
♀ Venus	♈ 23°27′12″
♂ Mars	♒ 10°58′41″
♃ Jupiter	♍ 24°12′47″ r
♄ Saturn	♋ 3°51′26″ r
♅ Uranus	♊ 9°10′13″
♆ Neptun	♎ 5°44′36″ r
♇ Pluto	♌ 8°26′23″ r
☊ Mondknoten	♋ 15°41′47″ r

	K	F	V
Fe	♀	⚴AC	
Lu	♆	♂	♅
Er		MC	♃
Wa	♄☊		⊙☿

Chart 4. Alan. The birth data has been withheld for confidentiality. Chart calculated by Astrodienst, using the Placidus house system.

house Uranus echoes this high-spirited quality. But the Moon-Neptune conjunction describes someone who lives for and through others, a kind of sacrificial victim, whose need to belong and to merge has outweighed her need to express her own individual talents. Saturn comes along and adds the component of duty, the woman who does the obligatory things because it is expected of her and she is too responsible—and too afraid of what people might think—to be irresponsible. I would guess that Alan's mother was, on the surface, a very good mother; she did all the right practical things, and seemed devoted and nurturing. But perhaps she didn't have much real feeling for mothering, and probably expressed a very collective and conventional attitude toward it all, rather than responding to the individual emotional needs of her child. And I suspect that she was very angry and frustrated underneath it all, and may have resented the bondage in which child-bearing trapped her.

One might suggest also that this complex combination of ingredients applies to Alan's own emotional nature; and it is not easy to create a lifestyle which grants permission for all of them to express. But in terms of the experience of the mother, I think it is a very insecure and unstable emotional atmosphere for a child. One can't really trust the mother, because she is never what she seems. The sacrifices have little strings attached, and the anger and frustration communicate themselves to the child's unconscious despite the good behaviour. From this I would suggest that you were never able to properly separate from your mother and your need of her—or your need of a mother-surrogate—because, on some deep level, you never really had her. Can you see why your mother's death might have triggered off something very deep and very painful in you?

Alan: Yes, I can. All that you say about her makes sense. She was very dutiful and self-sacrificing. But I always felt that somehow she was cold. Everyone else used to tell me what a wonderful woman she was. I thought there was something wrong with me because I couldn't feel it.

Liz: Well, that's just for starters. But I believe it is this problem with the mother, and the insecure child who still lives in you, which lie at the core of your depression. Now what about the opposition between Mars in the 6th house in Aquarius and Pluto in Leo in the 12th?

Audience: Pluto in the 12th suggests a very turbulent family background, with all kinds of unexpressed emotions and sexual conflicts going on even before Alan was born.

Liz: Yes, I would read it that way too. Being a Piscean, Alan would have been acutely sensitive to that powerful unconscious atmosphere throughout his childhood. It is as though one senses something always just on the edge of erupting that never quite comes out into the open. I think that the father is also bound up in this terribly insecure atmosphere as well, because the Sun is square Uranus. There seems to have been some great tension between these parents, and in the whole psychic background of the family, as though any minute it might all blow up. If we add to this the very intense passions of the Mars-Pluto, and the great frustration and rage which Alan must have felt in the face of all that tension and suppressed anger in the parents, then I think we can see how difficult it might be for him to put all this together. There is a great deal of gentleness in the combination of Sun in Pisces and Moon in Virgo; these are extremely civilised placements, and Mars in Aquarius is also rather refined and intellectualises aggression. How does such a nice decent person cope with such terribly violent feelings toward the parents – particularly if the mother is already suffering and the father is too distant to be reached?

Audience: Why do you say that about the father?

Liz: Because of the Sun-Uranus square. Remember the sky-god Ouranos in the myth, who couldn't be bothered with his children because he thought they were flawed and ugly? This is an aloof father-image which embodies very high ideals, sometimes too high for ordinary mortal children to attain.

Audience: All this would be awfully hard on the body, with Mars in the 6th house taking all the pressure. I think there is a big work ethic in Alan's chart, an ability to work very hard and a great emphasis on duty.

Liz: Yes, that is suggested by the 6th house Mars. Also there is a very strong trine between Saturn and the Sun-Mercury conjunction in Pisces. And the Moon-Saturn square echoes this. Work, responsibility and self-control would be extremely important, and since one usually uses one's trines to fend off one's squares and oppositions, I would expect Alan to avoid the issue of his anxiety and insecurity through plunging himself into work. This is of course precisely what the mother did as well, and probably the father too.

Alan: That is very true. When my mother died, I just went on working. It didn't seem to affect my work at all. Then, when my relationship first broke up, I still went right on working, and I thought everything was fine.

Liz: I am sure you have that kind of persona—capable, reliable, and hard-working. It is not only the 6th house Mars, it is the Taurus MC as well. But of course people don't see Scorpio with all its intensity of feeling at the IC. And I think we should look now at the transits when these events occurred, and observe that Uranus was crossing that Scorpio IC. At the same time, Uranus came into square with the Mars-Pluto opposition. That is what I mean by a trigger. Uranus released not only the intense emotions of the hidden Scorpio IC, but also the rage and destructiveness of the Mars-Pluto. I think, Alan, that your response to your mother's death was not only a sense of grief and loss which was repressed; I suspect there was also great rage that she could leave you when you never really had her to begin with. You can see that I am concentrating much more on the issue of the mother than on the relationship breakup, because the latter seems to have been part of the former. In some way perhaps you needed your girlfriend as a kind of mother, as much as a lover, without being conscious of these needs; and her leaving was, as they say, the straw that broke the camel's back. The anger is the dominant component here, as this planetary combination at the time reflects considerable passion and violence. Here is Uranus releasing blocked feelings which are too powerful for the kind Pisces-Virgo personality to initially cope with. This is what I think lies behind the depression. And the depression can equally be seen as an extremely creative experience, because it served to put you in touch with not only the deeper feelings which any person born under a water sign needs to acknowledge and express, but also with a great deal of rage—and somewhere in that rage lie the seeds of considerable strength of will and survival capacity. It is also worth noting that transiting Uranus, at the same time that it set off the natal Mars-Pluto opposition by square, was also forming a trine to the Sun in Pisces. I think this is also important, because the Sun is the symbol of the individuality, the sense of being a unique and worthwhile person in one's own right. So Uranus not only released powerful destructive feelings which had their roots in childhood; it also gave support to the Sun, to the sense of self.

Audience: I would like you to say something more about the mother as reflected by Uranus. I understand the issue of the double message, but I am not quite getting the feeling of who this Uranian mother is.

Liz: All right, I think if we want to get a sense of this figure we must first look at mythology. Ouranos is the original god of heaven in Greek myth, and he rules before there is a manifest universe. He is a personification of the Divine Plan, the Mind of God which conceives an image of creation before anything comes to birth in form. When his children are born to Gaia, he repudiates them because they seem to him flawed and ugly. They cannot match up to the perfect image. I have talked about this myth many times before. It encapsulates something about the value-system and feeling-tone of this planet. Uranus is not intrinsically malefic; it is a representation of an archetypal pattern. But it is lopsided, as every planet is, because there are many archetypal patterns, and it describes only one. We can see the positive contribution of this idealistic Uranian perspective on life for any individual, as well as for the collective. It allows us to conceive of potentials, of a future which might be better than the present. It is the Promethean spirit of enlightenment, which frees us from slavery to the instinctual realm. But what happens when this image is linked up with the experience of the mother? Uranus is innately opposed to biological fate, to the instinctual role of the mother. Its world is that of heaven, not that of earth and of the body. If we personify this in ordinary human terms, then we have the mother who struggles against the fate of her female body. The things of the earth are flawed and ugly; only the mind and spirit are pure and perfect. Such a mother may love the idea of a child; but the actual baby, complete with soiled diapers and vomit and wind and fits of crying in the middle of the night, is not such a pretty experience. It means imprisonment, the crushing of the spirit—in short, a kind of death. This message will be communicated unconsciously to the baby, even though the mother might do all the right things and even believe that she is totally devoted. The advent of contraception, legalised abortion, and a more enlightened attitude toward a woman's so-called destiny as mother has changed many women's lives in the last couple of decades, and offered much more freedom of choice. But even now it is still a painful issue, and for Alan's mother it would have been much harder to face these things honestly. The collective values of her own childhood would have been nearly insurmountable. And if the child of such a mother receives this kind of message—"My God, how did I get myself trapped in such a mess with this revolting screaming creature demanding things from me all the time?"—then there will be a deep anxiety and insecurity, because of the feeling that at any moment the mother might jump up and suddenly go. Of course the reality is that she would probably never have gone; her need of security and collective approval was too great, and perhaps also her love of her child, which is not mutually exclusive with all that I have said. But to the child on the unconscious emotional level, it feels as though all the time she is hanging on the edge. There is no sense of safety. And if a child does not experience the mother as safe, then he or she will not be able to readily let go of the mother, or the need for mothering, later in life. This is what I mean by an inability to separate. The real separation can only occur when the mother dies; and then the pain of never really quite having her will rise to the surface. Yet initially Alan blocked this feeling of pain and loss, because it was too threatening to the adult ego.

Audience: There is another transit you didn't mention which was operating at the same time as the Uranus transit. Transiting Saturn came into opposition to the Sun and Mercury, and squared natal Uranus. It was exactly the same month.

Liz: Yes, Saturn was involved at the time as well, which is characteristic of a period of depression. Here he was moving through the 2nd house, opposing the Sun in the 8th. That seems to suggest an experience of darker levels of the psyche—the 8th house realm—through Saturn's usual method of forcing the individual to confront issues via the house through which he is transiting—in this case, the 2nd, which is concerned with self-sufficiency, self-reliance, and the security one has built oneself. Alan is being pushed into discovering his own identity—symbolised by the Sun—through confronting his lack of true self-reliance. Here I think we can see some of the tracks of the profound alchemical symbolism I spoke about earlier. This is really a rite of passage—a period of suffering and a disturbing encounter with the unconscious, which results in the building of a strong sense of identity. The necessity of something of this kind happening at some point in Alan's life is implied by the presence of the Sun in the 8th house at birth. I think that perhaps this entire chain of experiences has been necessary for Alan, so that he can emerge out of the maternal soup as a man. I feel that in some way, before this relationship breakup and the death of the mother, he was not yet himself, but was secretly deeply dependent on women to give him a feeling of safety in life. This is understandable in light of the parental experience. But the psyche seems always to strive toward some kind of wholeness, and suddenly there is a convergence of inner and outer experiences which, although painful and difficult, points towards the establishing of an independent identity. Alan has been forced into isolation in order to become himself.

I have been nattering on without giving you a chance to speak, Alan. Would you be prepared to talk about your experience, and comment on all that we have said?

Alan: Well, my first reaction after the relationship broke up, when I started feeling anything at all, was an incredible sense of loss. I felt

I had lost something wonderful that I would never find again. But I went on working; it didn't affect my work at all. I functioned quite well there. Also, my girlfriend was Chinese, and a lot in my life is connected with China. Whenever I do something, I do it 100%, so about two years after the breakup I travelled to China to help exorcise the woman.

Liz: That sounds as though she was as much of a symbol for you as an individual woman.

Alan: I also think that. I began to realise that I believed she would never ever leave me, because she was so loving and devoted, in that Chinese way. Somehow I had a fantasy that, whereas a Western woman might leave, a Chinese woman never would. There really isn't much more I can say about it.

Liz: Do you see how much this has to do with the need for a safe mother? What you have just said is terribly revealing. It is the longing for a woman who can offer unconditional love, who can accept anything without ever changing—unlike the Uranian mother whom I was describing before. But I would guess that your own perception of your mother was not of the Uranian, but rather of the Neptunian.

Alan: That is true. I felt her coldness, but I must say that I find it quite difficult to grasp this other side of my mother that you are talking about. She seemed so devoted. She was a very practical woman, not an intellectual at all. She made many sacrifices for me.

Liz: That is really my point. I believe you; I am sure she was those things. But she was probably also something else, which was violently repressed and never lived out. I think you must consider why you should be so deeply insecure as a man that you must have a woman whom you believe can guarantee you total safety. There is such a deep mistrust reflected by what you said earlier, about needing a Chinese woman because you can count on her constancy and devotion. Where do you think this comes from? I believe it is very hard for any person to see a parent as complex and perhaps split in motivation. But I have learned that when the chart describes such a double face pertaining to the parent, then it is terribly important to bring the hidden elements into consciousness, along with the feeling reactions that the hidden side of the parent invoked. The Moon-Neptune-Saturn side of your mother was devoted. The Uranus-Jupiter side was not. The less aware you are of this issue, the more you set yourself up for precisely the kind of experience you had—which, at its deepest level, was a re-enactment of your experience with your mother. You thought you could trust her but then you had a terrible shock. There is often an unconscious dimension to the mother and the father which affects us far more powerfully than we can imagine. It is the business of psychotherapy to smoke these things out.

During the aftermath of the breakup you said you were deeply depressed. During this period, Pluto was transiting in opposition to Venus. Would any of you like to comment on this?

Audience: Perhaps that is the trip to China, the exorcism. Venus is in the 9th house in the birth chart.

Liz: Yes, there is that literal level of it—the 9th house of travel. But I cannot let you get away with that. What else does this mean?

Audience: Perhaps it reflects the death of an old pattern, an old way of loving. It seems to be a transformation of the whole way in which Alan views life. That is the 9th house too—the view of life. That would connect the period of depression with the alchemical symbolism, the long wait in the dark while something is slowly changed and rebuilt.

Liz: I would agree with you. There is a gestation period reflected here, and in a sense also the activation of Venus—a more individual way of loving, more connected with Alan's own soul and less with his mother-complex.

Audience: It's the end of all those Chinese ladies.

Liz: Lucky for you there are no Chinese here today, otherwise they might be very justifiably annoyed. I think, looking at the overall picture of Alan's chart, that this is not a personality which is pre-disposed to a depressive outlook on life, in the sense that I was earlier describing. Alan's depression was a kind of one-off—a way of resolving an unresolved childhood issue which is connected with separation from the family background and the formation of a strong individuality.

Alan: That is true, I have never been prone to depression. But I am very moody. I have mood swings, and periods of gloom and doom.

Liz: That is probably the price you pay for being a Piscean. All the water signs are naturally moody; water by its nature changes and shifts all the time, and the flow of feelings is never consistent. A watery individual lives from the feelings, and they ebb and flow. It may be that these moods are very creative; if you work with them rather than against them, you may find that the periods of gloom and doom precede new bursts of creative activity, and are in some way necessary. I am sure there is more to come in terms of your own development, as there is no such thing as finishing; and Pluto will soon be coming up to square the natal Mars-Pluto opposition. I suspect that you have not yet fully got to the bottom of what has happened to you, and it may be that you will have a chance to really own and live that very strong and self-directed quality reflected by the natal aspect. Perhaps there is still some bitterness in you which needs to be cleaned out, and some deep anger about the whole experience, even though you are not in a depression any longer.

Alan: I wonder whether some of that bitterness is innate in me—a sort of world-weariness, because I'm a Pisces.

Liz: I don't think I would call Pisces bitter. But world-weariness is perhaps an appropriate description. By the time one has got to the end of the zodiac, one has seen it all. There is a quality of sadness in Pisces, which is possibly one of the chief motivations toward the search for transcendent meaning which is so powerful in this sign. It is as though Pisces carries within it the experiences of the previous eleven signs, and has lost the capacity to get attached to any one path or object in life. This melancholy quality is innate, although it is not melancholy in the Capricorn way—it is more a quest for a higher or deeper reality which can make sense of the apparent transience of earthly life. It is this sadness, and an innate empathy with all suffering life, which creates such a fund of compassion in Pisces.

Alan: I also feel a deep loneliness connected with the Moon-Saturn and Venus-Saturn aspects in my chart. It isn't so much a desperate desire for company. It's an awareness that I must always be separate, which I sometimes find quite painful.

Liz: I think you are an excellent example of how inappropriate the typical collective reaction to depression can sometimes be. With a chart like this, you are hardly going to bounce about like Mary Poppins. Your world-view will be coloured by something sad and bittersweet, but there is also great depth and considerable insight into the depths of others. The aggressively cheerful extravert might suggest that you try to get over it; but how can you get over yourself? And why should you want to? The bitterness which you mentioned earlier, which I would relate to the Mars-Pluto opposition, is a rather different issue, because that is poison. But the natural world-view of the watery trigon is a rather melancholy one—particularly Scorpio and Pisces. It is not that the watery signs believe life is without joy; but they also perceive the sadness in it, and the loneliness in all people. When we consider the family inheritance in your chart, particularly the 10th house Uranus with its suggestion of many generations of frustrated and unfulfilled women who never developed their intellectual and creative potentials, it would be surprising if you did not feel sadness at the pathos of it. I think Pisces is always a poet at heart, and the poet's vision is a melancholy one. It is not tragic, but rather, tragi-comic, a little like Puck's famous line in *A Midsummer Night's Dream*: "Oh, what fools these mortals be." This is also the vision of the mystic—it is only union with the One which can make sense of the bittersweet transience of incarnation.

Alan: I am also very involved with Buddhism, which is an expression of all you are saying.

Liz: I am not surprised. Well, thank you for letting us examine your chart so deeply. I have another chart which I would like to put up on the board, which John has given me. (See Chart 5.) He said that we could look at it if the seminar started becoming too cheerful. Would you like to say something about this individual, John?

John: This is the chart of a singer, a man who achieved a small amount of fame in the late 60's and early 70's. He made three record albums and then his creative inspiration seemed to dry up. I don't know about his childhood because I have not actually met him. I did the chart for his mother. I know that he went to public school, where he learned to play the guitar. He then went on to Cambridge, where he was good at sport and seemed to have had a fairly happy life for a while. However, then, while he was still at Cambridge, he began to act out an exaggerated role, dressing in black and smoking dope and strumming his guitar. He became extremely depressed. He said he felt like a visitor in his own body, and found it very hard to dress or wash his hair. He became quite morbid. He found it very difficult to relate to people physically. He never had a girlfriend, and could not get on with women. Many of his friends thought he was probably gay, although repressed. But it seems neither sex interested him. He couldn't imagine physical contact with anyone at all. He was able to communicate only through his singing. If he had conversations they always circled around cheerful topics such as madness, schizophrenia and suicide.

He was also totally unable to express anger, which I think is shown by the weakly aspected Mars in his chart. Unless you take the very wide square to Jupiter, it makes no aspects at all. But he eventually got "discovered," and made a record album which met with critical acclaim. He found it very difficult to relate to his audiences, though. He tried touring, but became very despondent because people seemed to find his music difficult. Eventually he moved to London and produced another record which the producer declared to be a masterpiece. But it didn't sell, and this crushed him. He despised money. At times he went through great poverty. At one time he couldn't even afford to buy a pair of shoes. Throughout the period that he made this second album, in 1973, he was in a very deep depression. His parents persuaded him to see a psychiatrist, who prescribed antidepressants. But they didn't seem

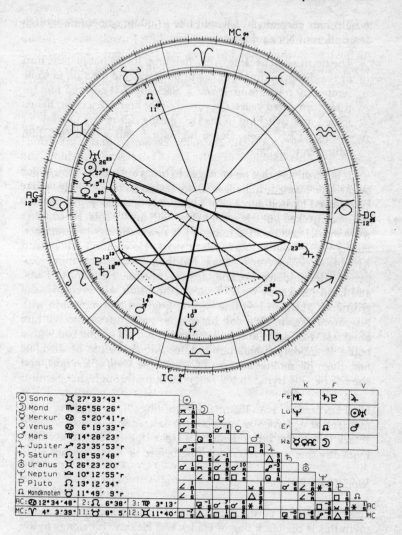

Chart 5. Nick A. is a musician. The birth data has been withheld for confidentiality. Chart calculated by Astrodienst, using the Placidus house system.

to help him very much. I would like to quote someone's written description of Nick's depression:

> The depression became overwhelming. It was not just the hurt or the disappointment or the understandable reaction to some temporary misfortune. It was a black fog that covered him for three tormented years. He would sit for hours in a chair, hands folded and twitching in his lap, gazing out of the window or staring at his shoes. Some nights a friend would find him sitting in total darkness.[3]

It is surprising that he managed to bring out a third record. But by the time he made it, he was so depressed he could barely speak. He checked himself into a local psychiatric hospital for five weeks. Then he checked out. He went to live with his parents. He couldn't write music, and decided to get a job as a computer programmer, but he walked out after a week of work. He couldn't understand why his records weren't selling. But then a remarkable thing happened. He suddenly became terribly cheerful. He went to Paris, and lived for a time on a barge on the Seine. He even found a girlfriend. But then he came back to England and moved in with his parents again. One day his mother went upstairs to tell him breakfast was ready, and found him lying dead on the bed with a bottle of antidepressants beside him. Shortly before he died, he had given his mother a copy of Camus' *The Myth of Sisyphus*, and she felt he was trying to tell her something through that gesture.

Liz: I am familiar with this man's recordings. I am thinking at the moment of a particular song on the last album, which is called "Black Dog." The lyrics describe a black dog coming to get him. Evidently this was written not long before he killed himself.

John: That's right.

Liz: I was struck by the symbolism of the black dog, because in myth this is the black dog of Hades and Hekate. It belongs to the underworld. It is the mythic image of a death-wish. The song is

---

[3]This quote comes from personal correspondence. Used here by permission.

very beautiful, but highly unpleasant. Do you have the transits for the period of bad depression?

John: Yes, Saturn was transiting over all the 12th house planets.

Liz: And Pluto, in 1973, was at the beginning of Libra, so it was going back and forth over the IC. Would any of you like to comment on your initial reactions to this chart? As John said, it effectively counteracts any inappropriate cheerfulness that might have broken out in the last hour.

Audience: That emphasis in the 12th house suggests that he was very tied to the family unconscious and to conflicts which he couldn't understand or cope with.

Liz: Yes, I am struck by the 12th house emphasis also. It certainly implies that he lived within the ambience of the family psyche, as though somehow he never quite managed to get born at all. He seems to have mediated much of this collective unconscious background through his music, which is very powerful; and perhaps this is emphasised by the Moon, which is the chart ruler, being placed in the 5th house of creative expression. But I think there was not enough of an ego for him to cope. He was a kind of vessel, but the unconscious overwhelmed him. There is no defined identity here, no structure which might have allowed him to cope with the overwhelming emotions. There also seems to have been a lack of solid fathering, which I would deduce from the Sun being conjunct Uranus and opposite Jupiter, and from Neptune in the 4th house. And with a Cancer ascendant, the mother is always much more powerful because the archetypal mother is one of the dominant mythic themes in the individual's life. He was completely at the mercy of the archetypal mother, with not enough masculine ego to balance her. And what you say about Mars, John, is quite significant here—a weak Mars cannot help him to fight her either. This is not about Nick having a "bad" personal mother. It is the archetypal Dark Mother, the life-devouring aspect of the collective unconscious, which possessed him, and out of which he was unable to emerge.

I think I have mentioned Erich Neumann's books to you in other seminars — *The Great Mother* and *The Origins and History of Consciousness*.[4] Neumann writes about a particular stage in the development of ego-consciousness which normally occurs around the age of seventeen or eighteen in the individual, and which he relates historically to that period of culture which we think of as matriarchal — the era of the great goddesses and of mother-worship, between 4000 and 2000 B.C. At this stage of development the individual ego is imaged as a beautiful youth, not yet a man. The beautiful youth is the son and consort of the great goddess. He is sacrificed at the end of every year and ploughed into the soil to ensure its fertility; and he accepts this death, because his consciousness has not yet evolved to the point where he can even conceive of a different fate, let alone have sufficient male power to free himself from the mother. There is a bittersweet and highly erotic feeling around the sacrificial death of the youth; it is both a sexual ecstasy and a doom. It is a kind of love-swoon. The Great Mother will take him back again, and there is something tremendously seductive as well as terrifying about such a death. One can see why the pre-classical Greeks linked together Eros and Thanatos, the gods of love and death. There are no fathers in this world; only mothers and sons. This is not the personal mother. It is the archetypal one, although the personal one no doubt colludes. In the adolescent, this stage is quite recognisable, because one is afflicted by the tremendous sadness and futility of life, and one things about suicide a lot. The pull of regression back to the mother is very strong, because the umbilical cord has not yet been broken. One has not yet embraced the loneliness of real separation, and one does not yet feel able to cope with adult life. Breakdowns are common at this stage, and are usually blamed on the pressure of university exams and such; but it is deeper than that. Nick's depression and suicide, in context of what we have heard and in relation to this dominant 12th house and Cancer-Scorpio emphasis and missing father, seem somehow a reflection of a mythic pattern.

---

[4]Erich Neumann, *The Great Mother: The Analysis of The Archetype* (Bollingen Foundation, Princeton University Press, 1955; and London: Routledge & Kegan Paul, 1955); and *The Origins and History of Consciousness* (Bollingen Foundation, Princeton University Press, 1954; and London: Routledge & Kegan Paul, 1954).

He never left the Great Mother; and when he moved too far away from her, by becoming happy in his own right and finding a girlfriend, she called him back again.

There are some other aspects in this chart which I think are relevant. The Moon is widely square Saturn, which might make a statement about a certain lack of relatedness between Nick and his mother. We have already looked at this aspect in Alan's chart. I think Nick probably felt lonely and isolated throughout his childhood. He was less equipped than some other children, perhaps, to cope with an emotionally unresponsive mother. She probably did all the right things, just as Alan's mother did, but somehow had no real feeling for mothering; or perhaps she was too unhappy herself. And Mars is the only planet in earth, which I also think is important. As John mentioned, Nick could not relate to his body at all. He didn't have a sense of his own physical reality. The body is a great container and protector against the onslaught of the archetypal realm, and I think one must be fairly well earthed to mediate the unconscious without being swept away by it.

Audience: It's interesting that he had such abhorrence toward money, with Saturn in the 2nd house. Do you think it would have made any difference if his albums had been successful?

Liz: I think this is very difficult to answer. I suspect that money and material success meant much more to him than he could admit; this is usually the case with 2nd house Saturns who claim to despise the material world. The materialism lies in the shadow, but the person fears experiencing this side of himself or herself, because it seems bad and dirty. This is especially the case in an idealistic chart, which Nick's is — since there is so little earth. But if one does begin to make money, one often feels worse. Nick did get good critical acclaim. If he had gone on writing songs, he probably would have had a hit sooner or later. But it seems he got worse when he began recording. The root of this problem is a lack of self-value. Don't forget that the 2nd house is about value, and money is the symbol we use to designate the worth of something — particularly ourselves. Saturn is in Leo, which means that he suffered a deep sense of inadequacy about his essential lovability and value as an individual. I suspect that a sudden success might have precipitated an earlier suicide. It would have proved that people only loved him because he was successful. There is also often deep shame about the body, which is the child's first sense of "I"—and this in turn is enhanced by the lack of earth. Perhaps this was also a problem in his mother, who may have had sexual confusion which translated itself into rejection of his body at an early age.

I have an uncomfortable feeling about this chart, which I did not have at all with Alan's, nor even with Barbara's—although Barbara's chart is, on the surface, more difficult. There is something mythic at work here, the beautiful youth wed to the Dark Mother. This is a true puer aeternus in his most tragic manifestation, gifted and yet doomed to die. It is not any one particular factor in the chart that gives me this feeling; it is the overall picture. Nick really acted out the myth to an extraordinary extent.

John: The transits on the day of Nick's death are remarkable. There was a conjunction of the Sun, Venus, Mercury, Mars, and Uranus at 28 degrees Libra, all in trine to Nick's Sun-Uranus conjunction in Gemini.

Liz: Those transits would have fallen in Nick's 4th house—the traditional "end of life." This would suggest that his death was really a release—at last he got to go home again. That is the feeling I have from those transiting trines. Sometimes death is represented as a tremendous conflict; one gets the feeling that the individual is struggling with something, and that perhaps the body cannot withstand the struggle. But here the implication is that he really had had enough; the battle to emerge as a separate individual was too wearying and painful, and he gratefully gave it up.

John: Saturn was transiting over his ascendant during the darkest depression.

Liz: So he was being called upon to define himself as an individual—to come out of the birth canal. This might have been a period of opportunity, since with Saturn in the 2nd house in the birth chart the issue of incarnating and coming to terms with physical existence was challenging him. But evidentally he couldn't, or wouldn't, emerge. Perhaps he could find nothing in life as seductive and appealing as a return to the womb.

Audience: This is interesting in light of what you said earlier—that the real time of danger is when the person seems to be coming out of the depression.

Liz: Yes, this is a sad example. Nick seems to have begun to make forays into the world—his trip to Paris, and the girlfriend. I think that making a relationship for the first time must have opened up all the possibilities of having his own life; but of course this would mean the necessity of leaving the mother, both personal and archetypal. The conflict must have been enormous. He chose the mother in the end. It is much harder for a person who has never been able to make a relationship, and who has lived in depression throughout youth, to begin to emerge into the light of day; because if someone finally gets through the barriers at last, the person feels unbearably vulnerable, and sometimes it is too late. Another person's warmth and love are experienced not as comforting, but as excruciating. That is why the emergence out of depression can be such a dangerous period for someone who has lived most of his or her life in a state of darkness.

Audience: How would you interpret the personal mother from this chart?

Liz: I would look at the Moon in Scorpio square Saturn, its only aspect except for two quincunxes to the Sun and Uranus. This would suggest to me a very passionate and deeply emotional woman with a powerful sexuality, blocked by her own conventionality, anxious to do the proper thing, and probably repressing considerable resentment and unhappiness. The Sun-Moon quincunx would suggest a problem in the parental marriage—an unease or lack of contact between the husband and wife. She may have been very unconsciously possessive of Nick, and poured her frustrated erotic feelings out on him while at the same time not relating to him in a genuinely warm way. Also, Nick was terribly sensitive, and was probably acutely aware of her unhappiness, even if she did not speak about it. I get the impression that he may have lost his father at an early age, through death or divorce or on a subtler level, perhaps around six or seven years, when the IC progressed onto Neptune. There is something quite uncomfortable about the intensity of a Scorpio Moon with no outlet except a square to Saturn; and I don't doubt that this same bottled up passion permeated the unconscious atmosphere around the mother. I think that Nick lived within his mother's aura for so long that he was completely subsumed by her, and by the archetypal figure behind her. It is not just her possession of him; it is also his longing for her. That is why I think the girlfriend must have provoked some deep and unendurable conflict—a separation which was too much for him to handle.

Audience: Is there any way of knowing from the chart whether his suicide might have been avoided?

Liz: I don't know of any way to determine that from a chart. It is a very old and difficult question. The whole issue of suicide is a complex one, and we have some very conventional and rather obtuse responses to it. You ought to read James Hillman's *Suicide and the Soul*,[5] which is a little outrageous at times but certainly challenges our assumptions about suicide always being "wrong." It a person identifies too closely with an archetypal figure, then he or she is fated by that figure, because an archetypal pattern is a fate. The puer always dies young. To what extent an individual is able to separate out from such identification is a huge question. Some people never experience such proximity to the mythic world. A full 12th house suggests that one lives within proximity, and must therefore try to develop sufficient strength in the ordinary personality to mediate it, rather than being subsumed by it. But perhaps some people do not wish to disengage from the archetype, for there is a kind of meaning and power to such a life, and it is a great sacrifice to become an ordinary long-lived mortal rather than a divinely chosen son-lover of the Great Mother. What Nick seems to have needed was a sense of reality—a set of boundaries, a sense of himself as a physically separate and worthwhile person. Perhaps he could have gotten that from a therapeutic relationship. But he

---

[5]James Hillman, *Suicide and the Soul* (Dallas: Spring Publications, 1964).

did not seek such a relationship, and I would question whether he would have allowed a therapist entry. I have no answer to these issues. I think one can only try to work with oneself, and do the best one can; and with others as best one can if that is one's calling.

Thank you, John, for depressing us so thoroughly. Shall we look at another chart? (See Chart 6 on page 158.)

Vicky told me when she gave me her chart today that she suffers cyclical, deep depressions for about two days four times a year, and as an Aries she finds these depressions a waste of time and wants to know why they happen so that she can get rid of them? Would you like to give us some more details about yourself, Vicky?

Vicky: I'm an artist. Both my parents are still alive. My mother is a very dominant and quite violent woman. I remember the depressions from around the age of five or six; it's quite a long-standing problem. I am now forty-one. They have recurred all through my life. When I get depressed, I lose all feeling and interest and desire. If I was in the middle of the road, I wouldn't mind if I was run over. I become totally inactive—no crying, no sleeping. It is a horrible state.

Liz: Any comments from the group on Vicky's chart?

Audience: My eye goes to the Moon-Pluto conjunction.

Liz: So does mine. I think that the things people tell you initially about themselves are very interesting. Vicky has said first that she is an artist, and second that she has a dominant and violent mother. Shall we, once again, look at the mother? She would inevitably be important, because depression is so deeply connected with the issue of separation and the birth of the individuality. The cyclical nature of your depression, Vicky, suggests that some common garden-variety transit, such as the Sun, keeps triggering something unconscious in the birth chart, and I suspect it is the Moon-Pluto that is triggered. Perhaps what you are really experiencing with your depressions is a kind of regression, a return to what your childhood was like on the emotional level. The Moon-Pluto is in the 12th, so we are back to the issue of the family

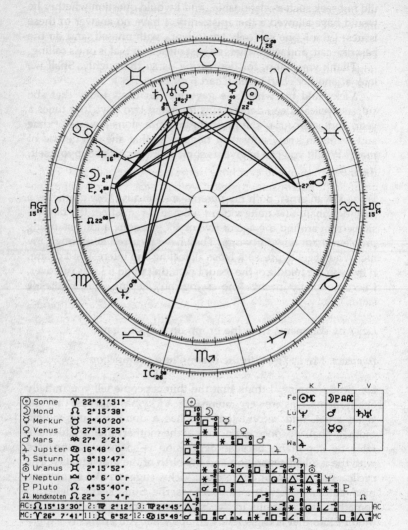

	Sonne	♈ 22°41′51″
☉	Sonne	♈ 22°41′51″
☽	Mond	♌ 2°15′38″
☿	Merkur	♉ 2°40′20″
♀	Venus	♉ 27°13′25″
♂	Mars	♒ 27° 2′21″
♃	Jupiter	♋ 16°48′ 0″
♄	Saturn	♓ 9°19′47″
♅	Uranus	♓ 2°15′52″
♆	Neptun	♓ 0° 6′ 0″r
♇	Pluto	♌ 4°55′40″r
☊	Mondknoten	♌ 22° 5′ 4″r

AC: ♌ 15°13′30″ 2: ♍ 2°12′ 3: ♍ 24°45′
MC: ♈ 26° 7′41″ 11: ♋ 6°52′ 12: ♋ 15°49′

Chart 6. Vicky. The birth data has been withheld for confidentiality. Chart calculated by Astrodienst, using the Placidus house system.

unconscious, and the lack of boundaries against it. I think it is very interesting that you have come today and wanted your chart looked at, because transiting Pluto is in exact square to this natal conjunction at the moment. Perhaps this will bring some realisations, and some surfacing of unconscious feelings over the next months.

Vicky: I have been very depressed just lately. I have also been feeling a lot of anger and hopelessness.

Liz: You are probably in better connection with your childhood at the moment than you ever have been since your childhood. That is an opportunity for something to begin to heal. But you will probably need to go down into all that stuff and explore it, rather than being ram-headed about it and calling it a "waste of time."

The issues of childhood are particularly emphasised in this chart because the Moon-Pluto conjunction is in the 12th house, which deals with issues inherited from the family past. There can also be an implication of pre-birth experiences, things which have happened to the mother during the months of pregnancy. I get the impression that there might have been some deep unhappiness around the mother before your actual birth, Vicky. Could you comment on that?

Vicky: My father was in the war when I was born, and I didn't see him until I was two years old. I am sure the whole period of pregnancy was a terrible burden on my mother, because he wasn't there to support her. And she had to take care of me totally on her own for those first two years.

Liz: Have any of you read a novel by Judith Rossner called *August*? I would recommend this novel for anyone interested in the therapeutic process. It's about an analysis. One of the strongest points which is made is the issue of very early experiences, even those which take place in the mother's life before the child's actual birth, and the ways in which these experiences communicate themselves via the unconscious and surface in all kinds of ways later in life. The young girl in the novel, who is undergoing a long and difficult analysis, has a mother who committed suicide before the girl remembered anything at all. Yet the image of the depressed, disturbed mother keeps coming to the surface, over and over again, because of the unity between the unconscious of the parent and the unconscious of the child.

I think that the depressed states which keep coming to the surface are connected with very early and very distressing experiences in relation to the mother. Perhaps some of this concerns the period of the pregnancy, but some of it no doubt relates to the difficulties of a woman trying to raise a child single-handedly while living with the constant possibility that her husband might be killed at any time. It is also sometimes interesting to look at lunar aspects such as this Moon-Pluto to see whether they are applying or separating aspects. If they are applying, as this one is, then one can work out how long it would have taken, by the symbolic motion of secondary progression, for the aspect to come exact. In Vicky's case, the Moon would have closed its applying conjunction to Pluto at the age of two months. I would guess that the very black, frightened, helpless, and hopeless feelings which rise to the surface during the times of depression are the feelings of a two-month-old girl, faced with a deeply depressed and anxious mother.

Vicky: I would like to ask you two things. The first is about my father. I sometimes wonder who in the hell my father really is. Even though I've known him almost all my life, I really don't know him at all.

Liz: I suspect he doesn't know himself either.

Vicky: I think you're right. The second thing I wondered about is a kind of telepathic link I have with my mother. I don't know if it has any bearing on what you have been saying, but it is such a close, weird link.

Liz: Well, we can see what sort of father-figure is represented in the chart. There are no planets in the 4th house, so we need to look at the Sun, by sign, house, and aspect. It is in the 9th house, and this would suggest an active, restless, visionary quality, someone who had to be on the move all the time. I suspect he probably enjoyed the war on some level, being away from home and fighting the good fight and tramping about with the boys. There are many men who, despite the horrors, felt as though they had lost something very precious when they had to come home again and settle down. I think your father might have been one of them. He seems to me to have been a boy, a delightful, exciting, energetic boy who lived all the time in a fantasy of greener pastures, and who didn't cope at all well with the extremely intense emotional needs of a wife and baby daughter. I am considering the Sun-Jupiter square and the Sun-Mars sextile, as well as the 9th house and the Aries.

Vicky: That sounds right. I remember finding him very exciting and glamourous. But my mother had a lot of anger toward him. I never really worked out quite why.

Liz: I would guess that she knew perfectly well, on a gut level if not consciously, that he would have got away as much as possible if he had had any justification for it. She must have felt deeply rejected. It is interesting to take this parental combination and look at it not only from the perspective of the parental marriage, but also what it might represent as two different sides of yourself. On the one side is the freedom-loving 9th house Sun square Jupiter, intuitive and longing for new life experiences and new knowledge. On the other side is the intense, passionate and deeply loyal Moon-Pluto in Leo. I am struck by the way in which this Sun-Jupiter father inside you calls your depressions a "waste of time." This must be how your father dealt with your mother's emotional needs, which no doubt pushed her even further into depression and rage. You seem to have little patience with your own pain, and I suspect he had little patience with hers.

Audience: Would you take into consideration Venus as the ruler of the 4th house, as part of the picture of the father?

Liz: Yes, I would consider it as an additional statement, although I feel planets in the 4th, and the placement of the Sun, are more important. But Venus as a father-significator would suggest a tie of love and perhaps strong erotic feeling. It is father as lover. This would fit in with the tendency of a person with the Sun in Aries to idealise the father's potency, and if it is a daughter with the Sun in

Aries, to project her masculine power onto him as the beloved and desirable object. I think it must have been quite a difficult situation for your parents, Vicky, when your father came home. On the one hand, your mother must have been deeply resentful about his absence, although the war was hardly his fault, and probably became even more resentful when she realised that he had got something positive from it while she suffered at home struggling to raise her child. But your powerful attraction to your father must have made it even worse. Previously, you were wholly hers, the compensation for as well as the cause of her suffering. It starts to become terribly Oedipal.

Vicky: I don't think my mother wanted my father. She shut him out sexually, during the time I was growing up.

Liz: Yes. But with Moon-Pluto as a significator rather than Moon-Saturn, or Moon-Uranus, I would guess that this was from furiously hurt pride, rather than lack of passion. My interpretation of this is that she was getting back at him. I would also guess that she tried to make it difficult for you to have any real relationship with him.

Vicky: That's right. I had to virtually ask her for permission to talk to him.

Liz: This I think was also a way of retaliating. Very often a parent who wishes to hurt his or her spouse will try to take the child away, emotionally if not physically. It is a common occurrence where there is a lot of suppressed anger in a marriage. Also, there is jealousy in it—your mother's jealousy of any potential relationship you might have with your father, because if she wasn't getting any, then she was damned well going to make sure you didn't get any either. None of this, of course, is conscious, or maliciously contrived. But the unconscious can be very primitive, and a Plutonian mother is very, very primitive. The problematic family inheritance on the mother's side, suggested by Moon-Pluto, is a problem of suppressed sexuality, frustrated passions, and generations of accumulated resentment. I think you were sometimes cast in the role of a football. The only way your mother could really hit back at your father's indifference to her feelings was to separate the two of you, and take over both roles.

Vicky: She certainly did that.

Liz: There is another facet to all this family drama, which is your own collusion with it. It always takes two to dance. This collusion I think is connected to your affinity with the mythic role of the champion, which is suggested by both the Sun in Aries and the Leo ascendant. Both these signs are related to the archetypal figure of the knight errant, the rescuer of damsels in distress and the seeker after the Holy Grail. Because the Sun, your chart ruler, is conjuncting the MC, albeit on the 9th house side, there is the suggestion that your mother needed you to play the role of her champion, and that you on your side colluded because it fit into your own unconscious mythology. Do you understand what I am getting at?

Vicky: Yes, I do. I was always expected to be strong for her, to do things for her. She has tended to try to live through me. Are you suggesting that there is some sexual confusion around this?

Liz: I would expect some sexual confusion to be one of the by-products of it, yes. It means you were pushed into living out the masculine side of your nature, at the expense of your own emotional needs.

Vicky: My mother was always telling me that men weren't worth the time of day. It took me a long time to get rid of that notion. I suppose it's part of the same thing.

Liz: I think so. This is what I meant by a football. Your fascination for your father and your deep obligation to your mother seem to have practically split you in half. There was no chance for your own child's needs to be met in the midst of that. This is what I would see as the background of your depressions—the frightened, angry child keeps coming to the surface, demanding recognition of her feelings.

Vicky: How do you explain the regularity of the depressions?

Liz: I think it probably has something to do with the transits of inner planets—Sun, Mercury, Venus—which would form conjunctions, squares, and oppositions to the natal Moon-Pluto conjunction four times a year. The Sun by transit is often a powerful trigger, especially if it coincides with the transit of a heavier planet. I have seen many people with cyclical depression—they always go into a plunge in October, for example, when the transiting Sun hits something hot in the birth chart. The Sun is particularly important for you, because it is your chart ruler. If Mars or Jupiter or Saturn happens to be setting off the Moon-Pluto at the same time because one of them is transiting in conjunction to the transiting Sun, then it is a particularly heavy patch. But then it goes away again. However, now Pluto is around, and Pluto does not go away before something is changed at a very deep level. I believe this whole issue is ripe for exploration at the moment. Pluto is a bit like Heineken's; it reaches the parts other planets can't reach. I would try to take the opportunity if I were you.

Vicky: But you are saying that I would have to tell the father inside me to shut up and stop denigrating my depressions.

Liz: Yes, something like that. Now you know who your father is. You're carrying him around inside. He's the chap who gives you your love of travel, your adventurous spirit, and your fascination with the world of ideas. He's also the chap who treats your emotional and instinctual life—your female self, in fact—as though it were nothing more than a petty nuisance. Your depressions seem to be very truthful expressions coming from a part of you that badly needs recognition, compassion, and time.

    I think we have come to the end of the seminar. I am grateful to both of you who have been brave enough to have your charts poked into in front of a group, since our theme today is a particularly sensitive one. I think it will be apparent how very deep and important this issue of depression is, when we begin to look at it as something meaningful rather than as an illness. I don't believe there are any shortcuts when trying to deal with these things, and I know of no fast-food route through the kind of regressive emotional pain that lies coiled within depression. But I do know that if it is taken seriously, and related to as a genuine expression of the unconscious, the rewards are very great—greater perhaps than simply a "cure." I will leave you with a reminder of the alchemical formula, which requires a nigredo in order to produce gold.

PART 3

THE QUEST FOR THE SUBLIME

We fear our highest possibilities (as well as our lowest ones). We are generally afraid to become that which we can glimpse in our most perfect moments, under the most perfect conditions, under conditions of greatest courage. We enjoy and even thrill to the god-like possibilities we see in ourselves in such peak moments. And yet we simultaneously shiver with weakness, awe, and fear before these same possibilities.

A. Maslow
The Farther Reaches of Human Nature

THE JONAH COMPLEX

According to Freudian theory, as children we possess certain innate drives and instincts—in particular, sexual and aggressive urges—which we feel nervous about expressing. One part of us has these urges; other parts of us hold them back.

Security is a child's basic need. Because we need the love and approval of those who care for us, we soon learn to defend ourselves against those drives which are not in line with what the environment condones. As a result, we inhibit our sexual and aggressive urges, and, indeed, any of our natural expressions which threaten to lose us love and security.

For instance, let's say that as a child you felt terrible destructive anger toward your mother because of something that happened. These feelings will make you anxious: you need your mother to feed you and keep you warm and safe, so it's not very wise to turn against her. She may not respond very lovingly toward you if you exhibit these feelings. What can you do but curb the expression of your anger?

In *Existential Psychotherapy*[1] Irvin Yalom maps it this way:

DRIVE → ANXIETY → DEFENCE MECHANISM

Certain drives feel dangerous. They give rise to anxiety, which then prompts us to employ appropriate defence mechanisms against their free expression. Drives can be repressed, projected, displaced or sublimated. There are a wide variety of defence mechanisms available to cope with our anxieties.

Freud believed that repression was one way of holding down what he termed the *id*, the inner reservoir of our so called "lower urges." Post-Freudians, such as Karen Horney, Erich Fromm, and Henry Stack Sullivan, took a slightly different view. They believed

---

[1]Irvin Yalom, *Existential Psychotherapy* (New York: Basic Books, 1980), p. 9.

that the child not only repressed the more obvious id urges, such as aggression and sexuality, but also learned to hold back some of his or her innate energy, curiosity, and even positive self-expression in order to conform to environmental wishes. So good things as well as "negative" things could be suppressed. For the sake of security, we compromise being true to the self. We opt for safety at the expense of freely expressing our real nature.

The humanistic psychologist Abraham Maslow extended the application of the concept of defence mechanisms even further. Not only do we fear, repress, and defend ourselves against our lowest possibilities, but we fear, repress, and defend ourselves against our *highest* possibilities as well. Maslow referred to this as "The Jonah Complex"—the fear of one's own greatness, the running away from all that one could be.[2] We all have within us an impulse to improve ourselves, to actualise our potentialities and attain greater fulfilment, and yet so often something blocks us or holds us up and gets in our way. Why?

In today's seminar, I want to explore this puzzle with you, both from a psychological and astrological point of view. Why do we fear our own greatness? Why are we walking around using only a fragment of our full potential? If the nature of life is infinite and unbounded, why (to borrow the words of Blake) has man "closed himself up till he sees all things through narrow chinks in his cavern?" We will be looking at how these fears and resistances show up in the birth chart, and how we can work with these issues both in ourselves and with clients.

Before going any further, it's necessary to define some of the terms we will be using today. All of us have so many different ideas about what "ego" means or what "the Higher Self" exactly is that we will end up very confused unless we come to some sort of understanding of what we mean by these concepts. Once we have defined our terms, then we will look more closely at *why* we resist our highest capabilities and also *how* we do this—the various ploys, strategies and defence mechanisms we use to defend ourselves against fully unfolding who we are and experiencing all that we could experience in life.

---

[2]Abraham Maslow, *The Farther Reaches of Human Nature* (New York: Penguin, 1985), p. 34.

THE EGO

The Concise Oxford Dictionary defines the word ego as that "part of the mind that reacts to reality and has sense of individuality." Jung defined ego as "the centre of the field of consciousness."[3] The ego gives us a sense of "I"; it is the feeling of there being a "me-in-here." In the womb we are in an egoless state, because we don't have an awareness of ourselves as separate individuals. Our experience of who we are in the womb is pre-personal, pre-subject/object. We think we are everything, or as Koestler puts it, to the developing embryo "the universe is focused on the self and the self is the universe."[4]

Gradually, after birth, a sense of ourselves as a separate and discrete entity begins to emerge. We eventually become aware that we have a body which is distinct from all other things and which is our own—this could be called a "body-ego." As time passes, we become aware that we have a mind and feelings which are our own—hence, we develop a "mental-ego." Once established, the boundaries of the ego or sense of "I" can keep expanding. So we start out with a feeling that we are everything. Through gradually differentiating the self out of the unbounded matrix of life, we begin to recognise ourselves as separate individuals. However, as we shall see, once we have developed a separate-self sense or personal "I," it is possible to expand the borders of the ego once more and re-connect to the rest of the universe from which we have previously differentiated. Albert Einstein gives a sense of what I mean:

> A human being is part of the whole, called by us "Universe", a part limited in time and space. He experiences himself, his thoughts and feelings as something separated from the rest—a kind of optical delusion of his consciousness. This delusion is a kind of prison for us, restricting us to our personal desires and to affection for a few persons nearest to us.

---

[3] Jolande Jacobi, *The Psychology of C.G. Jung* (Yale University Press, 1973; London: Routledge & Kegan Paul, 1975), p. 7.
[4] Koestler cited in Ken Wilber, *The Atman Project* (Wheaton, Illinois: Theosophical Publishing House, 1980), p. 8.

Our task must be to free ourselves from this prison by widening our circle of compassion to embrace all living creatures and the whole of nature in its beauty.[5]

In his book *Up From Eden* the American transpersonal psychologist Ken Wilber argues that human evolution progresses from a pre-personal state (in the womb and early months of life), to the development of a personal identity. Once we have established a sense of our own personal identity, the next stage is realising that we are in fact connected and inter-related to everything in the universe—the transpersonal dimensions of our nature. Pre-personal to personal to transpersonal.[6] Before you can transcend your separate-self sense and experience yourself as part of a larger whole, you first have to establish a personal self or ego. You have to have an "I" first, before you can transcend that "I." How can you transcend something you never had?

All this talk of the transpersonal and of transcending the separate self-sense may sound very mystical and up in the air to some of you. However, when we come to define what some people call the Higher Self, you will see that 20th century physics, mirroring mystical perception, also speaks of the individual's unity with the rest of life. Let's relate some of what we have been talking about back to astrological symbolism.

THE SIGNS AND HOUSES
AS A PROCESS OF DEVELOPMENT

The sign of Pisces and the 12th house both describe the experience of being part of something greater than the self or at the mercy of something bigger than the self. In fact, the 12th house is sometimes referred to as the collective sea out of which we all emerge, and is compared to the undifferentiated waters of the womb. We begin life immersed in an oceanic totality—what Wilber calls the pre-personal or pre-subject/object state.[7]

---

[5]Einstein cited in Peter Russell, *The Awakening Earth* (London: Routledge & Kegan Paul, 1982), p. 129.
[6]Ken Wilber, *Up From Eden* (London: Routledge & Kegan Paul, 1983).
[7]Wilber, *Up From Eden*, p. 25.

After Pisces and the 12th house, we come to Aries and the Ascendant and 1st house. The Ascendant relates to birth, which jolts us out of that state of primal wholeness. Being born means taking on a body, and when you take on a body you take on a specific form and boundary. You end somewhere and another person or thing begins somewhere else. Aries to Virgo and the 1st house to the 6th house define processes by which you further establish your separate-self sense. By the time you reach Virgo (the sign of detail, discrimination and drawing distinctions), and the 6th house of technical precision and attention to form and boundary, you have fully differentiated yourself from others. No longer at one with everything around you, you are now a concrete and distinct entity with your own particular mind, body, and feelings, performing your own particular tasks in the particular niche you have made for yourself in the world. You are firmly entrenched in the realm of the personal.

As we turn the corner from Virgo to Libra and from the 6th to the 7th house, a new process is set in motion: the urge to transcend the newly-found separate-self sense in order to merge again with something other than the self. From the 1st to the 6th, from Aries to Virgo, we have worked hard to build an ego-identity and define ourself as a discrete entity. But from Libra back to Pisces, and from the 7th to the 12th, we are asked to dissolve the boundaries of our acquired ego and recognise that we are indeed part of something bigger. In the 7th and 8th and through Libra and Scorpio we attempt to blend and unite with any number of significant other people in our lives; in the 9th and 10th and through Sagittarius and Capricorn we recognise that we are a part of an even larger unit which influences and defines us—society; and in the 11th and 12th and through Aquarius and Pisces we realise our interconnectedness with the rest of life and all of creation. So by the time we arrive back at Pisces and the 12th house, we are once again part of something much greater than the self. We are now in the realm of the transpersonal. Really, the ego hasn't gone away—it has just expanded itself to include more and more.

Aries (1st) to Virgo (6th) and Libra (7th) to Pisces (12th) describe two very distinct and yet related processes. On the one hand, we have the urge to develop a discrete ego-identity, while on the other, we have the urge to transcend that separateness and reconnect again to the larger whole, to something greater than the self. If you have Saturn in one of the first six houses or signs, then you have some fears or problems about being separate and defining yourself as an individual. However, if Saturn falls somewhere in the last six houses or signs, then your problems are not about defining the separate self, but stem from a fear of merging with others and letting go of separateness. Some people have difficulty establishing their autonomy and individuality, and will too gladly go along with the crowd or flow. Others are more tight and bounded, and have difficulty connecting and blending with others or acknowledging their universality.

THE HIGHER SELF

Now I have to confront the difficult task of trying to define what is meant by "the Higher Self" or what some people call the Transpersonal Self or the Pure Self or just the Self with a capital S. Mystics and philosophers have been attempting to explain this concept for thousands of years. We have about ten minutes.

Earlier we talked about the pre-personal state or feeling that we are the whole universe, which we experienced to some degree in the womb (or even at some point in between lives, if you believe in reincarnation). Two months after conception the developing embryo has a rudimentary brain which is capable of registering experience. One of the first things in life which we register is this sense of universality and wholeness with all of life. Even after we are born and take on a body and a separate existence, something within us recalls that our deepest and innermost nature—our Pure Self or Higher Self—is unbounded and infinite. Consciously or unconsciously, we still long to reconnect to that lost wholeness.

Getting to the Higher Self means letting go of our more surface identities. Most of us derive our sense of who we are through something external. We define ourselves by what job we do, by where we live, by how much money we make, by whose partner we are. But even if we lose a job or partner, we still exist—we still *are*. There is a deeper underlying you, which exists even when things you thought you were are taken away.

Some people discover this deeper and more eternal sense of self through meditation. Meditation involves reducing outer sensory experience and turning the awareness inward until you are left experiencing consciousness itself. If we compare the mind to an ocean, meditating involves shifting attention from the surface levels of the ocean to the deeper levels of the ocean and ultimately to the ocean bottom. If we compare the mind to a radio, meditating is like turning the volume of the radio down as low as it can go, but the radio is still on. Through meditation, it's possible to arrive at a state of pure consciousness or pure self-awareness. If there is any feeling or identity at all, it is a feeling of universality or at-one-ness with the whole of creation. You begin to experience that at some fundamental level, you and the rest of the universe are one and the same—your deepest Self or Higher Self is a Universal Self.

So the Higher or Transpersonal Self is both our innermost essence as well as that part of us which is universal. Jung referred to the ego as the centre of consciousness, but the Self as the whole circumference which embraces both conscious and unconscious.[8] All-encompassing and more powerful than the ego, the Self ultimately guides and oversees our fullest possible unfoldment. But there is a catch. In order to connect to the Self, we have to let go of our separate-self sense. And that's a scary prospect.

The symbol of Pisces—two fishes swimming in opposite directions—is an apt description of a basic human double bind: one fish is swimming toward individuality, while the other swims toward universality. One part of us struggles to form and maintain a separate and discrete ego-identity, while another part yearns to transcend that separateness to merge with the larger whole again. The ego doesn't want to be dissolved, but if we are to reconnect with the rest of life, then we will have to relinquish its tight boundaries. We don't have to lose our ego entirely—some sense of individuality is needed to function in the world—but we do have to put the ego in its proper relation to the Higher Self.

Audience: Don't some people swim the other way?

---

[8]C.G.Jung, *Memories, Dreams, and Reflections* (New York: Random House, 1965; London: Collins, 1974), p. 417.

Howard: Yes, the converse situation is possible. Some people prefer to remain amorphous and undefined, and their problem is not that of letting go of the ego, but forming one in the first place.

Assagioli, the founder of psychosynthesis, was fascinated by the different reactions people had when subjected to his "cosmic test." The cosmic test involves being shown pictures of the universe enlarging in scale until the earth is just a tiny dot disappearing into the immense void of space. Some people who take the test are oppressed by infinity, bewildered and frightened at its vastness. Others, however, when presented with the same series of pictures, experience a sense of expansion and opening up of the self, and the feeling that they participate in some grand cosmic scheme. But let's get back to explaining the Higher Self a bit more clearly.

A German Dominican monk, Henry Suso, once wrote: "All creatures . . . are the same life, the same essence, the same power, the same one and nothing less."[9] A 20th century scientist, Henry Stapp, writes: "An elementary particle is not an independently existing analyzable entity. It is, in essence, a set of relationships that reach outward to other things."[10] From either a mystical or scientific perspective, we discover that a unifying element connects all life, and that nothing exists in isolation. An experience of the Higher Self, Pure Self, Transpersonal Self, or Universal Self (these terms roughly mean the same) is an experience of that part of you which is universal and unbounded—that part of you which you share with everything else. The humanistic psychologist Carl Rogers once observed that the deeper you go into your own self, the more you discover the whole human race.[11]

If your awareness is permanently established in the Higher Self, then you might be called an enlightened or realised Being. Enlightened people would still function with an awareness of their own individuality, but along with it there would be an equally strong awareness of their oneness with the rest of creation. Universality does not exclude individuality. You can be in touch with that

---

[9]Suso cited in Russell, *The Awakening Earth*, p. 122.

[10]Stapp cited in Ken Wilber, *No Boundary* (Boston: Shambhala, 1981), p. 37.

[11]Carl Roger's ideas on psychotherapy are presented in his book *On Becoming A Person* (Boston: Houghton Mifflin, 1961; and London: Constable, 1977).

part of you which is unbounded and infinite and still maintain a sense of yourself as an individual as well. Peter Russell sums this up in his book *The Awakening Earth* when he writes: "Oneness and separateness become different perspectives of the identity."[12]

Audience: So an enlightened woman can feel at one with a tree and still see that the tree is different from herself.

Howard: Yes, she will see the tree as a tree, and herself as herself. And yet, she will also be fully aware and in touch with the reality that at some deep level, she and the tree are part of a single undivided whole. At the deepest levels we are all one, and everything shares the same reality or Is-ness—a concept referred to as "the perennial philosophy" by Aldous Huxley.[13] Your Pure Self and my Pure Self and a tree's Pure Self are the same, although my Pure Self will guide me to grow in a certain way, your Self will direct you another way, and the tree's Self unfolds in yet a different manner.

Most of us are not aware of the oneness we share with the rest of life because we have been conditioned, educated, and brought up to see our differences rather than our unity or at-one-ness. We are conditioned into a me-in-here versus you-out-there reality, and lose a sense of us-in-here. William Blake put it all much more poetically:

> If the doors of perception were cleansed, everything
>   would appear to
> man as it is, infinite.
> For man has closed himself up, 'till he sees all things
>   thro' narrow
> chinks in his cavern.[14]

Many of the breakthroughs and new insights of modern physics mirror the precepts of the perennial philosophy. Previously, according to classical 19th century physics, the universe was seen as a mass of separate things and events, each isolated from one

---

[12]Russell, *The Awakening Earth*, p. 138.
[13]Aldous Huxley, *The Perennial Philosophy* (New York: Harper & Row, 1970; London: Fontana, 1958).
[14]William Blake, *The Marriage of Heaven and Hell*.

another in both time and space. On this basis, scientists proceeded to measure, label, and put everything in its place.

Trouble arose, however, when they began exploring the nature of sub-atomic particles—protons, neutrons, and electrons. To their astonishment, scientists discovered that these particles, which were believed to form the basis of all life, refused to act in accordance with expected laws and formulas. In fact, sub-atomic particles, the very building-blocks of existence, actually defied location in time and space. In *The Awakening Earth*, Peter Russell explains the theories of a British physicist Richard Prosser. Prosser formulates "that what we consider to be a single, isolated, elementary particle can be considered to be an infinite wave pattern spreading out in all directions across the Universe."[15] These waves cancel each other out everywhere except in one tiny place, and it is in this place that we have what is known as a particle. The conclusion Prosser draws is that everything is everywhere, but only manifests at a particular point.

Do you see what is happening? Classical 19th century science had developed laws and formulated theories based on its belief in one thing being separate and bounded from another, but 20th century physics is now revealing that bounded, separate, and distinct things don't actually exist. The boundaries which science once believed existed between me, you, and this table are not as rigid as once thought. Ken Wilber sums it up this way:

> In short, the quantum physicists discovered that reality could no longer be viewed as a complex of distinct things and boundaries. Rather, what were once thought to be bounded "things" turned out to be interwoven aspects of each other. For some strange reason, every thing and event in the universe seemed to be interconnected with every other thing and event in the universe. The world, the real territory, began to look not like a collection of billiard balls, but more like a single, giant, universal field, which Whitehead called the "seamless coat of the universe."[16]

---

[15]Russell, *The Awakening Earth*, p. 127.
[16]Wilber, *No Boundary*, p. 38.

THE REALM OF THE SUPERCONSCIOUS

Some people associate feelings such as joy, bliss, or universal love with the Higher Self. But an experience of the Higher Self (one's basic Beingness or Is-ness) is not necessarily filled with ecstasy and intense emotion. Contacting the Higher Self is more usually experienced as a state of profound stillness or peace. Peter Russell compares it to being in a completely silent room where there is nothing to be heard.[17] You are conscious, but there is nothing to be conscious of except consciousness itself. When you are experiencing the Self, you are not focussing on, or experiencing anything in particular. You are not thinking about love or having feelings of joy. You just are. The Self is not a process—it is boundless Being.

But as you move closer to the Self, you pass through what is known as the *superconscious* dimensions of the psyche, the place from which feelings such as joy, universal love, and bliss emanate. For instance, at church or in private prayer or meditation, you may feel waves of rapture and be swept away by a love for all humanity. As total or perfect as this state might seem, strictly speaking it is not an experience of your Higher Self, but a superconscious experience. As I said before, the Self is an experience of pure Being, and is felt as just calm and serene. By contrast, an experience of the superconscious is more gushy than an experience of the Self. However, an influx of superconscious energy is a sign that you are coming nearer to the Self.

So compared to the Pure Self, the superconscious is more lively and active. The superconscious is associated with what are known as the higher emotional and intellectual processes—joy, bliss, compassion, and a heightened awareness of truth and love. A typical superconscious experience would be to feel that you are a channel through which some wider or stronger force flows. Delighting in beauty can be a superconscious experience, so are powerful feelings of universal love or creative inspiration. You have these kinds of experiences as you approach the Pure Self. They are signs that you are near the Self.

Although the Higher Self is devoid of any concrete contents, it nevertheless expresses itself through the qualities and experiences

---

[17]Russell, *The Awakening Earth*, p. 120.

of the superconscious. Assagioli compared the Self to a pivot point or hinge of a door. The door opens and closes, but the hinge stays steady. The Self is the focal point around which the superconscious processes take place. The Self is also the energy source which enlivens the superconscious. While the Self itself is unchanging and just pure Is-ness, it nonetheless sends out energies which are then stepped down and transmitted via the superconscious.[18]

Audience: I've heard an analogy for the relationship of the Self to the superconscious. The source of electricity in a large city is a national grid or a generator which has all the electricity for the city stored there. This electricity, however, is stepped down through cables and transformers into various areas. This is similar to how the Self channels its energy through the superconscious.

Audience: All this seems related to the idea that the Self speaks to us through symbols and dreams.

Howard: Yes. The Self sends messages through the superconscious. Dreams, symbols, and insights come from the Self via the superconscious.

Some people in their journey toward the Self become sidetracked and find themselves identifying with superconscious qualities, mistakenly thinking that these things are the Self. In this case, the "I" is not merging with the Self at all, but rather the sense of "I" is being identified with superconscious qualities like love, truth, beauty, or whatever. While this sounds nice, people who become too attached to these qualities (even though such things seem so positive) are not really experiencing the true unbounded and infinite nature of the Self. Maslow called this "higher sidetracking." You see it fairly often—people on a spiritual path veering off into the superconscious a bit too much and getting hung-up on too many psychic type things, or hearing angels and voices speaking to them or seeing visions everywhere. Their "I" is identified with the contents of the superconscious rather than with the Self, and they walk around thinking they are Love incarnate or Wisdom

---

[18]Assagioli cited in *The Superconscious and the Self*, a pamphlet available through the Psychosynthesis and Education Trust, 188 Old Street, London EC1.

reborn. But if you are thinking that you are the very embodiment of Love or Wisdom, then you are *not* having an experience of the Higher Self, because the Higher Self is contentless. In such cases, the "I" is deriving its identity from some superconscious content.

Vedic Indian philosophy stresses that you have to be without the three *gunas* in order to be enlightened. The three *gunas* are *tamas*, *rajas*, and *sattva*. *Tamas* correlates to decay, corruption, and things rotting and dissolving. *Rajas* means activity. *Sattva*, the third *guna*, is associated with feelings of expansiveness and positivity. While it is easy to understand that enlightenment means being detached from *tamas* (decay) and *rajas* (activity), it is more difficult to appreciate that enlightenment also means not being identified with *sattva* (goodness). In order to be truly enlightened, you must not even be identified or attached to *sattva*. While it seems noble to be attached to something so positive and life-supportive, it is still an attachment, and therefore not a true experience of the unbounded and infinite Self. So those people who are always running around and trying to do good all the time ("do-gooders") are possibly too attached to *sattva*, and this might be in the way of their having a true experience of the Universal Self.

Now that we have defined some of our terms, let's look at the quest for wholeness and the true Self from the perspective of psychological astrology. I'll draw on some mythology to help us.

KRONOS AND HIS CHILDREN

This myth gives insight into the relationship between the principles of Jupiter, Saturn, Uranus, Neptune, and Pluto, and highlights the whole issue of the repression and fear of the transpersonal realm. It all begins with Uranus and Gaea. Uranus is the first sky-god, ruling expansive and limitless space. He is married to Gaea, Mother Earth. Every night the starry heavens (Uranus) comes to lie on the earth, and, as a result, the couple keep producing children. They give birth to a race of giants known as the Titans, a number of one-eyed Cyclopses, and various other monsters. Uranus, disgusted at the sight of his own offspring, keeps shoving them back into Gaea's womb; in other words, he banishes them to the underworld. Uranus does this because the children don't live up to his idea of what they should be. This is a Uranian issue, and people with Uranus prominent in their charts will know what I am talking about.

Uranian types often have marvelous visions and ideals, and in their minds they are capable of imagining how wonderful something could be: they envision the perfect political system, the perfect relationship, the perfect state, etc. However, when an attempt is made to concretise that vision and put it into action by giving it form, the end results are often very different from what was hoped for. What can be abstractly imagined in the mind and what seems highly desirable and ideal may in actual fact disappoint or let down the Uranian person when the effort is made to make it real and bring it down to earth. I can see some of the more Uranian among us nodding their heads in agreement. A good example is the French Revolution, which took place synchronously with the discovery of Uranus in the 1780s. The revolutionaries tried to implement their noble ideals of a state based on the principles of liberty, equality, and fraternity, and ended up in a bloodbath instead. On the whole, people were just not ready to live up to such ideals and what was conceived as so wonderful turned very ugly indeed.

But back to our story. Obviously, Mother Earth isn't amused, her womb gorged with these banished children. Producing some steel out of which she fashions a sickle, she implores Kronos (Saturn) to castrate Uranus. What does this mean?

The myth suggests that the part of us which is more earthy or Saturnian—our caution, conservatism, sense of duty and responsibility to what is already existing, and our fear of the unknown—can actually "cut off" the creative impulse and imagination of Uranus. Saturn represents the principle of maintenance and is pitted against Uranian urges for the new and untried. Saturn builds and preserves boundaries; Uranus challenges boundaries, threatening to tear them down in the name of progress and for the sake of something new and better happening. Saturn reflects the ego's tendency to try to preserve and maintain things as they are. Saturn holds on, doing what it can to block and inhibit change. Psychologists use the word *homeostatis* to define the ego's urge to maintain the *status quo*. To some degree, we all have this conflict in us between Saturn and Uranus, between safety needs (maintaining what is known) versus growth needs. Being human and creatures of habit, we don't like to lose those things to which we have attached our sense of identity. People born with Saturn in hard aspect to Uranus will feel this tension all the more strongly. Also, those with a preponderance of earth in their charts won't take too kindly to Uranus wanting to break up what is existing.

There's more. Saturn castrates his father Uranus, but in turn, Saturn later fears that his own children might try to overthrow him. To avoid this, he swallows them. Saturn eats his own children—he won't even let his own creations exist. In much the same way, strongly Saturnian people will filter and censor any ideas they might have about breaking out of old moulds and patterns or trying to do things in a new way. Saturn swallows Neptune (Poseidon) and Pluto. In other words, Neptune and Pluto threaten Saturn. Because Saturn fears being overthrown by Neptune and Pluto, he doesn't want them, or the principles they represent, to exist. Psychologically, the forces of Neptune and Pluto threaten to overthrow our ego-boundaries (Saturn) and challenge the separate-self sense or existing sense of self which Saturn so dearly wants to maintain. You know this from your own experience. A major transit of Neptune or Pluto doesn't want to leave you the same way it found you. Transiting Neptune and Pluto "wipe out" so that something new can happen. You are not the same person afterward. They change your life. Saturn doesn't want this to happen. After all, the ego is not that keen about its own demise.

However, I don't want to be too hard on Saturn, even though it can be pretty hard on us sometimes. I've been dwelling on Saturn as the cruel tyrant, who defends the borders of the ego and won't let in anything too new or disruptive. But there is another side to Saturn—the Wise Old Man or the Celestial Schoolmaster, as Isabel Hickey was fond of calling him. Saturn transits can bring about profound psychological changes which deepen our awareness and make us more solid. Saturn transits are times when potential abilities and talents can be developed and expressed in concrete ways. We learn greater commitment and discipline, and are better able to accept the necessary limits and restrictions that being human imposes on us. Some people come into their own under transits of Saturn. We shouldn't forget this side of Saturn. But let's get back to our story.

JUPITER TO THE RESCUE

Rhea, Saturn's wife, is distraught. (Wouldn't you be if your husband kept eating the children you produced?) But she comes up with a plan. When pregnant with Zeus (Jupiter), she plots to trick Saturn in order to save the child. She goes into hiding, gives birth to Jupiter in a cave, and then offers Saturn a stone wrapped in swaddling clothes to swallow in place of the child. With the help of his grandmother Gaea, and Amaltheia, an amazing goat cum wet-nurse whose horns overflow with nourishing milk, Jupiter enjoys an almost idyllic childhood and soon grows old enough to challenge his father. The goddess Metis (Wisdom) gives Saturn a draught to drink which makes him disgorge Neptune and Pluto in what could only be described as one enormous belch, and together with Jupiter, the three of them eventually overthrow Saturn. With the old tyrant banished, Jupiter takes charge, assigning rulership of the oceans to Neptune, the domain of the underworld to Pluto, and (carrying on the tradition of his grandfather Uranus) establishes himself as the supreme Ruler of the Heavens.

The point I am stressing is that Jupiter is the one who is responsible not only for avenging Saturn's castration of Uranus, but also for the release of Neptune and Pluto. In other words, the Jupiterian principle supports the progressive urges of Uranus and also makes it possible for the forces of Neptune and Pluto to overcome the restraints and restrictions of Saturn. Translated into plain English, what does this mean?

We know from any astrological textbook that the Jupiter principle corresponds with the urge for expansion and growth. Jupiter is the planet associated with broadened vision and expanded horizons. Saturn wants to maintain the *status quo* and preserve the existing sense of self. But, in the end, it is the ego's own desire to expand, grow and broaden its horizons (as represented by the Jupiter principle) which compels the ego to change and open up, eventually allowing for the breaking down of its rigid boundaries. That part of us which is Saturnian wants to preserve the tight boundaries of our ego and the sense of our separateness from what we think is not-us. But that part of us which is Jupiterian urges us to grow and expand, eventually making it possible for Uranus, Neptune and Pluto to break down and transcend the existing borders of the ego and put us in touch with the higher, all-inclusive Self we have been talking about.

Let me spell this out step-by-step with you once more. You start out in life in a more or less egoless state in the womb, where you have no clear sense of being a separate "I" (the pre-personal stage). Then you are born and begin the process of defining yourself and building your separate-self sense. You develop the sense of a me-in-here or ego-identity, along with the Saturnian urge to preserve your own discrete I-ness (the personal stage). However, there is a problem. While one part of you wishes to maintain your discrete ego-identity, the Jupiterian part of you wants to keep expanding your sense of self to include more and more. Ultimately, the urge to expand your already existing sense of yourself takes you to the point where you will have to forfeit your separate-self sense in order to merge with something greater than the self (the transpersonal stage and realm of the outer planets).

Audience: So we are back to what you have explained before, when you talked about the Piscean dilemma of the two fish swimming in opposite directions: one wanting to define the sense of individuality and the other wanting to dissolve or transcend separateness to reconnect to the larger Whole again.

Howard: Right. I am coming at it from a different angle this time. But remember that Jupiter is the co-ruler of Pisces, so we have the linking of the Jupiter principle with that of Pisces. However, I would draw one major distinction between the workings of Jupiter and Neptune. Jupiter seeks fulfilment by adding more and more things to it: "If I gain more, if I do more, if I see more, if I acquire more, if I explore more, if I expand my ego boundaries then I will be fulfilled." Jupiterians can't get enough but Neptunians can't let go of enough. Neptune is not so concerned with gaining and adding things to itself, but has more to do with giving up and letting go of things: "If I let go of things and give them up, if I sacrifice what I have attached to myself, if I relinquish and dissolve my boundaries (rather than keep expanding them), then I will be spiritually redeemed." See the difference? Jupiter gets there by going after more and more; Neptune by letting go of more and more. Jupiter adds and Neptune takes away.

THE SEARCH FOR MEANING IN LIFE

The derivation of the Greek name Zeus comes from the Sanskrit root *dyaus* and the Greek *djeus*, which means the light of the heavens. Zeus or Jupiter is the bringer of light. The Roman name Jupiter comes from the root *diu-pater*, which means God the Father. Jupiter was a god of the sky, residing in the ethers, the upper part of the air, and on mountaintops. He was "all-high," and worshipped in elevated spots. Jupiter was considered omnipotent and all-knowing. Looking down from on high, he dispensed good and evil on all mortals. You can see how the astrological Jupiter is associated with foresight and vision, and with having a higher perspective on things. The planet Jupiter has come to be connected with the drive to find truth and wisdom, and what some people call religious urges. Freud believed that these aspirations were a sublimation of "lower" drives and the sexual instinct. Jung and other psychologists, however, felt that the religious urge was a basic drive in the human being—as basic as any of the biological impulses, and not just the result of sublimated instincts.

Jupiter has to do with the drive to find meaning in life, and represents the symbol-making capacity of the psyche; the ability to imbue an event, object, or experience, with meaning and relevance. Jupiter is our capacity to invent symbols and then find meaning in them. In ancient Greece and Rome, Jupiter was prayed to for help, guidance, inspiration, benevolence, and preservation— he delivered people from plagues. If we combine all these connotations of Jupiter, we come up with idea that giving meaning to what we are going through is a way of helping us endure even very difficult times.

Jupiter can be understood as the psyche's tendency to attribute meaning to things: the urge to fit your experiences and your whole life into a greater explanatory framework. Jupiter gives you the ability to view what you are going through or having to endure from the perspective of the larger context of your overall unfoldment. The need to find meaning in life is so important that we had better dwell a little longer on it. Jung wrote:

Absence of meaning in life plays a crucial role in the etiology of neurosis. A neurosis must be understood, ultimately, as a suffering of a soul which has not discovered its meaning. . . . About a third of my cases are not suffering from any clinically definable neurosis but from the senselessness and aimlessness of their lives.[19]

The psychologist Viktor Frankl also stressed the need to find meaning in life. In his book *Man's Search for Meaning*, Frankl wrote about his grim experiences in Auschwitz from 1943–45.[20] He observed that, aside from pure chance, the ones who survived the concentration camp ordeal were those who could find some sort of meaning or purpose in what they were going through. The meaning might be something like "God is testing me," or "I have to get out of here to see my family again," or "I have to survive in order to tell the world about how awful it has been." Those who could find no meaning were less likely to survive.

Freud had emphasised the pleasure principle or will to pleasure as a human being's most basic motivation. Later, Alfred Adler postulated that our underlying drive was the will to power and a striving for superiority.[21] Frankl, however, believed that the will to meaning (the striving to find a meaning in one's life) was the primary motivational force in human beings. Without meaning, we feel we have nothing to live for, nothing to hope for and no reason to struggle for anything. Meaning gives us direction in life. Some people believe that the whole cosmos has meaning and it is our job to discover what that is—God has a plan and we are part of that plan. Other people believe that there is no ultimate meaning or grand design, and yet it is still necessary for us to invent some meaning in our lives in order to survive. Nietzsche once wrote, "He who has a *why* to live, can bear almost any *how*."

---

[19]C.G. Jung, *Collected Works*, Volume 16 (Princeton, NJ: Bollingen Series, Princeton University Press, 1985), p. 83.

[20]Viktor Frankl, *Man's Search for Meaning* (New York: Washington Square Press, 1984).

[21]Alfred Adler, *Superiority and Social Interest* (London: Routledge & Kegan Paul, 1965).

MASLOW'S HIERARCHY OF NEEDS

It wouldn't be fair to discuss the will to meaning without mentioning the work of Abraham Maslow. Back in the 1950's, Maslow had a very bright idea: why shouldn't psychology study happy and fulfilled people? Up to then, sick people were the ones who were studied, tested, measured, and evaluated. Psychology was developing a pretty good idea of what sick and neurotic people were like, but didn't really understand what made someone healthy or what the fulfilled person was like. In his book *Towards A Psychology of Being*, Maslow writes:

> Contemporary psychology has mostly studied not-having rather than having, striving rather than fulfillment, frustration rather than gratification, seeking for joy rather than having attained joy, trying to get there rather than being there.[22]

Maslow turned his attention to people who were successful and fulfilled, and one result of his research is something now known as Maslow's Hierarchy of Needs.

Maslow saw human needs as multi-layered, and devised a pyramid of needs. At the base (level one) are those needs which are purely physiological—survival related needs such as those for oxygen, food, sleep, and sex. As you move to the second level of the pyramid, safety needs preside—the need for order, stability, and some sort of economic or job security. Level three gives belongingness and love needs—the need for affection, family membership, physical contact, friendship, etc. Level four covers self-esteem needs—the need for autonomy, competence, and mastery as well as the need for esteem from others—things like praise, recognition, and status. Finally, you arrive at level five, what Maslow calls meta-needs or higher order needs—the need for self-actualisation, the search for truth and understanding, the creation of beauty, and the desire for justice. The level you are on will vary according to age and circumstance; for instance, a child is probably more concerned with the lower levels, and a person who is starv-

---

[22]Abraham Maslow, *Towards A Psychology of Being* (New York: Van Nostrand, 1968), p. 73.

ing is not so caught up with sexual needs or the pursuit of wisdom. However, Maslow proposed that if you succeed in fulfilling one level of the pyramid, then you naturally want to move on to the other level needs.[23]

For our discussion, the most important deduction to come out of Maslow's work is his belief that the urge for self-actualisation and for something spiritual is an innate part of our make-up, as innate as the desire to be fed or the need to belong. Like Jung and Frankl (and unlike Freud), Maslow concluded that spiritual needs were part of our biological inheritance. Maslow also pointed out that we are often ambivalent about growth and fulfilling our higher needs. Humans, as he saw it, are caught between the desire for safety and staying with what is known versus the urge for growth and unfoldment. We are pulled in these two directions. In order to grow, the delights of growth have to be more tempting than the delights of safety. We have to minimise our anxieties about growth and maximise our anxieties about staying the same.

Audience: Would you associate Jupiter with Maslow's higher-order needs?

Howard: Yes, because Jupiter symbolises both the urge to grow and the need for a belief system. Along with other factors in the chart such as the 9th house and the placement of the outer planets, Jupiter's sign and house will suggest something about where we look for the Truth with a capital T or where we seek God in some form. Any planet aspecting Jupiter will colour our "God-image" as well as describe how we go about our search for truth and what we encounter in the process. For instance, Saturn square Jupiter may have more difficulty, frustration, problems or issues with rigidity when forming a belief system; while Venus trine Jupiter is likely to have an easier time of it.

---

[23]Maslow's theory of a hierarchy of needs and his research on self-actualising people can be found in his book *Motivation and Personality* (New York: Harper and Row, 1970).

JUPITER'S SIGN AND HOUSE
IN THE QUEST FOR MEANING

I plan to talk more about aspects to Jupiter later in the day, when we discuss the kinds of problems people experience on the path of self-realisation or spiritual development. For now, let's look at Jupiter by sign and house with regard to the search for meaning in life.

Jupiter in Aries/Jupiter in the 1st

If Jupiter is in Aries or the 1st house, you may feel as if you have been assigned to initiate some divinely inspired mission. In other words, you believe in yourself, which is a healthy enough thing. Taken to an extreme, however, it could mean that you think *you* are the truth.

Audience: I've noticed that people with Jupiter in Aries will get very excited about what they believe in—they have to tell everyone and enthuse about it all over the place.

Howard: Yes, that's a good point; the sign position of Jupiter not only gives clues about what a person believes in or is enthusiastic about, but also tells us something about the way in which he or she shares those beliefs and enthusiasms.

Jupiter in Taurus/Jupiter in the 2nd

If Jupiter is in Taurus or in the 2nd house, you may look for God in the acquisition of money or in the material world in general. You believe in being secure. But this isn't the only way this Jupiter expresses itself. Some people with these placements can find Heaven right here on earth, through a deep love and feeling for the natural world. For them, communing with nature is a way of connecting to something Higher. The 2nd house doesn't only indicate material values. More broadly, it denotes how we find security in life. If you have Jupiter in the 2nd or in Taurus, possessing a definite philosophy or world-view will provide you with a sense of safety and well-being. And whether your values are material or spiritual, you'll stubbornly hold onto and defend them until you're good and ready to change.

Jupiter in Gemini/Jupiter in the 3rd

God or "the Truth" is sought in knowledge, education, or learning. You may believe that thinking *per se* and the analytical process itself is all that is needed to solve problems, or that the answer to life lies in improving your ability to communicate. You aspire to know as much as you can about everything around you, and may talk a lot about what you believe in. Of course, with Jupiter in Gemini, this could change from day to day.

Jupiter in Cancer/Jupiter in the 4th

For you, the meaning in life and sense of fulfilment may be linked with establishing a happy and secure home base. Unlike Jupiter in Gemini or the 3rd, God (or the Truth) is not sought via the intellect, but rather through the feelings and emotions. You may believe that the only true gods are the ones which your distant ancestors worshipped—in other words, things from the past have a great deal of value to you. Some with this placement may feel that having children or looking after others is the answer to everything. Others will believe that having their own emotional needs fulfilled is the be-all and end-all of existence.

Jupiter in Leo/Jupiter in the 5th

Those with Jupiter in Leo or in the 5th house might believe that the meaning of life lies in the importance of giving creative expression to the self and finding out who you are in your own right. Rather than looking for God (or the Truth) in groups or organisations, it is to be found inside you. God might be sought in art and culture, pomp and circumstance, royalty and fame, or through noble, dignified, or dramatic gestures. As with Jupiter in the 4th, Jupiter in the 5th could find meaning in life through the creative act of procreation and raising children, although others with this placement may see the pursuit of pleasure and romance as the main goal of existence.

Jupiter in Virgo/Jupiter in the 6th

With Jupiter in this sign or house, you believe that the meaning of life is connected with being productive, useful, and of service to others. Work itself may be worshipped as a deity. Technical efficiency, craftsmanship, or becoming an authority in a chosen field of interest could assume great significance in the overall plan of things. Or God is sought through orderliness, and an adherence to routine and ritual. The meaning of the universe could be found in a grain of sand or speck of dust. For some it indicates the belief that the body is the temple of the spirit, and therefore gives a preoccupation with inner and outer purity and cleanliness.

Jupiter in Libra/Jupiter in the 7th

Relationships give your life meaning and you could put great faith in them. Love and beauty might be sought as the most important goals in life, along with a belief in co-operating peacefully and harmoniously with others. The God-image will most likely be imbued with qualities of fairness and justice. The purpose of life may be to redress discord and injustice, and in some way make the world more true and beautiful. However, if Jupiter is not well aspected in this sign or house, then your perspective could be off, and you might be dominated by the desire to impose your own personal view of what is beautiful and just, at any cost to others.

Jupiter in Scorpio/Jupiter in the 8th

God is found in Scorpionic or 8th house matters—in that which is hidden, mysterious, occult or taboo, or in those things which other people turn away from. For some, the fulfilment of religious goals may involve the transformation or sublimation of the sexual and darker side of the nature. For others, the sexual act itself may be linked with the numinous. Sexual exploration and conquest may be high on the list of what makes life meaningful. Wielding greater power and influence over others could be what spurs you on; or you might believe that the way to God and fulfilment is through penetrating deeply into the hidden recesses of your own psyche— exploring, mastering, or coming to terms with your own shadowy bits. Your philosophy in life is intensely felt, and could embroil you in battles and conflicts, both within yourself and with others. Some people believe that God can only be found through struggle, crisis, and suffering.

Jupiter in Sagittarius/Jupiter in the 9th

You look for meaning in life through Sagittarian or 9th house things. There is the belief that if you could find the right philosophy, it will give you all the answers and you will be fulfilled. God is sought in a system—finding a system or set of laws which will guide your conduct and way of life. For some with these placements, travelling the world and having a wide variety of experiences in the name of seeking the truth is what gives meaning to the life. Knowledge, education, and "higher" wisdom could be looked upon as the keys to heaven. You might promote your philosophy and beliefs in an overly enthusiastic manner, pushing what you believe in as the answer to everything.

Jupiter in Capricorn/Jupiter in the 10th

Some with these placements find meaning in life through achieving in conventional ways—through money, status, and power. Being successful is what gives the life meaning, purpose, and direction. Establishing yourself in a good career or helping to maintain the smooth and proper functioning of society is what you seek after or believe in. Discipline and structure may be worshipped as a God. Your philosophy in life could be quite straight and narrow, or your philosophy has an earthy quality to it. Like Jupiter in Virgo, it gives a belief in that which can be seen, measured, and tested.

Jupiter in Aquarius/Jupiter in the 11th

You find your faith in ideologies or isms. Like Jupiter in Sagittarius or in the 9th, you look for a system which will guide you and lead you to the truth. God is sought through groups, friendships, and ideals. Promoting social change or helping to bring new trends into society may be the way you give meaning to your life. You might worship humanitarianism, or believe that the only way to make your life meaningful is to participate in some endeavour which serves the larger body of humanity and not just your own personal needs. Your philosophy could border on the utopian, and you may need to be reminded about the more instinctive or primitive side of human nature.

Jupiter in Pisces/Jupiter in the 12th

The urge to find meaning in life is connected with Piscean or 12th house things. You look for the Truth and are opened to something greater than yourself through music, art, poetry, or other forms of creativity. Sacrifice, love, and charity may be what give your life meaning. You might believe that transcending your separateness through service and compassion will lead you to God. There is the danger of being swept away by your beliefs, a kind of effusive faith which gives up everything for the church or your guru.

PLACEMENTS IN THE NINTH HOUSE

The 9th house is the area most directly concerned with philosophy, religion, and the search for meaning in life. It is in the 9th house that we seek the truth and attempt to fathom the laws underlying existence. The 9th house describes something about the way in which we pursue religious or philosophical concerns. The planets and signs which we find in the 9th also suggest what kind of God we worship, or the nature of the philosophy we formulate. Let's run through some of these quickly. After lunch, when we look at why and how people resist living their highest, we will discuss many of the issues raised so far more fully, both from an astrological and psychological point of view.

Sun in the 9th

The Sun is where you find yourself—where you distinguish yourself as a separate, unique individual. If it is in the 9th, then this can be done through an interest in and the pursuit of philosophy, religion, or spirituality. In your search to find meaning in life, you will discover a sense of who you are, or feel empowered and vitalised.

Moon in the 9th

If you have the Moon in the 9th, then you probably feel quite comfortable or "at home" contemplating the meaning of life. The philosophy is experienced not just via the mind or intellect, but through the heart and feelings. The image of God will be coloured by the Moon and the sign it is in. For instance, if you have the Moon in Capricorn there, then your image of God might be an entity who demands obedience and duty. The Moon in Pisces might worship a God who emphasises more Neptunian qualities, such as compassion or a love for all of humanity.

Mercury in the 9th

The urge is to try to understand God and figure him out. In other words, God is sought intellectually. Issues of philosophy and religion can be scrutinised very carefully, and will usually be debated and argued over with vigour. A variety of different beliefs and philosophies may have to be explored in a restless pursuit of truth. You may want to tell others about what you believe, either through writing or teaching.

Venus in the 9th

If you have Venus here, then you are capable of attaining peace, happiness and equilibrium from this area of life. Your philosophical belief-system is likely to have symmetry, taste and proportion. It could be very neat. More likely than not, God would have to be fair and just, dispensing authority in a reasonable way from high above. Loving and respecting other people will probably be a basic premise upon which your philosophy rests. Unless Venus is difficultly aspected, there needn't be much anguish in your pursuit of truth or philosophy.

Mars in the 9th

Those with this placement pursue their philosophy, religion, or search for Truth with ferocity. You would be willing to fight to defend your beliefs and, in some cases, actively go about forcing others to take your side. It's possible that God could be seen as angry and fiery, demanding action and assertion. You need to be careful that you don't displace responsibility for what you do onto God—some people justify pillaging and killing in the name of the Lord. In some cases I have seen with this placement, the person was actually angry at God or the cosmos for not running the show as he or she would see fit.

Jupiter in the 9th

We've already touched on this one briefly when we discussed Jupiter in Sagittarius. If you have Jupiter in the 9th, then what you believe in is belief systems. You have faith in your philosophy. When working on The Twelve Houses[24] and looking through Lois Rodden's The American Book of Charts,[25] I was struck by the number of murderers and assassins who were born with Jupiter in the 9th. It is as if those with this placement can justify anything they wish to do on the basis of their philosophy or belief system. In other words, the belief system can be construed in such a way as to rationalise any action: "If God didn't want me to kill that person, then He wouldn't have invented guns. . . . He wouldn't have allowed me to go so far as to get one in my hand." In short, if Jupiter is in your 9th, then you should be careful about getting

---

[24]Howard Sasportas, The Twelve Houses (Wellingborough, England: The Thorsons Publishing Group, 1985).
[25]Lois Rodden, The American Book of Charts (San Diego: ACS Publications, 1980).

carried away by what you believe. (Wherever Jupiter is by house, there is the danger of going over-the-top.) You might think your belief system is the answer to everything, and look down upon other people who don't see it your way. Or you feel that it is your mission to show them the true way. People with Jupiter here usually believe that every event or occurence has some sort of significance and fits into a larger scheme of things. Things don't happen randomly; they have meaning. Behind everything that happens is God's purposeful intention, plan, vision, or wish. God is cast in the likeness of Zeus—he is omnipotent and all-seeing, dispensing justice from on high.

Saturn in the 9th

Those with Saturn in the 9th may fear that they are not good enough for God, or that God doesn't like them. The God-image is tied up with Saturn: the Supreme Being may be viewed as someone who is harsh and stern, demanding obedience and discipline, and who will punish you for putting a foot wrong. What God likes or dislikes may be very clearly defined and spelt out, and woe to those who dare to transgress the law! If you have Saturn here, religious or spiritual issues are usually taken pretty seriously, and approached in a methodical or apprehensive way. For those with this placement, philosophising is not taken lightly: it's not something you do just because you are bored or enjoy being fanciful. Wherever Saturn is in the chart is where we have to work hard. Saturn doesn't make things comfortable for us—we have to exert some effort in its domain. Some may play it safe, and cling to conventional or well-established dogmas, or dedicate their lives to studying philosophy and religion in order to be certain of the Truth. Others may try hard to avoid the whole issue of philosophy altogether, either by denigrating its importance in life, or by denying that there is anything "higher" or anything "out there" to believe in. This is called nihilism. The French existentialist writer Albert Camus was born with Saturn in Gemini in the 9th: he believed that events had no higher or absolute meaning, other than what the individual happens to attribute to them.

Uranus in the 9th

Those with Uranus in the 9th are not likely to buy someone else's belief system wholesale. They need to find the answers for themselves, and be free to experiment with different philosophies and systems in their search for the Truth. Mirroring Uranus in mythology (who banished his creations to the underworld because they didn't live up to his expectations), those with a 9th house Uranus may periodically cast off one set of beliefs for what they think is a new or better one. Some people with this placement may be attracted to rather odd or unusual explanations of the whys and wherefores of existence, or go for philosophies based on unconventional tenets or premises. The image of God might be cast in the likeness of the mythological Uranus—the starry heavens—something very high up there and hard to grasp. Even though God or the cosmos might be difficult to figure out, don't forget that Uranus is associated with the fixed air sign Aquarius—a sign dedicated to the search for systems, ideologies and isms through which to better understand and order life. (Albert Einstein, with Aquarius on the cusp of the 9th, once remarked, "I cannot believe that God plays dice with the cosmos.") People with Uranus here normally believe that finding the meaning or truth in life will set them free. Knowledge liberates. No matter where they might have to search for it, those with Uranus in the 9th still believe that a system must exist, somewhere or someplace, which will explain everything or make sense of the universe. I'd give them plenty of room to look for it.

Neptune in the 9th

Those with Neptune in the 9th are seeking redemption and salvation through their belief systems. They may believe that in order to find God they have to make sacrifices and give things up. Their philosophy will usually entail some sort of surrender or devotion to God, to the church, to the guru, or to a way of life. I have observed that some people with Neptune in the 9th succumb to what Rajneesh called "the buddha disease," the belief that if you imitate your guru, then you will be enlightened. They try to find out what the guru eats, what television shows the guru watches, what soap the guru uses. If their guru only eats vegetables which grow above the ground, then they will only eat vegetables which grow above the ground. If their guru says peanuts are bad for you, then they will believe that peanuts are bad for them. If the guru happens to enjoy bathing with Badedas, then they will bathe with Badedas.

As I understand it, their basic misconception is the mistaken belief that consciousness is the result of behaviour: by trying to behave in a certain way, they think it will automatically produce a certain level of consciousness. They try to "mood-make" themselves into enlightment. I tend to see it reversed—on the whole, behaviour is the by-product of consciousness, not the cause of it. Your level of consciousness naturally gives rise to your behaviour, not the other way around. Those with Saturn in the 9th will act in certain ways out of obedience to their guru, but people with Neptune in this house go a step further and try to merge or become one with him or her. Some are easy game to anyone who offers the keys to heaven, opening themselves to disappointment and disillusionment in this area. Hard aspects from other planets to Neptune in the 9th could give rise to various forms of spiritual inflation—thinking that they are Love Incarnate or that they are God's chosen messenger.

Pluto in the 9th

In certain ways Pluto in this house is similar to Saturn there. Those with Pluto in the 9th often approach philosophical issues and the question of meaning in life with a seriousness or reverence. Pluto was the god of death. We may be unconscious of it, but Pluto's house is where we believe that life/death issues are at stake. If you have a 9th house Pluto, you might believe that your very survival depends on figuring out how God or the cosmos works. You could become obsessed with the need to evolve or be driven by a compulsion to fathom the deeper laws which govern existence. There could be a total and all-consuming commitment to your beliefs or spiritual path. Nothing else will matter as much.

I've observed a number of people with Pluto in the 9th who are frightened of what the future might bring, and it strikes me that they have "projected" Pluto onto God. They fear that God is ruthless—ruthless enough to turn on them and make life pretty terrible or destroy them altogether. Even if they are good and do everything right, God or life could just turn around and betray them. Or suffering, breakdown, pain and crises are seen to play a crucial part in the drama of spiritual unfoldment. In other words, for them (and whether it is conscious or not), God has a dark side: He or She is not all beauty, justice, and light.

Like Saturn, Pluto doesn't make life easy for us in the house it is in. In an attempt to evade the issues of the 9th house, those with Pluto here could turn nihilistic, and deny that there is anything higher. Pluto destroys so that something new can be born. Those with Pluto in the 9th may periodically undergo radical changes of philosophy or belief system, wiping out one way of ordering and finding meaning in life in order to replace it with a new and revised view.

URANUS, NEPTUNE, AND PLUTO
AS SUPERCONSCIOUS QUALITIES

The closer you get to an experience of your Higher Self, the more you tap into superconscious energies. Here is a list of some of the qualities we could assign to the superconscious or transpersonal realm: beauty, compassion, courage, creativity, freedom, liberation, an awareness of truth, good-will, harmony, light, and love. These are the kinds of qualities you make contact with when you have a peak experience—an experience which puts you in touch with something higher.

Jupiter—the urge to grow and expand—opens us up to the energies of Uranus, Neptune, and Pluto. Jupiter and the outer planets correlate with superconscious qualities. The outer planets, in particular, put you in touch with things beyond the sphere of the ordinary, everyday ego. If you have Uranus, Neptune, or Pluto aspecting the Sun, Moon, Mercury, Venus, Mars, Jupiter or Saturn, then something transpersonal or something from the superconscious level is trying to enter into your life through the nature and sphere of the planet which is being aspected. For instance, if Uranus, Neptune or Pluto should be aspecting your Mercury, then it is through Mercury that you are meant to be opened up to something beyond ordinary, everyday reality. What could that mean?

Audience: You can be opened up to the superconscious through Mercury things—through your mind or through what you study.

Howard: Right. Mercury also rules brothers and sisters, so it might even be through a relative or sibling that you discover superconscious qualities. Also, what you have to say or communicate (Mercury) might tap into that realm. Now, what if you have an outer planet aspecting your Moon? How would superconscious energy find a way into your life with the Moon being touched?

Audience: The way in would be through your feelings or your emotions—through Moon things. Maybe even from your mother!

Howard: Don't laugh. I have seen many charts with Moon-Neptune aspects, and the mother has been interested in things of a spiritual or psychic nature. But, in short, if an outer planet touches your Moon, then you are prone to emotions, feelings, and perceptions which are more subtle or refined than usual. So with the outer planet touching Mercury, the superconscious qualities come in through the mind; but when the Moon is aspected, these things find their way in through the emotions.

Uranus, Neptune and Pluto open us up to what some people call the higher mind. If you resist and don't allow the kinds of awareness associated with an outer planet into your life, then you may find that your life is disrupted in some way so that you are forced to grow and open up. For example, if Venus is aspected by Uranus, Neptune, or Pluto, then it is through love, relationship, or creative expression that you are opened up to the higher mind, or the qualities of the superconscious realm. Now, in the case of Venus, if you are conducting your relationships in such a way that you are only concerned with your personal ego-needs and nothing else, then you are not really letting in the transpersonal dimensions of Uranus, Neptune, or Pluto. You are not learning what you are meant to learn through love. So in some way the relationship will be disrupted or challenged in order for you to gain greater awareness, wisdom, and understanding of life—that is, to allow in the superconscious.

In a similar fashion, the house placement of Uranus, Neptune, or Pluto could show where we have to undergo a certain amount of pain or crisis (where we may even have to fall apart altogether) so that we can rise again with a higher understanding, broadened vision and a different way of looking at life than we had before. Uranus, Neptune, and Pluto are inimical to the homeostatic side of Saturn: they are against keeping you the same, or keeping you stuck in old forms or narrow ways of seeing things—those "narrow chinks" Blake wrote about.

Audience: What specific superconscious qualities would you attribute to Uranus and what other ones would you give to Neptune or Pluto?

Howard: Qualities I would assign to Uranus relate to a sense of freedom, liberation, detachment, originality, light, will, truth and wisdom. Uranus also stands for respecting your own individuality and independence and the individuality of others—and yet working as part of a team with a sense of co-operation, brother- or sisterhood. If Uranus aspects a planet, then any of these qualities are trying to come into your life through that planet. For example, if Uranus aspects Venus then it is through the sphere of love, creativity, or relationship that you are receptive to the superconscious attributes of Uranus. Through love, you discover truth or wisdom, or you learn detachment. With Uranus in aspect to Venus, it is possible, in relationship, to liberate yourself from the grip of your personal ego's needs, wants, jealousies and fears, and arrive at a place where you see things from a broader, more detached or transpersonal perspective. If Uranus aspects Jupiter, then you discover those superconscious qualities associated with Uranus through Jupiterian things, such as your belief system or through travel. Your philosophy may embrace ideas which challenge the more conventional or established codes of thought of your society—ideas which originate as a result of seeing things from a broadened awareness.

The transpersonal or superconscious qualities which come through Neptune are those of beauty, compassion, creative inspiration, generosity, inclusiveness, joy, bliss, love, devotion, serenity, peace, acceptance, silence, and service. If Neptune aspects a planet, then these qualities are trying to enter into your life through that planet. Of course, Neptune also is associated with confusion and deception, but right now I want to focus on the more positive superconscious qualities of this planet. Even if you go through a Neptunian period of being confused and foggy, it may wear your ego down in such a way that you end up more open to spiritual and transpersonal dimensions. So even the supposedly more negative manifestations of Neptune can serve something higher. Someone once said that human extremity is God's opportunity.

If Neptune is in aspect to Venus, then you are meant to learn compassion and service through love. (This is different from Venus-Uranus aspects that teach detachment and liberation.) While Uranus wakes up, shocks, and challenges you to face things as they are, Neptune soothes, calms, and acts in ways which protect and care for others. If Neptune aspects Mercury, then your mind is open to the superconscious qualities of Neptune—love, beauty, silence, compassion, and peace. You say and think things which show how sensitive and empathetic you are with others. However, with Uranus in aspect to Mercury, you say things which wake others up or challenge their old restricting views. In either case though, whether you have Uranus or Neptune aspecting Mercury, it means that your mind doesn't work in ordinary ways. You may not particularly want to study and learn those things that might interest someone with Saturn in aspect to Mercury. Mercury, Venus, and Mars all represent functions basic to everyday life. We think and communicate (Mercury), we relate and form unions (Venus), and we assert ourselves (Mars). The outer planets in aspect to Mercury, Venus, or Mars challenge us to go beyond the ordinary way of seeing and doing things.

The superconscious qualities I associate with Pluto are those of courage, power, strength, depth, will, regeneration and renewal. So if Pluto aspects your Mercury, then your mind can probe deeply, your thoughts have added power, intensity, and strength. With Venus-Pluto aspects, you learn about strength and courage through relationship. If Pluto aspects your Venus, then you can be transformed through love—torn down and rebuilt. You meet Pluto through love. Pluto is the god of death and rebirth, but he is also the god of the underworld, of what is buried in us. So with this aspect you meet, through relationship, what is buried in you. This can mean unfinished business from childhood—infantile rage and destructiveness or early, primal pains. However, in contacting, working with, and integrating these deep complexes, you are presented with the chance to grow and be transformed.

If Pluto aspects your Mars, then the superconscious qualities of Pluto will express themselves through your actions and how you assert yourself. If Neptune aspects Mars, you act with compassion and sensitivity; but if Pluto aspects Mars, then you act with power, will, and strength. Through Mars, you connect to or discover the superconscious principles associated with Pluto. There may be other, less pleasant principles associated with Pluto—such as violence, tyranny, and other extreme expressions of power, but right now we are focusing on Pluto as an agent of transpersonal qualities. Even so, as with Neptune, having to experience the more negative manifestations of Pluto may be necessary in the process of growing more whole or becoming more spiritual. You have to accept your darker nature before you can transform it. How can you transform anything you deny is there?

Audience: You assigned the will to both Uranus and Pluto?

Howard: Yes, there are different kinds of will. Power can stem from different sources. Uranus is wilful, even stubborn. Uranus "knows" something is true, and cannot see it any other way. I usually associate Uranus with energy that is felt in the head or the upper chakras. You've seen those cartoons where someone has an idea that's depicted by an electric light bulb in a bubble over the person's head. That is what Uranus is like—a sudden flash of intuition which hits like lightning. You are certain of its truth. Pluto is different—not a light bulb in the head—but something you feel down here in your gut or in the lower chakras. Pluto feels something in its bones, and therefore is going to be pretty adamant about it. Even Neptune has a will, but it is generally softer; Neptune feels things strongly in the heart.

Audience: Some people say that Neptune is the higher octave of Venus.

Howard: Yes. Venus is a more selfish love: "I'll love you if you love me." Neptune is a more selfless love: "I'll love you no matter what you do or say and even if you can't give me back exactly what I want." Venus enhances its identity and worth through a relationship—the ego is bolstered by being someone who has someone else, especially if the other person is considered a good catch for whatever reason. Neptune, on the other hand, rather than deriving, enhancing, or bolstering identity via a relationship, actually seeks to lose itself through blending or merging with others. Venus wants equality and fairness with another; but Neptune sacrifices itself for the sake of others. Neptune transcends separateness by being what others need. Venus is more personal and ego-bound, embellishing one's identity through others rather than abnegating or transcending the self in the way Neptune is prone to do.

Audience: Could you say something about Uranus being the higher octave of Mercury?

Howard: We can look at this in a number of ways. Mercury has to do with how your individual mind works, while Uranus is associated with the workings of the group mind. Do you know what I mean by the group mind? It is a concept that Alice Bailey and the Theosophists often talked about. Teilhard de Chardin believed in it as well, and more recently the work of a British scientist, Rupert Sheldrake, also brings in this concept. In his book *A New Science of Life*, Sheldrake talks about invisible organising fields which he believes connects one member of a species to all the others of the species.[26] Furthermore, if one member of a species learns some new behaviour, the invisible organising field for that species changes. As greater numbers learn the new behaviour, it makes it possible for other members to follow suit—they "pick up" on it through the connecting field. The group mind is also in evidence when one person in San Francisco, one in London, and another in Tokyo all come up with the same new idea at roughly the same time. Dane Rudhyar once wrote that Uranus gives insight into the divine mind or the mind of God—into what God has in mind for each of us.

---

[26]Rupert Sheldrake, *A New Science of Life: The Hypothesis of Formative Causation* (London: Blond and Briggs, 1981; and New York: State Mutual Books, 1981).

Uranus can also be understood as the higher intuitive and mental processes; while Mercury is associated with the lower mind, or pure reason. Uranus glimpses something whole, all-at-once or out-of-the-blue; while Mercury is busy trying to string logical facts together. Uranus says "I've just had a flash — Aunt Margaret is coming to visit tomorrow." Mercury asks, "How do you know that — does she always come on Tuesdays?" Uranus shrugs, "No, but I just know." Bewildered and slightly infuriated with Uranus, Mercury goes off to do something else. Guess who comes to visit the next day?

Audience: You talked before about people being sidetracked into identifying with the contents of the superconscious — such as people thinking they are the embodiment of Supreme Love or Wisdom. Are there any particular aspects or placements in the chart which would incline someone to fall into that?

Howard: Strong placements in the 9th or 12th could indicate a sense of identity is too mixed up with far-out things. The sun in configuration with Uranus, Neptune, or Pluto means that the sense of identity is linked to the nature of the outer planet involved, so we should keep an eye out here for possible higher sidetracking.

Audience: What about Saturn in difficult aspect to an outer planet? Does that block the superconscious qualities associated with that outer planet coming through?

Howard: Yes, that is possible, although a number of different things can happen with Saturn in aspect to an outer planet. For example, take Saturn square Neptune. Saturn concretises what it touches, and in this case it could try to crystallise Neptune. Treating Neptune too rigidly, Saturn might try to turn Neptune into an ought or should: "You *should* always be loving and compassionate."

However, it is also true that Saturn in difficult aspect to Neptune or an outer planet could inhibit that planet and block the expression of the superconscious quality coming through. The person has something to learn (Saturn) about the nature of the outer planet involved.

THE REAL SELF

In *The Reality Game*, John Rowan, an English humanistic psychologist, distinguishes between what he calls "the real self" and "the higher self."[27] Some of what he has to say is relevant to this afternoon's discussion. According to Rowan, the aim of the various humanistic psychotherapies is to help a person contact the real self. What we normally show to the world—our mask or persona—is not who we really are. The real self is who we are under that mask.

We all wear masks. The mask is the "everyday you"—those parts of you that you let others see. Rowan calls the persona or mask "your positive but phoney self-image" (see figure 1 on page 208). Beneath the positive but phoney self-image is what Rowan names your "negative self-image," and what the Jungians refer to as the shadow. If you are honest with yourselves, most of you here would be willing to acknowledge that there is a lot more going on inside you then you are exposing at any particular time. I've seen this operate again and again in therapy groups. For instance, when you first meet a man attending the group, he may appear very confident and together. You might even be envious of him: "If only I were that person wouldn't it be wonderful." Then in the course of the group, he starts to open up to all the different things that are going on inside him. He reveals that he is frightened and scared, that he thinks he is ugly, and that he can't stand the frustrations in his life any longer. Just by looking at what he previously had shown you, you never would have guessed all that was underneath the surface. When his mask is down, however, you can see a little deeper into him, into this second level—his negative self image or his level of distress.

Those of you who are doing charts for people know what I'm talking about. The masks people wear usually consist of those parts of their charts that they like and are willing to publicly display. A woman may be quite willing to show her Moon-Neptune conjunction in Libra to the world while trying to hide her more pushy or disruptive Mars square to Uranus. Our mask is made of

[27]John Rowan, *The Reality Game* (London: Routledge & Kegan Paul, 1983), Chapter 5.

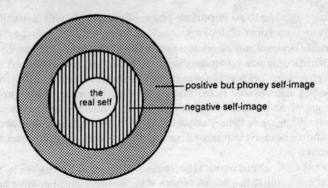

Figure 1. The real self. As you can see, the real self is shielded by the negative self-image (▥), which in turn is covered by the positive-but-phoney self-image (▦).

those bits of our charts we are willing to show at any time. Just to complicate things, there are some of us who hide our nice bits. We may not like the fact that a part of us is soft or compassionate, so we don't own or show those parts of the chart. Maybe we were brought up to believe that if we are too nice, people will take advantage of us. The parts of our charts we like, we are willing to show to the world, and the parts of the chart we don't like or can't accept will go into the shadow or negative self-image.

Rowan writes that every person will have different ideas about what his or her "badness" consists of, and he gives three examples which I would like to highlight:

a) If they knew how nasty (evil, bad, horrible, hating) I really am, they would all hate me;

b) If they knew how inadequate (weak, worthless, inept) I really am, they would all reject me;

c) If they knew how needy (insatiable, sucking in and then destroying, attracting and then devouring) I really am, they would all avoid me.[28]

---

[28]Rowan, *The Reality Game*, pp. 59–60.

Now we come to an important point. Many people will resist therapy or any form of looking inside themselves because they are afraid they will not be able to face what is negative in them. Even when people are committed to the process of therapy, they will often set up resistances against looking more deeply into their hidden motives and fears. The problem is, however, that in order to get to your real self, you have to let down your mask and confront what is behind it. Because of their apprehensions about doing this, many people never experience the self that is underneath it all.

As Rowan and many other humanistic psychologists see it, the real self is what lies beneath both your positive and negative self-images. Existentialists would call it your *authentic self*. In order to experience the real or authentic self, you have to break through parental and societal injunctions about what you *should* be like. It takes a certain amount of courage to do that—the courage to be who you are. Contacting the real self doesn't mean you are in a permanent state of bliss or happiness. It just means you are free to experience life, with all its joys and pains, and you are not hiding behind rigid defences and facades. Earlier in the day, we discussed how as children we often lose touch with our true selves in order to adapt to what our parents would like us to be. Getting close to your real self may feel threatening and scary because in order to get to it you have to own and express things you fear won't win you love and which you normally try to hide. You will have to confront and change much of your early conditioning and habitual personality patterns which barricade you against your self.

As an astrologer, I often find myself in the position of giving people permission to live out parts of their charts they are frightened or hesitant to express. Very often they have suppressed those parts because in childhood and the developmental years no one encouraged or allowed them to be that way. One person may need permission to be more assertive, while another may need permission to show his or her more vulnerable or sensitive side. In any case, letting them know that it is okay to be that way is the first step toward their re-connecting to parts of themselves they have disowned. Because of their (often unconscious) childhood fears about being who they are, they may be able to take only small steps at first. And yet I'm inclined to feel that any step toward the real self, no matter how tentative it is at first, is an important one.

Audience: What you are saying sounds an awful lot like self-acceptance.

Howard: That's exactly what it is.

THE REAL SELF VERSUS THE HIGHER SELF

It is important not to confuse the real self with the concept of a Higher Self. The real self is the innermost part of your individual nature—it's who you are underneath all the trappings. It is your selfhood: who you are as a separate, individual being. Finding your real self is a process of letting go of the false self that you took on in the course of growing up. To get to your real self you will have to break through and change many old personality patterns. And, as I have already explained, it can be quite frightening to do this—to risk exposing yourself and lifting the lid off your defences. So naturally people resist the real self, because of all they have to go through to get there.

The real self is not the same as the Higher Self. Contacting the real self does not necessarily mean that you feel a mystical oneness with the rest of life. An experience of your real self does not entail transcending your separate-self sense and merging with the greater Whole. In other words, the real self is not the final break-through. Having come to the real self, there is still farther to go. Through more work on yourself and through various forms of psychotherapy, meditation, religion, introspection or whatever, you can go beyond the boundaries of the real self (which is still an individual self) and experience an even deeper all-inclusive Self. Finding the real self is what Maslow called self-actualisation. Finding the Higher Self is what he called self-transcendence. The real self gives you a sense of who you are in your own right; but the Higher Self is the sense that at your deepest level you are the same essence as the rest of the Universe, that you are part of something much greater than yourself.

According to Maslow, self-actualised people feel an inner sense of liberation and freedom which others don't neccessarily experience. But when self-actualisers have these feelings of freedom they often ask themselves, "Freedom for what? I can be who I am, but for what?" It is at this point that they receive a "call" from the Higher or Transpersonal Self to use their energy for the sake of something greater than themselves. They feel a pull to service and a sense that there is meaning to the universe and they have some part to play in making the world a better place. Rather than just the freedom to be oneself, they are thinking in terms of obedience and surrender to something Higher. In this way, they move from self-actualising to self-transcending.

Audience: Can a person be a self-transcender before self-actualising?

Howard: Yes, I believe so. Some people have a great deal of higher awareness, spiritual vision, and a sense of their oneness with the rest of life but no channels through which to bring this awareness into everyday life. They have transcended the separate-self sense before they have really developed a solid and integrated personality centre or "I." They may have no job or place to live, but they can tell you all about the spiritual meaning of the universe. Their challenge is to further develop the personality and everyday self so they can give these high ideals and visions some sort of practical expression. Of course, the reverse situation also exists. There are those who are quite self-actualised, but have no sense of being part of something larger, although Maslow would say that sooner or later these people would run up against a "crisis of meaning" and start asking what being here is all about.

Breaking through to either your real self or your Higher Self means you have to pass through certain boundaries, and it is always scary when we have to give up an existing sense of identity for another. People defend themselves against their real selves because they are afraid to change and face things in their own natures. People defend themselves against the Higher Self as well; not neccesarily for the same reason, but for a variety of different ones—the first on the list usually being the fear of losing one's individuality and separate-self sense. Shortly, we will be examin-

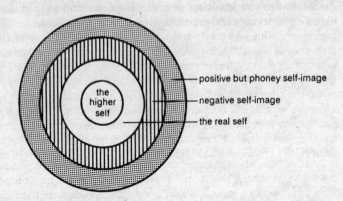

Figure 2. The Higher Self.

ing other reasons why we defend ourselves against experiencing the highest possible in ourselves – what has been called the resistance to the sublime. Having said all this, we can alter figure 1 to look like figure 2.

There is another way to explain the different levels of the psyche. David Boadella, a Reichian therapist, speaks of three broad divisions: the mask; distress; and peace.[29] The surface level of the psyche is the mask which we all wear. The mask is what we present to the world, what we let people see. Under the mask, there is very often distress. We usually try to hide the distress – the frustration, hurt, anger, and pain. Underneath the distress is peace. The deepest level of the psyche is peace – the peace of pure being, the silence and pure Is-ness that is underneath everything, no matter what else is going on. In order to get to that peace, we have to go through the level of distress. Many people never find peace, because they are unwilling to look at what is hidden or buried in them. They don't want to pass through the zone of distress, because they are afraid of getting stuck there.

---

[29]David Boadella discussed this concept of the three levels of the psyche in a course I attended on "Self-Formation" in 1985 at the Minster Centre, 57 Minster Road, London NW2.

Audience: Are you implying that it is better to find your real self first, before trying to break through to the Higher Self?

Howard: As a rule, yes. Some people only wear a mask of peace: their "positive but phoney" self-image is that of being enlightened and realised. But they haven't explored their level of distress or looked into the level Rowan calls "the negative self-image." They haven't looked deep enough into their own psyches. Lurking beneath their mask of spirituality, there are a host of unresolved complexes, drives, and pressures, from which they are cut off. Sooner or later, these suppressed parts will cause trouble. Finding the real self means that you have done some work on yourself. This puts you in a safer position from which to explore the transpersonal.

Audience: So what you are saying is that you could turn to spirituality as a way of trying to avoid facing pain or distress.

Howard: Yes, and this is not uncommon. A few months ago I lectured about astrology to an organization involved in psychic and spiritual studies. As a result of the talk, a number of people from the group came for readings. I was struck by how painful and difficult their early lives had been, and how much unresolved anger and depression still festered there beneath the surface—in spite of their spirituality. Many of them were out of touch with their bodies. It is a well known psychological fact that as infants, if things become too painful or unbearable, we cope with those feelings by splitting off from the body and going up here—into the head or into fantasy. Similarly, some people turn to spirituality as a way of avoiding pain or in order to avoid being in the body. They fear their own pain or rage, and look for possible ways to transcend these emotions.

In the name of spirituality, some people repress what they think is negative in themselves. But I don't believe that we can transcend or master anything we are denying or condemning. There is a fine line between self-mastery and repression. You could repress something and think you have mastered it. But how can you master something you've repressed or denied is there? Pain, anger, depression, frustration, and *the body itself* need to be accepted. They are part of life, and have to be explored and accepted before they can be transformed or transcended.

In *No Boundary* Ken Wilber emphasises an important point—the way Western civilisation splits heaven and hell.[30] We tend to see heaven as the place where all the positive ends of opposites reside. Good lives there—not bad; light—not dark; love—not hate. And we see hell as where the negative ends of the polarities exist. Wilber argues that it is wrong to define heaven as the place where only the positive halves of such oppositions are. Rather, he defines heaven as the place where all opposites are transcended.

You can't have good without bad, light without dark, or love without hate. These polarities go together; they define one another. By accepting both sides, it is possible to transcend getting caught in the net of duality. If you think you are all good, then you suppress what you deem bad. If you believe that you are all bad, then you deny what is good in you. But if you could accept that you contain both good and bad (and light and dark, and love and hate), then you are not one or the other, but someone who includes both. In this way, your centre of identity and awareness shifts to a higher or more inclusive place which transcends duality.

In an unpublished paper on spirituality ("Self-actualization and Spirituality: Wilber or Hegel?"), John Rowan discusses Hegel's concept of God as a trinity. "God as the One" is all loving and positive. "God as the Other" represents pain, suffering and negativity. "God as the Third" reconciles One with the Other.[31] To give you a very simple example, look at it this way. Something negative might happen to you; and yet, because of that experience, you develop some wisdom or understanding you might not have otherwise realised. If this is the case, how can you still call that original experience bad, when what it produced was positive? This is one way that opposites are reconciled.

---

[30]Wilber, *No Boundary*, p. 20.
[31]John Rowan, "Self-Actualization and Spirituality," June, 1981, unpublished.

PSYCHOSYNTHESIS AND THE BIRTH CHART

In psychosynthesis, a distinction is made between *personal* psychosynthesis and *transpersonal* psychosynthesis. Personal psychosynthesis is the phase in which you work on sorting out your personality. In groups or with your guide, you explore your mind, body, and emotions. You look inside and get to know your subpersonalities; you explore your strengths and weaknesses and try to find out as much as possible about what exists inside you. The object is to develop a strong personal centre—a more solid sense of "I." After working on yourself in this way and developing a good degree of personality integration, you move on to the exercises and techniques of transpersonal psychosynthesis, which help you to explore the superconscious realm and your relationship to the rest of the cosmos. If your personality is unbalanced, and you haven't worked on your subpersonalities or your more shadowy bits, there is a greater danger that you will not properly handle or contain the kind of energy associated with the transpersonal and superconscious realms. For instance, if you have a subpersonality that wants a lot of power and you haven't done any work on it, then this part of you could distort the way in which superconscious energy is channelled down into the personality. A man with a power-hungry subpersonality might go around demanding that other people listen to and obey him because a higher voice has told him to deliver a particular message to the world.

Audience: I study psychosynthesis. Just as Rowan draws a distinction between the real self and the Higher Self, Assagioli talks about the "I" or personal centre in comparison to the Transpersonal Self. He says that the "I" is the outpost of the Transpersonal Self in the personality.

Howard: Yes, we're back to the distinction between the ego or personal self in contrast to the Self with a capital S. To explain this better, it might be useful to elaborate further on the principles of psychosynthesis.

As I said earlier, the first phase of psychosynthesis is the development and integration of the personality. You explore as fully as you can everything that is going on inside you. You look at how your mind, body, and feelings work. You assess your personality weaknesses and strengths. This involves working with your sub-personalities. If you remember from the seminar we did on this topic last term, subpersonalities are like different people inside you—you can have the bitch, the martyr, the critic, the hurt child, etc. They are different parts of you which come out in different situations. Each subpersonality builds up or forms around various astrological placements in your chart. For example, the critic might form around a Mercury-Saturn conjunction in Virgo; or the martyr could relate to Neptune on the Ascendant. You tend to favour certain of your subpersonalities more than others. In astrological terms, this means you are in touch with some bits of your chart while other portions of it remain obscure or undeveloped. For instance, you may be more connected to your cautious Taurus or Virgo side, and not so in touch with your more adventurous Aries or Sagittarian planets. Psychosynthesis involves getting to know more of your subpersonalities and finding out as much as possible about everything that is going on inside you. In this way, you eventually become aware that you can shift your sense of identity from one subpersonality to another. As you do this, it finally dawns on you that who you are is not one or the other subper-sonality, but an "I" who can move from this one to that one. Rather than lodging your sense of "I" in any particular subpersonality, you can disidentify (or remove your identity) from any of them. As you disidentify from your various subpersonalities, you begin to consciously identify with the "I" that is doing the shifting.

Now you are not just deriving your identity from this or that sub-self, but from the "I" that moves around the various subper-sonalities. The "I," or personal centre as it is called, is like a conduc-tor of an orchestra, and the subpersonalities are the different instruments in that orchestra. The good conductor gets to know all the members of the orchestra and then helps them to play more harmoniously together. For example, I counselled a woman who had the Sun in Gemini and Aquarius rising, with many of her planets in air signs. But she also had Moon in Taurus opposing Saturn in Scorpio both square Pluto in Leo. She was strongly iden-tified with her more cerebral, objective, fair thinking airy side: that is, she mostly came from those subpersonalities which had built up around her air sign placements. She had more or less disowned the kinds of feelings associated with that rather tricky, pent-up T-square. As with anything that is not lived out in one's chart, her tendency was to see or attract her disowned traits in other people. So while she perceived herself as fair, easy-going and reasonable (Gemini and Aquarius), other people were seen as potentially nasty, conniving, or threatening (the T-square's Scorpionic and Pluto traits). Over a number of sessions, we worked on getting her in touch with the more intense and "messy" feelings suggested by the Moon, Saturn, and Pluto configuration. She began to recognise parts of her nature she hadn't wanted to acknowledge before, and discovered within herself the kinds of emotions the T-square suggested. In this way, her sense of identity gradually grew to include not just the detached Gemini and Aquarius side, but also her subjective emotions and deep instincts. Previously, her "I" was with the airy subpersonality and the T-square was mostly unconscious. But through work on herself, her "I" shifted from residing predominately in the air element and expanded to include not only her airy side but the T-square part of her nature as well as shown in figure 3.

Although psychosynthesis practicioners don't necessarily use astrology, what I've just described is similar to the kind of work involved in the phase known as personal psychosynthesis, which prepares the ground for transpersonal psychosynthesis. Having strengthened an identification with your "I" and personal centre,

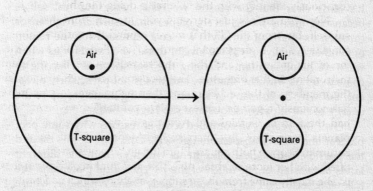

Figure 3. *A shift to a more inclusive "I." The self is shown by the dot.*

the next step is to open up to and align yourself with the Transpersonal Self—that bit of you which is universal and unbounded, and inter-connected to the rest of life. Aided by various exercises, reflections, and meditations, you explore and contact the superconscious and transpersonal realms of your psyche. In this way, you become more receptive to the will and purpose of the transpersonal dimensions of life. By aligning yourself with the transpersonal, you make it possible for the will and purpose of the Higher Self to find expression in your personality. Your personal "I" opens to the pull or call of your Transpersonal Self.

It is a basic law of evolution that integration is accomplished by the increasing dominance of higher order centres. We have just looked at an example of how this law works. The personal centre or "I" is a higher unifying centre which can co-ordinate the various subpersonalities co-existing inside us. However, as we strengthen our identity with the Transpersonal Self, this takes over as an even higher, or more encompassing unifying centre, which includes—but also transcends and supersedes—the "I" or personal self.

RESISTANCE TO THE SUBLIME

It's fairly clear that the reason we resist being our real self is because it means facing facets of personality which frighten or threaten us—parts of ourselves we have repressed for one reason or another, usually to win the love of those who cared for us when we were helpless infants. Freeing the real self means having to come to terms with the shadow, and this is not particularly pleasant. But why do so many of us resist opening ourselves up to the energy of the superconscious and the Higher Self?

Over the years, I've compiled a list of reasons why some people fear and resist transpersonal growth. Let's look at this list and the possible astrological placements which go with the different kinds of resistance. For much of the psychological material in the following sections, I am indebted to Lady Diana Whitmore, whose seminar on "The Pathology of the Sublime" stimulated my thinking in this area.[32] Acknowledgement also goes to Piero Ferrucci, whose book *What We May Be* provided me with further insight.[33]

THE FEAR OF CHANGE

The Transpersonal Self and the forces of the superconscious are such strong energies that they stir up fears in the personality. Your personal ego has its own laws, rules, and ways of going about things. While a sudden invasion from the transpersonal realms of the psyche might feel pleasurable and expansive, the impact of these energies threatens to disrupt the *status quo*. The ego doesn't like that. So when transpersonal inspiration begins to stir, your personality, in an attempt to maintain the existing framework, tries to find ways to neutralise this influx by putting up blocks against it. Before you can let these new energies into your life, you have to deal with *why* you are afraid to grow and change—with *why* you are frightened to become all that you could be.

For example, you may fear that if you come from your Higher Self then you will have to disrupt your life. The statement that goes with this fear is, "If I go to my Higher Self or let in superconscious energy, then I will have to change everything, and it would be too painful to do that." You might be frightened that your Higher Self will tell you to leave your partner or change your job. Very often, the fear of change results in inertia.

Now, I don't believe that the Higher Self gives orders quite this way. But many of us have a tendency to confuse messages from the Higher Self with the oughts and shoulds of the *superego*. The superego is that part of your nature which points a finger at you and insists that you *should* or *shouldn't* do this or that. The danger is projecting your superego onto the Higher Self. So you get messages such as, "In order to evolve you *have to* stop smoking," or "In order to be spiritual you *should* give up sex," or "In order to honour

---

[32]Lady Diana Whitmore runs the Psychosynthesis and Education Trust, 188 Old Street, London EC1. Her seminar on "The Pathology of the Sublime" (which I attended in 1980) is part of the Trust's professional training.
[33]Piero Ferrucci, *What We May Be* (Wellingborough England: The Thorsons Publishing Group, 1982), Chapter 14.

your Higher Self you *must* leave your wife." I don't think that the Higher Self comes through heavy oughts and shoulds or necessarily wants to hit you over the head. If your Higher Self wanted you to do something, it would coerce you more gently and naturally, not chastise you. If your Higher Self wanted you to stop smoking, for instance, you could get the message, "Well, maybe it would be good to give up cigarettes," or it would give you the feeling that it was time to let go of smoking. Unlike the often harsh and punitive superego, the Higher Self prefers to nudge and entice you in certain directions (at least, at first). If you are hearing lots of "you *shoulds*," it probably means that you've mixed up the superego with the Self. However, it's possible that if you repeatedly ignore what the Higher Self wants to make happen for you—if you are not respecting something that's really needed for your growth and unfoldment—then the Self may become impatient and bring some pain into your life so that you sit up and listen. In this case, pain is a messenger informing you that some new growth is needed. If you keep resisting what needs to happen, then the Higher Self may resort to forcing you to change.

I've seen people with Saturn in the 9th house or Saturn in aspect to Jupiter project the superego onto the Self. This is also possible with Saturn in Sagittarius or with Jupiter in Capricorn. Their philosophy in life (as represented by Jupiter or the 9th house) gets entangled with Saturn (the planet most closely aligned with the superego). When Saturn is linked to the Jupiterian principle in this way, moral and ethical issues infiltrate the belief system. People with these contacts can become very depressed, guilty, and self-critical if they believe they have failed to live up to their highest. They feel judged by the Higher Self, which is seen as authoritarian and dogmatic.

People with Uranus, Neptune, or Pluto in aspect to Jupiter, or with any of these planets in the 9th house, could have the attitude that, "If I open up to my Higher Self, then I will have to change and let go of everything that gives me security." They anticipate that the Higher Self will demand very extreme things from them or radically disrupt their lives. In some cases, the Transpersonal Self may ask that certain things in your life do change or go, and this can feel terrible, but that loss will allow something else to open up. Your Higher Self is that part of you which is universal and connected to the Greater Whole, so how can it ultimately leave you stranded? The Self doesn't lead you to a place of greater separateness, but a place of greater connectedness with life. In the end you'll find you gain much more than you give up.

Audience: What about those people in World War II who lost their whole families in the holocaust? How can you tell them they didn't lose anything?

Howard: You're right. They did suffer great loss and it is tragic. There is the need to grieve and mourn, and the ego or personality may never be able to understand why it happened or ever come to a place of forgiveness. I certainly can't give you very clear reasons why they had to go through such suffering. That's a major philosophical or metaphysical question. But what I am talking about now is slightly different—that some people fear opening to the Self because they are afraid certain things will be taken away and they will be left permanently empty-handed or bereft. The point I am making is that I don't believe the Self would land you in an empty place any longer than you needed to be there.

I'm thinking of a chart I did a few years ago where Saturn was conjunct Neptune in Libra in the 9th square Uranus in Cancer in the 7th. This woman had been in a relationship for seven or eight years. She came to see me in the middle of her Saturn return (with transiting Pluto in Libra not far away). During our session, she told me she was having strong feelings her relationship wasn't right for her—it was holding her back from developing in certain ways. She was having dreams which highlighted her need to break out. All this was painful for her, because she was frightened to let go and lose security. It was two years before I saw her again, and I hardly recognised her. She emanated a kind of strength and presence which just hadn't been there before. In fact, she had left the relationship. The first year on her own wasn't easy; but looking back after a couple of years, she felt no doubts or regrets about what she had done—the change had developed her in ways she never even imagined.

Hers was a case of having to trust the Self. When you open to the Self, you are opening to a part of you which guides and oversees your unfoldment and which is inter-related to the rest of life.

From the perspective of the Self, difficult phases might be necessary in order to develop in certain ways that you wouldn't develop if you didn't go through these times. So the loss of her relationship and the experiences which ensued are relevant and meaningful when appreciated in the context of her overall unfoldment.

Not trusting the Self could be related to patterns left over from childhood—especially if the Gods of the Nursery (Mother or Father) didn't support us in the way we needed back then. It's possible to project an image of the negative Mother or the negative Father onto the Self. Take the case with mother, for example. When we are infants, mother is the whole world to us, and we need her in order to survive. If she lets us down and repeatedly isn't there for us in the way we require, then we could formulate a belief or life-statement that the universe (remember, mother is the whole word to us) is not on our side. We form the opinion that life can't be trusted. The betrayal by the mother and the feeling that the world is out to get us could later be projected on to the Higher Self—and, in this way, we end up fearing what the Higher Self might do to us. Difficult aspects to the Moon often show problems with the early bonding to mother. If a problematic Moon is tied up with the 9th house (Moon in the 9th in difficult aspect to Saturn or the outer planets, or Cancer on the cusp of the 9th and the Moon difficulty aspected anywhere in the chart), there is a strong possibility that unfinished business with mother might be projected onto the image of God or the Higher Self.

We have to trust that God, the Atman, the Tao, whatever you call it, is on our side. Many people fear that if they open up to the Higher Self, they'll have to face where they are most vulnerable. This is a very legitimate fear: the Higher Self may very well ask that, at some point in our lives, we face what is weakest or most vulnerable in ourselves. But it doesn't do this just to torture us. It doesn't set this up for the sake of punishing or harming us, but in order that we can grow beyond our existing boundaries and enjoy a greater communion with life.

Saturn has been referred to as the Dweller on the Threshold—what you must face before you can be opened up to the Higher Self. Wherever Saturn is in the chart is where you feel weak and vulnerable; but you have to pass through Saturn's gateway in order to arrive at the outer planets, where you can be connected to something greater than yourself. I'm thinking of a man with Saturn conjunct Pluto in Leo in the 10th house who had intense fears about failing in his career. He tried to do everything he could to avoid something like this happening, but one way or another he managed to get involved in a business venture which collapsed on him. Now, at first, you might think how terrible and unfortunate for the poor man. However, in actual fact, what he gained through facing and coming through his fears was so valuable that in the end he not only accepted what had happened, but was glad it occured. He discovered he could survive his worst fears and learn a thing or two in the bargain. The way his wife and close associates stayed by him and helped him through the ordeal led him to re-evaluate the whole meaning of friendship and relationship in his life. Eventually, a new line of employment came along which suited his nature better than the previous work. So even though he suffered a blow to his ego, he wasn't destroyed. On the contrary, he could look back on the experience and perceive value in what he had suffered. Through this mishap, many things opened up to him, not the least of which was the feeling that the whole affair was necessary and meaningful. To paraphrase Jung, this man found out what supported him when everything he thought supported him didn't support him anymore. Through Saturn, he discovered the supportive nature of the Higher Self. Or if you prefer to put it in another way, his extremity was God's opportunity.

Audience: So Saturn is where we might resist change because we are afraid of being hurt, but also where we can grow through what we have to face up to in that area.

Howard: Precisely. Saturn shows where our ego is vulnerable. Because of that vulnerability, we try to protect ourselves. And yet, through the pain of Saturn, many of us come to view life and our own selves in a very different way. Going beyond Saturn means we enter the realm of Uranus, Neptune, and Pluto. The outer planets make us aware that we are part of something much greater.

People with a predominance of earth in the chart would also have a resistance to change and could fear opening up to the Transpersonal Self for that reason. The personality wants guarantees, but the Higher Self doesn't necessarily offer these—at least, not in very concrete terms. Your deeper Self may ask you to change or let go of something in your life, and yet you may not know exactly where these changes are going to lead you. For some people, an influx of superconscious energy, such as joy or universal love, feels like an invasion of a foreign substance into the personality, and they are frightened to let these intruders in—they don't know where these kinds of feelings will take them. In the end, you have to trust that the Self knows better than the ego. By definition, the Self can't lead you to a place of greater separateness.

THE FEAR OF LOSING INDIVIDUALITY

As we discussed earlier, the pure Self is the interface of individuality and universality. The pure Self is that part of us which is unbounded, infinite, eternal and which we share with the rest of creation. If you are in touch with this level of being, you are in tune with the cosmos. Acting from this level means acting in accord with the needs of the universe. If you feel your oneness with the rest of life as a living reality deep inside you, harming others or the environment would be as difficult as cutting off your own ear or finger.

Obviously, this is a positive state of consciousness to be in, not only for your own sake, but also for the sake of others. However, letting go of separateness and merging with something greater is also frightening for some people. Opening up to the Transpersonal or Universal Self could activate a fear of getting lost in the infinite— a fear of formlessness. Ken Wilber beautifully describes the fear of losing one's individuality:

> Now according to the perennial philosophy, the rediscovery of this infinite and eternal Wholeness is man's single greatest need and want. . . . But, at the same time, he is terrified of real transcendence, because transcendence entails the "death" of his isolated and separate-self sense. Because he won't let go of and die to his separate self, he cannot find true and real transcendence, he cannot find that larger fulfillment in integral

Wholeness. Holding on to himself, he shuts out Atman; grasping only his own ego, he denies the rest of the All.[34]

We want to transcend our separateness, and yet we are afraid of losing our individuality. The fear of formlessness is especially strong in people who have "tight" personalities (what psychosynthesis calls Will-types)—people who like to feel they are in control, and whose boundaries are rigid and defined. Astrologically, this could show up in the charts of people with a prominent Saturn or lots of earth. They fear losing control over their own lives and being at the mercy of whatever is happening around them. They fear that if they let go of what they are in charge of, they will be powerless. They are afraid of losing their defences and ending up a victim to the universe. It's hard for these types to make the shift from *my will* to *THY WILL*.

Wherever Neptune is placed in the chart is where we are asked to give up our separate-self sense and acknowledge that there is something greater than the ego's will. Some people do this readily, while others are terrified of anything which smacks of sacrificing the ego. Because the latter type find the dissolution of the ego so scary, they are likely to seek substitute gratifications in an attempt to fulfil the yearning for self-transcendence. Losing the self in drugs or alchohol is one way of doing this. Love and sex could also be sought as a way of transcending the isolated ego: "If I can be held, loved, or included then I have a sense of going beyond my separateness." Some people seek power as a substitute gratification for wholeness: "If I can expand my sphere of influence over more and more people and things, then I feel my connectedness to the rest of life." Whether it's through power or love, they are searching for fulfilment and wholeness outside of the self or through others. In mythology, Poseidon (Neptune) tried to do the same thing. He had a beautiful golden palace under the sea, but he thirsted after more worldly possessions. He fought with Zeus and other dieties for temporal power and the ownership of land. And yet, whenever he went after worldly possessions, he lost. He imagined all sorts of places and things which would satisfy his yearnings for completeness, but he never succeeded in having them.

---

[34]Wilber, *Up From Eden*, p. 13.

Angry and dejected, he would retire again beneath the sea, only to rediscover his vast golden palace there, which no one ever contested. Wherever Neptune is placed in the chart is where we might look for our lost wholeness in external things. But it is only by looking inside that we can find the kind of fulfilment we are seeking.

Others with a strong Neptune, unwilling to relinquish the separate-self sense in order to merge with something greater, would rather believe that they, themselves, are God. It's true that your deeper nature is infinite and eternal, but it's wrong to assume that your individual ego is omnipresent, all-powerful and unbounded. Again, I would like to quote Wilber, who puts it very well:

> Every individual *correctly* intuits that he is of one nature with the Atman, but he distorts that intuition by applying it to his separate self. He feels his separate self is immortal, central to the cosmos, all-significant. That is, he *substitutes* his ego for Atman. Then, instead of finding timeless wholeness, he merely substitutes the wish to live forever; instead of being one with the cosmos, he substitutes the desire to possess the cosmos; instead of being one with God, he tries himself to play God.[35]

It's just not wise to mix up the levels of the psyche in this way. As hard as the ego may try, it will never quite make the grade, or, in Wilber's words, "the ego can never quite pull off the charade that it is stable, permanent, enduring, and immortal."[36] On one level we are infinite and eternal but on another level we're not. We're mortal. We rot. We die. The ego can be a channel for the expression of transpersonal inspiration in everyday life, but it is not the same as the Higher Self.

People with Saturn in conjunction or hard angle to Neptune could suffer from a fear of formlessness. Neptune wants to merge with the larger Whole, but Saturn is terrified of letting go of boundaries. The same situation could exist with Saturn in the 12th house or Saturn in Pisces. Here, you have a fear of being over-

---

[35]Wilber, *Up From Eden*, p. 13.
[36]Wilber, *Up From Eden*, p. 15.

whelmed by something bigger than you. Saturn worries that if it lets go, it won't come back again.

I've taught a number of people with these kinds of placements to meditate, and I noticed a definite pattern. Just as they were going deeper into meditation and moving closer to experiencing that part of their nature which is unbounded, they would pull themselves out of the meditation. They'd open their eyes and say something like, "I've just remembered, I left my car on a yellow line," or, "I forgot to feed the cat." Frightened by the feeling of unboundedness, their Saturns connived to bring them back into the everyday world of form.

The fear of losing individuality and the fear of formlessness ultimately boil down to a deeper, underlying fear of death and dissolution. The prospect of the dissolution of the ego arouses the same kinds of anxieties we might feel about death itself. I would look to the 8th and 12th houses to see where a person stood in relation to death. The 8th house describes not only our attitudes towards a literal or physical death, but what happens whenever we have something akin to an ego-death, or major shift of identity. In the 8th, the house of intimacy and sharing, you die as an "I" to be reborn a "We." You give up something of yourself to merge with another. The 8th is a rehearsal for the 12th. In the 12th, we are asked to give up our sense of individuality and merge not just with a few significant others, but with the whole kit and caboodle—with everything, with the cosmos. We've already mentioned that someone with Saturn in the 12th could have a fear of opening up to something greater than the self. A similar situation exists with Saturn in the 8th. Those with Saturn in the 8th (or in Scorpio) could have problems letting go of the ego and merging with others. This could also manifest as a fear of death—holding on to the ego for dear life.

Of course, it is possible, through facing these fears, to arrive at a new level of understanding. Through working hard at something we can become masterful in that area. Elisabeth Kübler-Ross, who has done more to promote confronting death than anyone else I can think of, was born with Saturn in Scorpio in the 8th. Someone with Saturn in the 12th or in Pisces could end up teaching others how to open up to what is beyond the ego. If you have had to struggle to come to grips with something, you are better able to help others over the same difficulties later on.

Those with Pluto in the 12th might harbour a fear of being overwhelmed by anything greater than the self; and yet they will also be fascinated by the prospect of forces and powers beyond the ego. Similarly, Pluto in the 8th is both a fear and fascination with death and what lies beyond bodily existence. Earth signs on the cusp of the 8th or the 12th might have more difficulty letting go of the ego-identity than other signs in these houses. They'll want to hang in there as long as possible. By contrast, those with Jupiter or Neptune in the 8th or 12th (providing these planets don't pick up any hard angles to Saturn) are usually eager to open up and venture beyond their existing sense of identity.

A strong Aquarian or 11th house slant also gives the desire to identify with something greater than the self. People with these placements join causes and groups promoting aims for the good of the whole. But if you have Saturn in Aquarius or the 11th, you might fear merging with a group, because it means having to give up some of your individuality. Both Leo and Virgo have strong needs to develop the separate-self sense and define the identity. If planets in these signs are in opposition to planets in Aquarius and Pisces, there could be obvious conflicts between the building and forming of a strong sense of self versus the need to let go of the ego enough to open up to something beyond the self. A similar dilemma could exist if you have planets in the 5th or 6th houses opposing planets in the 11th and 12th. Squares between the expansive sign of Sagittarius and the more cautious and bounded sign of Virgo also create a tension between that part of us seeking universality and that part which wants to define and maintain individuality. This could also apply to planets in the 9th in square or hard angle to planets in the 6th.

Audience: What if you had a client with a fear of formlessness or a fear of losing individuality? How do you work with these dilemmas?

Howard: I would probably suggest they read the works of Ken Wilber, or Peter Russell's *The Awakening Earth*. These writers convincingly argue that universality doesn't exclude individuality:

experiencing your Universal Self doesn't deny that you also have a separate and distinct identity as well. You are neither one nor the other; you are both. That would give them something to chew over. An intellectual acceptance that universality and individuality can go together would be the first step in working through these kinds of resistance to the Transpersonal or Higher Self.

THE FEAR OF RESPONSIBILITY

People with these fears think like this: "If I open up to my Higher Self, I won't be able to be little anymore. I'll have to grow up. I won't be able to get away with indulging weaknesses in my personality." Being in touch with the Transpersonal or Universal Self carries with it a heavy duty and responsibility. Some people shut down knowing their true connection to the rest of life because of a fear of the responsibility involved. If you know that on some level you are connected to the starving people of Africa, then you feel an increased responsibility for their plight—it becomes more difficult getting away without doing anything about it.

Many people believe, and rightly so, that gaining knowledge is a way of reducing anxiety. If you can figure out how something works, then you might be less afraid of it. But what we are talking about now is the reverse of this situation. We're talking about greater knowledge giving rise to anxiety because knowledge carries with it the burden of responsibility. Knowing about something means you might have to get off your backside and do something about it.

Some people fear that living up to the Higher Self will be too much for them. They would rather not know about the existence of the transpersonal dimensions of life, because if they did know, then they might have to do something to develop their higher potential. Knowledge carries responsibility. If an ordinary man breaks the law, that is bad enough; but if a high court judge, who should know better, breaks the law, then the punishment is far more severe. Knowledge is the basis of action. Behind the fear of knowledge is a deeper fear of doing—a fear of "the burden of consciousness."

Astrologically, I would link this fear to Saturn in Sagittarius, Saturn in the 9th or Saturn in difficult aspect to Jupiter. People with these placements think that they would like to expand and grow, but they are often afraid of the hard work involved. Their 9th house, Jupiter, or Sagittarian qualities envision all sorts of higher things and higher possibilities, but Saturn balks at how much effort it would take to arrive there. You might also find this dilemma in people with a split between earth and fire in the chart. For instance, someone with the Sun in Sagittarius or Aries, but the Moon in Taurus, or people with a number of planets in fire signs along with a number of planets in earth. Fire has the aspiration, but earth may not be that keen to stretch itself. Earth tends to be a little wary of fire's idealistic vision.

Audience: But couldn't the combination of fire and earth give the ability to have the vision and then the steadfastness to go about realising it?

Howard: Yes, I was just getting to that. It's possible for earth to help out fire. People with a lot of fire or with a strong 9th house, Jupiterian or Sagittarian influence could have a great deal of inspiration, but if there were no earth (or if Saturn were weak), then they might just dream about what could be and never get around to making it a reality. So people with Jupiter trine or sextile Saturn (or even people with the hard aspects between these two planets) could ultimately have the stamina and discipline to get up at 6:30 every morning and follow a very structured meditation routine in order to open up to the Higher Self. However, it is also possible that the earth might slow down or even put out the fire. The earthy side may say, "Why bother, why do you have to be a god—can't you accept just being ordinary?" Fire/earth conflicts are one form of the mystic-pragmatist dilemma I talked about in the Subpersonalities seminar. Whether the earth puts out fire, or the earth helps the fire, will depend on the other placements in the horoscope and how well the person is working with his or her chart.

I have observed that people with Jupiter in hard angle to Saturn often have to put a lot of effort into realising their goals and objectives. I've seen it in the charts of dancers who suffer from trouble with their knees, or musicians who have arthritis in the fingers. Karmically speaking it may be that they have had opportunities for growth and expansion (Jupiter) in previous lives, but they turned their back on these and now have a debt of having to work extra hard (Saturn) to realise their potentials. This is why some of them would rather not know that they have any potential at all, because then they don't have to worry about achieving it.

Audience: I have Sun in Aquarius and Moon in Taurus and I can relate to this dilemma. My Aquarian Sun can envision all sorts of possibilities which my Taurus Moon is too lazy to do anything about. The Taurus Moon part of me thinks my Aquarius Sun is a bit pie-in-the-sky.

Howard: Yes, the fear of the responsibility of knowing something could be an air/earth dilemma as well. However, air and earth could help each other. I've seen people who had strong combinations of Capricorn and Libra in their charts, who have worked very hard (Capricorn) to live up to their Libran ideals and visions.

THE FEAR OF POWER

Some people fear they couldn't handle the power that opening up to the transpersonal realms and the Higher Self might give them. It's probably not power itself they are frightened of, but rather *the abuses of power*. Usually a fear of power is actually a fear of *misusing* power.

The closer you move to the Self, the more powerful you become. The Self gives off a stronger vibration than the ego. When you connect to the Self, you radiate something which attracts and influences other people. Certain people are afraid they won't use that power wisely. They worry that they might use it for their own personal ends, rather than for the good of the whole. Or they are afraid that their power and strength might cause them to hurt others in some way.

I've observed these fears operating in people who have the Sun in aspect to Pluto—in particular, the Sun conjunct Pluto in Leo, the Sun in Aquarius opposite Pluto in Leo, the Sun in Scorpio or Taurus square Pluto in Leo, or the Sun in Capricorn or Pisces inconjunct Pluto in Leo. These people worry about using power destructively. While one part of them wants power and influence, another part shies away from anything that might put them in a position of authority, just in case they mess it up. I don't always work with past lives, but in these instances I sometimes have the feeling that they have had power in a previous lifetime and didn't handle it very well, or ran into trouble because of it. They might have been in a position of authority and used their power selfishly. In between lives, they review what they have done in the past; seeing their mistakes, they reincarnate apprehensive of misusing power again. As a result, they try to avoid circumstances which might cause them to repeat the old pattern. When I see Sun-Pluto contacts in the charts of people who aren't doing anything to develop or use their power, I usually assume that they have conscious or unconscious fears about abusing authority. In most cases, I will discuss these issues with them. My tendency is to encourage these people to go for positions of some authority or power—this would give them a chance to learn about handling these situations better than last time.

Something similar could exist for people with Saturn conjunct or in difficult aspect to Pluto, especially if Mars is linked to these aspects in some way. There are a whole group of people born in 1948 with a conjunction of Mars, Saturn and Pluto. Or sometimes you find Mars, Saturn and Pluto in a T-square, such as Mars in late Capricorn/early Aquarius opposing Pluto in Leo square by Saturn in late Aries/early Taurus. That one was there for a while in 1939. With these kinds of aspects, there could be a *karma* around power. They might have misused it before, or, conversely, they might have suffered at the hands of someone else exercising brutal power over them. In any case, there is an association of power with trouble and pain, and therefore fears about owning and developing personal authority.

Looking at it more psychologically than karmically, fears around the misuse of power could stem from difficulties with the father in early life. If the Sun is in difficult aspect to either Mars, Saturn, or Pluto, then the father might have been experienced as violent, overly authoritative or destructive. Even if the father didn't behave openly in this way, children with these aspects could have felt the potential for such extremes dangerously lurking just beneath the surface level. Jungians call this a *negative animus*. The animus represents the masculine principle, and these kinds of aspects give problems with the animus. It's possible that the negative father or negative animus image can be projected onto the Higher Self or onto God. The Higher Self is so boundless that you can project almost anything onto it. If your father was potentially or actually violent and destructive, or if you have a negative animus image in your chart, then you could project that image onto the Higher Self. The Self, father, and God get all mixed up together. If this is the case, you could imagine that your Higher Self will make you do things you don't like or that it will somehow cause you to hurt other people. You may fear that if you come from your Self, you may have to say or do things which will be hard for others to take. You fear being dominated by the Higher Self—that the Self will *make* you do things you don't like doing. In actual fact, I don't believe the Higher Self really works like that. If you have something to say to someone which is truly coming from your Higher Self or from your heart, you usually say it in such a way which doesn't wipe out the other person. It's not done in a blaming or attacking manner.

People who are strong love-types (an emphasis of Cancer, Libra, Pisces, or a prominent Moon, Venus, Neptune, or a predominance of water) might be afraid of the power the Higher Self could give them. Love-types have problems with the will. Rather than risk confrontation, they often go along with whatever is happening, disowning the more wilful or directive sides of their natures. But what we don't own in ourselves, we project "out there." So love-types could project their own unlived needs for power and assertion onto the Higher Self. They end up frightened that the Higher Self might make them do things which could upset or hurt other people. You can see why it is important to do some straight personality work on the self (as in personal psychosynthesis) before opening up to the whole realm of the transpersonal.

THE FEAR OF INADEQUACY

This goes, "I'm not good enough for my Higher Self; I don't have a wise person inside me, and even if I did, my wise person wouldn't love me." In psychosynthesis and other forms of transpersonal psychology, there are techniques devised to help you contact your wise person. All of us have a wise person somewhere inside, a part of us which knows the truth for our lives and is a source of healing and nourishment. The wise person is a symbol of the Self. Contacting the inner wise person helps us connect to the Self. Some people suffer from such a poor self-image, they can't believe they have a wise person. They also project their negative self-image onto the Higher Self, and fear that it would never like or accept them.

Strong feelings of unworthiness make them feel they don't deserve anything higher. They imagine the Self as something way up there and out of their reach. They fail to see that the Higher Self is *inside*—that it is in everyone. We all have a Higher Self, but sometimes we forget it's there. You don't have to be a saint to contact that Self. You can even be eating loads of junk food and still have an experience of the Self. One Zen Buddhist Master used to say that you are already enlightened, all you have to do is wake up to the fact.

This brings us to a slightly sticky point: the Self is always there—going on all the time—and yet it is something that you have to get to. Paradoxically, you are already the Self and yet you need to get there. It's like looking for a path to take you where you already are. Maharishi used to speak about "the pathless path to the Self." Those people who see the Self as firmly inside them and everything, already there and happening all the time, are sometimes called "imminent mystics." The imminent mystic will say that no matter what happens or what you do, it's all Higher Self. So you could stay at home all day eating chocolate chip cookies and entertaining erotic fantasies about your next door neighbour and that would be fine—you'd still be coming from your Self. "Transcending mystics" however, believe that you have to find your Self: there are paths you must take which lead to the Self. Imminent mystics are not that motivated to do things—just *being* is enough. Transcending mystics feel that you have to work hard to realize the Self. For them, the key is *becoming*. Very (and I emphasise *very*) generally speaking, Jupiterian and Sagittarian types tend to fall into the category of imminent mystics, who believe that everything that is happening is all right—all is for the best in the best of all possible worlds. Some Neptunians are like that as well.

People with prominent placements in Virgo or Capricorn, or with Saturn strong, will usually fall more into the category of transcending mystics, who believe that you have to improve yourself and work hard to reach enlightenment.

Transcending mystics who see the Self as something you must work hard to get to are more likely to suffer from a sense of inadequacy than imminent mystics. Transcending mystics are more prone to the "look what I am compared to what I could be" syndrome. They don't believe they are all right as they are. The imminent mystic, by contrast, thinks that the Self is there all the time anyway. Diana Whitmore (of the Psychosynthesis and Education Trust) suggests that people who believe they aren't good enough for the Self should meditate visualising the Self already inside them. It's certainly worth a try.

If you suffer from a fear of inadequacy, it's helpful to cultivate the thought, "I'm okay just by virtue of being," or, "I deserve love just by virtue of being." We have a basic right to be loved, but some of us might not have been offered that basic right as children. We might have been loved not for who we are, but for how much we lived up to somebody's expectation of what we should be. People who felt unloved as children or not good enough for the parents are likely to project that onto the Self, and feel they are not what their Self requires. Astrologically, we are talking about such placements as Saturn in the signs of Aries, Cancer, Leo or Capricorn; Saturn in the 1st, 4th, 5th or 10th houses; or Saturn in difficult angle to the Sun or Moon. People with Saturn in the 9th or 12th might also feel that a rather exacting and demanding Higher Self judges them unworthy or low. I've also seen this pattern in the charts of those with Saturn in difficult aspect to Jupiter or Neptune.

Audience: I have Jupiter square Pluto, and I feel that until I get rid of my dark and nasty thoughts, I could never be enlightened.

Howard: Yes, that is a variation of what we are talking about. I guess this fear of not being good enough for the Self is a pretty common one. There is a lot of irony connected to this particular fear as well. If you think you are inadequate, you tend to run around desperately looking for people to love you – and yet, even if hundreds of people swear undying love to you, you still don't feel worthy of that love. Like Ixion on his wheel, it's a vicious circle. The more inadequate you feel, the more you need to open up to your Self; and yet if you don't feel good enough for the Self, it's very difficult to let the Self in. See what I mean, a psychological Catch-22? Somehow you have to break the pattern. It will probably require looking into your early life and working through what made you feel unworthy or unlovable in the first place.

Ultimately, we all need to find love from the inside rather than trying to import it from outside. Somebody out there loving you can help you learn to love yourself, but if there isn't a healthy enough sense of self-love in the first place, it is difficult to believe that someone really loves you. As I said before, if this is an issue for you, try telling yourself that you deserve love just by virtue of being. If you keep telling yourself you are no good, then the unconscious has a way of reflecting, "Okay, you are no good," back to you. If you can break that pattern and start telling yourself you deserve love, then eventually the unconscious will pick up the message and feed back, "Okay, you deserve love." Doing this will help clear the way for letting the Higher Self in. It's a short-cut, but sometimes short-cuts work.

Of course, some people have an investment in being no good, in being miserable and unhappy—a kind of attachment to suffering. It's true that there are times when suffering and pain serve to wear down your ego and help you open up to the Self. But there are some people who are so attached to suffering that they don't find it easy to let the Transpersonal or Higher Self in at all. Letting the Higher Self in might mean they would have to feel good about themselves and then they wouldn't get the secondary gain of other people feeling sorry for them or other people running around doing things to try to make them feel better.

Audience: That sounds like a strong Neptune or Piscean element, or even someone with lots of Cancer.

Howard: Yes, we had better add these to our list of astrological significators under this particular fear. This could be a little confusing. Some Neptunian types are imminent mystics who believe that no matter what is going on, it's okay; while others are prone to feel inadequate and insufficient compared to what they imagine they could or should be. You'd have to weigh up the whole chart to see which category fits.

THE FEAR OF LOSING OPINIONS

This one goes, "If I open myself up to superconscious energy or the Universal Self, then I will become soft and undefined. People will take advantage of me. I will see the essence of everything, but not the differences. I will lose my ability to be critical and discriminating; I'll lose my point of view."

This fear is based on wrong thinking. We talked about this earlier in the day: it's true that if you were enlightened you would perceive the unity in all life, but you would still retain the capacity to see the differences between things. On one level, you would still be you, and somebody else would still be somebody else; but on another level, you would be fully in touch with the interconnectedness of all life. This is called holistic perception—you see the *form* as well as the *essence*.

In fact, as you move closer to the Self, you can actually see things more clearly and objectively. Let me explain this better. It is related to what Maslow called "need-interested" versus "need disinterested" perception. If your sense of identity is reliant on something external to yourself, then you need the outside world to be a certain way in order to reinforce who you are. For instance, if you derive your sense of self by mothering others, then you look for situations which would give you a chance to re-affirm yourself in that way. You will view life in terms of your need to mother, rather than from an objective stance. However, if your identity is firmly established in the Self, then you are not dependent on the external world to bolster your sense of who you are. Accordingly, you can relax and see people and circumstances as they are, not as you need them to be. Krishnamurti called this choiceless awareness. Choiceless awareness (or desireless awareness as Maslow referred to it) doesn't mean you don't have any choices or opinions.[37] Rather, choiceless awareness means you can be more fully recep-

---

[37]Maslow, *Towards A Psychology of Being*, p. 40.

tive and appreciative of *what is*—you can see events around you and other people more truly as they are, unobstructed by your own investment in what something should or shouldn't be.

The astrological significators which go with this fear of losing opinions are similar to the ones we discussed under the fear of losing individuality. I've seen it operating, for example, in people who have oppositions running across the 5th and 11th or the 6th and 12th houses. The 5th and 6th houses establish your separate-self sense, or your own unique identity, while the 11th and 12th ask that you are aware of being part of something greater. Those with oppositions between the signs of Leo and Aquarius or Virgo and Pisces could also be frightened of losing their boundaries if they open themselves up to that part of them which is transpersonal or universal.

FEAR OF BEING ON THE WRONG TRACK

Some people are afraid of being swindled or jilted by the Self. A person might start to make a connection to the Self or superconscious energy (such as unconditional love or a feeling of oneness with others) and then pull back: "What if I am just fooling myself? What if all this is just one big fantasy trip? What if I am just trying to convince myself all this is true?" In other words, you start by having a breakthrough: "Yes, I must be more loving and accepting of people." You proceed to behave accordingly, but then you think, "I must be crazy—I'm sure to be taken advantage of it I carry on in this way." Fearing you might be on the wrong track, you backpeddle by denying the validity of the course you are taking.

Watch out for this particular fear in people who have Mercury in difficult aspect to Jupiter or Neptune. Their rational left-brain mind (Mercury) is at odds with the more intuitive and holistic right-brain mode of thinking (symbolised by Jupiter or Neptune). I've also seen it in charts where there is a strong Virgo or Saturn emphasis along with an equally strong Pisces, Neptune, or Jupiter. Their Pisces, Neptune or Jupiter parts readily open up to new ideas and inspirations. But just wait, a few days later after the Virgo or Saturn backlash takes effect, they can't believe how gullible they have been.

Audience: I have Uranus square Saturn and I go through that quite often. I have a breakthrough (the Uranian side) and then I pull back (Saturn).

Howard: Yes, it's a tug-of-war in the psyche between two very different ways of looking at life. Saturn, Mercury, or Virgo generally like the concrete and tangible. Neptune, Jupiter, Pisces, and in many cases, Uranus, can deal more readily with the abstract and intuitive. If both sides are emphasised in a chart, then you have a conflict.

THE FEAR OF BEING SEEN AS CRANKY

Some people resist opening up to the superconscious or transpersonal realms because they are afraid they'll be looked upon as cranky or eccentric. What kinds of aspects might show up in these charts?

Audience: People with strong Saturns or a heavy weighting in earth.

Howard: Yes, and especially if Saturn is in difficult aspect to Uranus or Neptune. Uranus is open to all sorts of new ideas, trends and currents, while Saturn prefers what is safe and known. Neptune is willing to let go of structures and rules and flow where it may, but Saturn wants to maintain existing boundaries.

People with such conflicts are sometimes hesitant even to talk about their superconscious experiences, for fear of being looked on as strange. One man I know with Saturn square Neptune sits in a psychic group and studies Kirlian photography, but keeps it secret from his more conventional friends and colleagues. The other day a woman rang up for a reading. I booked her in and asked for her phone number in case I might need to alter the appointment. She said I musn't call during the day because she didn't want her husband to find out she was spending money on something like this. Her chart has Saturn conjunct Uranus in Taurus.

Audience: My sister is a very earthy person (strong Virgo and Capricorn). She is always saying to me that I must be careful whom I talk to about astrology—they might think I am a crank.

Audience: Could it be in some cases that a woman, for instance, might live out her need for convention and security through her husband; and the husband lives out his own unintegrated Uranian or Neptunian interests via the wife?

Howard: Yes, and the other way around. I did a chart for a man with Saturn in the 10th opposing Neptune in the 4th. He worked as a government official (Saturn in the 10th), but was also very much involved with meditation (Neptune in the 4th). His wife was terrified of his interest in spiritual things. She was afraid he would get carried away with it all, leaving everything behind and disappearing off to India. She did everything she could to stop him going to mediation meetings or retreats. He partially resolved this problem by forming a meditation club at the large government office for which he worked. The club was very successful—a lot of people working there must have had a similar type pull between Saturn and Neptune!

You are right, though, when you say that projection comes in here. A person with Saturn in difficult angle to Neptune or Uranus may live out Saturn and attract Uranus or Neptune in a partner. Or the person could identify with Uranus and Neptune and project Saturn onto the other person. This happens frequently with couples, but also between parents and children. A parent with Saturn square Uranus might side with Saturn, and the child grows up with a compulsion to live a more Uranian life style. Or it happens the other way around. Recently I did a chart for a woman with Saturn in Cancer square Neptune in Libra. In the mid to late 60's, she was a hippie. She raised her eldest son on her own, and they moved around from one commune to another. During his growing up years, she was heavily involved with the peace movement and things like meditation. Her son is in his early twenties now. A few years ago he joined the Navy and fought in the Falklands War. Now he is back in England and his main concern is to make as much money as possible.

I've seen a number of relationships where the Saturn-Uranus split works very well. The husband provides the security and convention, and he doesn't mind his wife going off here and there to do astrology or meditation courses. In fact, sometimes the husbands rather like the space it gives them—more time at the golf club. The wife enjoys being inspired and expanded by interesting talks and groups, and yet wouldn't think of giving up the security offered by her merchant banker husband. Some husbands enjoy hearing about what their wives have been learning, although they would never dream of being caught cross-legged on the floor or anywhere near the vicinity of an astrology group.

Audience: But how do you resolve the dilemma without projecting one side?

Howard: You make room in your life for both Saturn *and* Uranus-Neptune. Some people make a work or career (Saturn) involving Uranus or Neptune. They work as astrologers (Uranus) or meditation teachers (Neptune). Or you could be an accountant or business manager (Saturn) for a spiritual group. I've seen a number of people with Saturn-Uranus or Saturn-Neptune contacts who act as bridges between conventional people and more unconventional types. They are Saturnian or respectable enough that conventional people don't find their unusual ideas so threatening. A lawyer who practises meditation will be more likely to convince other professional people about its value than someone who is so Neptunian that he or she has never been able to hold down a job for any length of time. There are businesses who employ astrologers to help with personnel management and selection. Some hospitals use meditation as a possible way of alleviating certain ailments. Conversely, some esoteric groups could benefit from a more down-to-earth approach. A Saturn-Uranus or Saturn-Neptune type person could be the one to help spiritual organisations to operate more practically and efficiently.

The fear of being eccentric shows up in earthy charts with little fire or air. But have you noticed when people with a predominance of earth do get involved with spiritual things, they often go overboard and do it in an extreme way? Liz talks about this in *Relating*, where she discusses fire as the shadow of earth.[38] Fire (intuition) is earth's inferior function. When earthy people do discover the intuitive or spiritual side of life, they may go over the top at first. They might think they have to burn all their possessions and move to the Himalayas, or they totally give themselves over to a spiritual group or guru. Some gravitate to the more psychic or occult side of spirituality, making the rounds of every psychic in town, or throwing the *I Ching* twenty times a day.

Audience: I have Saturn square Uranus and I enjoy being a crank. A crank is one of those bits of the machinery that brings about revolution!

HOW THE PERSONALITY
RESISTS THE SUBLIME

We've looked at various reasons why the personality resists the sublime: the fear of power, the fear of formlessness, the fear of inadequacy, and so on. These are reasons *why* we resist the transpersonal. But exactly *how* do we resist—what mechanisms do we use to avoid opening up to the Higher Self and the superconscious?

You'll remember that at the beginning of the day I talked about defence mechanisms. The personality is survival orientated: when we have an urge or drive which is threatening to our ego-identity, we bring in a defence mechanism, literally to defend ourselves against what we perceive as dangerous. We normally use these mechanisms to hold down sexual or aggressive urges. However, opening up to the transpersonal means our perception and identity will change. The ego doesn't like that, so it employs defence mechanisms not only against letting in the so-called "lower" drives, but also to keep out the "higher" drives as well. In *The Aquarian Conspiracy*, Marilyn Ferguson writes about the entry point experi-

---

[38]Liz Greene, *Relating* (York Beach, ME: Samuel Weiser, 1977; and Wellingborough, England: Thorsons Publishing Group, 1977), Chapter 3.

ence.[39] Something happens and we are opened to the possibility of a richer and more meaningful dimension of life. Some people are haunted by that glimpse and will go on to pursue more. Other people hesitate or stop dead at the entry point, terrified to go further.

Let's have a go at listing some of the defence mechanisms which are used to prevent the Transpersonal or Higher Self taking over the personality.

REPRESSION

This one is easy—you simply deny there is anything higher. Some people call this the repression of the sublime. If there is no such thing as your Higher Self, then you needn't be afraid or worried about what it might mean to open up to it.

Audience: Can you see a tendency towards this in somebody's chart?

Howard: The 9th and 12th houses are the ones most directly concerned with receiving superconscious or transpersonal energy. If Saturn or Pluto is in either of these houses (or linked to them by rulership in some way—such as Capricorn or Scorpio on the cusp), then you may, out of fear of that area of life, try to repress the sublime. However, if people with these kinds of placements do eventually open to the transpersonal realm, they end up fascinated or even obsessed by such things. For example, I did a chart for a man with Pluto in the 12th. I talked about the possibility that we carry over issues from previous lives. He adamantly denied the feasibility of reincarnation. Two years later he returned to me with a list of all the things he had done in his past existences, and how these were affecting his present life. He had become obsessed with the whole idea.

Saturn or Pluto in difficult angle to Jupiter, or Saturn in hard aspect to Neptune could repress the sublime for similar reasons to

---

[39]Marilyn Ferguson, *The Aquarian Conspiracy* (Los Angeles: Jeremy Tarcher, 1981; and London: Granada, 1980), p. 93.

Saturn or Pluto in the 9th or 12th. In these cases, expansion (Jupiter-Neptune) is associated with fear and apprehension (Saturn and Pluto).

PROJECTION

Normally we project onto other people those aspects of our nature which we think are negative and don't like to admit are there. For instance, we may be frightened that a friend will betray us, when in actual fact, it is our own ability to betray which is projected onto that person. If we cut off from any facet of ourselves, then we will perceive that part as belonging to others. But it is also possible to disown and project unintegrated positive qualities in one's own nature onto other people. In fact, it's possible to project the sublime onto another person—that is, we could deny our own inner spirituality and wisdom, and attribute these qualities to someone else. One's own Higher Self can be projected onto a guru, a therapist, or even an astrologer. Very often I hear people say things like, "My guru told me I should leave my wife," or "My astrologer says that I'm meant to do this or that." Projecting the Higher Self onto another person means we can stay small, and we don't have to face the responsibility of developing our own highest possibilities.

If you project the sublime onto another person, then you expect that person to act according to the image or ideal which you want to see. A transpersonal therapist once told me a story about this. She had a male client who saw her as all-knowing and all-wise, a kind of goddess. One day he came early to a session and caught her hanging out her wash. Shortly after the incident, he stopped coming to therapy: he couldn't bear to think of her as ordinary.

Audience: If you have Jupiter in the 7th, could you project the sublime onto someone else?

Howard: Yes, People with Jupiter or Neptune in the 7th may see such qualities in others rather than in the self. Also, if you have the Sun, Moon, or Venus opposing Jupiter or Neptune, you might see the Jupiter or Neptune qualities more easily in others than in yourself. A woman with Sun opposing Jupiter, for instance, could perceive her father in the image of the almighty Zeus. A man with Moon opposing Jupiter, or Moon opposing Neptune, might project the divine or numinous onto certain women. Those with Venus opposing Jupiter or Neptune could over-idealise a loved one. Whatever you greatly admire or appreciate is also there somewhere in you. Otherwise you wouldn't get so charged up about it.

RATIONALISATION

Rationalisation means thinking superconscious experiences away. You have a peak experience—something along the lines of feeling your oneness with the rest of life, or sensations of overwhelming love for everyone; but then you explain it away by saying that it's really just due to the fact that you didn't get much sleep last night or it must have been something you ate. Rationalisation involves trying to make superconscious experiences less important so that you don't have to fully acknowledge what these might mean or entail.

Audience: I work as a therapist. Sometimes people have a breakthrough in one session. They open up to a whole new way of being and viewing life. But it often happens that when they come back for the next session they've closed down again, or they say that what happened last week was a lot of bunk.

Howard: Retrospective devaluation—looking back over an experience and trying to belittle it's importance—is a form of rationalisation. To devalue something means you don't have to take it seriously. It keeps you safe. You don't have to change.

The main perpetrators of rationalisation and devaluation are people with a predominance of earth or air in the chart. Earth, with its resistance to change, will play something down; while air, mistrustful of emotions, will go up into the head as a way to interrupt flowing with the feelings.

Audience: Rationalisation reminds me of how some doctors and psychiatrists try to find neurosis in spiritual people. I worked in a

mental hospital where some of the people had definite superconscious things happening to them. The doctors always interpreted
what had occurred from a purely pathological point of view. They
couldn't appreciate the spiritual or transpersonal element contained in these experiences.

Howard: Yes, it also reminds me of those B-grade science fiction
movies where something very strange is happening in the town,
but almost everyone keeps looking for logical explanations. You
know the ones I mean – the main scientist always has a pretty niece
who falls in love with the handsome man they send in from out-of-
town to investigate what's happening.

DEFENSIVE PESSIMISM

Because some people fear being changed by the Self or by an influx
of superconscious energy, they often defend themselves through
pessimism: "I'm too old to change." "I'm not intelligent enough for
such things." "I'm too neurotic, how can I let love and joy into my
life?" Or, "How can I pursue a spiritual path when I have a family
to look after?"

Astrologically, defensive pessimism can show up with Jupiter
in difficult aspect to Saturn or when Saturn is in Sagittarius or in
the 9th house. The principles of Sagittarius, Jupiter, and the 9th
house all involve growth, expansion, and evolution, but Saturn
puts the brakes on. Those with Saturn in difficult angle to Neptune
also have trouble reconciling where they would like to be (Neptune) with the reality at hand (Saturn). Defensive pessimism also
comes up with oppositions between Gemini and Sagittarius, or
between Virgo and Pisces. The Mercury ruled signs of Gemini and
Virgo are good at finding reasons to put a damper on the expansiveness of Sagittarius or Pisces. I'd also watch for this defence
mechanism operating if you have squares between Gemini and
Pisces, or Virgo and Sagittarius.

DOGMATISATION

Some people open up to the superconscious and the Higher Self, but then dogmatise these experiences into rigid systems. For instance, certain religious groups or cults crystallise their perception of what it means to be spiritual and become extremely bureaucratic about it. They devise all sorts of rules about what is spiritual and what isn't. What was originally a vibrant and lively experience turns into a list of oughts and shoulds or strict routines demanding adherence: "You *should always* be loving," "you *should always* meditate in the lotus position twice a day," "you *should always* be radiant." I've heard this referred to as "Stalinism of the Spirit."

Some groups organise themselves around an inspired leader, but after the leader dies, they fail to preserve the true meaning of his or her teaching. In *What We May Be*, Piero Ferrucci writes about Dostoevski's *The Brothers Karamazov*. In one section of this novel, Christ returns to earth and is condemned by the Inquisition for his heretical beliefs![40]

Certain groups believe they have the only way to the truth. If you don't follow their path, you can just forget about getting anywhere. In *The Aquarian Conspiracy*, Marilyn Ferguson warns of the danger of believing that any one path is the answer to everything.[41] For instance, you might be opened up by some practice or technique—a form of meditation or something like Rolfing (a very powerful type of deep massage). As a result you come to believe that the thing which has worked for you is the answer to everything and everyone must do it: "If the whole world went out and got rolfed, all the problems in life would be solved."

Or one day you wake up early and catch a beautiful sunrise, which triggers a peak experience of the joy and meaning in life. Then you think, "Okay, if I get up early every day and watch the sunrise, I'll be sure of having this experience again." You set your alarm and are there by the window the next morning. The sun rises as usual and you are poised to be vaulted to the heights of ecstasy.

---

[40]Ferrucci, *What We May Be*, p. 158.
[41]Ferguson, *The Aquarian Conspiracy*, p. 97.

But nothing happens. It doesn't work. It's better to take the joy and expansion which the earlier experience of the sunrise has given you, and find other ways to gradually integrate these qualities into your life, rather than relying on the actual sunrise itself to always stimulate the same reaction.

Mars, Saturn, or Pluto in the 9th could be rather fanatical about spiritual issues and beliefs. Remember, Saturn and Pluto may be reluctant at first, but once set on a path, these planets are usually very determined about getting there. The tendency to fanaticism and dogma can also show up with Mars or Pluto in aspect to Jupiter. Uranus in hard angle to Jupiter sometimes gives excessive zeal as well, along with an "I *know* what the *real truth* is" attitude. If the Sun or Mercury were in the 9th and linked to Mars, Saturn, Uranus or Pluto, a person could also have fixed philosophical beliefs. In such cases, the spiritual isn't denied; it is accepted, but stifled and taken over by the superego.

Audience: Could Jupiter in a fixed sign be more fixed about beliefs as well?

Howard: Yes, that is possible. I've done a number of charts for people with Jupiter in Scorpio square Saturn and Pluto in Leo. When Uranus transited Scorpio and was approaching Jupiter, I remember telling some of these people that they might have a revolution in their philosophical belief system. They looked at me in utter disbelief, as if I were crazy—they would never change their guru or philosophy! Uranus came along and a new guru swept into town, and guess who were the first in the queue for a new mantra? Nothing like a Uranus transit to make you eat your words.

Something similar can occur when Uranus or Pluto transits the 9th, or transiting Pluto aspects Jupiter. A few years ago, Pluto moved into my 9th house by transit and my whole belief system collapsed. I didn't know what was the truth anymore. At first I was frightened and dizzy—I had no ground to stand on. Looking back, I see now that it was a good experience. The loss of my old belief system made me curious to find out what other people chose to believe in, and I kept going around asking everyone how they gave meaning to their lives. Eventually I pieced together some new viewpoints, and combining these with what I had salvaged from my earlier beliefs, ended up with a broader and more flexible understanding of life than I had previously.

CRISES AND CONFLICTS
ON THE SPIRITUAL PATH

In the time we have left, I'd like to look at the kinds of crises and conflicts people encounter on the path of spiritual or transpersonal development. Assagioli divides these into a number of stages: a) crises preceding the spiritual awakening; b) crises and reactions caused by the spiritual awakening; c) phases of the process of transformation.[42]

CRISES PRECEDING THE SPIRITUAL AWAKENING

It can happen that people suddenly experience a change in the direction of their lives. This can be triggered by a major disappointment in work or career, or the loss of someone close. Or sometimes people wake up and find themselves experiencing inner dissatisfaction, an emptiness inside. They may previously have coped very well, confidently going out there every day into the world; but suddenly they are gripped by a nagging sense of the futility or lack of meaning in their lives. Everything goes dead and loses its vitality. They are suffering what is commonly called a crisis of meaning: "Why am I here? Why am I bothering? What's it all mean?" It may even look like a nervous breakdown. But just beneath the surface level of these doubts and disturbances, spiritual or transpersonal aspirations are poised and waiting for entry into the personality. Something has to die for something new to be born.

The transits of Uranus, Neptune, and Pluto, or progressions involving these planets, are usually around at these times. When

---

[42]Roberto Assagioli, *Psychosynthesis* (Wellingborough, England: The Thorsons Publishing Group, 1965), Chapter 2.

the outer planets activate the chart or are touched off by progression, the cosmos doesn't want to leave you the same way it found you. The old is disrupted, or goes stale and doesn't work anymore. It is only then that the new has a chance to get in.

Life is questioned; going along as you always have just isn't enough. Very often we experience this kind of thing around mid-life when Uranus opposes natal Uranus, when Neptune squares natal Neptune, or Pluto squares natal Pluto. But it can happen at any time of the life—I've known people who have had a spiritual crisis at seven, and others who go through it at seventy.

CRISES AND REACTIONS CAUSED BY THE SPIRITUAL AWAKENING

The opening up of superconscious or transpersonal energies is often experienced as uplifting and as a wonderful release. At the same time, however, some people have great difficulty assimilating the influx of energy, light, and power that comes from these levels of the psyche. The nervous system can literally be overwhelmed or blown-out by an inflow of superconscious energy. In the 1960's, a number of people were "blasted" in this way by LSD and other psychedelics. Even without mind-expanding drugs, a powerful release of superconscious energy into a shaky or imbalanced personality could produce extreme forms of behaviour. In some cases, people snap—they run into the street, take off all their clothes and burn their passports. If we are universal and unbounded, who needs passports? Some people hear voices telling them what to do, or have visions which they can't properly handle or integrate. The inner experience of a Universal Self can lead to feelings of greatness which might become mixed up with unresolved infantile issues around omnipotence. A person could lose the ability to distinguish between the ego and the Self, and start thinking that he or she is God or the chosen centre of some all-encompassing divine plan. With such dangers along the path, you can see why a healthy, balanced ego or sense of "I" is necessary in order to better channel transpersonal inspiration.

There are other problems. You can have a spiritual awakening and mistakenly believe that what you have glimpsed in yourself is already a manifested reality. You have a peak experience and then you think, "Great, now all my problems are solved—I've risen above it all, I have all possibilities and am free, I have arrived." Unfortunately, you soon realise that it is only the beginning—you are not there yet. Temporarily you may feel unbounded love and see everything infused with a golden light, but all this soon ceases in intensity. Things normalise and you slide back into your former personality and its old ways.

Transpersonal energy, like everything in life, is cyclic. It ebbs and flows. When it flows in, you feel good—synchronicity abounds and magical things happen. When transpersonal energy recedes, the old limitations re-appear. You had it all and now the world looks dull again. Your old problems seem all the more frustrating because you have glimpsed what life would be like to be free of them.

What's more, scaling the heights has a way of stirring up the depths. Contacting the light of the higher mind brings what is dark in you into clearer view. Following an influx of superconscious energy, demons from the depths of the unconscious are awakened. You have an experience of light and love and two days later you find yourself angry as hell at something that happens. You come down and feel more depressed and empty than ever before. Was the peak experience just a fant:sy or illusion?

I once overheard a nun (No, I don't make it a practice to listen in on nun's conversations) telling a woman who was leaving a convent after a week's period of retreat, "Watch out, you'll meet the devil in a few days." As a meditation teacher, I discovered something similar. After a deep and powerful meditation, people come out feeling very clear and at peace; but even a few hours later, they might experience a patch of what we called stress release. The profound rest of a deep meditation brings out pockets of stress and tension buried in the hidden recesses of the psyche. Old stresses come to the surface and are sometimes re-experienced in the process of being released. Compared to the peace and equanimity of the powerful meditation, stress release makes you feel as if you are moving backward rather than forward in spiritual growth. St. John of the Cross talked about the dark night of the soul:

And when the rays of this pure Light shine upon the soul in order to expel impurities, the soul perceives itself to be so unclean and miserable that it seems as if God has set Himself against it and itself were set against God.[43]

Some of you may get people coming for readings who are in the middle of this kind of crisis. You can help by reminding them that what they are going through is a natural part of the process of spiritual growth and unfoldment. An exalted state usually will not last forever.

Crashing from such peaks can be depressing and disheartening—that is, until you realise that an influx of transpersonal inspiration has served to show you the direction in which you need to go. Now you can begin the work of doing what is necessary to ground your vision, and make it a more permanent reality in your life. We fall from the heights of superconscious awareness and then must start the slow climb back up again, step by step.

PHASES IN THE TRANSFORMATION PROCESS

The transformation process involves getting down to the work of developing and integrating the higher functions, and balancing these with the rest of the personality. For most people, this is a time of fluctuation between light and dark, high and low, and joy and pain. Obstacles to the flow of superconscious energies will need to be examined and cleared. Furthermore, in the course of Self-realisation, you will have to face and deal with some of your deepest and most painful childhood wounds and complexes.

So much of your energy goes into these processes, you may actually appear less efficient operating in the world than you previously have done. Other people might perceive you as going backward or falling apart. "Ha, so much for your spiritual ideas—you were much better off *before* you started meditating," or "I don't know what good therapy is doing for my wife—she's so much more difficult than when she began it." You are being tested. Can you stick with your commitment of growth, even while others are

---

[43]St. John cited in Underhill, *Mysticism* (London: Metheun, 1913), p. 26.

teasing you or mocking your progress? Joining up with fellow travellers on the spiritual path, who understand the ins and outs and with whom you can share your experiences, can be very helpful during this phase.

In *Psychosynthesis*, Assagioli makes a good point: the caterpiller is luckier than we are. It goes through its transformation in the relative peace and security of a cocoon. We, however, may be in the middle of a profound shift in our unfoldment and growth, and yet, more often than not, are expected to go on with our daily life as if nothing is happening.[44] Assagioli compares this to trying to rebuild a railway station without bothering to stop the existing traffic. For a while, everything is more of a mess.

In *The Aquarian Conspiracy*, Marilyn Ferguson underlines a valid point about spiritual and psychological development—that we go after transformative experience in the only way we know how, as consumers and competitors.[45] We worry about going fast enough; we shop around for all sorts of techniques, aids and practises to get us there more quickly; and we keep comparing how far we are with those around us.

It's virtually impossible to give specific astrological significators to all the various stages of psycho-spiritual development. It's different for different people. Anyway, it's time to end. All I can say is that Jupiter, Saturn, Uranus, Neptune and Pluto start the ball rolling, but as to where the journey ultimately takes you—only your own deeper Self can tell you that!

---

[44] Assagioli, *Psychosynthesis*, p. 50.
[45] Ferguson, *The Aquarian Conspiracy*, p. 97.

PART 4

ALCHEMICAL
SYMBOLISM
IN THE HOROSCOPE

That is indeed what men most seek on earth:
'Tis rust alone that gives the coin its worth!

Thales

Our gold is not the common gold.

Rosarium philosophorum

Alchemy as a Psychological Metaphor

The symbolism of alchemy is alien to us today, and therefore the theme of this seminar may seem strange to those of you who are unfamiliar with a psychological approach to it. Not only does alchemy initially appear to have little to do with the study of astrology; even worse, the layman who has never dipped into contemporary writers on the subject generally believes that alchemy was concerned with turning actual lead into actual gold. Since modern science has put paid to this apparently naive medieval fantasy, alchemy has wound up on the rubbish heap with the flat earth and other relics of our reputedly ignorant ancestors. I would like to briefly touch on some of the historical aspects of alchemy first, before I begin to explore its relevance to us as a psychological map, and its close connections with astrological symbolism. At the end of the day you might still have some reservations about rushing into the kitchen to transmute lead into gold, but I think you will see that alchemical imagery is as important a tool for understanding astrology as myths and fairy tales—and as you know, I feel these are extremely important methods of entering imaginatively into the meaning of astrological symbols.

The study and practise of alchemy was not limited to Western civilisation; there is a very old Chinese tradition in it, and it was also known to the Arabs throughout the first centuries of the Christian era. In the West there were two great flowerings of alchemy, one occurring in the first centuries A.D. and primarily centred around Alexandria, the second occurring during the Renaissance and primarily centred in Italy and Germany. This latter flowering continued up through the 18th century, at which point alchemy and chemistry parted ways, just as astrology and astronomy did. The inner or psychological content of both alchemy and astrology became separated from the outer or physical study, and since the Enlightenment chemistry and astronomy, which are branches of what we now call science, have disowned their earlier antecedents.

Now, Jung was quite fascinated by the alchemical texts of the Renaissance and the writings of the Gnostics of the first centuries A.D. because he felt that anything which contained so much power and numinosity must have had some profound psychological truth encapsulated within it. He applied the same kind of perspective to alchemy that he did to the symbolism of myths and fairy tales – in other words, the imagery of alchemy is a map of psychological development, and in particular a map of the dynamics of the unconscious unfolding its process of what Jung called individuation. Alchemy, like mythology, seems to have arisen as a naive and spontaneous product of the unconscious. It is really a form of mythology, which makes use of pictures quite different from myth but which emerges from the same sea of the collective unconscious which has given birth to the stories of the gods over the millennia.

The point over which the modern mind seems to stumble in understanding alchemy is the strange fusion of physical and psychic, which does not differentiate between inanimate matter and inner states. Physical gold and psychic gold are the same in alchemical writings, and base matter is likewise both inside and outside the alchemist. We have, on a rational level, split the physical realm from the psychic since the Enlightenment, and have accepted this split as a statement of truth about the nature of reality. But there are many important questions about the validity of this Cartesian duality beginning to arise within the scientific community now, and the unconscious appears to ignore the split absolutely, despite our intellectual efforts. The realm of substance and the realm of psyche are, in terms of the unconscious, indissoluble; they are merely different manifestations of a central, "psychoid" reality. It is this perspective which we need to remember if we are to penetrate beyond the oddities of alchemical writings. But for that matter we need to keep this perspective in mind when we deal with astrology too, because what we call a planetary influence can express itself on a bodily level, as an external event, as an inner emotional or spiritual state, as an ideology, as another person with whom we engage in relationship, or as any combination of these diverse levels.

So, bearing in mind that alchemical lead and alchemical gold are dimensions of ourselves, and that the alchemist and his opus are symbols of the process of individual unfoldment, we can begin to see that a very important map of our inner development is offered by alchemy. All alchemical writings strongly make the point that alchemy accomplishes what Nature leaves imperfect. In other words, left to her own devices, Nature, or human nature, muddles through somehow in a state of inherent conflict and confusion; but the alchemist saw himself (or herself, for there were women alchemists) as the transformer of this natural chaos, the individual who stepped in and interfered with God's noble but imperfect creation in order to accomplish its ultimate evolutionary design. You can see how very advanced a psychological perspective this is for the early Christian mind, because it is, in effect, a gross heresy. Implicit in this belief is the conviction that somehow God depends upon human consciousness for His redemption, rather than the other way around, and that individual effort in some way accomplishes what the divine in unable to do in the manifest world. This great heresy naturally made the Church's ears prick up, because from early Christian times through the Reformation, the Church, and not the individual, held the key to salvation. The alchemists were not unchristian; but they were a very special kind of Christian, and therefore subject to persecution. So they cloaked their doctrines in some very florid and strange symbolism in order to conceal the enormity of the heretical statement they were making. Alchemy presented a world-view in which the individual is no longer a poor sinner, helpless and damned without the succouring arms of Mother Church; he or she is a noble participant in God's creation, and in fact can enhance or transform that creation through individual effort, self-honesty, integrity and moral responsibility.

These are deep and difficult concepts, but I would like you to think about them carefully. You will see, if you reflect for a while on this key issue of transforming nature through individual effort, that this is also the same perspective held by modern psychotherapy, although more overtly religious in its language. The underlying theme of alchemy is not really about making gold. It concerns transforming the raw substance of human nature and releasing its potential for inner divinity, not through repression or transcendence but through inner confrontation and integration. Alchemy was not preoccupied with "getting rid of" the baser aspects of the psyche. Instead, it was directed toward unification and wholeness. You can see why Jung devoted three volumes to the psychology of alchemy, because he equated the process of individual development with the great alchemical opus.

Now, another interesting feature of alchemy is that it is heavily astrologised. Astrology features constantly in all alchemical texts, because it belonged to the same world-view—that outer and inner reflect each other and are part and parcel of one whole. The famous Emerald Tablet of Hermes Trismegistus, the alchemical and magical text written in the second and third centuries A.D. which became the alchemical Bible of the Renaissance, states with beautiful simplicity that what is above is like what is below and what is below is like what is above; and thus the miracle of the One is accomplished. This Hermetic World-view is familiar to all astrologers who have studied the antecedents of their art, because it is based on the law of signatures or correspondences. You can find this same perspective in many astrological texts of the 20th century, because the schools of Theosophy, Rudolph Steiner, Alice Bailey et al. have retained the old Hermetic vision of reality. So the principle of Mars, for example, is not only a planet; it is also found in the earth as iron, and in the human body as the adrenal glands, and in the psyche as the aggressive instinct, and so on. Saturn is not only a planet, but also lead in the earth, and the human skeletal system, and the impulse for self-protection. The Sun can be found not only in the heavens but as gold in the earth, and as the human heart, and as the capacity to love. The vision of a unified cosmos with interconnections via a finite number of archetypal lines was fundamental both to alchemy and to astrology, and so the two were never separate. The metals upon which the alchemist worked were not only actual substances, subjected to cooking processes; they were also seen to be the planets themselves, and the great cosmic principles behind them. So if you were transmuting lead, you were transmuting Saturn, and in turn working on the defensive, dark, depressive and barren aspects of Nature and of yourself in order to release the solar gold of a loving heart and a joyful vision of life.

Many of you will be familiar with this Hermetic perspective in astrology. From this ancient tenet of astrology it is not a big leap to understand that alchemy stated the same things about life. The natural conflicts to which alchemical texts refer—the imperfections in Nature—are the natural conflicts which we see astrologically represented as the squares and oppositions of the birth chart, the element imbalances, and all the other lopsided features which are a characteristic of every individual horoscope. There is no such thing as a perfectly harmonious horoscope, and there is no such thing as perfect harmony in Nature. So it was to these natural conflicts that the alchemical work was addressed—to take these warring aspects of creation, and of the individual, and try to effect some kind of change which might allow them to work more harmoniously together without destroying the integrity of each. I will talk in much more detail about the astrological correspondences to alchemical images later on. Right now I am trying to give you the overview of just what we are dealing with. Astrological timing also figures importantly in alchemical writings, because it was assumed that the alchemical opus could only be performed at certain optimum moments. In other words, there are favourable and unfavourable times to tamper with God's creation. The right moment depended upon the right transits. If the alchemist tried to perform his or her work when the planets were particularly antagonistic, that was asking for trouble, and the work was botched. But a better set of planetary configurations at least meant you could expect a little help from Nature. Once again we can see a parallel here to the various experiences which the individual encounters at different times in life. There are optimum moments for conscious efforts at development, and there are times when it is better to leave well enough alone. So a great deal of alchemical literature focusses on the unity of above and below not only in terms of the components of life, but in terms of Nature's timing.

Now I am going to give you a short alchemical glossary, so you can begin to familiarise yourself with the language. You may never use these words again, unless you want to terrify your friends at parties, but the language itself is highly evocative. Trying to understand alchemical language is like trying to understand mythic language. You need to let your imagination play with it rather than trying to cage it with too many rational interpretations. The alchemical work, first of all, was referred to as the *opus*, which is simply the Latin word for "work." We use it in everyday language in terms of an artist's effort—Beethoven's *magnum opus* or "great work" is considered by some to be the 9th Symphony, for example. The opus is also called "the Art." This opus was understood as a sacred or holy task, which merited a lifetime's effort. It was not something one did on Sunday afternoons after walking the dog. It was a process to which the alchemist dedicated nothing less than everything. Also, the opus was not something one did for gain; the fact that physical gold might be one of the by-products was not really the point at all. The opus was an offering to something divine.

Audience: To be an alchemist, did you have to be an astrologer as well?

Liz: Yes. The two things were not separate. If one learned alchemy—and the only place to learn it was as a student with some alchemical master—then astrology was an inseparable part of the language, the timing and the work. You will also find, later on in the alchemical tradition as it developed in the 16th and 17th centuries, that alchemy and astrology were also inseparable from medicine. These three were bound together because the body was one of the chief working grounds for the alchemical process. Paracelsus was one of the most important figures in Renaissance alchemy, and one who fascinated Jung more than any other; and the repercussions of his work stretch today into the field of medicine as well as into astrology and psychology. Paracelsus' work has had its modern flowering in homeopathy, which is ultimately based on the same idea of signatures that alchemy and astrology were. The perspective of alchemy turns the horoscope into a map of a process rather than a listing of static character traits. This is the link which I want to explore most fully during the course of the day.

A good way to get the flavour of some of the alchemical texts is to look at their translations in Jung's *Psychology and Alchemy*.[1] Some

---

[1]C.G. Jung, Psychology and Alchemy, Vol 12. The Collected Works (Princeton, NJ: Bollingen Series No. 20, Princeton University Press, 1968; and London: Routledge & Kegan Paul, 1953).

of these texts sound as though the alchemist has bumped into a medieval Timothy Leary and has taken acid. You find the strangest images, like the green lion who must be put into a sealed vessel with his paws cut off. Light a fire beneath the alembic and the King will first be consumed by the wolf, and then the wolf will devour itself. And so on. These images, some of which are very violent and grotesque, arise straight from the unconscious. They are the language of dreams, psychotic states, and primitive myths. Another term which is essential in alchemy is the *prima materia*, which simply means primal substance. This prima materia forms the basis of the opus. No one really knows just what physical substance the alchemists considered "prima." Different writers refer to different things. Very often the prima materia is referred to as Saturn, or as lead, or both. The implication is that lead, being the manifestation of the Great Malefic, is the basest substance in the universe. Some alchemists refer to the prima materia as faeces, and one wonders what the kitchen must have smelled like during the opus. This equation of faeces with the base and undifferentiated yet potentially fertile dimension of the psyche is an idea well beloved by Freud. Faeces are equated with baseness, but they are also the raw creative products of the human being, so shit therefore contains the seeds of the alchemical gold. We might understand the prima materia as the raw, primitive instincts that erupt from the unconscious, the emotional compulsions and conflicts and fears and passions which drive all of us at one time or another in life. It is really Freud's concept of the *id*. This prima materia is in a state of conflict all the time, blind, potent, undirected, but full of raw power, and constantly embattled. There is a very beautiful engraving of the prima materia reproduced in *Psychology and Alchemy* which portrays the universe in its natural state before the alchemical opus. It is an image of great clashing rocks, huge cosmic boulders blundering into each other, and mixed in are the different animals of the zodiacal signs fighting each other. On one rock a bull and a scorpion battle, and that rock is colliding with one on which a ram is trying to butt a pair of scales. The whole picture contains a feeling of furious confusion, aggression, and conflict. This is what alchemy envisioned as prima materia. I don't think we have to look very far to discover where it might lie inside us, because it is our natural unreflective state of being. Whenever we are beset by affects, compulsions, irrational eruptions of any kind, there is the prima materia.

There is an extremely interesting series of articles which Edward Edinger published in *Quadrant*, the New York journal of analytical psychology.[2] These articles deal with the different stages of the alchemical opus in relation to analysis. Edinger makes the statement that the prima materia is the symptom which drives the patient into analysis. We might consider the same thing in relation to the person who comes for an astrological consultation. Whatever the mess is, the crisis, the issue that forces the individual to begin to question his or her real nature—that is the prima materia, the life wound, the life conflict. The declared reason for a client's desire for a consultation may sound superficial enough, but underneath there is usually a much more profound dilemma. Sometimes this issue is equated in alchemy with Saturn, although not always; but there is inevitably a shadowy quality to it, something dark and inferior and undeveloped within the person and, from the alchemical perspective, within Nature itself. In individual terms, this is of course the shadow, the unconscious bit of us which is so often socially embarrassing because it is unpleasant or infantile or terribly vulnerable, yet which contains all the unlived potentials of the personality. So the prima materia always has an apparently negative or shadowy connotation.

One of the things which Jung explored in his work on these themes is the appearance of typical alchemical imagery in the dreams of modern individuals who know absolutely nothing about it consciously. I have also frequently seen this in the dreams of the people I work with, as I think every analyst does. One of the most common alchemical dream-motifs is shit, which is often an embarrassing topic to discuss with anybody but which in dreams often heralds the beginning of facing some previously undeveloped and unconscious aspect of oneself. Toilet dreams are extremely common, particularly the dream where one is trying to find a loo in order to have a shit, but there is no loo, or there are already fifteen people in it, or it doesn't flush, and so on. When one begins to actually work on the personal associations connected with dreams

---

[2]This series of articles, entitled "Psychotherapy and Alchemy," ran over a period of four years, first appearing in *Quadrant*, Vol. 11, No. 1, September, 1978, and ending with Vol. 15, No. 1, Spring 1982.

of this kind, they open up all kinds of feelings of shame, embarrassment, vulnerability and guilt which lead straight to a confrontation with the shadowy aspects of the personality. If we approach dreams of this kind through the lens of alchemy, then we can see a potential in the shit—a herald of something to come, the beginning of a process. And as astrologers, we can also look at Saturn in the birth chart, and in transits and progressions, from the same perspective. This opens up a highly creative approach to what otherwise might be considered a very unpleasant and awkward area.

The prima materia is the beginning of the opus. At the end of it stands the *lapis*, which is Latin for "stone." Once again, we are not really sure just what this stone was which alchemy put such great store by. Sometimes the lapis is called gold, but alchemical texts are forever stating that their gold is not ordinary gold. The mysterious lapis, which the alchemist attempted to release from the confusing matrix of the prima materia, is equated with all sorts of extraordinary things. It is sometimes called the Philosophers' Stone, sometimes the Garden of the Philosophers, sometimes a rose or a lotus flower, sometimes a diamond. It is equated with Christ, with the unicorn, and with the bizarre image of the crowned hermaphrodite. Through all these diverse portrayals of the lapis a single thread runs, of something holy which must be extracted from the base stuff which comprises the beginning of the work. So far as I can understand this lapis psychologically, I think it is connected with a sense of individual essence, what Jung calls the Self. It is both individuality and divinity, a feeling of unique destiny and meaning in life. In religious language it is the inner god, the individual spirit. This is the thing which gives us a sense of permanence, which can sustain us through the flux of life's changes. If a person does not have this sense of inner validity and uniqueness, then he or she is at the mercy of the collective and of external events, and can find no continuity or purpose to life. Life is then full of dangers, and one is afraid to give anything of oneself, and also afraid to love. One cannot love or create anything original without a little of that sense of self. The alchemists believed the lapis to be immortal and imperishable; and they also believed that it had a catalytic effect on the world around it. In other words, if the alchemist could produce the lapis, the lapis would transform other base substances simply by being what it was. This is the same as the Chinese idea of being in Tao. The lapis reproduces itself, and has a permanent and ever-extending effect on life. So there is something about this inner authority on a psychological level which gives an individual a profound effect on the environment, not because he or she is struggling to achieve power or has arrived at a state of spiritual perfection, but because somehow that core of self acts as a trigger on the psyches of other people. Then we say a person has "mana," some quality of inner authenticity and wholeness which affects others very powerfully. I think this lapis, and the longing of every person to find it, stands behind many of our powerful projections onto religious and political figures. You can see not only the positive side of these projections of the lapis onto figures such as Christ and the Buddha, but also the negative side of them when a whole nation projects what is essentially an inner and individual responsibility onto one charismatic leader like Hitler or Khomeini.

The lapis is, as I have said, sometimes portrayed as a hermaphrodite. In other words, it has both male and female aspects. This divine hermaphrodite is also referred to in alchemical texts as *Mercurius*. Now Mercurius is one of the chief symbols of alchemy, and it is worth spending some time trying to understand what they might have meant by it. In some ways there is a relationship between the figure of Mercurius and our astrological symbol of Mercury, because the processes of perception and comprehension which are linked with Mercury—in other words, the capacity for consciousness—are part of the magic of the lapis. But Mercurius is much more than Mercury. He-she is a deeply paradoxical image. Try to bear with these apparently nonsensical circular metaphors, because it is worth it for the glimmering of understanding one can find. In alchemy, Mercurius is the lapis—the goal of the work, the spark of divinity encapsulated within raw Nature, the gold which is our true essence and our experience of meaningful individuality. Mercurius is also the androgynous Christ, the progeny of God, the divine spirit made human by being incarnated in flesh—in other words, in mystical language, every individual contains Christ and is a child of God. These are deeply religious sentiments, and so far they are not anti-Christian. However, Mercurius is also the prima materia—the base, smelly, devilish and conflict-ridden animal in us all. There is a secret unity between Mercurius as base substance and Mercurius as alchemical gold. The faeces which cause such shame and guilt are secretly the same as the luminous figure of Christ. This is getting very heretical indeed. The alchemist is therefore not engaged in changing something into something else; he or she is releasing what was always there, shrouded in a darker and more primitive form. This makes nonsense of the idea that one must leave behind the baser aspects of one's nature in order to reach the spirit, because the spirit IS base nature, transformed in its manifestation rather than its essence through the magical power of consciousness. Put in more ordinary language, it is not the strong, developed, and well-adapted aspects of the personality which yield the greatest inner rewards, but the despised and infantile parts that we spend so much time trying to hide from others and from ourselves.

One can often hear artists trying to express these feelings about releasing an essence—one does not sculpt a horse out of a piece of stone, one reveals the horse that was always locked up within, awaiting the eye and hand of the sculptor. It is a revelation of the unique individual essence which has always been hiding within the apparently chaotic, painful, blind unconscious mess that we call our problem or our symptom. Something has changed, but on the other hand nothing at all has changed. One still has the same horoscope one had to begin with, and one is still the same person. So the alchemists wrote that Mercurius was the prima materia and Mercurius was also the lapis. Nothing is added and nothing taken away. But a chemical, or alchemical, transformation occurs. What becomes even more deeply paradoxical is that the alchemist considered himself or herself Mercurius as well—the conscious worker who elects to tamper with base substance is secretly the same as the base substance, and also the same as the gold which is the goal of the opus.

The alchemists saw their opus as being a process inevitably fraught with suffering. It was not considered to be fun and games, to say the least. The opus was said to sometimes drive people mad, and only a considerable and unusual degree of integrity and honesty and moral decency could help the individual through the labyrinth of confusion and danger which attended all the stages of the work. The unconscious is protean in nature, and can enchant and delude as well as devour; and only solid moral fibre and a capacity for commitment could see the alchemist through his own morass. Thus one could not perform the opus in order to get rich on the gold. I think this is a very important issue in context of why people are motivated toward self-development, because our motives are always mixed. There is no such thing as pure altruism, and even the loftiest spiritual aspiration carries a shadow component at its back—thirst for power, craving for being loved, and so on. Alchemical texts stress great importance on the conscious qualities required for performing the work, including both moral and physical stamina. If the alchemist did not possess sufficient of these qualities, then he or she was better off doing something else instead, because the opus taxed the whole person. It put pressure on everything, particularly the weak links in the chain; and unless the container was very strong the work went wrong and the fumes became poisonous on every level. It is probable that there were actual physical as well as psychic casualties among the alchemists, because these people knew very little about toxic chemical combinations, and very likely some of them got sick from lead poisoning or accidentally blew up their kitchens. But it is the moral risks which are stressed most frequently, and I think these moral risks await anyone who elects to tamper with Nature by entering the realm of the psyche. And tampering includes doing astrological charts. The issues of power and inflation and seduction on various levels always attend the creation of the lapis. No one is exempt. One finds repeated over and over in alchemical writings the injunction, "*Deo concedente*," according to the will of God.

Audience: What do you mean by moral risks?

Liz: I don't mean the obvious ones like winding up in bed with one's clients, which because they are so obvious are not the trickiest ones. By tampering with God's creation, one is unconsciously identifying with God. That is the great moral risk, which Nietzsche knew all about: the problem of inflation. This is really about the use and abuse of psychological power. It is a risk for any astrologer as well as any psychotherapist, because one does gain power through self-knowledge and knowledge of others, and the shadow is always eager to get its hands on that power for its own purposes. The shadow is infantile; it is the repository for all the childhood wounds and humiliations which all of us have suffered in one degree or another. The child rejected in his or her Oedipal fascination for the mother or father will secretly crave sexual power and the humiliation of all rivals, real or imaginary; the child unbearably humiliated by thoughtless or insensitive parents will secretly dream of ruling the world, and will become spiteful and envious toward anyone who seems to have more than he or she does. Any increased sense of potency, beauty, lovability, or creative power brings with it, along with healing and enhancement of life, the danger of inflation. This is why the alchemists go on ad nauseam about how it is not them, but rather Mercurius, or God, who allows the work to be performed. Any progress is not due to the personal excellence of the alchemist, but to the deity. This is a very wise injunction for the psychotherapist or astrological counsellor, because it is very easy to believe that one has healed the patient due to being exceptionally good and clever, rather than through the agency of the unconscious, *Deo concedente*.

Audience: In esoteric schools they often stress that the motive for work must be for others, rather than for oneself.

Liz: Yes, they stress it. Everyone stresses it. Who wants to be caught with his pants down? But consciously promising this is not enough. One needs a very long spoon to sup with the devil, and anyone who tampers with the unconscious will, sooner or later, be infected by it. As you say, this is stressed in many esoteric schools. But there is not sufficient follow-up in the form of real self-confrontation, because in the same paragraph the individual is told to stop thinking nasty thoughts, to be selfless and sacrificing, and to ignore or repress the "lower nature." Not all teachings are this naive, mind you. But a good many of them are. And the problems of inflation and a very dirty shadow are prevalent throughout the esoteric field, as well as throughout the psychological and astrological ones, and of course in the Church.

Throughout the body of alchemical writings, this issue of the dangers of inflation, seduction and corruption is stressed. Another feature of the opus is its extreme unpredictability. Not only suffering and moral risks accompany the alchemist all along the way; so do surprises. Mercurius is here truly Hermes of Greek myth, because he-she is a very slippery and mischievous daemon. Mercurius is not only androgynous, but also morally ambivalent, which is why the alchemist has to be the one who clings to some sense of moral integrity. The unconscious cannot, so the alchemist must. Sometimes Mercurius shows a beneficent face, and everything seems to be going along fine, and one has the right dreams and the right insights, and then all of a sudden the psyche turns around and plays a truly dreadful trick which costs dearly—an act of "fate" where everything goes badly wrong. One of the roles of Hermes in Greek myth is the seducer who leads men astray in the dark night. Mercurius can appear as an enchanting siren of either sex who is really corrupt underneath, and leads straight to castration and death; and everything is suddenly back to front and upside down. What seemed loving is revealed as manipulative and selfish, and what seemed hard and cruel is revealed as deeply compassionate; the outlaw becomes the saint and the virgin the prostitute, and one can trust nothing any longer, at least not for a time. As one of the witches says in *Macbeth*, "fair is foul and foul is fair." Or as an analytic colleague of mine once put it, "I try to make all my decision from a spirit of deep uncertainty."

The process of individuation is not, in alchemical imagery, something which can be guaranteed to fulfil its potential. One does not know whether it will work out or not; one can only pray, Deo concedente, and get on with it, and if it all goes wrong, then one can try to see where one blew it, and can start again, hopefully in the same incarnation. Have any of you seen Tarkovsky's film *Stalker*? This film is a wonderful portrayal of that spirit of uncertainty, humility, and inner integrity which must accompany the individual on the journey to the centre, which in the film is called "The Zone." For the alchemist, one was constantly in danger of losing one's way, because Mercurius came during the night and changed all the signposts. This is the most difficult dimension of working with the psyche, which is probably why we create psychological and esoteric schools with rigid doctrines and highly structured terminologies. It makes us feel safer, and helps to protect us from that primal anxiety of dealing with something which one cannot define according to any known conscious laws.

Mercurius is really an image of the unconscious itself, and the strange triple face of this figure—the raw life of Nature, the divine essence or Philosophers' Stone, and the conscious ego which attempts to make sense of it all—is encapsulated in the bizarre imagery of alchemy. The alchemist must trust Mercurius, but Mercurius is intrinsically untrustworthy according to any ordinary definition of the word. Yet there is nothing else to trust, and ultimately there is nothing to do but follow the circuitous meanderings of this surprising archetypal character. I think these perspectives, alien and lofty though they may at first seem, are very worthwhile to bear in mind when we look at a natal horoscope. For the whole birth chart is in a sense the prima materia, the raw stuff out of which the individual shapes a life. The alchemical work begins at birth on this raw stuff; the child's developing ego gradually finds its way through some of the labyrinthine passages, slowly forming the solid centre of the stone as it goes, through frustration and suffering as well as through joy and reward. Alchemy postulates a process at work within Nature itself, an intelligent pattern which attempts to knit together its own conflicting opposites. This is a natural process; it is imperfect, as the alchemists say, but it is a process nonetheless, and every individual sets forth on it whether he or she is aware of it or not. But the unconscious and unreflective person will enact that chart as only prima materia, and the lapis is imperfectly formed if formed at all; and then the person's life is quite predictable, and utterly at the mercy of exteriorised fate. The very unconscious person is extremely predictable. If you have a client who never reflects on his or her own motives at all, then you can make a much better job of offering concrete predictions than you can with the person who has begun to tamper. For example, someone might come along who is very unformed as a personality, and very identified with collective rather than individual values; and that person has just fallen in love. He or she really thinks it is going to unfold just like the magazines and romantic novels say. And you can see that in a few years' time, transiting Saturn is going to conjunct that person's natal seventh house Pluto square Venus. Of course it is predictable that this marriage made in heaven will break up, because the individual is so oblivious to the unconscious dimensions of the attraction and the unconscious dynamics of the relationship. Like the prima materia, there is an inevitability about Nature when it is blind human nature. So predictability is a property of the primal substance, even though in essence it is chaotic and full of blind passions.

But the moment the person begins to reflect on his or her own inner nature, then a tampering has begun. The natural process which has gone on in the darkness has now suddenly had light cast on it by the alchemist—the conscious ego which is striving to understand. The ego begins to ask important questions—Who am I? How have my parents shaped my values? How much am I connected with my own feelings, my own motives, my own needs? How much do my actions reflect my secret need to please, my fear of rejection, my terror of being alone? And so on. These are psychological questions, but they are, in an older metaphor, the work of the alchemist. What did that dream mean? Where can I see that figure within myself? Where am I being unconsciously destructive, repressive, cold? Who is this unknown child full of potentials? Where do I project bits of myself on friends, lovers, enemies, governments, races? I think you can get the picture. A chart analysis can often provide the trigger for a change in perspective; and changes in perspective because of encounters with the unconscious are precisely what alchemy is about. Any attempt we make to improve ourselves and our lives through understanding the dynamics of the birth chart is a piece of the alchemical work, particularly if it starts approaching the domain of psychotherapy, because this is taking the raw materials of the psyche as portrayed in the horoscope and transforming them through the intervention of consciousness. But now you can perhaps see better what I mean by moral risks. The attitude one takes toward these raw components is critical, and no alchemist would have been stupid enough to set himself or herself up in arrogance as a judge of the unconscious realm; for that would have been, in effect, judging God, which means being God oneself. The horoscope is an opus, a life's work. We run the same risks, and have the same kind of dreadful uncertainties, although we may not blow our kitchens up. To try to remain wholly detached and intellectually barricaded is no more effective now than it was in the 16th century. One is infected anyway.

Audience: I can see the problem of being too uninvolved. But there is also a danger of getting too involved.

Liz: Yes, of course there is. A vast terrain lies between identification with unconscious components, and dissociation from them. Alchemy has its metaphors about overinvolvement as well as underinvolvement. If you stir the stuff in the cooking pot for too long, you begin to hallucinate and inhale the poisonous fumes. But you cannot just go away and leave it, because it will spoil or burn or explode. There must be a constant commitment but also a sensible distance from it. There is also the inevitability of periods of difficulty. This dimension of working with the psyche is well known in analytic circles, but appears to be left out of many other self-help programmes. It is expected that there should be no confusion, no mistakes, and no setbacks; and all the answers should be clear and defined from the beginning. That is not how Mercurius behaves. The religious feeling in alchemy is very deep, because it is an approach to God which combines awe, fear, worship, and yet, at the same time, confidence in one's own value. Neither the divine nor the human is undervalued.

Are there any other questions about the alchemical terminology I have been using, before we move on to the astrological dimensions?

Audience: You mentioned something called an alembic.

Liz: The alembic is the vessel in which the alchemical work is performed. It is also called a retort. Usually these were glass vessels, rounded at the bottom to rest in a metal rack, and with a long neck, sometimes curved. There is a wonderful collection of these at Heidelberg Castle, if any of you ever have occasion to travel there; a room has been set aside and reconstructed as a laboratory, since a lot of alchemical experiments were going on at Heidelberg during the late 16th and early 17th centuries. Illustrations of alchemical texts always show these vessels. There are many of them among the engravings in Psychology and Alchemy. The alembic is suggestive of a womb, and sometimes one finds it referred to as the uterus. The idea is that the work is like a gestation of new life, and is performed within a sealed vessel. Whatever is contained inside is subjected to heat and great pressure, but the seal must under no circumstances be removed, or the work will be spoiled. And the alembic must be strong enough not to crack under this pressure. I think you can see what this might mean in psychological terms. The alembic is an image of containment, of being able to hold on to the affects and emotions and conflicts as they bubble up to the surface, without exploding and running around acting out all over the place. The alembic represents a middle place between repression, which disowns these powerful unconscious eruptions, and possession, which drags the individual down into the stew and overwhelms the capacities of the ego to make responsible choices. The alembic is in some ways an image for the containing capacities of consciousness. If it cracks in the middle of the work, this is a vivid image of a psychotic state, because the unconscious spills out all over the place without any container to hold it any longer. If the seal is removed, then the individual has relinquished responsibility for his or her own dilemma, and the conflicts are spewed out all over everybody else within range.

The symbol of the alembic is very relevant to psychotherapy. When unconscious conflicts begin to come to the surface, a person is compelled to want to act them out in the environment. We all want to break the seal at some point. We want to change therapists, leave lovers, enter or exit from marriages, quit jobs, rob banks, have quarrels, blame people, emigrate—just to get rid of the intense heat. I think many of you can recognise this need to act out which springs from the tension of the therapeutic situation. It is very different from making a decision with all of one's faculties. It is the "I shall go mad if I can't have this, or do that . . ." syndrome. There is a desperation in it. But if one is really engaged in inner work, one cannot break the seal. Repression is inappropriate; it is repression which has, at least in part, caused the problem in the first place. But breaking out is inappropriate also. It is a terribly difficult situation. Some of the images used to describe what goes on in the alembic when things begin to heat up are pretty hideous, and very violent. Wolves eat Kings, and lions get their paws cut off, and animals scream in agony as they burn. These are very exotic, raw portrayals by the psyche of its own suffering when conflicts are contained within rather than projected outside.

Audience: Can you explain the difference between repression and containing something within the alembic?

Liz: I can try. I think repression — although not "deliberate" in the sense of sitting down and saying, "I will now repress such-and-such" — involves a disconnection from some part of oneself. It is a split, an unwillingness to be conscious of what is essentially one's own issue. Freud used this word to describe the mechanism by which highly charged sexual feelings and memories, usually incestuous in nature, were blocked from consciousness. They were repressed; they were censored, not allowed in. I think every individual represses things at one time or another, sometimes necessarily so, because to go through the experience at the wrong time might shatter the ego, or be so painful that it paralyses rather than heals. But chronic repression of a psychic component causes deep problems, because nothing in the unconscious can truly express itself or develop without the participation of the ego. This is what I believe the alchemists meant when they declared that God's creation needed the opus to achieve what Nature could not. Nature is the unconscious — raw primordial life. Without consciousness, it cannot evolve or express its potentials. Repression cuts off those potentials, and the unconscious eventually rises in rebellion.

In alchemy, constant participation is required in the work. One could not put things into the alembic, seal it, light a fire under it, and then go on holiday to the Costa del Sol. The transformations which occurred required the involvement of the alchemist. Otherwise they would not take place. We have a parallel to this in quantum physics, where the development and outcome of an experiment depends completely on the involvement of the observer. Conscious involvement, which means experiencing feelings as well as gaining insights and making connections, is absolutely necessary for any movement to take place. The alchemist could not turn his back on the tormented animals being burned in the alembic, which are really images of his own tormented instincts being subjected to transformation. So one has to feel what the creature in the alembic is feeling. The agonies of the wolf being consumed are the agonies of the alchemist. The radiant light of the dawn in the "reddening" stage of the process is the radiant hope and joy of the alchemist. And these people wrote about it in precisely this way. They suffered the pain of the wolf, and were scorched by the fire, and were fertilised by the heavenly dew. Repression is a kind of "No, thank you," to these experiences. One observes from a distance, but one feels nothing. It looks great in a textbook. I have heard this from many people who believe they have insight. They say, "Oh, yes, I know my mother didn't have much time for me," or "Oh, of course I adored my father, but he was never there," but they feel nothing. They have no memory of the pain and rage and loneliness that attended that mother's neglect, or the intensely erotic fantasies that focussed on that absent father. And insight without involvement is quite useless when we are concerned with issues of healing, transformation, and, to use the language of alchemy, the making of the stone.

Another alchemical term which I will talk about in more detail later is the *coniunctio*. This word simply means union, a conjoining of male and female. We get our astrological term "conjunction" from the same Latin word. In alchemical images, this union takes place between the King and Queen who are enclosed within the alembic. The coniunctio is a symbol of inner union, but it is also an image of union with another, and a representation of the deepest meaning of marriage. It is not only the savage and tormented creatures crying out from within the alembic which must be held in by the seal. The divine marriage cannot take place either, if the seal is broken. The problem of the seal is also the problem of commitment—whether this is to an inner process or to a relationship. Many people have a deep fear of involvement which keeps them from staying in the fire and working something through. Even though they may technically remain loyal to a relationship or a job or a therapist, they are somehow not really in it, and nothing scorches or uplifts. This is the dilemma of the puer aeternus, who is frightened of the suffering and conflict which occur in that sealed vessel, and whose negative shadow-side, the senex or old man, has no real faith in the process of transformation, despite all the optimistic talk. The puer or puella breaks out all the time, and runs away. I have often heard people with this kind of conflict saying, as they reach mid-life, that they feel they are unreal somehow, and lack substance. There is no stone forming, because they will not leave the seal intact. We could go on for a long time about the imagery of the alembic, which is similar to the temenos or sacred enclosure of Greek temples. Dream images often throw up this theme in the guise of a room with a locked door, a prison which is really a sacred container. These motifs come up all the time: "I dreamt that I was wandering through a wood and came to a circular clearing and met another person," or, "I dreamt I was in a garden with a high wall around it." The enclosed and often walled-in space, in which something mysterious happens, is the sacred cooking-pot of the psyche which alchemy portrays as the alembic.

Are there any other questions about the terminology?

Audience: Is the Philosophers' Stone the same thing as the Grail?

Liz: That is one way of interpreting the Grail, and it is the interpretation which appeals most to me. In Wolfram von Eschenbach's poem *Parzifal*, the Grail is not a cup; it is a stone. Von Eschenbach's poem was the first representation of this myth in Western literature; the more familiar romances of Chrêtien de Troyes came later, and the Grail became Christianised into the cup from which Christ drank at the Last Supper. But in the beginning, it was a stone, and many of the Grail motifs can be found in alchemical writings. The search for the Grail is an inner search, a metaphor parallel to the alchemical opus; and the stone is one's own self, which, according to alchemy, cannot be painlessly found in beautiful places, but only in the dung-heap of the prima materia.

THE STAGES OF THE ALCHEMICAL OPUS

Now I would like to spend some time on the different stages of the alchemical process, because these link up directly with astrological symbolism and are particularly helpful when we consider the deeper meaning of transits and progressions across a person's natal chart. I should stress first of all that the alchemical stages, although I have to talk about them in some sort of order, do not necessarily follow in that order either in the literature or in life. These stages are cyclical as well as individual in pattern; we keep repeating them on different levels throughout life. Different people do things in different ways. In other words, the order of any individual's inner process varies individually. But the stages themselves are archetypal; they are basic life experiences through which it seems we all must pass, and which, if they are engaged upon with open eyes and heart, move steadily although apparently circuitously toward the goal of the opus. However, because we are all different, some of us appear to pass through particular stages more frequently, or find them more relevant, depending upon the emphasis of the birth chart.

CALCINATIO

The first of these stages which I will discuss is called the *calcinatio*, and it is a process of burning. This stage is steeped in the symbolism of fire. The idea is that the alchemist heated the prima materia until the liquid evaporated from it, and it was reduced to ash. I think this very vivid symbol needs little explanation. The imagery around the calcinatio almost always involves the frustration of desire, until the emotions exhaust themselves and the old King or savage animal is burned down to the bare essence. Fire cleanses away dross, and here the dross is liquid—water, the image of longing for union. The animals connected with the calcinatio are usually the wolf and the lion. these have been from time immemorial animals connected with the passions, with hunger and pride and arrogance and desire. In their natural state, these animals are not evil; but they wreak havoc and destruction because they are wild and savage and destroy whatever gets in their way. The passions in their natural state are not considered evil or devilish in alchemy; but they are dangerous, and need to be transformed into the gold which was always potentially contained within them. The lion in Egyptian myth is connected with the goddess Sekhmet, one of the vengeful "Eyes of Ra" who embodies the burning heat of the desert sun. The lion personifies the lordly passions, the "I want"; it is the greedy imperious infant who is the centre of the universe, wielding absolute power and destroying what it cannot have. And the wolf, who is one of the animals of Kybele, the voracious mother-goddess of Asia Minor, is perpetually hungry.

Audience: What is the significance of the lion's paws being cut off?

Liz: I think one way of looking at it is that it is an image of deliberate frustration. The lion cannot claw at anything, or pursue its prey, if it has no front paws. It is a symbol of the curtailment of the passions by an act of conscious volition. This frustration of desire is not based upon conventional moral grounds; one does not shake one's finger at the lion and say, "Naughty, naughty." Here frustration is a painful but compassionate contribution to a process which is trying to unfold. There seems to be a popular feeling in our post-Victorian era that desire ought not to be frustrated in any way; this is our modern backlash to the old ethic that desire should be repressed on moral grounds because it is greedy, selfish, and morally reprehensible. The backlash is understandable and probably very necessary in the light of centuries of repression. But what is reflected in the calcinatio is not repression or moral condemnation; it is a voluntary sacrifice of something so that something else can emerge. The morality in it is very subtle, and without judgment. Alchemy offers an extremely sophisticated model here, which was never taken up by the collective of the time and which unfortunately has not yet been taken up by our time either.

One of the most characteristic areas of life in which the stage of the calcinatio occurs is the area of frustrated love. This experience burns away a great deal of dross, if it is entered into with some consciousness. Normally if a person cannot have the object of his or her desire, there is great anger, and the other person or some outer circumstance is blamed; or there is a kind of sodden self-pity and self-denigration. But if the response to such a situation contains some recognition of its potential creativity, and the person can experience and contain the frustration and rage without blame falling on either the beloved or oneself until something begins to transform from within, then this kind of experience can become one of the greatest shapers of a solid sense of personal identity. The individual who has never experienced such frustration, or who has experienced it but has interpreted it solely as one's own or someone else's fault, can never grow beyond the lion and the wolf—there is a basic uncompromising greed and destructiveness which festers in the unconscious, often quite out of reach of the person's awareness. This in turn can be triggered by all kinds of external situations, to the horror of the individual involved; or else he or she may instinctively avoid deep involvement with others for fear of what will happen if the lion or the wolf should be unleashed.

The only alternative to this state of affairs, which is a pretty typical one, is for the wolf or lion to be burned in the fire, or have its paws amputated. The wolf, as well as being one of the animals associated with the mother-goddess, is also connected with Mars. In Roman myth, the twins who founded the city of Rome, Romulus and Remus, were the children of the war-god Mars, and they were suckled by a wolf. Mars represents the desire-nature, and it is interesting that Jung focusses on this Martial aspect of the alchemical process. He writes about Mars being the hot, male, sulphurous principle in the prima materia, which is also portrayed as the lion. The lion is an early, primitive form of the renewed King, the alchemical gold. In other words, the primitive passions contain the potential for kingship, for true individuality; but they must be burned first, so that they are transmuted. These metaphors are extremely useful when we consider Mars in the birth horoscope, and even more useful when we examine progressions and important transits involving Mars. Very often dreams will arise during such a period which reflect the problem of frustrated desire. Any trigger to Mars is a triggering of the desire-nature, and many people protect themselves from the heat of the passions for much of their lives, until such a trigger finally catches up with them. So movements involving Mars herald an important stage of the process of development. The detached, uninvolved individual who avoids commitment and considers raw passion beneath him or her often goes through experiences which reflect the alchemical calcinatio during strong transits and progressions of Mars. There is always a risk with the experience of passion, because the object might refuse the offer or elude possession; and even if one gets one's desire, the reality is almost always somehow short of the fantasy. So the element of frustration is somehow built into the experience of passion. You can see why this calcinatio stage of the alchemical opus is particularly important for the individual with a "problem" Mars—Mars in the signs of its detriment, or in difficult aspect to repressive planets such as Saturn, or deflecting planets such as Neptune and Venus. The astrological timing which is reflected by progressions and transits involving Mars may provide an opportunity for the primitive, infantile passions to be experienced for the first time; and such an experience, according to the symbolism of alchemy, is a necessary component in the opus. Without it, there is no possibility of the gold.

Another planet which I associate with the calcinatio is Pluto. Where Mars is concerned with individual desire, Pluto is a more blindly instinctual drive; it links us not only with other human beings, but with the kingdom of the beasts as well. Pluto reflects passion, but it is the very archaic instinct of all organisms to survive and reproduce. This can be especially disturbing to the individual who has dissociated from the drives of the body, and considers himself or herself to have transcended such things. Images of burning also seem to be bound up with strong movements of Pluto in the chart, and often there is a combination of Mars and Pluto at work during such periods. I should caution you, by the way, not to be too rigid in applying these alchemical symbols to the chart. The idea is not to look in the ephemeris, notice that transiting Mars will conjunct your Moon on Thursday, and wait for a calcinatio. The alchemical images are very potent amplifications to help us understand the real depth of an astrological placement.

For example, one of the birth configurations which I associate with the alchemical calcinatio is the conjunction of Mars, Saturn, and Pluto which occurred in 1948. A great many people have this natal configuration. There is something about the feeling of it – particularly because it falls in a fiery sign – which seems to point to the archetypal issue of transforming primitive passions into individual creative expression, and which suggests that at some point in life the individual with this configuration may be required to undergo a very difficult and very formative experience of intense frustration and denial of someone or something passionately desired. Transiting Pluto, which is now in Scorpio, will be coming up to square this conjunction in the charts of people born around 1948, and this piece of astrological timing might reflect the period in life when the calcinatio process will be most emphasised. Not everyone goes through such a process as his or her chief method of development. It is peculiarly emphasised in some lives and not so much in others, although sooner or later we all experience it in one form or another. The alchemical imagery helps us to understand that however frustrating the experiences might be which occur in relation to such a passage, they are part of an intelligent process which aims toward a goal of individuality. They are not just a random assortment of painful events.

A birth chart in which fire predominates also suggests that the issues of the calcinatio—powerful desires, arrogance, and the inevitable frustration of passion which can potentially yield enormous inner integrity and self-confidence—will come up again and again during life. Some fiery people fly away from this quality of passion which is innate in them, and try to clamber up into the intellectual and spiritual realms to avoid the burning. Powerful Saturn transits and progressions hitting a fiery birth chart also suggest calcinatio experiences. There are physical manifestations of the calcinatio as well as emotional ones; sometimes particular kinds of illnesses, such as infections and fevers, seem bound up with the issue of frustrated desire. The images of alchemy are, as I have said, quite often violent, and the image of sealing a wolf in a container and then lighting a fire under it is not an attractive one. The wolf will of course become unbearably enraged. But there is a road through this fire which purges and transforms, and this is what the calcinatio process seeks to achieve.

The calcinatio is also associated with purgatory in alchemical texts, because it is a purification process which burns away sins. Fire, as well as burning and frustrating, also purifies and enlightens. Enlightenment, or a sense of the meaningfulness of experience, is one of the goals of the calcinatio, as well as the purity which springs from absolute self-honesty. What is left is indestructible, because one cannot be corrupted or got at from behind through self-delusion. That is another potential of this stage of the opus, and it is a potential which is peculiar to the fire signs and also to the Martial and Plutonian personalities. Fire signs are by nature initially unreflective, and the calcinatio forces a kind of introversion which results in a capacity to look beneath and within. Once again the dream imagery is very typical: dreams of burning houses, where an old self-image or set of attitudes is destroyed in the conflagration.

Now are there any questions about the calcinatio? I should stress again that this is not necessarily the first stage of the opus. I have simply mentioned it first. But for many people it is the experience which sets people on the way toward inner development.

Passion is a great catalyst, perhaps the greatest we have, and frustration of passion is the essence of this stage of the opus.

Audience: If a person goes through this kind of experience, does it repeat? I mean, if I have the Mars-Saturn-Pluto configuration you mentioned, will I have to go through this kind of thing every time a transit hits it?

Liz: I think these alchemical processes are cyclical, but they are spiral rather than circular. Each time they come back around, a little bit more of the stone is formed; and once there is even a tiny piece of it, one does not suffer in the same way. Perhaps one does not have to suffer at all, in the sense that we usually think of it, because there is a conscious cooperation with what is happening, and it feels like more of a choice. But yes, I think we meet the same characters in our individual myths, and undergo the same characteristic experiences which are our greatest spurs to growth. What might always get me moving might not affect you strongly at all, and vice versa. Just as we meet ourselves in certain kinds of external experiences, we also meet ourselves in the developmental processes which make us deepen and expand.

Audience: What happens if this burning actually makes you physically ill?

Liz: It sometimes does. Physical illness, as I said earlier, is often an aspect of this stage of the work. Physical symptoms of various kinds are a common occurrence in analysis, and they are part of the process. I mentioned fevers earlier, and I suspect that glandular fever, that perennial companion of the student about to take his or her examinations, is a particularly vivid example. The student who is faced with examinations is right on the threshold of adulthood with all its frightening new responsibilities, and there is often deep anger and ambivalence about such a rite of passage, particularly if there is still hunger for a parental love which was not forthcoming earlier in life. I suspect that the psychic burning which hides beneath glandular fever may often be a powerful desire to regress, to go back home again to the parental womb, and a great rage because life and the inevitable passage of time make this impossible. As far as what one can do about it, perhaps very little—except strive to become more conscious of the ambivalence and conflict expressing as a physical symptom. But being able to connect with the internal conflict may help more than one might suspect, and may make it unnecessary for the body to carry the whole burden.

The period of life when glandular fever so commonly occurs is around the time of the buildup of transiting Saturn approaching the second square to its own place. I think this reflects a terrific collision between the need to move out into life and the longing to go home again, to remain merged with the world of childhood and the parental womb. Some people make that passage without much trouble. But others fight violently against the new life. Often the person in such a conflict will sabotage his or her work, and will fail the examinations. But any refusal to part from the realm of the mother is doomed to frustration, because we cannot turn back the chronological or the psychological clock. Sooner or later it catches up with us. The wolf is greedy for the breast, and for the constant assuagement of hunger without interruption. If you want to view this through Freudian eyes, it is the original Oedipal passion, which is by its nature regressive. It longs for satiation, rather than relationship.

The stage of the calcinatio is often a factor in psychotherapy, but it is, in my view, not properly dealt with in many more superficial therapeutic approaches. It is in the transference, and the feelings of the patient (or client if you prefer) toward the psychotherapist, that the wolf or lion appears. The different schools of analysis address this issue in great depth, but many of the humanistic approaches do not. It is the patient's passionate, ambivalent, and often all-consuming obsession with the psychotherapist that provides the ground for the calcinatio, and the therapeutic structure is the alembic which contains it. This situation is very common and often very necessary, and needs to be handled with respect and honesty, because it most frequently happens to a person who has never allowed himself or herself to feel intensely about anyone since childhood. Because there may be a deep, albeit unconscious, sense of safety with the psychotherapist, the person can begin to get in touch with these ambivalent feelings of love, hate, aggression, and longing again through the transference. This situation is not limited to one sex or the other, either; it crosses sexes quite readily, because it is a primal passion which does not differentiate. Often a tremendously powerful emotional attachment will develop, with many fantasies which at first seem embarrassing and humiliating, but which are extremely important and worthy of exploration. Naturally there is also rage and frustration, because the psychotherapist must sooner or later draw boundaries of one kind or another. This element of passion and deprivation is a feature of a great deal of therapeutic work, and many psychotherapists are afraid of it and do not allow their patients to express or acknowledge these feelings. But if they do spontaneously arise — which is not always the case — then they can be seen as an important and necessary part of the process, because if both therapist and patient can stay in the middle of the burning-ground and see it through, the alchemical transformation takes place. If a person is too fearful of undergoing this process in ordinary life, then he or she may save it for the psychotherapist, who can hopefully be trusted to behave in a fashion different enough from the original rejecting parent to allow the patient to develop a new attitude.

Audience: I would like to ask about a woman whom I am currently counselling. She is the sort of person who burns, but none of it ever comes out. She implodes rather than explodes. She has had one operation for a malignant tumour, and now she seems to have developed a second tumour. I feel that somehow she must get these emotions out in her therapy.

Liz: How often do you see her?

Audience: Once a week.

Liz: I suspect that you may need to see her more frequently. She will probably need to become very angry with you, and the container, the alembic, is probably not strong enough with a once-weekly visit. Although some of you might find this a harsh comment, I feel that the conflict and rage hidden in cancerous growths are often quite murderous. It is possible that she has been displaying indications of her anger toward you in covert ways, but you might need to draw them out onto yourself rather than letting them slip by. If you feel equipped to do this, then I should think you will recognise when a gauntlet has been unconsciously dropped. But if you don't feel equipped to handle great anger in a client, then you should refer her into deeper psychotherapy. Do you think you might be colluding with her to keep her anger quiet?

Audience: I suspect so. Up to this point our relationship has been quite nice, and that is partly my doing.

Liz: This is probably also what her parents did, so any possibility of bringing that fire into the consulting room should be encouraged — provided you feel you can handle it. If it is coming out in cancerous lumps, then I suspect, as I said, that it is a very hot fire, and it will be very destructive when it comes out into the open.

Audience: She is also seeing a sex therapist about specific problems, but I get the impression that he is also keeping it very nice.

Liz: It isn't easy to contain another person's destructiveness, to provide a safe alembic, unless one has faced one's own. It can be quite terrifying, and one should not underestimate the client's desire to wound and destroy. There may be quite a lot that you need to think about, not only in relation to your client, but in relation to yourself. But I think that if some of this anger was able to come out in the safe container of the therapeutic relationship, the wolf would transform. In your client, the wolf has turned against the body, and is beginning to devour it from within. There is no shame in not wishing to work with this level of anger in a client; it does not make you a bad counsellor. But I think one needs to be equipped to handle a very intense calcinatio in the therapeutic situation. Otherwise it is better to pass the person on to someone who is trained to contain such emotions. Unconscious anger in a client, whether therapeutic or astrological, is always unpleasant. An astrological consultation is perhaps not the appropriate place for it to be unleashed. But it must be unleashed somewhere, for otherwise the person is caught with a part of himself or herself trapped in a perpetual burning without release.

In alchemy, the calcinatio eventually burns itself out. But that is with the cooperation of the alchemist. One doesn't throw water on it by trying to offer motherly tea and sympathy, or blow it out with airy intellectualisations, or bury it under a lorry-load of practical advice. One waits for it to burn everything that can be burned, and when there is nothing left to burn, then it burns itself out. I think that it is only when the fire is trapped in the unconscious that it just goes on burning, and begins to break out in the body. But people's reasons for fearing the wolf are often perfectly legitimate. The wolf is dangerous.

Audience: If my client doesn't face the wolf, she will die.

Liz: Yes, the wolf will destroy her. But you can see the great difficulty of facing such a primitive destructive force in oneself, and then containing it while it burns with frustration until it has been consumed. The ego must first be strong enough to stand its ground, and sometimes years of preliminary therapeutic work are necessary before the wolf can safely be confronted without the entire personality being shattered in the conflagration. Sometimes the calcinatio must burn itself out in a psychotic breakdown, and if this is sensitively contained then it can herald a new beginning. Freud was once asked what qualities he recommended in a person undergoing deep analysis, and he replied: "Courage, courage, and courage." Freud and Klein were particularly concerned with the fires of the calcinatio, and the same challenges face the analyst as well as the patient. Your client is afraid the wolf will destroy her; you are afraid it will destroy you. But if you look closely at this wolf, it is the primal form of the capacity for individual relationship. This is horribly paradoxical, but these malignant tumours are in some strange way an inversion, or perversion, of passions which perhaps reflect your client's innate capacity to love another person deeply.

Audience: Do you think guided imagery exercises might help?

Liz: I don't know. There is another alchemical stage, which is called the *sublimatio*, which is concerned with this kind of activity, and which I will talk about later. But I am not sure whether a contrived attempt to push such primitive feelings up onto the imaginative level is always very helpful. If this occurs spontaneously, as it often does in dreams, then that is the way the psyche is trying to go. But to try to get someone to contrive images may be a means of circumventing the heat. Once your client begins to feel her own feelings, then the process of symbolisation, the sublimatio, becomes very important. But she is not there yet. She does not experience her feelings; her body has lumps instead. The capacity for genuine spontaneous visualisation is something which emerges when there is already some little chunk of the individual stone released from the chaos of the prima materia. Otherwise it is artificial, to please the therapist. If your client were able to say, "I feel dirty and disgusting and rejected and angry," then one can begin to encourage images for those feelings. But if she can say nothing except, "I have an illness and it has nothing to do with me," and you try to get her to visualise images, then you will get an intellectualisation. The feelings are not in it. Above all, the calcinatio deals with powerful feelings. You need to try to resist the urge to rescue her from her burning. She needs to feel her burning, rather than making safe tracks around it. I suspect it would not be helpful to say to your client, "Try to get an image of the cancer." In a way, that is breaking the alembic, or more accurately, turning the heat off. Too much heat all at once might be unbearable; but it is possible to draw it out into the open in manageable puffs, through her feelings toward you.

SOLUTIO

Now I would like to move on to the second of the four alchemical stages, which is called the *solutio*. This stage does not necessarily follow the calcinatio. It may come before it, or some time after it, with another stage in between. Like the calcinatio, the solutio, which simply means dissolving, results in a death and a transformation. But here we are dealing with the element of water rather than fire. Astrologically, I would associate the alchemical imagery of the solutio with Neptune, just as I associate the imagery of the calcinatio with Mars and Pluto. In the opus, the prima materia is put into the alembic and dissolved in water. The prima materia then breaks down and disintegrates. It loses its defined shape and properties, and becomes fluid, or part of a fluid mixture. One way of looking at this psychologically is that the solutio is an experience of the boundaries of the ego breaking down. It is also an experience of surrender. Now, initially this does not sound nearly as terrifying as the calcinatio with its horrible images of de-pawed lions and charred wolves. And often the solutio is not at all an agonising experience. But for many people it is, particularly those who have defined their boundaries very sharply and fear the loss of control. The very Saturnian or earthy individual often fears the solutio, and so, paradoxically, does the Martial one, because of the loss of one's autonomy.

The stage of the solutio will probably be a familiar experience to many of you. One's sense of boundaries begins to dissolve, and there is sometimes a feeling of missing a layer of psychic skin. One is suddenly very vulnerable and permeable, and feelings come up which threaten to swamp the rational ego. There are characteristic dream motifs which echo this stage of the opus, and they almost always contain the imagery of water. The boiler has burst and the basement has flooded; a tidal wave is rising up to flood the shore; one is in a frail boat on a turbulent sea; and so on. The advent of the deluge is a mythic theme which corresponds to the alchemical image of the solutio, and which appears frequently in dreams when there is a lot of Neptune about because of transits or progressions. Like the calcinatio, the solutio is often experienced through love. But it is a very different kind of experience. The burning passion which calcinates does not belong to the realm of water. Love in the solutio is expressed as surrender and submission, the losing of oneself in the identity of the beloved. One becomes powerless, devoid of a self, fused with the other. In a sense, one's individual identity is eroded. Feelings of passivity and fatalism often accompany the solutio. One's soul has flowed out of oneself and has merged with someone or something else. It is very uroboric. Do you know this word? The uroboros is a mythic image of the origin of life—the cosmic serpent eating its tail which forms the world-egg out of which all manifestation comes. It is also an image of the womb, as well as of paradise. Dwelling within the uroboros means dwelling in the original Garden of Eden before the fall. It is a lovely, sweet, blissful place, a return to the source of life. There is no separation and no separateness. This solutio experience is also a powerful component in many religious or mystical states. The "oceanic" peak experience, which encompasses a feeling of being at one with the whole of life, is another way of expressing the imagery of the solutio. Romantic love and mystical union are here mixed and indistinguishable. For many people, this stage of the opus is the most profound and transformative experience of their lives. This is particularly the case with the individual who is very defended behind rather rigid boundaries—as I mentioned before, the Saturnian person, or the highly intellectual temperament who comes strongly under Mercury and Uranus. And it is also very alien and transformative for the Martial nature who is accustomed to having his or her own way in all things. The imaginal world, the ocean of the collective unconscious, floods the boundaries of the ego.

But the solutio is not always pleasant, or it may be beautiful at first and then increasingly anxiety-ridden, because of the sense that the ground has dissolved under one's feet. One is being subjected to forces beyond one's control or rational understanding. I think there is often considerable fear accompanying this stage of the opus. Edinger, in his article on the solutio, remarks that for the individual whose ego is weak to begin with—in other words, the person who has never really properly formed as an independent personality, but who still lives in the magical uroboric embrace of the mother—the solutio is experienced as a wonderful thing, because one does not have to struggle any longer. It is a kind of death-wish, a return to unconsciousness and sleep and the waters of the womb. There are certain kinds of psychotic states, such as some forms of autism, where there seems to be a perpetual solutio, and no ego emerges. The drug addict and the alcoholic also seek a perpetual solutio from which they do not ever have to emerge. The experience of oneness with another, which forms part of "falling in love," is also felt as a wonderful thing, at first. The feelings at the beginning of a love affair can sometimes have a powerfully mystical quality. One has known the person in some other incarnation, there is no conflict, it is like two hearts beating together. And so on. There is the fantasy that the two of you are really one person. But this has little to do with relationship. It is an experience of the unconscious flooding the ego, bringing with it the feeling of containment within the mystical uroboros.

One of the most powerful alchemical images of the solutio is the image of drowning. This appears in many alchemical engravings. The old King, who is the prima materia, the Saturnian base substance, is in need of regeneration and transformation, and he is portrayed drowning in the sea. He waves his arms wildly from the water, calling for help. But the alchemist stands on the bank and lets him drown. This is a very suggestive image, because the presence of the alchemist reflects that act of conscious participation in the process which seems such a necessary part of the opus. It is not enough simply to drown; there must be something which can reflect on the drowning, feeling it yet not identifying with it. The old entrenched attitudes toward life, rigid and stagnant, must be dissolved in the sea. The solutio can be a very fear-ridden experience, and often, in psychotherapy, phobias arise, because it seems as though the unconscious is seeping up through the floorboards and threatening from all sides. One fears the dark, one gets agoraphobic, one gets claustrophobic, one fears spiders, one fears aeroplanes. The solutio is very welcome to those who do not wish to be born. But it is questionable whether anything can come of a permanent solutio, any more than anything can come of a permanent calcinatio. It is a stage which moves toward a goal. For those who have a strong ego, the solutio is a frightening journey, fraught with anxiety although perhaps also bittersweet and deeply moving.

Audience: I gather that the earth signs don't like this stage.

Liz: No, they don't. The water signs are more comfortable with it, except for Scorpio, which partly welcomes it and partly fights like mad against it. But I think the individual who has a strong Neptune, particularly if it forms strong aspects to the Sun or Moon or Venus, will find the solutio a dominant theme in life. One keeps meeting it over and over again. There is also a lunar quality to the solutio, rather like the imagery of the card of the Moon in the Tarot deck—a moonlit fog of confusion through which one can travel only by instinct, and not by clear sight or maps. But the symbolism of water has always been associated in myth not only with dissolving and drowning, but with resurrection and new birth. One is baptised in water and one's sins are cleansed. The deluge comes and all the evil on earth is swept away, and the human race can begin again. Water cleanses, just as fire does, merging the individual with the collective unconscious and then gently abandoning him or her on the shore, newly born and ready to start a fresh life. The purpose of the solutio is to release new life, cleansed of the corruption and cynicism of the old. This is the purpose of all the alchemical deaths; they lead to births. The solutio represents death by drowning. When the prima materia eventually coalesces again, it has been cleansed of its impurities, and the gold can be seen.

So the solutio leads to a kind of death, just as the calcinatio does. There is often a depression waiting for the individual who has drowned in the experience of mystical union or erotic fascination. The old self has dissolved, but there is not yet anything new to replace it. One waits in the womb of the unconscious, with only moonlight to illuminate the landscape. I would suggest, for those of you who are particularly concerned with this kind of Neptunian journey, that you read Jung's *Psychology of the Transference*.[3] This essay addresses the dilemma of the transference in analysis, but it is also applicable to all deep and transformative human relationships. Jung used an alchemical text, the *Rosarium*, and used the illustrations in this text to amplify the experiences of both analyst and patient. It is a text which focusses primarily on the solutio as the medium of transformation. There is no calcinatio in *the Rosarium*. The first alchemical picture portrays a fountain – the Mercurial fountain of the unconscious, the prima materia which is the beginning of the work. This picture announces the entire alchemical opus to be under the governance of Mercurius in the form of water. In the next picture, the King and Queen, the protagonists in the opus, are shown, fully dressed and confronting each other formally. But they are shaking hands with their left hands. There is already a collusion on an unconscious level: something is going to happen. The King and Queen are sulphur and salt, the male and female aspects of the primal substance. They might be seen psychologically as analyst and patient, or two lovers, or the two aspects of oneself – conscious and unconscious. They are all of

---

[3]C.G. Jung, "The Psychology of Transference," in *The Practice of Psychotherapy*. Vol. 16. *The Collected Works* (Princeton, NJ: Bollingen Series, No. 20, Princeton University Press, 1966; and London: Routledge & Kegan Paul, 1954).

these. In the next picture, the King and Queen are naked. Now the erotic fascination has begun, and the formal persona has been stripped away. It is interesting to contemplate, when you reflect on the beginning of any important relationship, just when that left-handed handshake occurred. When did it happen? When one of you said, "Would you like to have a coffee later?" At what point do two people secretly, unconsciously know that they are going to have a profound effect on each other's lives? At what point does the real analysis begin?

Sometimes one can see these things heralded in dreams, and often there is the imagery of water, the Mercurial fountain or the flooded basement or the tidal wave coming. Something has started to happen, although both people may heatedly deny it. The patient may say to the analyst, "Oh, this isn't working, nothing is going on, I want to stop coming." But the solutio has begun, and the person is frightened, and the dreams reflect the advent of the deluge. That is why he or she wants to leave so quickly. In the next alchemical picture of the *Rosarium*, the King and Queen are sitting naked in a bath. Here is one of the classic images of the solutio. The bath is like an alembic, or a womb. The royal pair are now in a state of blissful oneness. "I feel as though I've known you all my life." In the next picture, the King and Queen are copulating under the water. Alchemical images don't mess about. The royal pair are now in the coniunctio, the state of union. But it is an underwater union. It is a merging of personalities, which is happening in the unconscious, rather than a conscious relationship between two separate individuals. And in the next picture, the King and Queen have fused into a hermaphrodite which lies dead on a slab. They have died. This is the depression I mentioned, which follows the drowning. In the magical fusion of psyches, the individual consciousness has been snuffed out, and the person goes into a depression because he or she is not a separate person any more. The sense of independent identity has gone away, and with it the capacity for choice and action.

Often in therapeutic work there is a period where the patient feels everything is now fine, the therapist is wonderful and perfect and the problem is solved. But what has really occurred is a kind of fantasy where he or she has returned to the welcoming womb, and the therapist will do all the work, and there will be no conflict. Yet this stage of bliss—it is sometimes called a "flight into health"—is important, because it is a dissolving of the defences, and it allows the person to become vulnerable. When the depression sets in afterward, there is a memory of something beautiful that has been shared, and that is often strong enough to sustain the person through the next stage. Sometimes a person will try to leave psychotherapy when the solutio begins, because of the anxiety. Sometimes the person is seduced by the solutio, because it can be an experience of enchantment, and he or she becomes extremely angry when the water in the bath starts to grow cold. Bug there is always a death, and it is important, just as the burning is important with the calcinatio. If one can sustain the depression which lies at the bottom of the bath, after the ecstatic phase of the union has passed, then one forms a little bit of the stone. The bliss of total union is not the object of the alchemical opus. It is the lapis, the stone, the sense of self. There is no such thing as total union with another person, except in the womb, from which one is eventually expelled by Nature, if not by one's mother's physician.

Audience: I can relate this to my experience of being in therapy. At first I thought it was wonderful. But then I reached a point where I began to find things wrong with my therapist, and then I wanted to leave. But I managed to stick it through, and all sorts of stuff started to leak out.

Liz: You deserve credit for sticking it through. It is harder than it seems. You can see what I am getting at from your own experience. Very often there is a wild fantasy about the therapist, who can initially appear as a composite of the Great Good Mother, the Great Good Father, Christ, Dionysos, and one's future husband or wife all rolled into one. The dreams are all very numinous, and one feels healed. Then one day the therapist makes a mistake of some kind, or is a little distant, or has a cold, or one discovers that there is a partner in the house, or one simply changes in one's feelings. Then the therapist is not the uroboros any more. He or she is incompetent, and a fraud, and has no feelings, and is charging too much, and could never possibly help you. That is when something creative can really start to happen.

Audience: There is something I can't seem to work out. Does each person go through one of these stages as a major life experience, or do we go through all four to a greater or lesser extent? And can they overlap?

Liz: I think that, as with all symbolic maps, one has to be loose and flexible with this one. The alchemical stages describe, in pictorial imagery, archetypal stages or processes of psychological development. They are very powerful and truthful, because they not only portray the emotional quality of that process; they also portray an inherent meaning, as part of a larger overall process. Since we all have all four elements somewhere in us, albeit in differing proportions and differing degrees of consciousness, some taste of all the stages probably awaits us all. We experience the transits of every planet, and sooner or later face all the essential archetypal experiences which life can offer the human being. But different people, I think, tend to develop more along one line than another. This is the statement of the birth chart, rather than of the transits or progressions. Some dimensions of the solutio experience – the dissolving of boundaries, the merging with another – are likely to come the way of anybody who has a strong transit of Neptune, and everyone gets this kind of transit at some point in life. But the person in whose birth chart Neptune is strong – where it aspects the luminaries, or where the 12th house is full, or where there are dominant placements in Pisces – may be predisposed toward a development pattern which repeats this experience of dissolving and merging and disillusionment, in both positive and negative forms. Is that a little clearer?

Audience: Yes.

Liz: As far as your second question is concerned, I think these stages do overlap. Once again, they are meant as symbolic portrayals, rather than as rigid structures which move from A to B to C. One can be inundated with water and consumed by fire at the same time; it is often the case that a Neptune transit will activate a natal Sun-Mars conjunction, or Pluto will transit something at the same time that transiting Neptune aspects something else in the chart. We never get only one planetary movement. There is an

entire dance occurring at any point in time over any birth chart. Or
one can react from a fiery natal chart to a strong watery transit.
Different people also react differently to the different alchemical
stages, with comprehension or fear or both. A watery temperament will go along with the solutio process, because there is a deep
understanding of its necessity and its healing power. But that same
watery person will react with panic and resistance to the stage
which is called *coagulatio*, which I will deal with a little later, or to
the *sublimatio*. Fire can usually make sense of the burning of the
calcinatio, because there is an innate understanding of this kind of
strenuous conflagration. Fire is the element of grand drama, and
even though one suffers, there is meaning and passion in it. But
the fiery nature hates the stage of the coagulatio, which is earthy.
The earthy signs appreciate this latter stage, because it is in their
nature to give it value. But they fear the solutio, when all those nice
clear boundaries that earth signs love so much begin to disintegrate
into chaos. If a person has a configuration such as a T-cross involving Neptune, then the solutio is a symbol of a repeating experience
which is profoundly important and likely to occur many times in
life on different levels.

Audience: You described the solutio as a blissful experience for
some people. But it seems to me that it is very frightening. Drowning is a horrible image.

Liz: I am interested in Edinger's comment that the individual with a
weak ego tends to long for the solutio as a means of escaping life. I
think that all the alchemical stages imply a kind of death, a sacrifice
of old attitudes and a relinquishing of some cherished ego viewpoint. The strong ego meets all the stages with resistance. But
there is an inevitability in the process, so that the resistance is not
only futile. It is also necessary, because the creative release of
energy emerges out of the battle. Can you understand this? We
have to fight, but at the same time we also have to understand that
the fight will have an inevitable outcome. The portrayal of the King
drowning is indeed a horrible image. In the picture, the alchemist
has turned his back on the King. There is enormous protest within
many people at such an experience, and rightly so, because the ego
has had to work hard for its little patch of ground, and this is no

mean achievement. But for the person who has not been able to separate from the fantasy of the uroboric mother, there is a kind of death-wish inside, a longing to give up the struggle and return to a state of sleep. Then the solutio seems wonderful. This is the psychology of the heroin addict, and also, to a lesser extent, of the falling-in-love addict. If one tries to work with an addict or an alcoholic, one runs up against a powerful death-wish, a longing for sleep, which is often stronger than the fragile ego's impetus to live. The person says he or she wants to get better, but this voice is only one part of the psyche, and the part that does not wish to leave the bath sits there and is determined to defeat any efforts at help or transformation.

There is also the opposite extreme, where the ego is so defencive and crystallised that the experience is shut out altogether. I think this is when these alchemical stages tend to break out in the body. They have nowhere else to go. Or they appear as "fated" events in the world outside, over which we have absolutely no control. The solutio contains feelings of helplessness and impotence and dependency. It is an infantile stage, where the baby is not yet separate from the mother. The mother is, to use the trade jargon, not yet an internalised object. There is no sense of having the capacity to look after oneself. In therapeutic situations as well as in relationships, this dependency and weakness can be a frightening and shameful thing. Some people kick furiously against this kind of dependency. The humiliation of this stage is reflected in the alchemical picture, which shows the proud King flopping about on his belly with his crown askew, splashing water everywhere as he drowns. The royal personage who is accustomed to absolute control is suddenly at the mercy of the primordial element of water, the collective unconscious; and no one comes to help him. Of course one fights this experience, and if there is a difficult Neptune in the birth chart, the fight begins in childhood with the parental relationships. Often there is an early experience of having been dependent and having been humiliated or used through that dependency. So if the individual with this kind of inner constellation then discovers that, in adult life, another person has become desperately important, it can provoke great anger. People in whom Uranus is strong find this solutio stage a dreadful problem. They would much rather detach and conceptualise the experience. This takes me back to the question about guided imagery which was asked earlier. If you are a therapist with a strong airy bias, or a strong Uranus, then the client in a stage of infantile regression can be extremely uncomfortable. Probably you are reacting just as the person's parents did to the dependency of the baby. The guided imagery techniques then seem very handy; one can turn the person's dependency upon an image, so that one is not inundated. But I have grave questions about the real depth to which these kinds of techniques can go with a person who needs to experience such feelings in real life. It may be necessary for that individual to experience the dependency and anxiety in a relationship with an actual human being, not with an image of a constructed kind. It is uncomfortable for both therapist and client to sit in the gluey liquid of the solutio. Yet if one cannot do it when it is necessary, then perhaps one must look to one's own problem. Perhaps working on this level is not the route for every counsellor. But one ought to be aware of one's own issue with it. I think you can see the connections of this alchemical stage with the fear of deep water that many people suffer from. But along with the imagery of drowning, there is also the imagery of baptism, annointing, redemption, and resurrection. One offers oneself up to something higher and one is cleansed in the experience of fusion.

My purpose in discussing the imagery of these alchemical stages is that, like fairy tales, they throw light on the hidden meaning and intelligence contained within painful and apparently random or unfair experiences. Whether you use the language of alchemy with an astrological or therapeutic client depends totally on the client and the appropriateness of it at that moment. Probably it is unnecessary, because you can find your own words. But it is the deep implied purposefulness of these processes, and the way in which they link together and move into another stage, which tell us so much about the way in which the psyche works. They also can offer the astrologer a sense of continuity when interpreting transits and progressions. Each movement across the birth chart does not occur in isolation. It builds upon the results of the last one. There is a story line, of which each transit and progression forms a chapter or sub-chapter. Having a feeling for this continuity makes an enormous difference when you interpret transits and progressions. Without it, they seem piecemeal, and not connected to the person's life.

Audience: The solutio seems to require a state of total devotion and self-sacrifice. It's as though one needs this devotion to get the best out of it.

Liz: I think you are right. I am not sure whether "total self-sacrifice" is quite the right phrase, but certainly deep trust is required in that which cannot be seen or comprehended by rational consciousness. At some point it is necessary to submit to that which is greater, and submission does not mean humiliation; it implies a willingness. Religious teaching circles around this theme of accepting the will of God. For some people, the experience of the solutio occurs in the context of a mystical or peak state. For others it might happen through having a child. For many women the birth of a child is an experience of the solutio. One is in the hands of Nature, and one is connected with the archetypal world at that time. Often it is possible to love a child in a way which is difficult with an adult, because of the empathetic response to the child's helplessness. Childbirth can be a profoundly healing experience for some women. So the solutio can occur in many spheres of life experience. And it does require a voluntary act of relinquishment, to permit its most creative dimensions to unfold.

Audience: What about the timing? How long do these stages last?

Liz: That is an impossible question. The alchemical stages are descriptions of very basic psychological experiences. They can last for an hour or for twenty years. It depends upon the person, the situation, and the transit. A long transit of an outer planet can take anywhere up to four or five years, if one includes all the stations and retrogradations, and allows an orb of approach and departure. But a transit of Mars square Uranus can last for a day or two. The timing and the depth vary enormously. One can live in a kind of permanent solutio, and be kicked by the advent of other stages or processes. I know many of you would like a nice, practical, concrete map where one can say, "Aha, I am about to go through a calcinatio and it will last for two months, one week and two days."

I think it would be wrong to use the alchemical imagery in that way. It is meant for amplification, to open up one's imaginative response to experience. It is not meant to provide a train timetable.

Audience: I can relate to all you are saying about the solutio. I have had my progressed Sun conjuncting Neptune for the last two years, and I started off feeling terribly confused. Through a Piscean friend I was introduced to a spiritual organisation and a guru. I was fighting this, thinking it was a load of old rubbish, because of all the talk about surrendering the ego. It makes me very uncomfortable. I am an Aquarian. But from what you say, it might be important for me to make the effort.

Liz: Perhaps it is important. If you fear it so much, then there is perhaps something of value in the experience, even if it is a rite of passage rather than a permanent commitment. Whether one offers oneself to a guru, God, or a lover, the solutio requires a relinquishing of control. Sometimes one is disillusioned at the end of it. But that doesn't matter. The issue is not to find an external person who is the repository of all truth, but to find a source within which can be trusted. Very often the thing or person for which one has sacrificed one's control turns out not to be worth it, or one is not able to possess the desired object in the end. The solutio contains a sting in its tail. Reality may not change because one has let go. But the experience may cleanse ancient poisons that nothing else can release, and ultimately the water seeps away, leaving one with a deep knowledge of one's own resources. One discovers that one can love. That is much more healing than acquiring an object which one is driven to possess. There is exhaustion, disillusionment, and resignation lying in wait at the end of the solutio. But something has changed.

Audience: I would have thought that, because of the mystical experience, a person would not be disillusioned, but would be left with more than before.

Liz: In a sense, that is true. That is the thing that changes. But one must come back into the world again. There is often a depression which follows deep religious experiences, because of the inevitable comparison with what life was before and must be after. One has been transformed and cleansed by the experience, but then life begins to encroach again, and the truths are tested. This is the problem of earthing the vision through an ordinary mortal personality. One can see the same thing with post-natal depression. The experience has been transformative, but it also implies mortality, and there is a disillusionment after the glory. The physical challenges begin to appear, and so do feelings of ambivalence.

The aftermath of each of these alchemical stages is often imaged as a death, and this death is referred to as the *nigredo*. There is often a hiatus, a gap between the end of one stage and the beginning of the next and the discovery that a new journey has begun. There is a feeling that something irrevocable has been lost, and there is not yet a perspective which the ego can take toward that loss. Many creative people express this situation in the feeling of depression and emptiness that follows a burst of creative effort. When the work is finished, there is often a nasty feeling of letdown. However difficult the experience was, one was intensely alive. There is no one quite an unhappy as an actor who has finished the successful run of a play. Alchemical engravings often show this nigredo or death as somebody lying dead. The King and Queen, in the *Rosarium*, are shown lying dead on a slab, after the coniunctio or mating which has taken place under water. Catullus understood this when he wrote that after coitus, all creatures are melancholy.

Audience: There seems to be a great difference between the random encountering of these experiences in life, and the deliberate intentions of the alchemists.

Liz: The difference lies in the participation of consciousness. The alchemist could not force the stages of the work; he or she depended, according to the wording of the texts, on the will of God and the propitious configurations of the heavens. That is also what we depend upon, however we wish to define God. But the alchemists tried to cooperate with, and enhance, the process through conscious involvement, through suffering what the prima materia suffered. In this way, they believed that a little extra was added to the process of Nature, which made it more perfect. The process goes on with or without conscious agreement, just as we experience transits whether we know astrology or not. But it is the involvement of the individual that makes the difference between the natural evolutionary process and the priceless alchemical gold.

Audience: Could you say something about the history of alchemy?

Liz: Yes, perhaps we need a little interlude. We have covered two of the four stages.

AN HISTORICAL INTERLUDE

I find the history quite interesting, although I am not a scholar and therefore cannot give you much detail about the origins. In the West, alchemy seems to have emerged along with other magical techniques just after the dawn of the Christian era. It arose in Alexandria, which was a melting pot of old Egyptian magical rituals, new gnostic Christianity, and a strange mixture of pagan beliefs culled from Greek, Roman, and Arab philosophy. The Egyptians had their own alchemical tradition involving the embalming and resurrection of the dead, portrayed in the myth of Osiris; and they also had a tradition of magical talismans. One of the most ancient Egyptian beliefs involved the transmutation of inanimate substance through magical operations. That is the origin of all the modern Hammer House of Horror mummy stories — that the sacred scarabs, amulets, statues, and so on have been imbued with life through magical rituals and have an intense dislike of British tomb robbers. This tradition seems in early Christian times to have become mixed with Platonic philosophy. The alchemical traditions of Alexandria in the first centuries A.D. developed side by side with Neoplatonic and Hermetic philosophy. Astrology was part of that world-view, which postulated a unity of all things, and a law of signatures or correspondences by which the archetypal or "ideal" realm of God or the gods revealed itself through progressively denser material forms.

Alchemy went underground during the early medieval period, because of the opposition of the Church. Its philosophical tenets found their way into many creative works, such as Dante's *Divine*

Comedy, but it was primarily practised in secret. There was a period of temporary flowering during the 13th century, because during the time of the Crusades there was an influx of the Hermetic philosophy from the Middle East. The Arabs had continued to develop alchemy and its accompanying philosophical perspectives outside the jurisdiction of the Christian world. The Crusaders, in particular the Knights Templar, brought it back again into the West. But it was still unorthodox and still hunted; what happened to the Templars, thousands of whom were burnt at the stake for practising black magic, is a case in point. When the Renaissance erupted, it was directly linked to the resurgence of the Hermetic philosophy and its astrological and alchemical adjuncts. When Constantinople fell to the Turks in 1453, hundreds of magical and alchemical texts in Greek, which had been preserved by the Byzantine Empire during the period of the Roman Church's persecution in the West, found their way back to the capital cities of the West with the refugees fleeing Constantinople. In Italy, Cosimo de' Medici, the lord of Florence, was particularly interested in acquiring these texts, which he then had translated. The powerful philosophical and cultural movement which we call the Renaissance, and which included alchemy, resulted directly from Cosimo de' Medici's acquisition of these Neoplatonic and Hermetic texts, many of which came originally from Alexandria.

So all the forbidden magical texts came back into the West with the fall of Byzantium, and among them was a volume called the *Corpus Hermeticum*. This was written at some time during the first and second centuries A.D. and was full of alchemical recipes, magical procedures, instructions on the making of talismans, rules for the invocation of planetary deities, steps for the transmutation of metals, and so on. This work was believed at the time to have been written by a great and ancient sage called Hermes Trismegistus, Thrice-Greatest Hermes, who of course is the Mercurius of alchemical symbolism. This book, along with the works of Plato and the Neoplatonic philosophers, was translated into Latin, and suddenly everyone could read about these things. For a brief period, in Florence and other sympathetic city-states, alchemy and magic came out into the open. But the Church still did not like it, and persecuted where she could. There was a terrible backlash in the 16th century, although the alchemical movement was still very strong in Italy and particularly in Germany. The counter-Reformation erupted, linking together the heresy of alchemy with the heresy of Luther and Calvin, and important figures such as Giordano Bruno were burned at the stake. But in Germany, which was heavily Protestant, the Church did not have its Inquisition. It is out of the 16th and 17th centuries in Germany that the great alchemical writers like Paracelsus and Gerhard Dorn come. While the Church clamped down on Italy and France, alchemy continued to flower in Germany and also in England, where it had inevitably travelled and taken root during the reign of Queen Elizabeth.

Germany at this time—the end of the 16th and beginning of the 17th centuries—became the seat of tremendous conflict around these issues. Many of the independent German princes, who were Protestants, played about with alchemical experiments themselves, or patronised alchemists and astrologers. In Bohemia, the Habsburg Emperor Rudolph held an alchemical court. But the Catholic Habsburgs who ruled the old Holy Roman Empire were violently opposed to this kind of activity. The Rosicrucian movement, which was alchemical in nature, became very strong in Protestant Germany at the beginning of the 17th century, and in this movement one can see the beginnings of the scientific method combining with the old magical Hermetic world-view. This movement flowered, and came to England through John Dee and Robert Fludd, although it was already strong enough in England to find its way into the creative works of figures like Shakespeare. But eventually war erupted in Germany, which we now call the Thirty Years War, because a German Protestant Prince, Friedrich of the Palatinate, who was himself deeply involved in alchemy and Hermetic philosophy, tried to take the crown of Bohemia after the Emperor Rudolph had died. The Habsburg armies invaded Bohemia and the German Protestant states, and then all hell, literally, broke loose. The whole of Western Europe was drawn into this conflagration. It is also parallel to this time that the great witch hunts of the 17th century began, largely spawned by the Catholic reaction to the Rosicrucians and their offshoots. The Church succeeded in driving the movement underground again in Europe. But in England it survived despite the opposition of King James I and the period of Cromwell—for the Puritans, although not Catholic, were equally virulent toward these things. When the Restoration came, Charles II, who was himself deeply immersed in what was called the Perennial Philosophy, had the Royal Society founded, and the whole alchemical tradition landed in the lap of Isaac Newton. Newton's sources were astrological and alchemical, although there is some embarrassment about this in more scientific circles. By this time alchemy had become a philosophy, and had separated itself from chemistry. People had become more sophisticated about the nature of matter, and began to approach the subject symbolically. And then we enter the Age of Enlightenment, and hear no more of alchemy except in Freemasonry and other movements of this kind which began to arise in Europe in the 18th century. Now its inner content is back again disguised as analytic psychology.

There is a long-standing tradition of alchemy in China, which I know little about, and likewise in the Arab countries. But that is its potted history in the West.

Audience: What about reference books?

Liz: Marie-Louise von Franz has written an excellent book called *Alchemy*. Jung's three volumes, *Psychology and Alchemy, Alchemical Studies* and *Mysterium Coniunctionis* are more or less required reading. Frances Yates is also a good source, particularly her *Giordano Bruno and the Hermetic Tradition* and *The Rosicrucian Enlightenment*. For those of you who are interested in the connection between the Hermetic philosophy and Shakespeare, try Frances Yates' *Theatre of the World* and *Shakespeare's Last Plays*.[4]

Audience: What about the connection between alchemy and witchcraft?

Liz: They were not the same thing. No astrologer would like to be called a witch, and the alchemists didn't like it either. But as we all know, there is a certain stupidity demonstrated by those who have an emotional investment in battling with the nonrational or the heretical. Witchcraft is based on a very different tradition, although the use of talismans and magic spells is shared by both. There is no

---

[4]See Suggested Reading on page 361 for complete references.

focus on the Devil, or on power over others, in the alchemical tradition. The entire concept of evil is different. The witch hunts also involved a dreadful element of projection onto women, which seems to have been part of the ferocious sexual repression of the time. Anyone whom the neighbours didn't like was considered a witch; and this was usually an old woman or a particularly attractive one who lived alone. The psychology of the witch hunt is a very interesting issue, but it does not have much bearing on the alchemical tradition.

The influences of alchemical philosophy are wide-ranging and deep on Western culture. Goethe, for example, made Faust the protagonist of an alchemical journey. Goethe was profoundly influenced by the work of Paracelsus. Mesmer, who is considered the founder of modern psychology, is another recipient of the alchemical tradition, and he, too, was influenced by the work of Paracelsus and other alchemists. Most summaries of the history of psychology begin with Mesmer as though he were the first enlightened thinker in the field, who appeared out of nowhere. But he was deeply involved with astrology, alchemy, and the peculiar Hermetic Freemasonry of 18th century Vienna, in company with Mozart, who belonged to his Lodge. It is extraordinary how little we know about a subject which has influenced so many great thinkers and artists over the centuries.

COAGULATIO

Now we can go on to the alchemical stage called the *coagulatio*, which is exactly what it sounds like. When a liquid coagulates it begins to solidify. This stage of the process involves the transformation of a previously fluid or gaseous substance into a solid one — in other words, feelings and images and intuitions and ideas becoming concretised in actual life. The coagulatio is associated in alchemy with the planet Saturn, which is not surprising to us, and psychologically it represents a process of incarnation, of incorporeal things coming to birth in physical form. The images connected with the coagulatio are all related to this basic idea of incarnation. Food, money, and sensual pleasure are directly bound up with it. And, in company with all mythic images of incarnation, there are also associations with sin, carnality, heaviness, and a fall from grace or an expulsion from Paradise. Earthing anything involves both positive and negative emotional experiences. On the one hand, the coagulatio brings things into concrete manifestation, so it is concerned with integrating unconscious images and movements into the ego and into actual life. But the act of bringing potentials to birth in this way also implies limitation and even imprisonment, because the moment you concretise something, you have cut short its potentiality. It is no longer full of limitless possibilities, but has become an actuality, and has crystallised. Because the form is now definite, there is a sense of depression around the coagulatio. The physical world is Saturnian, the domain of Rex Mundi. It is full of limits, problems, failures, and separations, as well as the joy of seeing the products of one's efforts becoming real, tangible, and rewarding in ordinary daily life. The domain of the coagulatio is that of Adam and Eve after they have eaten the apple. There is an awareness of guilt, sin, isolation, and separation from the uroboric container of the universal spirit.

Where the solutio implies an experience of merging and loss of individual ego identity, the coagulatio implies an experience of separateness and the formation of ego identity. In terms of the stages of a child's development, this is the process by which the young child begins to recognise the ambivalence of his or her own feelings. Good and bad are no longer neatly split and half projected onto the mother; the ego has begun to form through a recognition of one's own badness as well as goodness. It is an acceptance of mortal limits, of basic humanity. This stage of the alchemical work is described as "heavy," and the motif of entombment or imprisonment runs through the texts. To the free-flying spirit, the world of matter is a tomb, and to the individual who is very airy or an air-fire combination, concrete life is frequently experienced in that way. The intrinsic badness of flesh, the corruption of the body, are themes which run through the alchemical texts in relation to the coagulatio; we are separated from God through the sinfulness of our mortal bodies, which contain the seeds of death. The desires of the body are seen as lustful and lecherous, goatish, and therefore alienated from God. Crucifixion is also a motif of the coagulatio, because the spirit suffers through being nailed to the cross of material incarnation. This crucifixion is about accepting one's mortal fate, one's burdens, responsibility for one's own life.

The stage of the coagulatio may follow after the solutio or the calcinatio. Then it is the gradual integration, in actual life, of the experiences and insights and changes acquired through the painful waters or fires of the previous stage. You can see how naturally this stage follows on the heels of that dissolving of boundaries and inundation by the unconscious which the solutio describes. The transcendent love affair, the mystical initiation, the disintegration of the ego in the face of a breakdown, the creative exaltation of producing a work of art—all these things must ultimately be followed by a confrontation with reality and one's own limits. Thus the coagulatio both depresses and makes permanent. It is also a natural sequel to the passionate burning of the calcinatio, where one gradually discovers the truth about oneself and about the mortal limits of others after the flames have died and the dross has been burned away. The frustration of desire eventually leads to the acceptance of self-responsibility, and the ability to stand alone and take life as it comes. Compulsions have been burned to ash, and one is never likely to be so driven by them again.

The coagulatio can also precede these two stages, because what has become solid may become too solid, and will need to be broken down again in further transformations. We can see this process in the natural development of the ego, which by the time of the Saturn return at around 29 has begun to crystallise, and which by the time of the Uranus opposition at about 40 is ready for new invigouration through the discovery of further unknown potentials. Often, at the time of the Uranus opposition, the personality has become too rigid and entrenched, and a dissolving or a burning occurs—frequently through problems with a marriage or a love affair, or through a shift in career focus because of a kind of desperate feeling of suffocation—which springs the individual out of this state of stagnation. This in turn is followed by yet another coagulatio as Saturn moves into opposition with its own place and the experiences of the Uranus opposition must be integrated into concrete life.

The process of making solid what has previously been liquid or gas is one which is the special and natural gift and task of the earthy signs. These signs strive to manifest everything, for nothing can be left in the realm of ambiguous potential. For such a nature, the other stages are more of a shock. For the airy and fiery signs, the advent of Saturn can be a great nuisance, because these two elements do not want to crystallise. It seems a kind of death, and an apparently permanent loss of joy, spontaneity, and creative potential. Deep commitments that in theory ought to bring joy, such as marriage, or the birth of a child, or even the buying of a home, are a kind of coagulatio, and are often accompanied by the transits of Saturn; and they are therefore not wholly joyful, if one is honest with oneself. I have sometimes been fascinated by the fear and trepidation which some people seem to experience around the buying of a home and the taking up of a mortgage. Although the actual money required each month may be no more than what one pays in rent, there is something terrifying about the solidity of a mortgage—although, of course, it is not in the least solid, because one can sell the house two weeks later. But it feels as though it is. It feels as though one will never be able to be free again. Rented premises suit the puer aeternus—even though they also require a financial obligation, one does not own them, and one is therefore not truly responsible. There is always a landlord somewhere who in the end keeps ultimate control.

I have met this same irrational fear around the issue of saying things. This is often a critical time in therapeutic work. One might recognise and acknowledge certain feelings, but saying them—putting them into concrete form through the use of words—means crystallising them. Once you have said it to someone, you cannot unsay it, although you can try to lie about it later. This is also the issue behind many people's creative blocks. You can see how deeply related the stage of the coagulatio is to the issue of commitment, on every level. And although the stage of coagulatio in turn moves into something else, and the house is sold and new things said, one cannot go backwards. Something has happened, it has become history. One can move on, but one cannot erase it. It is now an irrevocable part of the past. It is very much like baking bread—and the baking of bread is an image which the alchemists used to describe the process of coagulatio. Once bread is baked, it cannot be separated back into its original components. It provides food and nourishment, and the body digests it and breaks it down into what is useful in the form of vitamins and minerals, and what is useless in the form of shit. But it cannot be turned back into eggs and flour and yeast and salt and butter again.

The coagulatio reflects a stage in the psychotherapeutic process which both therapist and patient look forward to. It is the time when the client or patient who has been grappling with a particular inner problem for a long time finally makes a decision, and begins to put the insights into action. The person sells his or her house, or moves out of a destructive relationship, or finally leaves an unfulfilling job, or begins a new and exciting course of study or training, or writes a book. At last something is being done with all that effort that has been going on for so long within the alembic of the consulting room. The emotional affects and fantasies and dreams need more than understanding; they need actualisation. There is a point where one must, to put it crudely, put one's money where one's mouth is. It is a time of taking responsibility for oneself; the child has at last matured and crystallised into an individual capable of action in the world. For some people, this is a painful time, because it seems, as I have said, like a kind of death. The dominance of the puer aeternus comes to an end. It does not mean the spirit of the puer dies, but the reality function now contains him. One must make choices at last, and even though a choice may be right on every level, it means the exclusion of another possibility.

The coagulatio also deals with issues around the body, and with becoming aware of inhabiting a body. Earthy people do not have an issue with this, but the more ethereal nature comes down to earth with a bump and discovers that the body must have as much say in choices as the intellect, or the spirit, or the feelings. I think it is possible for a person to try to avoid the coagulatio, just as some individuals try to avoid the solutio and retain their precious autonomy and sense of control.

Audience: Do you think eating disorders such as anorexia might be seen in this way?

Liz: One could use alchemical symbolism to gain further insight into them, certainly. I think the more immediate emotional and family problems underlying anorexia must be looked at; it is not enough to look at it alchemically. But if you want to envisage the anorexic as a person who is desperately struggling with the dilemma of "coagulating" or crystallising into an individual, then yes, I think the symbolism can be helpful, because it points to the underlying archetypal problem of incarnation. This is the problem of sin and loneliness, both of which the individual must bear himself or herself. It is the price of individuality. No god or godlike parent can redeem one from oneself. Issues which circle around food and eating problems are, I think, often connected with the problem of separating from the mother; and that, expressed in alchemical terms, is the coagulatio, which is separation on the deepest level.

Dream motifs which reflect this stage of the process are, once again, quite characteristic. Food, eating, and throwing up are common images; so are the images of building, buying, or renovating houses, repairing floors, and roofs, and foundations. Clothing is also connected with the coagulatio, because in dreams it often suggests our persona, the public face which we wear to the outside world. Those dreams where the dreamer suddenly discovers he or she is naked in a street full of people suggest that somehow one has not yet developed an appropriate interaction with the Saturnian world. One has not yet coagulated into a self-confident individual in relation to the collective, and therefore one is naked, one is vulnerable. Dreams of shit also pertain to the motif of the coagulatio. Freud placed great importance on faeces, because this is the first thing that the young child produces alone, without mother's help. It is the first display of individual creative power manifesting as a concrete object. Mummy didn't make it, I did. For this reason, gold and shit are often analogous in alchemical texts, because the coagulatio is often the stage which produces the gold—the individuality crystallised here and now in actual life. Alchemical gold is found in living life, not in transcending it.

The coagulatio is a very complex stage of the opus. For many people, it is not an issue; when it comes time for this process to be undergone, the earthier personality moves forward willingly. But for many others it is a nightmare, and feels desperately lonely. It is a crucifixion, an imprisonment, and a death of all that is beautiful and ethereal and transcendent.

The coagulatio seems much easier to understand than the other stages, but it is not really easier. It is just more concrete. It is interesting that equal value is given in alchemy to all the stages.

The coagulatio is not "lower" than the sublimatio. It may be higher, depending upon where the prima materia starts. Some alchemical writers pay more attention to one or two stages, but that is natural, because of the personal bias toward different kinds of experiences. I mentioned that the *Rosarium* primarily describes a solutio process. There is also a good deal of the sublimatio, which we will deal with next. But in other texts, the fiery images are dominant, and in still others, the images of entombment and imprisonment. Alchemical texts vary enormously. That is what might be expected, since they were written by individuals, and were never collated into a definitive text in the way the Bible was, or the state-approved mythology of different nations of antiquity. I think it is important to remember this issue of equal value being given to all the stages, because it is easy to think that the coagulatio represents a somehow less exalted stage of the process. Ironically, as I have said, it is often further down the line than the others, and directly produces the alchemical gold.

SUBLIMATIO

We have been influenced in our use of the word "sublimate" by Freud, as though somehow sublimation were a bit of a cheat, an attempt to escape the darker instinctual aspects of oneself. When we talk in ordinary language about sublimation, there is consequently a certain ring of sarcasm to it—"Oh, well, he's obviously sublimating." If you sublimate something, in this sense, you are repressing it and trying to live it out through displacement onto an intellectual or spiritual level, in order to avoid the dilemma of dealing with it on a concrete or emotional level. But in alchemy the sublimatio does not have any implication of escape or avoidance. It is associated with the element of air and with the planets Jupiter and Mercury, although now we might consider Uranus an equally important astrological representative. The imagery of the sublimatio often involves birds or winged figures. It is the process of an instinctual content transforming into an image, and it is not a deliberate contrivance such as a guided imagery exercise, but rather a spontaneous psychic function. One cannot "make" an authentic symbolic image out of psychic stuff. It "makes" itself. It is the psyche portraying itself symbolically, and this is a transformation of the prima materia because the symbol allows detachment and objectivity while preserving the meaning. The sublimatio of alchemy is thus very different from sublimation in the psychoanalytic sense, because nothing is being repressed.

The process of the sublimatio most often arises out of one of the other three stages—the calcinatio, the solutio, or the coagulatio. The movement from calcinatio to sublimatio is a movement from frustrated desire for an external object to the transformation of that desire into an internalised image which contains meaning, purpose, and regenerative capacities for one's own life. To give you a crude example of what I mean by this, you might think of the extremely common situation of a powerful sexual attraction to someone whom one cannot have—either because the desired person is elsewhere or someone else's partner or disinterested, or because one is oneself already committed elsewhere. Acting this passion out, which a great many people do, may result in temporary pleasure and some realisations, but often the price paid is too high for what one gets unless some deeper level of meaning can be extricated from the situation. This is an old story. Acting out has its rewards, but by itself it has little to do with the processes we have been looking at today. Repressing such a passion does no real good either, for it is sure to pop up someplace else and on someone else, or forms a pocket of bitter unlived life which eventually poisons whatever relationship one is currently in. The alchemical alternative is to remain conscious of, and loyal to, the feelings, but to contain them—in other words, not to act them out. This is the wolf in the alembic, who howls and protests and burns. If the ego can contain the burning, then the beloved object begins to internalise— in other words, one begins to see what undeveloped and unlived part of oneself got projected outside, because it returns inside in the form of an inner image. This sounds simple, but is dreadfully painful, as any of you will know who have been through it. Yet this internalisation of the outer object into an inner image, and the realisation that this beautiful beloved is a dimension of one's own soul, is the work of the sublimatio. It cannot come about because one wills it. But it may come about if the preceding stages are handled with some integrity and honesty.

In the *Rosarium*, after the dissolving into an ecstatic underwater sexual union, the King and Queen now appear lying dead on a slab, joined in a single hermaphroditic body. The solutio has merged them, but they are dead. In the picture following this nigredo or death phase, they are still portrayed dead on the slab, but there is a little winged creature flying upward from the corpse into the ethers. It goes up somewhere and vanishes. In the next picture, a dew has formed, a heavenly fluid, and it begins to drip moisture onto the motionless corpse beneath. Then, in the next picture, the little winged creature is shown flying back again, ready to reanimate the dead couple. This is a bizarre and initially baffling sequence of pictures, but it portrays the process of sublimatio. The depression which follows the coniunctio is something I have already touched upon—the disillusionment which follows the fantasy of total union with another, or with God. There is no feeling of life; there is only a kind of numbness and apathy, and a sense of loss, even though the desired object has been attained. But something is being activated up above, out of the frame of the picture. The soul has flown upward and is opening up the capacity for symbolisation, or, to put it another way, the capacity for imagination.

There is a considerable amount of psychoanalytic literature on the stages of separation from the mother, where she moves from being experienced as an extension of the child toward being a "part-object"—neither wholly independent, nor wholly united. Bits of the mother, or what the mother represents, begin to be internalised. The child discovers that he or she can be relatively independent, and can survive. Mother is no longer the sole sustainer of life; one can begin to sustain oneself, eat by oneself, walk by oneself. Also, the bad destructive feelings which were previously experienced as being split off and the sole property of either the mother or the child begin to become internalised and integrated with the good, loving feelings. The child discovers that he or she is angry or sad, loving or hateful, and has independent feelings, separate from those of the mother. This area, as I have said, is well explored by the different schools of psychoanalysis, and one of the most important ideas which has emerged from this exploration is that the process of separating from the mother involves the spontaneous making of images which are "part-objects" — in other words, an inner image of mother, or of her life-sustaining qualities, begins to become as safe and nourishing as her physical presence once was. Likewise, an inner image of her life-destroying qualities begins to become tolerable as an aspect of oneself, so that one is not so terrified of and split off from one's own aggression and rage. Once there is a capacity to image, there is a capacity to concretise the image, and the sublimatio leads directly into the coagulatio — the picture of the soul returning from heaven.

I think if you can try to grasp these issues, you will see that the capacity to unlock and confidently explore the imaginal realm depends upon separation from the mother. In other words, so-called "creative blocks" are usually connected with problems of separation. One cannot confidently explore the realm of the imagination when one is still connected by an umbilical cord which is two feet thick. It is too frightening, and too risky. The capacity to image spontaneously is an in-between stage, a movement from identity with the mother to autonomy and crystallisation. Hopefully, it is a stage to which we retain access, because too much separation makes us blocked and closed. It could also be argued that what I mean by "too much" separation is really an inability to separate, masked by a kind of rigid defenciveness to one's own and other's feelings. The child, or the child in the adult, can respond to an image with the same emotional authenticity as he or she responds to a physical object. It is not "just" an image. This capacity to symbolise gives a kind of "as if" quality to the perception of life. Another way of putting it is that the sublimatio represents a capacity to play. If you listen to a child explaining a drawing, or a dream, or a fantasy, there is a magical quality of utter belief mixed with utter play. It is very serious, and yet it is not. This capacity arises out of the space between mother or child; and, in alchemical terms, it arises out of the pressures and transformations placed on the base substance by fire, water, or earth. One relinquishes one's compulsions through these pressures, there is a death and a sense of loss, and out of this loss arises the capacity to form spontaneous pictures in the imagination.

The imagination comes into play when a separation has begun, and the image is a kind of intermediary between oneself and the outer object with which one has previously identified. So the function of the imagination, in relation to the alchemical opus, is that it permits separation and the formation of a sense of individuality— the alchemical gold. There is breathing space, a middle ground which can contain the fears and needs in such a way that feelings are not repressed, but are not acted out either. The sublimatio can only occur when there has been a death, a relinquishing of the fantasy of merging. This is the sequence of the pictures in the *Rosarium*. Only after death and disillusionment can the soul escape upward and fertilise the heavenly realms. There can be no sublimatio when there is a fantasy of fusion. The image of the beloved appears between the person and the actual beloved, so that the person begins to get a glimpse of what this beloved really means to him or her. There is freedom and detachment in it, because it is the great dissolver of instinctual compulsions.

I would see this function as being in part Jupiterian and Mercurial, and in part Uranian. All three of these planets are connected to our capacity to formulate symbolic pictures and concepts. They translate life from concrete experience and emotional identification into meaning through symbols, insights, and maps.

Audience: Is the sublimatio then the ability to be able to translate experiences into a creative activity?

Liz: Yes, exactly. The sublimatio transmutes experience into imagination, which is the prerequisite for any creative work. Then the coagulatio is needed to bring it into form.

Audience: And would the separation from the mother and the emerging symbol of the muse as an alternative be part of that?

Liz: Yes, it is the issue of what Jung calls the anima or animus—a transformation of these psychic functions from external objects toward whom we have an overwhelming compulsion into an inner capacity to receive inspiration from the unconscious. The poet's muse, which might be male for a woman, is the source of inspiration, but it is not a physical person. It is only loosely hooked onto an object. Dante, for example, never even spoke to Beatrice; he merely saw her across the Ponte Vecchio one day. But she became for him an image of beauty, purity, and heavenly virtue, and inspired him to produce the *Divine Comedy*. Dante was forced into this by 'fate, because Beatrice died. But some artists instinctually know that it is better not to get to know the actual person upon whom the anima or animus fantasy has landed, because it will surely turn out to be a disappointment. It is what the person represents as an inner image full of meaning that is important. But one cannot do this with one's head, and sit down and say, "Look, it isn't really that 16-year-old, it's my anima." This is simply a way of avoiding the painful process of containing the compulsion, and generally it does not work.

Somehow longing and grief and loss were transformed, in Dante's case, into poetry. Geoffrey Chaucer, incidentally, was wildly but hopelessly in love with the Duchess of Lancaster, the mother of King Henry IV, who was utterly beyond his reach as an actual lover; and he wrote and dedicated innumerable poetic works to her. One might also see the *Canterbury Tales* as the outgrowth of this process at work in Chaucer. We are not all Chaucers or Dantes, but they serve as good examples of this strange phase of the alchemical process, which holds the key to every person's individual form of creativity.

The sublimatio is a very mysterious process. I would suggest that you read Jung's *Symbols of Transformation*,[5] which addresses precisely this issue, although he wrote it long before he became involved in alchemical texts. One cannot inaugurate the sublimatio with an act of will and a clever intellect, nor even with a good capacity to consciously construct images. Very often the sublimation emerges spontaneously out of Uranus, and to a lesser extent, Jupiter, transits or progressions. When Uranus comes along, the individual often becomes obsessed or fascinated with someone or something, or there is some kind of blow-up or disruption to his or her basic security. There is frequently a burning frustration, a kind of calcinatio, or a drowning in erotic fantasies, but not long afterward, during the course of the transit, there is a dawning insight, which is best reached if one can bear to sit still rather than rushing about like a chicken with its head cut off. This new insight reveals meaning, and the sense of a pattern at work, which often takes the

[5]C.G. Jung, *Symbols of Transformation*, Vol. 5. *The Collected Works* (Princeton, NJ: Bollingen Series, No. 20, Princeton University Press, 1967).

initial form of an image in a dream. One begins to look differently at things, from a higher and clearer place where the air is fresher, and one can begin to ask some very pertinent questions: "What does this have to do with me? How am I connected with the events taking place? What inside me has constellated this situation? What part of myself have I been avoiding living?" Uranus has a way of opening up one's vision and imagination through separations, which free energy and allow new levels of the mind and spirit to be fertilised and activated.

The sublimatio lifts one out of one's mess and confusion. But it is not a comfortable stage for everyone. The airy signs of course favour it, and to some extent so does Sagittarius, which is, in a manner of speaking, the airiest of the fire signs. But a watery or earthy temperament finds the sublimatio initially cold and frightening. Earth needs its concrete objects, and finds it terribly difficult to take images seriously. They are "merely" fantasies. This kind of nature finds dreams a problem, because they are somehow not "real" in the way that lunch is. Even with the best of intentions, a dream is "merely" a dream. Earth panics at the boundless imaginal realm. After all, one might get lost in there, and never come out again. There is a kind of vertigo, which is sometimes experienced physically. There are many individuals who are very resistant to working with images and fantasies; they just close down, because deep down they are frightened. Images are like air, or like the alchemical birds which appear in so many engravings. They are too insubstantial to place one's trust in them. So the very literal-minded individual may resist the sublimatio, and resist the meaning of an experience, because there is a feeling that if one relinquishes one's grip on concrete reality one will go mad, or become a fool.

The watery signs may fear the sublimatio because it is essentially a solitary experience. One cannot move into the domain of the imagination with a crowd tagging along behind. I have had quite a few people say to me, "Oh, it must be so terribly lonely sitting at a typewriter writing a book. I could never do it, I've tried and find it frightening." I don't experience it in that way, but some people do; constant external companionship is a necessity to them, and the companionship of the imaginal world seems cold comfort, because it is so strange and alien, and requires withdrawing from people for a while. The watery signs are themselves highly imaginative by nature, which makes it seem a bit of a paradox. But often they do not develop this wonderful gift, because of the deep solitude necessary for exploring the inner realm. All the imagination then pours out through romantic fantasy, or is stifled. To allow an image to form within means letting go of the dependency upon the concrete object outside. Uranus transits often coincide with a forced letting go, which is very distressing to a watery temperament. But you can see, from this material on the sublimatio, that Uranian separations are not just hurtful random experiences. They have a profound meaning and teleology, and can open up all kinds of potentials of an imaginative and creative kind.

Audience: All these processes sound like different stages in the Easter story. I am still trying to understand why alchemy was such a heresy in the eyes of the Church.

Liz: It was a heresy because it was an individual opus, and involved a highly individual communion with a very ambivalent God. It therefore made the role of the priesthood superfluous, and indeed the role of the Church herself, because the direct relationship between the alchemist and the opus supplanted any need of such a collective authority. But the alchemical stages and their imagery lie at the core of every religion, because they are archetypal stages of development; and if a religion is living and relevant to many people, it draws its imagery from the same pool of the collective unconscious. The four elements of astrology likewise emerge from the same pool. These four stages are the cornerstones of human experience. One finds them not only in Christian myth, but in every mythology from every culture. But the heresy of alchemy was that it made it possible for an individual to form his or her own relationship to the deity; and the deity that was met in this way looked rather different from the one which the Church taught was God. The alchemical God is Mercurius, who is not *summum bonum* at all, but is a peculiar mix of light and dark, male and female. Having glimpsed this, the alchemist could no longer wholly swallow the collectively defined picture of God, nor the collectively defined paths to salvation.

The alchemists were very nervous about all of this, and many of them considered themselves good and upright Christians and described themselves as such, sometimes ad nauseam. Some, like Cornelius Agrippa, courted danger and openly rejected orthodox doctrine. Others, like Paracelsus, were extremely heretical in their writings, but refused to acknowledge the significance of what they were saying in relation to orthodox doctrine. For the same reason the Church went after Luther, who was not involved in alchemy, but whose attitude was: "Yes, I will obey the Pope, as long as the Pope is in accord with my own conscience. If the Pope is not in accord with my conscience, then I must obey my conscience, so here I stand, so help me God." That in essence was also what the alchemist was saying, although often he or she couldn't bear to realise it.

I cannot argue about the rightness or wrongness of these viewpoints, because religion is to me an individual rather than a collective matter. The real nature of God seems to keep eluding us anyway. But the experience of God is a human experience, and therefore falls into the realm of psychology; and the alchemists were courageous enough to face their own individual experiences, rather than clinging to statement of things they were taught they were supposed to experience. Alchemical texts imply that God is not perfect, because Nature, which is the creation of God, is not yet perfect; and therefore God depends upon man for the perfection of creation. Therefore the fault does not lie in man; he is not a poor worm of a sinner who must seek redemption through the intermediary of the Church. Man is part of creation and is a noble co-creator with God, and has the freedom to say, "Look, Our Father Who art in Heaven, with all due respect and humility, you've not got this quite right. You seem to be a little confused, and there might be something I can contribute."

The medieval Church was very understandably worried about the collapse of society, since the Church conceived her role as the emissary of God's will on earth; and the idea of obeying one's own conscience is a very dangerous one if you don't happen to have a conscience. There were heretical movements during the Middle Ages, such as the Brethren of the Free Spirit and the Anabaptists, who really made a mockery of conscience, and were incredibly destructive. There is a case to be argued on behalf of the Church.

But alchemy required considerable moral integrity, as I have mentioned before. So does its modern equivalent, depth psychotherapy. There is often a sense of shame around a person entering psychotherapy, not just because people might think one was "sick," but also because it is in some way a rejection of collective values as a basis for life's decisions. One is effectively saying, "Look here, I am not going to do what everyone does, I am going to take the lonely, painful road of finding out what I am first, and then I will decide." There is a feeling of it being somehow not quite right, somehow slightly renegade. Alchemy has a rather shady component; it is somehow unclean, because of the dark phases of the process, and the confrontation with one's own devils. So is psychotherapy. This is often reflected in dreams of criminals breaking into one's house, or black men or women coming in uninvited, or dreams of being poisoned by a snakebite. It is the sinister, left-hand way, not quite orthodox. Are there any questions about the sublimatio?

Audience: I am having some trouble understanding it in practical terms. Can you give an example?

Liz: In practical terms? That is just what it isn't. But I will try to illustrate it. Let's take a person who has come into analysis, and spends a few months being a really perfect patient, arriving on time and paying all the bills immediately, and always being polite and bringing lots of dreams and so on. Then the person starts to become angry, and feels that you, the analyst, are not responding, not coming forth with the goodies which all this excellent behaviour was really meant to be buying. So there is a lot of suppressed anger in the atmosphere, although nothing much is said about it, until finally the patient bursts out with, "You don't care about me at all! You only see me because I'm paying you! I'm just one of dozens of people you see!" And so on. Now, if at this point you, the analyst, react defencively, and answer, "Of course I care, let me make you a cup of tea," you have broken the alembic just when the contents are coming to the boil. But if you can wait, and contain the person without either rejecting him or her, or trying to compensate or wriggle out of it, then the patient will get angrier and angrier; and then all the feelings of childhood will rise to the surface, and the person will begin to remember how much it hurt to have an unresponsive parent whose love he or she had to "buy" through good behaviour. All the fury and humiliation of being trapped in a situation where anger could not be shown for fear of losing what little there was, all the loneliness, all the unfulfilled emotional needs will begin to emerge. This is not really a personal attack on you; but if you try to interpret too quickly, or deflect this eruption too early, then it short-circuits the process for the sake of your comfort but at the patient's expense. Until these feelings of burning and dissolving have been re-experienced, insights are not yet rooted inside. They are merely conceptual. But after a time it may begin to occur to that patient, spontaneously, that the cold, rejecting person is not actually you. This may be because of an image in a dream, or a fantasy. There is a realisation of the familiarity of the experience. Then the connection is made. And at the same time comes the realisation that not everyone is like one's parents, not everyone will respond to the child in the same old way. A chain of associations has been made, and a thread of meaning; and a considerable amount of energy can then be freed. At the same time, you, the analyst, have also been forced into your own internal dilemmas, because being the object of such an onslaught will activate all your own childhood issues. So there is a kind of alchemical soup, which is what Jung writes about in "The Psychology of the Transference" in relation to the alchemical pictures of the *Rosarium*. Spontaneous insight of this kind is part of the alchemical sublimatio. But it can only arise if the previous experiences have been faithfully faced.

Audience: At the moment you are talking about, might it then be useful to suggest using meditation or visualisation in order to ease some of the pain?

Liz: Yes, I think that when this kind of perception has already begun in the person, then it can be encouraged very fruitfully. Of course, you can suggest it earlier; but I would never require it, nor give the impression that it is a kind of "ticket" to a successful psychotherapy. You can suggest getting some paints out, or try an "active imagination," but the problem with this, if it has not arisen spontaneously from the patient, is that the person might try to produce something to please you, and then it is not really any help at all. Probably everything depends, in the end, upon timing.

If an individual has already begun to find that space between identification with the mother and a strong, autonomous identity, then imaginative work of any kind in psychotherapy is very helpful. But a therapist cannot push a patient into the sublimatio because the therapist wants the patient to feel better, or because the therapist wants to feel better. There may be a temporary alleviation, but this comes from the feeling that the therapist, like the implacable parent, has been pleased. But then anxiety comes up again, because the patient has to keep thinking of more and more things to please the therapist. It is deadly to collude with this kind of thing. It is better to allow a person to become angry, frustrated, and upset, because these are the true feelings which have lain hidden beneath; and anger is one of the most creative tools for separation. Remember the function of Mars, which is not only concerned with anger, but also with self-actualisation. The sublimatio arises as a natural process out of other processes, and trying to force it does not really accomplish anything at all. In many ways it is the kindest of the alchemical stages, not only for the individual but also for the therapist. But the soil must be fertile. The same thing applies to the coagulatio. One can say to a person who needs a better connection with the body, "Why don't you try a yoga class? Or exercise?" But if the person has not yet arrived at the stage of wanting, from within, to come down to earth, then these suggestions will meet with a polite smile and agreement, and then the person goes off and does nothing about it, or does one class to please you and then never continues. If a person has already begun to make these connections himself or herself, then such a suggestion can have an immediate and genuine response, because the preparatory stages have been accomplished. Of course these things are always worth trying, and one does not always know — especially in an astrological consultation, where you see the person once — where that individual has got to. But we should not be upset or disappointed when our good advice is ignored. Once again, I find alchemical symbolism extremely helpful in illustrating the intelligence and autonomy of the psychic processes. The ego may know a great deal, but one cannot stand over the psyche and shout, "Grow, you bastard." Everything lies in the timing.

EXAMPLE CHARTS

We might now look at some example charts to try to earth some of this very colourful and very abstruse material on alchemical symbolism. I must stress once again that alchemy is a metaphor for psychic processes, and should be kept in mind in much the same way as mythology: to amplify astrological placements in order to get a deeper and rounder understanding of them.

Someone from the group has given me a chart for us to examine. (See Chart 7.) Sheila, do you want to say something about what you are after? Are there particular issues connected with alchemical themes which you wanted us to discuss?

Sheila: I feel very uncomfortable when you talk about the solutio, about dissolving and losing one's boundaries. At the moment I am caught between having lots of fantasies about future possibilities, and having trouble actually manifesting the fantasies. I also feel as though I am in the middle of a calcinatio, because I can really relate to the image of the wolf being burned. I tend to do a lot of analysing and intellectualising, but it isn't helping at the moment. Probably that is my natural way of dealing with things.

Liz: Perhaps it would be useful to begin with the transits which are moving across your chart right now. That should give us a picture of just what is happening inside you. Also, we might look at the natal balance of elements, to see how you are likely to react to the transits. Would anyone like to comment on either of these issues?

Audience: The planets in air are nicely aspected in the birth chart. Venus and Uranus in Gemini are in trine Jupiter. And there is a strong emphasis in the 9th house. I would have thought this might be connected with Sheila's tendency to use her intellect to cope with things.

Liz: I would agree. The process of abstracting and imaging—what alchemy calls the sublimatio—would come quite naturally to you. When a person is really pressed by life, it is the trines in the chart which are mobilised, because this is where the natural gifts lie. The

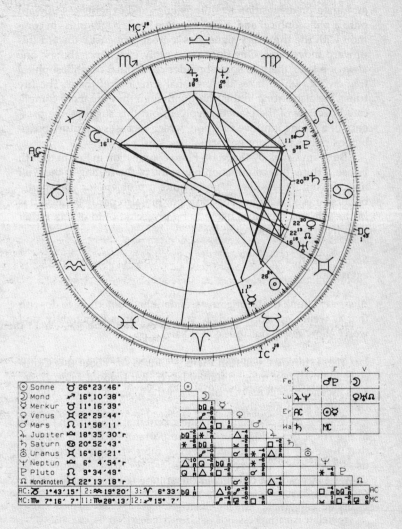

Chart 7. Sheila. The birth data has been withheld for confidentiality. Chart calculated by Astrodienst, using the Placidus house system.

Moon in Sagittarius echoes the 9th house emphasis, and points to an innate predisposition to shift feelings and experiences upward onto a philosophical and more objective level. Sagittarius, in common with the three airy signs, has a great propensity toward this upward movement. One does not simply experience things; one always relates them to some broader conceptual or philosophical framework, which takes the personal sting out of them. The fire trines are also strong in this chart, although they are more complicated because of the planets involved; but this suggests the presence of a strong intuitive function, which focusses on future possibilities rather than present actualities.

But I am struck by the Mars-Pluto conjunction in Leo in the 7th house. I think this conjunction has some of the feeling of the wolf in it. I would guess that it poses quite a problem for you, partly because it is a rather hot combination, but also partly because it is in the 7th and therefore likely to be projected onto others rather than lived out in your own life.

Sheila: Yes, that's true. I have a great problem showing anger and aggression.

Audience: I think the Capricorn ascendant has something to do with that as well. Capricorn tends to structure things very tightly, and won't allow much out unless it is safe.

Liz: Yes, I think we will find there is a lot to say about this Capricorn ascendant on many different levels. But I would again agree. This ascendant will make it harder for the Mars-Pluto, the wolf, to find expression directly.

There is only one planet in water, and that is Saturn in Cancer in the 7th. I think this is also very important, because it suggests that those airy trines will operate even more strongly; they will be used to protect your very vulnerable feelings from exposure. This vulnerability is most obvious in the sphere of relationships.

Sheila: It certainly is.

Liz: I would also look at the Sun in Taurus, which is potentially a great builder and actualiser in the world. You have said you have a problem in making your fantasies real in concrete terms. I think everyone has a problem living out the Sun-sign, although the degree of the problem varies. The Sun is a symbol of the individuality, and that is the whole point of the alchemical process: the emergence of a true individuality. A particularly problematic issue is suggested in the chart when other factors mitigate against the innate values of the Sun-sign. Here the strong fiery emphasis pulls you up into the intuitive world of possibilities, and will battle against the earthier, more prosaic values of the Sun. Just the combination of Sun and Moon signs here reflects the dilemma you have expressed—translating fantasies and intuitions into actualities.

In order for you to become the individual who is reflected by that Taurus Sun, you will probably have to deal more deeply with the issues suggested by the Mars-Pluto conjunction. This I think would be true in any case, because the Sun needs Mars in order to fully manifest. Mars is a kind of primitive Sun, a basic instinctual function of self-assertiveness that is necessary before a more conscious realisation of self is possible. But it is especially true here because the Sun disposes of that hot conjunction. So sooner or later the issues of the wolf will come up. These are issues of desire, aggression, hunger, and emotional needs. When we start looking at the transits, you will see that it is upon you right now.

Audience: I think we should also consider Sheila's relationship with her father, because of the Sun being in the 4th house.

Liz: Yes, I think we should, too. We are darting around this chart rather quickly, but I think we need a preliminary picture before we tackle the transits and look at the alchemical imagery in relation to them. What about the father?

Audience: Well, he seems to be awfully important. There is some kind of identification there with the Sun in the 4th.

Liz: All right. Let's look more carefully at the meaning of the Sun in the 4th. One's own sense of individuality is projected upon the father at the beginning of life, so the father carries the image of the potential self, of the alchemical gold. This may not be conscious, and often isn't; I have heard many people with the Sun in the 4th say they did not relate to their fathers, or that the father left when they were young, or that he was weak, and so on. But this placement describes a subjective feeling, and if you remember the solar radiance of the sun-god Apollo, and the spiritual intimations of the solar alchemical gold, then you will see that the father is indeed terribly important as the carrier of the self. It is especially powerful if such feelings are unconscious. On a deeper level, it is the father-archetype which is so important, and this placement describes a challenge to make manifest in life a profound sense of transcendent order and meaning. It is, for lack of a better term, a true sense of the spirit, although there is also a need to manifest that spirit in the world in practical terms, because the Sun is in an earthy sign. But initially, because the personal father is the first hook upon which the child hangs this perception, a woman with this placement will look for her meaning and order in a partner who can be a father-surrogate.

Sheila: I know I keep doing that. But every time I think I have found one, the person always lets me down.

Liz: There is no person living who could be an archetypal father for you. That is partly why they let you down. In the end it has to come out of you. No one can live the Sun for us. I think we should also look at the Capricorn ascendant here as well, and its ruler, Saturn, in the 7th. Here again is the principle of father, although more the earthy side of the archetype—the ability to define limits and create order in the world of form. The mythic divine father is not only an image of spiritual meaning. He is also a symbol of creation and structure in the material world. He combines spirit and matter, and makes his law manifest in actuality. This is the ancient symbol of kingship, where the King is the divine vessel for the will of God on earth, and the hierarchical social order follows in accordance with the law and structure of the cosmos. We don't believe in these things any more. Even countries with Kings know that the King is human, and if one reads the seedier representatives of British journalism, one might even think he (or she) was subhuman. But as a symbol, kingship is alive and well in the psyche of every Capricorn ascendant, or, for that matter, every

Capricorn Sun. I think this combination of 4th house Sun and Capricorn ascendant points the way toward those qualities which need to be developed, and which describe your true individuality. But they are likely to be threatening and unpalatable to the fire-air combination, because they are contradictory to it, and would require some sacrifice of a certain kind of self-image in order to be integrated. In order for you to produce anything with your talents, you would sooner or later have to face the world of the fathers, which requires toughness and good survival capacities as well as realism and self-honesty. You need the Mars-Pluto conjunction for that, as well as a knowledge and acceptance of your emotional needs. Can you see what I am getting at? You can't have the one without the other. But the fire-air combination is highly romantic and idealistic. It recoils from the grit of the other. There is a split here, to which the Mars-Pluto conjunction is one of the keys for healing.

Audience: Would you see the coagulatio, the coming down to earth, as the major task because of the Capricorn ascendant?

Liz: Yes, I would read it that way. The ascendant seems to have a forward-looking quality to it. It is the nature of the journey, the quest, the task. A Saturn-ruled chart demands incarnation. Sheila would prefer not to have to, for many reasons—not least because, I suspect, there was no real support from the father to provide her with a positive model. It might even be suggested that the father was faced with the same challenge, and could not meet it in a creative way. Do you feel that is the case?

Sheila: Yes, I do. I found my father a great disappointment. He is a very stubborn man, with very old-fashioned values, and very rational and materialistic. We had constant fights. I have a lot of anger toward him.

Liz: The more we discuss this, the larger the father gets. You are perhaps more like your father than you would like to admit. I suspect that both of you are extremely stubborn, and sure that you are right. But can you see how your anger and rebellion toward your father might be making it difficult for you to internalise this archetypal principle of father and just get out there and get on with your life? It is as though you will refuse to incarnate until he, or someone like him, comes along and gives you the thing you feel you need but did not get in childhood. That wolf is very much in evidence, because there is a great hunger here for love and recognition. I think you have secretly been in a terrible angry sulk, because you did not get the father you wanted. So you will not actualise that father-principle through work in the world, and this is a kind of retaliation against him. You are going to injure him through being a disappointment to him. But it is you who are being hurt by it.

Sheila: I feel as if I act this out all the time in my relationships. I meet a man and think he's wonderful but then after a while I start feeling unappreciated and neglected, and then I get very angry.

Liz: That is what alchemy means by the wolf. It is the furious child, the greedy infant. Give me, give me, says the wolf. Recognise me, love me, make me the centre of your world. The needs of the wolf are valid enough, and they are a perfectly legitimate requirement of every child. But as long as they are sought outside in adult life – and this usually happens because the parents cannot recognise these needs in the child – the wolf remains hungry, and cannot transform. The thing is that you probably don't recognise yourself yet. And that will take you into the issue of your feelings about your body and your sexuality, because the Sun is in Taurus. That is where you have been most hurt. If you project this self-rejection onto your lovers, then you will always feel crushed and unwanted. The anger you feel is toward the father, but not for the reasons you think. I doubt it is because he was conservative and worldly. I think it is because you loved him deeply, as a little girl – which means full of a little girl's sensual and erotic needs – and he did not respond to this aspect of you. Or he may have done so unconsciously; but was frightened by it and therefore pushed you away. Now you push these needs away yourself.

Sheila: So you feel the issue of my relationship problems and the issue of my inability to do anything with my talents are connected.

Liz: I feel they are most definitely connected. Behind both issues lies the wolf, who needs to be faced and felt and understood. Otherwise this whole complex keeps getting acted out, without making any sense at all. Your capacity to be effective in the world is potentially very great, with an earthy sun and ascendant, and the Sun is, in addition, sextile Saturn. And there are also the strength and survival capacities of the Mars-Pluto conjunction. You have all the right ingredients. But I fear you will need to burn a little, to contain that wolf and find out what it really involves, rather than living it out through disappointments in love.

Audience: So this Mars-Pluto conjunction is a kind of prima materia.

Liz: Yes. The unconscious passions and emotional needs are a kind of prima materia. It is this dimension of Sheila's personality that can yield up the gold, not the attractive trines in air, which are very bright and inventive and artistic but which, in themselves, do not lead down that road to the centre.

Sheila: I sometimes feel that my anger, although it keeps erupting toward men, has also been my salvation, because it got me to leave home early and get away from my parents.

Liz: Anger is a great asset, if it is handled creatively. It is a spur to movement and creativity. I suspect, although it is a slightly unorthodox viewpoint, that one cannot really create anything without having a fair-sizes wolf inside. That does not mean having to spend one's life burning. But without some feeling of anger and frustration, and even envy, one is not driven into doing anything at all. Of course, some people do not wish to create anything. They simply wish to be happy. But for someone with such placements as a Mars-Pluto conjunction and a Capricorn ascendant, there is a great need to produce and achieve. And there is also a lot of anger at life, because one's desires are powerful and therefore inevitably frustrated in some way, sooner or later. All that tremendous energy is at the moment caught in father-bashing and lover-bashing, because all these men have apparently let you down.

It is worth looking at the image of the wolf more carefully. The wolf eventually needs to be humanised, because in its wolfish form it is not capable of conscious decision-making. It is a creature of pure instinct, and is therefore under the complete compulsion of Nature. But it has a wonderful survival capacity. Wolves manage to live in the most unpromising places, and can survive extreme cold and terrible conditions. They are nocturnal animals, which suggests that they know the hidden routes and passages of the unconscious; they can see in the dark. And they are only truly vicious when they are starving. The wolf comes from the same family as the dog, and there is something in the wolf which can relate to human beings. It is possible to tame a wolf. Myths such as that of the founders of Rome, Romulus and Remus, and even Kipling's wonderful story of Mowgli the jungle-boy suggest that the wolf is not so far away from humankind; in these tales it will suckle a human baby with great devotion.

As an image of untamed nature, the wolf is destructive, but it is not malevolent. It is one of the animals sacred to the Great Mother, as an image of eternally hungry instinct. But in Egyptian myth, the wolf was seen as a symbol of fertility, and in Roman myth, as we have seen, it is sacred to Mars. The wolf therefore contains extraordinary paradoxes. It is lustful and avaricious, yet also courageous and full of valour. And the story of children being reared by wolves is worldwide, not just Roman. So the wolf is also a protector of children. Alchemy unconsciously chose an extremely rich image to describe the prima materia.

Now let's consider the transits.

Audience: I notice that Saturn is hanging around the MC at the moment. [Note: This seminar was originally given in November 1983.] And it will soon come into opposition with Mercury and square the Mars-Pluto conjunction.

Liz: How would you interpret that?

Audience: Well, the MC has to do with career issues. Maybe it is now becoming necessary to make some sort of definite move to choose a direction in which Sheila can properly establish herself.

Liz: Yes, that is one level of Saturn crossing the MC. One must crystallise something or begin to build something permanent in the world. But this transit is more than just a transit across the MC. It touches off the Mars-Pluto conjunction, and will eventually come into opposition with the Sun.

Audience: There is likely to be a lot of anger about.

Sheila: There is already a lot of anger about. I was thinking of spending Christmas with my parents, but I decided that it would be pretty intolerable. I am in a very aggressive mood at the moment.

Liz: You need to contain that burning somewhere where it is not inevitably dragged out into scenes with other people. The imagery of the calcinatio is very appropriate for you at the moment. You said that at the beginning. Do you have some idea, after all we have been saying, what its goal might be?

Sheila: What I hear is that somehow I am not looking at the real roots of my anger, nor taking responsibility for it myself.

Liz: That is a fair summary.

Sheila: I don't like the sound of that sealed alembic.

Liz: You would be very peculiar if you did. But you have quite a long period of Saturn coming up. It will go retrograde across the Mars-Pluto conjunction, and perhaps it might be a good time to explore some of these feelings, with another person or in writing or painting, so that the injured and angry child can get a hearing. I would repeat once again that it is you yourself who reject that hurt Taurus child with her powerful instinctual needs. You have turned your anger toward your father into an ideology, which is what we all do at some stage, but attacking Saturnian conventions and traditions in the world only denies your own need for convention and tradition. And I think it is a blind, a kind of red herring. A displacement, as Freud would have said.

Sheila: I wanted my father's respect.

Liz: That is the adult speaking. A child does not think in terms of respect. For her it is an issue of love, of affection and loyalty, and of a genuine response to her developing femininity, both physically and emotionally. The adult in you is liberated and wants respect in an adult sense. But the little girl craves validation of her girlhood, of her female identity. She is a little girl first.

By the time Saturn reaches the opposition to the Sun, there is a chance for that burning to have moved into a more structured phase. The imagery of the coagulatio might then be highly appropriate. What begins now will culminate then, and you will probably need to define yourself in worldly terms, as has been suggested already. And I would think that Saturn moving in opposition to Mercury could be very productive for you, because you are likely to become unusually thoughtful and reflective, and the tendency to fly up into abstractions may be balanced by a much more realistic and truthful way of looking at things. That is there in potential anyway, because Mercury is in Taurus, but it is in the 4th house, so your father once again has to carry your own undeveloped capacity to look at things in a more realistic way. The combination of Mercury in Taurus with the trines in air is a lovely one, but they need to blend, rather than battle with each other. It is possible to be idealistic and practical at the same time. You seem to have a strongly developed intellect and a natural intuitive feeling for the symbolic world. This broader vision is potentially well balanced by the earthy Mercury, which can approach all metaphysical and philosophical issues with common sense and discrimination.

There is a kind of mixture going on here with these transits, a combination of a calcinatio and a coagulatio. Saturn triggers off the wolf, and ignites the fire; but at the same time it is Saturn and not Pluto or Uranus, so there is an implication of the need to face your own feelings more honestly and build into your own life a set of values that has previously been projected. That is the coagulatio.

Audience: Pluto will be coming along.

Liz: Yes, but perhaps that is not as ominous as you make it sound. If one does the preliminary Saturnian work, then a deeper level of confrontation with that wolf might mean a period of enormous creative energy. That is why I pay so much attention to the process of alchemy. One thing builds upon the next. Also, Pluto has an irrevocable quality, as though something is finally paid up and finished. Perhaps it is time for the power of the family complex to finish. The Pluto transit needs to be taken in context.

There is also the issue of pride involved with a Mars-Pluto conjunction. The wolf is a very proud creature, just as proud in its own way as the lion. I suspect that you and your father are cut from the same cloth. Both of you are too proud to admit that you love each other. Hell will freeze over before that stubborn pride in both of you will acknowledge hurt and vulnerability. You may need to have a showdown with him at some point during the proceedings, but one which is different from the usual arguments. If you can face your feelings truthfully, then you can be truthful with him.

Sheila: I can't imagine admitting to him that I want his love.

Liz: Why not? He is only a person, not a god, and he is an old man now. It's no shame to you that you can love him. It's a strength. You might find something out that surprises you.

There are other transits imminent which we can look at with some help from alchemy. Uranus is beginning to make its approach toward conjuncting the Moon and opposing its own place. And Saturn, as it moves through Scorpio, will trine its own place. As you have said, Pluto will eventually touch the Mars-Pluto and cross the MC, and Neptune will creep over the ascendant. That is quite an active picture.

Audience: Could I ask something before we discuss these transits? Do you think a natal Mars-Pluto opposition would mean the same thing as a conjunction?

Liz: There is a similarity in meaning. I would find the image of the wolf useful for both. The opposition contains more tension, because there is a split between the personal will and the will of the instincts, which is a property of the species, and not the individual. With the conjunction, the two drives work together, and form a very powerful desire-nature with great endurance. When they oppose, the voice that says "I want" sometimes runs into conflict with the basic desires of the body and the instincts. This often emerges as sexual conflict. One wants to be special and different in one's needs, not the same as every other animal. There is a feeling of fighting against fate sometimes. But in general I would say yes, they are very similar. Now does anyone have any comment on some of these transits I mentioned?

Audience: We haven't mentioned Sheila's mother. I am looking at Uranus coming up to conjunct the Moon.

Liz: Quite. That is the other half of the equation, as always. What do you make of the natal picture?

Audience: Perhaps a woman with a great deal of passion and imagination, because of the fiery Moon trine Mars and Pluto. Maybe much more independent than she was able to show. You often call a Moon-Uranus opposition a mother with a trapped spirit. But the Moon is in the 12th. So perhaps she was too submerged or self-effacing to live out any of that.

Liz: I think that's an excellent reading of it. Sheila, would you like to say a few words about your mother, into the microphone?

Sheila: Oh, God. Not really. My mother was a martyr. She was desperate for material security, because her family were poor. She did everything to please my father. She was sick a lot of the time. But I never felt comfortable with her. I always felt manipulated.

Liz: Probably you were. You seem to be exhibiting all her anger, rebelliousness and independence as well as your own. I would take the transit of Uranus over the Moon to suggest an emergence of this submerged mother into consciousness—who she really is, what she really wanted from life—and at the same time a separation from her. On some level, perhaps, you are secretly acting out her martyrdom as well, hoping that some man will come and take care of you. That is what she did. I am also interested in the Moon-

Venus opposition, which I have found often reflects a split in the mother between erotic feelings and maternal needs. She is driven into having to choose between being a sexually alive and attractive woman and a mother, rather than realising that she can be both. The result is often a secret rivalry between such a mother and her daughter, who, if the mother identifies solely with the maternal pole, must carry the erotic one to the exclusion of all others. This means that the daughter, which would be you, Sheila, must play a kind of hetaira, never settling down and never able to commit herself, even if there are strong factors in the chart which suggest a need for domesticity and family life.

Sheila: I suppose I have a problem about commitment. I become very resentful if I am taken for granted, and I tend to leave relationships. I have always been afraid of having children.

Liz: That is what I mean. With the Sun in Taurus in the 4th, you may need stability and security and a peaceful family life more than you can admit. But if your mother has appropriated all these spheres, then that leaves you with only the hetaira, the eternal girl. The sad thing is that I don't think your mother was actually very maternal. With the Moon in Sagittarius in opposition to Uranus as one of her significators, had she lived in a different generation, she might have tucked a lot of experience in before she settled down— if she ever settled down. Perhaps the sublimatio which often accompanies the transits of Uranus will help you to get a broader and clearer understanding of the dynamics at work in your family, probably going back for many generations, since the Moon is in the 12th house and suggests an inherited issue. That may help to free you from the more compulsive aspects of your relationship patterns. Although this issue of the mother may not seem directly connected with your original query about actualising your potentials, I think it is. Before you know what potentials you want to work at, you need to be a whole person, more or less, and that includes the issue of your sexuality and your relationship with the mother as well as the father. I don't think that what we call choices are really choices at all until there is a relatively complete person making the choice.

Audience: Then the Saturn transit trine natal Saturn might mean more issues of the coagulatio—facing the truth about unconscious patterns in relation to others, and learning to make decisions on one's own.

Liz: That is good reading of it. It is a helpful and supportive transit, which occurs after Saturn stirs up the Mars-Pluto conjunction with squares, and before it comes into opposition with the natal Sun, although all of this seems to belong to the same process as the opposition does. I think this transit will activate the natal Sun-Saturn sextile, which suggests an excellent potential for self-sufficiency and a capacity to ground potentials in the concrete world. The whole feeling of the pattern of transits occurring now and into the next few years is one of quite a lot of heat, but also of finally making peace with the father inside you, and accepting your earthiness as well as your intellect and spirit. There is certainly a feeling of some burning, and perhaps also some dissolving, because of the approaching Neptune transit. Maybe some of those Capricorn defences, which are sometimes as thick as rhinoceros hide, might gently loosen. The Neptune transit occurs after the Saturn transit has finished, so this advent of a solutio does not fall under the same constellation. It is a new and different phase, coinciding more with Uranus transiting over the Moon. After all this anger yields its results, there is quite a different feeling coming in.

I think Sheila's chart is a very good example of the sequence of stages which I have been talking about. You can see how each one builds upon the previous one. The discomfort and heat of the calcinatio is unpleasant, but it can burn away all the false assumptions, leaving the true core of the hurt, and consequently making it possible for Sheila to take an individual and more compassionate attitude toward that hurt. Until it is really seen, and felt, she cannot take any attitude at all. At the same time there is an urgent call to ground whatever has been learned, as though all the pressure will lead to some kind of dynamic drive to begin participating in the material world.

Are there any further comments about Sheila's chart? You can see that I have been using the alchemical imagery very loosely, but it helps to put together the picture of transits as a reflection of a series of processes at work within.

Karen, would you like to say something about Chart 8? (See page 340.) I take it that it isn't yours, since it's called "Peter." Is this someone you are involved with?

Karen: No, it's a work colleague and a close friend. He was interested in any comments which might be helpful to him. Also, I'm concerned about him.

Liz: I am not surprised, given the transit of Saturn moving over those Scorpio planets.

Audience: What does he do?

Karen: He's a doctor. He's got involved in holistic medicine.

Audience: Maybe the transit of Saturn is changing his beliefs and values. It's moving into his 9th house, where most of those planets are. Would you read the Mercury-Mars conjunction as being in the 8th or the 9th?

Liz: I think I would read it as both. Its roots are in the 8th, but it will release itself through the 9th, because Mars is very close to the cusp and is also being pulled into the next house by its conjunction to Venus.

Audience: Well, maybe the transit of Saturn over those two in the 8th would suggest a coming to the surface of a lot of anger. But the anger wouldn't come out in emotional and sexual issues. It would come out in ideological or philosophical ones.

Liz: Yes, there is a feeling of a tremendous amount of energy beginning to break loose. I think there may be issues around authority which are starting to plague him, and a lot of personal resentment may be unleashed toward establishment structures to which previously he was only too happy to adhere.

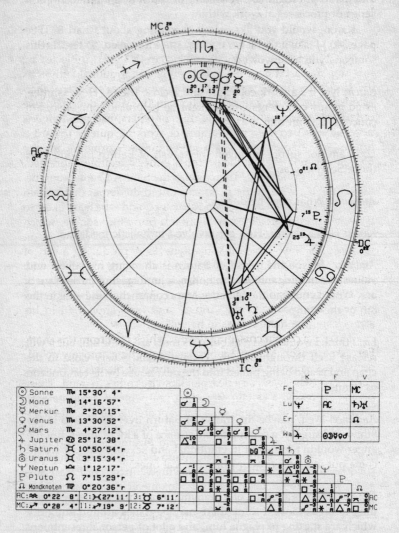

Chart 8. Peter. The birth data has been withheld for confidentiality. Chart calculated by Astrodienst, using the Placidus house system.

Audience: Where do you get the implication of an authority problem from?

Liz: Several things. The great emphasis in Scorpio, to begin with. Although there is a strong rational bias in this chart, reflected by the Aquarian ascendant, Scorpio itself has an irrational faith in its own inner law. the Scorpio personality—and Peter's is a very characteristic one because of the stellium in the sign—does not take orders gracefully, nor follow the rules of others, except when it is necessary as part of a programme of working quietly toward a future goal of autonomy. If you see a humble Scorpio towing the line, then you know that the person is either dreadfully repressed, or biding his or her time. There is also the Saturn-Uranus conjunction at the IC, which reflects issues around the father that pertain to a conflict between anarchy and structure, and which are likely to be rather uncomfortable. And there is a Sun-Pluto square, which never bows to anybody. Even if Sun-Pluto is operating in an unconscious way—which it sometimes does, producing a sort of "victim" personality which always seems to attract others who dominate—it is deeply and relentlessly unforgiving in the face of enforced submission. I get the impression that the deeper he becomes involved with the "fringe" and feels supported in his iconoclasm, the more renegade he will go.

There is a certain crusading flavour which I get from this chart. For some reason Martin Luther keeps popping into my mind, probably because he also had a great clump of planets in Scorpio. Paracelsus, who was also a Scorpio, likewise comes to mind. These people expressed a certain crusading zeal which I associate with the martial side of Scorpio. One day, apparently all of a sudden—although nothing with Scorpio is ever really sudden—they had enough of other people's hypocrisy and incompetence and ignorance, and they begin to do battle with the big Behemoth of the collective. For Luther, Behemoth was the Church. For Paracelsus, as for your friend Peter, it was orthodox medicine as taught at the universities of his time. Do you know the famous story of Paracelsus' short-lived teaching post at the University of Basel? It was a very brief tenure. On the morning of his first lecture, he came out before the students holding a big bowl covered with a cloth. He then told them to throw away all their books by Galen, the great

Greek and medical authority whose teachings were never questioned, and to consider the real miracle of nature that he held in his hands. He then whipped the cloth away and displayed to his students a big bowl of shit. Presumably it was his own, although history is silent on this point. Naturally he was immediately dismissed from his post, and driven from Basel. That is the sort of spirit I am talking about.

Something very potent is beginning to erupt in Peter, and we should remember that the transit of Saturn will be followed immediately by the transit of Pluto. This eruption begins as a deep and perhaps very personal issue, but it emerges in the arena of the 9th house, which always seeks to convey a message of enlightenment to society. The 9th house is the house of the teacher and the preacher. It belongs to Jupiter or Zeus, and the name Zeus comes from an Indo-European root word which means "enlightener." This archetypal figure of the bringer of light and consciousness is a major figure in Peter's life, and now it is being powerfully activated, possibly for the first time and probably to the point where he will initially identify too closely with it, and see himself as a kind of persecuted messiah or bringer of truth. I think he is likely to make a few enemies, because he will also probably project his 7th house Pluto outside – not only onto those close to him, but onto the public. Don't forget that the 7th house is other people in general, not just one's partner. All his own unconscious prejudices and rigidity and need for power will initially be projected outside, before he begins to understand that the dragon lies within himself as well. He is waging a war against evil in the collective, but he has not yet come to terms with his own evil. Here is an impending calcinatio with a vengeance.

Karen: People are never lukewarm about him. They either hate him or adore him, but nothing in between. The more he shows his determination and intensity, the more he sets off the people around him. I think he used to be much more Aquarian, much more reasonable. He never offended anyone. He has the common touch, he can communicate with most people, and that was what showed. Now another person is emerging. He is ethical enough, and dedicated enough, to avoid deliberately hurting people. But he is giving off a definite atmosphere of eagerly preparing to step on toes all over the place.

Liz: Perhaps the real issue, with this transit of Saturn, is that it is time for him to face himself and see that he is not just a decent medical man with a common touch, but that he has many other levels to his personality, and great depths, some of which are pretty dark. Perhaps also he needs to face his own motives in becoming a healer. But he does not want to go through this confrontation, so it is all being acted out in the arena of the external world, where there are naturally some very good hooks.

Once again I would associate Saturn with the alchemical stage of the coagulatio, so something is attempting to come into incarnation—perhaps a more honest, solid, and realistic personality. But Peter has no earth at all in his birth chart. That, I think says a great deal. He is likely to avoid the pressure that Saturn puts on him to face his own reality, and may try to unstopper the alembic because it is getting too hot looking in the mirror.

Audience: How can he be a doctor and have a bad relationship with reality?

Liz: Easily. Do you know many doctors? One can be a very intuitive physician, with a great feeling for the suffering of others, and yet have a poor relationship with the limits of ordinary life. Also, with many people working in the healing fields, there is often a deep conflict around the body and its mortality, which forms one of the unconscious motives in taking on the difficult task of working with disease and death in others. Our vocational choices are almost always bound up with our own complexes; that is why we care so much about them. I would guess that Peter carries some of this problematic issue of the mortality of the flesh, which may be exacerbated by his idealism. It also seems that he might lack a clear sense of just what he can and cannot get away with. He used to be a good obedient son, and now he is becoming a violent rebel. Neither of these postures is really related to reality. Both are reactions to inner stress and insecurity and anger. Perhaps he is fighting his father. First he displayed a typically Saturnian adherence to structure, now he is an iconoclastic Uranian. Probably his father had both sides, but could not resolve them, so the son has inherited the split. I doubt that he has ever genuinely accommodated himself to the rules of the game in the medical profession. He has merely paid lip service, for complicated reasons most of which have been unconscious.

Karen: I am very afraid that he will make powerful enemies.

Liz: I think you are probably right. He is likely to get himself into some rather hot water. He lacks the calm realism of earth, which might allow him to contain his passions and work more slowly toward his goals; and he will need to develop this kind of realism. But he will initially fight against having to develop it, because something in him has become inflated and does not want to accommodate the laws of the Saturnian world. I think that he is basically not very tactful, with a Mercury-Mars conjunction in Scorpio. He can be manipulative, but not tactful. Mercury square Pluto is one of the most manipulative of Mercury placements; one pries out the secrets of others, but gives nothing away oneself. And Mars is also square Pluto. Here is the wolf again. Underneath that civilised Aquarian veneer with the "nice chap" persona, I think he is deeply convinced that he is, has always been, and will always be right, and that the means are justified by the end. This is his shadow side, the more primitive person hiding behind the dedicated and ethical doctor. He is both. He is a complicated man. When he finally does come out fighting, I expect that he will come out with a big club. Yet he will always have devoted followers. It seems you are one yourself.

Karen: Yes, I suppose I am. I believe in him. But I am also afraid some of this enmity he stirs up will rub off on his colleagues, and come flying at me.

Audience: Can you say something more about Pluto conjuncting the descendant?

Liz: Well, let's break it down to essentials. If something is opposite the ascendant, then it feels as though it belongs to other people and not to oneself. The ascendant is deeply bound up with one's personal destiny in life, one's individual path. The descendant appears in the guise of others. It reflects both what we try to obtain from others to make us complete, and what we oppose in others as the enemy who threatens our individual journey. The Plutonian force which Peter sees outside is both a great attraction and a great threat to him. Pluto is a kind of primordial will to survival and power, an instinctual force of nature. Here he opposes it because it seems to oppose him. Yet he was drawn into the world of healing, because of that same placement of Pluto. He saw the pain and outrage and humiliation in others, although he might not have recognised it as also his own, and he needed to become involved with it in order to feel complete. His temperament is, at least superficially, reasonable and fair. That reflects the ascendant, which he appears to have identified with, at the expense of many levels of his Sun-Moon conjunction in Scorpio. Perhaps he developed this persona because he needed to please others, and that may go back to his early relationship with his mother and father.

Audience: Could it be that when Saturn finishes its transit through the 9th, and comes into the 10th, he will be able to ground all the new ideas better? And make some kind of real commitment to a new line of work?

Liz: It could come out that way. I hope so. He will need to build something in the world. At the moment he is trying to tear something down. He is discovering his own need for power, but does not yet know how to handle it in a balanced fashion. There is a tremendous desire to have power over life and death, which I think attracts many Scorpios to the healing professions. The power problem is a dominant theme in this chart.

Karen: He is opposing the kind of power the orthodox medical establishment wields over ordinary people.

Liz: He is opposing what he sees as power because he wants it himself. This is what he does not wish to look at. He is projecting his own will to power onto the establishment. Aquarius is the great voice of the "we." One rarely hears Aquarius saying, "I want that for myself." Instead, Aquarius says, "I want that for others, because they are being unjustly deprived." Some of this is a genuine feeling for the needs of the group. Some of it is the unconscious undertow of Leo, its opposite. Probably the transit of Pluto will bring him much deeper insight. But at the moment he is busy acting it all out, and he does this because the heat is on but he is poorly related to the earth. He cannot yet contain his own affects. I suspect he really wants a great conflagration. Something in him is begging for a burning-ground from which he can emerge as a solid individual. If anyone can survive such a burning-ground, this man can.

Audience: You said earlier that he was inflated. What did you mean by that?

Liz: I am using the term "inflated" to mean that there is something in this man which identifies with the archetypal realm. It is the figure of Zeus, the enlightener who is also king of the gods, that I am thinking of. Somewhere within himself I think he secretly believes he ought to be exempt from the rules of the earthbound world which limit other people. Inflation is a psychological term which implies just what it sounds like: blown up or puffed up. One usually finds it sitting side by side with deep feelings of inadequacy. It is a natural compensation for the child who feels inferior and unloved. There is a fantasy of being divine, the child of the gods, the misunderstood genius who really knows better than everyone else. We tend to identify with the archetypal in those areas of life where we secretly feel inferior or less than human. Inflation can occur in different areas, just as feelings of inferiority can. It is a kind of spiritual inflation in Peter's case, because of the accent on the 9th house, and it compensates, I would think, for feelings of inferiority on a physical and perhaps sexual level, a sense of impotence in the face of life. You can see this kind of inflation in many religious teachers, particularly those of the Fundamentalist cast in America. They would never dream of questioning whether their views might not be universally applicable. Other people are considered intellectually or spiritually inferior or unevolved, and are therefore incapable of seeing the truth as clearly as the inflated person can. One can also see it occasionally peeping out from behind some individuals of a more mystical bias, who teach or lead groups where the emphasis is on spiritual development. They believe they are enlightening the unevolved, but never question the hidden arrogance in the assumption of who is evolved and who isn't, or even if there is such a thing at all.

Astrologically, I get the whiff of this inflation in Peter's chart from the lack of earth combined with the new Moon in Scorpio in the 9th square Pluto. A new Moon has a great deal of dynamism and will, but it can also sometimes be rather insulated and impervious to others. It has a kind of Aries flavour to it; it is the beginning of a new cycle. Even a new Moon in Pisces has this rather closed and self-absorbed quality. I think it is very difficult for anyone to really reason with Peter. He seems reasonable, but actually he is very fixed and certain of his own rightness. A little earth might have offered him some healthy cynicism about his own limits. But there is nothing to provide ballast here. Also, there is considerable pain suggested by the Moon-Pluto square, as though he has inherited a deeply despairing world-view from his mother. This is perhaps another reason why he was drawn into healing. The entire chart has a very peculiar feeling, because it falls into distinct configurations which have little connection with each other. The Scorpio group of planets aspects only Pluto, with Mars and Mercury making out-of-sign squares to Jupiter; and the Saturn-Uranus conjunction aspects only Neptune by trine. It is as though there were two people here, an airy one and a watery one, and the right hand doesn't really see what the left is doing.

Karen: I think you are right. Although I admire Peter and am concerned about him, I can see that he doesn't listen to anybody at all. He only seems to.

Liz: Well, he is asking to be burned, and will no doubt come out quite transformed from the experience. Being a good and competent doctor is not enough for Peter. It is not extraordinary enough. He wants to traffick with the gods, to be something great and glorious, to be a mouthpiece for the truth. You can see why the coagulatio stage of alchemy is such an important experience for a person who has a problem with earth. One learns some very precious and hard-won lessons.

It is also possible that Peter is picking up on collective issues which are bubbling under the surface at the moment, and that these collective unconscious movements are adding fuel to his own personal crusade. He is sensitive to underground issues because of the Saturn-Uranus conjunction. I think anyone with Saturn conjuncting an outer planet is peculiarly receptive to mass movements and trends before they rise to the surface of collective consciousness, and Uranus governs the realm of those great upheavals of ideas and ideologies which have so often created disruption and transformation in the structures of society. Also, he has a strong Pluto, and that connects him with the cyclical laws at work in the collective unconscious which call for the ending of particular world-views and social structures. There is a destroyer in him, but this destroyer is not wholly evil; it is also an intuitive knowing that the time has come for something to change. I think he is being pushed along not only because of his own personal issues, but because of this deep connection with the collective unconscious. In this sense he is right—something will have to change in the medical profession, and soon. But his way of approaching this larger issue is to generalise and cast a black cloak on the whole establishment. That reflects his complex, because in reality individual medical practitioners are all very different in their approaches, and many are open to alternative ways of looking at healing. There are a good many excellent and sensitive general practitioners who are well aware of the psychological component in the patient's illness, and who are working along these lines without making a great deal of noise about it. There are of course a few baddies, but one will find those anywhere, including the alternative medical field. It is not as split as it looks, and there is movement and progress. Moreover, Peter has forgotten that it is also the patient who requires the doctor to offer a black-and-white, concretised definition of illness with a bottle of pills. In all professions there is collusion between parties, and this is no less the case with medicine. I have done charts for people whose symptoms seem to me, from the layout of the astrological configurations, to spring from a largely psychological base, but who tell me they have been informed by their doctor that it is "an illness." When I begin to suggest that there might be some emotional strands woven into the physical ones, and that these emotional strands, if explored, might perhaps lead to a change in the physical situation, I sometimes have met the most violent resistance—not because the terrible orthodox doctor has coerced the patient into believing that everything is physical, but because the patient has an unconscious investment in not looking at the real nature of his or her problem. I have also done charts for doctors who suffer intense frustration in their attempts to help the patient recognise that the whole personality, including the personal life situation, is involved in the illness, because the patient is terrified of rocking the family boat by confrontation of any kind with the real issue. But because Peter has a split within himself, he does not recognise the subtlety in these dilemmas, and polarises what he sees outside him. He has a rigid and doctrinaire shadow which he attacks outside, but which in reality is within, making him stubborn and inflexible.

I get the impression that he is quite a brilliant man, with an exceptionally quick mind and very penetrating and profound insights. The problem is that he is exploding, when he ought to be imploding.

Karen: Is there anything I can do for him?

Liz: Probably not. I don't know what kind of relationship you really have with him. You can try talking to him, but at the moment I doubt that he can hear you. In the end he must follow his course through, and he certainly does not lack courage or resilience. He will survive whatever demons he unleashes. He will no doubt start to feel persecuted at some point, and you might be able to help him see that he is creating the very thing he accuses others of doing. Paranoia is a characteristic Scorpio problem, and also the problem of a 7th house Pluto. Having gone out and clubbed everyone over the head, he will become very hurt and offended when they hit back. But if he can't take a few punches, then he should stay out of the ring.

Scorpio is a peculiarly split sign, perhaps because of its dual rulership, and the oddity of being a watery sign with a fiery nature. Faust is a wonderful image of the Scorpio dilemma, because he contains extreme good and extreme evil. One end of this is usually projected. In Faust's case his evil manifests as Mephistopheles, his good as Gretchen. He becomes very dirtied, but at the end he is redeemed and forgiven, because he is worth it. Some Scorpios will look within, and are reflective enough to understand their own complexity. Others are more extraverted and act it out, and then the evil is always out in the world someplace – in some dreadful government or some dreadful nation or some dreadful ideology or some dreadful husband or wife or lover. But never in oneself. In Scorpio, the healer and the disease are both within the person. They cannot be separated. Scorpio as a sign has a greater affinity with alchemical thinking than with orthodox Christian thinking.

Audience: Would you say it's fanatical?

Liz: By nature, no. I would prefer the word "intense." Fanaticism, which I would define as intolerance of others having a different viewpoint, is usually the result of deep doubt or insecurity, which the individual tries to overcome by going overboard in the opposite direction. The impulse to forcibly convert others usually springs from a desperate inner compulsion to convert one's own Mephistopheles, without recognising that he is inside. Many people are fanatical without being Scorpios. But if the makings of fanaticism lie within the person, and they are also very Plutonian, then there is an enormous intensity and charisma about the whole business. I have known many quite fanatical Sagittarians as well, because sometimes a conflict arises between the natural optimism and faith of the sign and a deep cynicism and bitterness that may be connected with other, contradictory astrological significators. Fanaticism is also a quality I have encountered in some Aries people, once again because of conflict – between the natural self-will and aggression of the sign, and some other factor in the personality which suggests fragility, impotence, or inability to separate from others. In Peter's chart there is a Sagittarian emphasis because of the accented 9th house.

Karen: Sometimes I think Peter would have made a wonderful actor.

Liz: I am sure you are right. But in a sense he already is. I am not sure what drew him to medicine rather than psychology or the theatre—since these fields often overlap—but perhaps, in astrological terms, it is the MC ruler, Jupiter, in Cancer in the 6th. There is a strong sympathy for others reflected by this, and perhaps too much idealism for him to have entered a profession such as the theatre which apparently does not "help" people. I think good theatre is enormously transformative and healing, but many people do not realise this because they think of "help" as overt, obvious service which can be demonstrated in a collectively acceptable way.

There is also a great lack of patience in Peter. He is highly intuitive, and he can sense that something is happening. But he thinks it's happening now, right this minute, and he is in a hurry. Things are indeed moving in the collective unconscious, but like a pregnancy, time must be allowed for it all to ripen. Peter doesn't know how to wait. Earthy signs sometimes wait too long. Peter may have to learn through a certain amount of personal suffering, a true alchemical calcinatio and coagulatio, that he cannot save the world all by himself before next Thursday.

So, we can look once again at the transits which are approaching. In the midst of the Saturn and approaching Pluto conjunctions, Uranus is also finishing its opposition to its own place and to Saturn. This Uranus transit I think is very important, because it is releasing a great deal of energy which was previously bound up in Peter's unconscious relationship with his father. In a way this is a potential sublimatio, a period where major insights could utterly change Peter's view of himself and his life, if only he could make the connections—because he has broken out of the role of the good, obedient son, and is struggling to express his own individuality. But he does not yet see how much his impatient crusade is connected with breaking free of the parental background. This Uranus transit, which has already crossed the MC, has shaken loose a family complex as well as his identification with orthodox medicine, and I think what we are seeing is a kind of reaction to that freed energy. He is undergoing tremendous inner changes. He will probably have a bad fall, but I am sure he will pick himself up again, and will probably come out of it much more solid and better balanced. He will no doubt have to go through the fire, and then he might ground a few insights, and learn to live in the world rather than solely in his world. One doesn't know what form this calcinatio will take. There is bound to be a self-destructive impulse at work, because he is riding for a fall. Perhaps he will get himself in trouble, or struck off the medical register, or will fail to cure somebody because he has given them comfrey instead of penicillin and will wind up in court. But once he gets over the problem of bitterness and paranoia, I think he will come out very changed in a creative way.

All right, perhaps we can look at one more chart before we finish. Alison, would you like to say something about Chart 9?

Alison: This is Nick, a friend of mine. Over the past few weeks he seems to be going into some kind of breakdown. He has never been very stable, and is always moving from one flat to another, never settling anywhere. He does not work very regularly. I noticed that Neptune is transiting over his Sun at the moment, and I thought this might indicate something. From what you said, this is a state of solutio.

Liz: Yes, it has that sound. He is dissolving. This is the more frightening aspect of the solutio, because if the ego is not strong to begin with, the person can literally disintegrate and the unconscious can flood in. But I think we need to look at more than a Neptune transit across the Sun. Not everyone with this transit experiences it in this way. Is there anything that strikes any of you initially about Nick's chart?

Audience: There isn't any earth in his chart either.

Liz: Yes, I think that is a very important factor. These examples which you have given me seem to underline the importance of earth for the alchemical process. I don't think I need to keep repeating the issue of grounding and relationship to reality.

Alison: Nick constantly talks about girls. He had a relationship which lasted for about five years, which split up about a year and a half ago. His girlfriend left him. I think this was a terribly painful experience. He actually had a complete breakdown about six years ago. He was in hospital for quite some time.

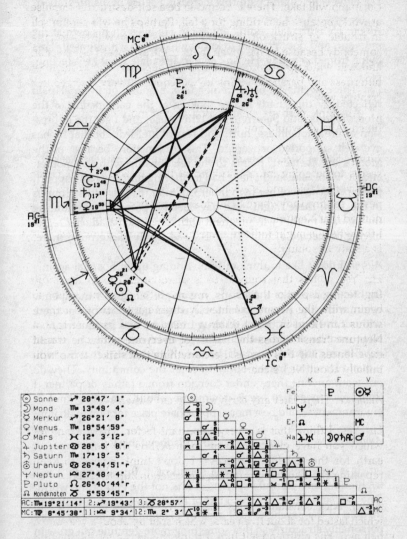

	Sonne	♐ 28°47' 1"
☽	Mond	♏ 13°49' 4"
☿	Merkur	♐ 26°21' 8"
♀	Venus	♏ 18°54'59"
♂	Mars	♓ 12° 3'12"
♃	Jupiter	♋ 28° 5' 8"r
♄	Saturn	♏ 17°19' 5"
⛢	Uranus	♋ 26°44'51"r
♆	Neptun	♎ 27°48' 4"
♇	Pluto	♌ 26°40'44"r
☊	Mondknoten	♉ 5°59'45"r

AC: ♏ 19°21'14" 2: ♐ 19°43' 3: ♑ 28°57'
MC: ♍ 8°45'38" 11: ♎ 9°34' 12: ♏ 2° 3'

Chart 9. Nick B. The birth data has been withheld for confidentiality. Chart calculated by Astrodienst, using the Placidus house system.

Liz: How is he coping with this increasing sense of disintegration?

Alison: He isn't really doing anything. He lives on his own at the moment, and doesn't seem to know what to do with himself. He's living from day to day. He isn't able to articulate what he is feeling.

Liz: There seems to be a tremendous amount of internal pain reflected by this chart. I keep looking at the conjunction of the Moon, Venus, and Saturn in the 12th house, and I get the impression of great loneliness, hurt, and fear of life. I doubt that he has ever felt supported or wanted. This conjunction, because of the Moon's involvement, points to the relationship with the mother, and problems she might have had in offering him any real support, perhaps because of her own inner isolation. Because this group is in the 12th, there might even have been events occurring during the time his mother was pregnant with him which made her regret having conceived a child. There is a sad family background there.

Alison: I don't like to think of him winding up in hospital again.

Liz: No, nor would I. Perhaps you might suggest a therapeutic community like Arbors to him. He would get containment there without the constrictions and drug treatment of a psychiatric hospital, and he would get constant psychotherapy. But he would have to ring them up himself, because Arbors insists that the individual himself or herself apply to enter the community. They do not want anyone there under coercion from a family or partner. I think Nick needs to break down and rebuild, and this kind of environment would be a more appropriate place for him to do it in.

Audience: Do you think a breakdown is inevitable?

Liz: It is very possible, from the sound of it. But although it is a frightening and painful experience, it is not the end of the world. One can sometimes see this kind of breakdown as an attempt on the part of the psyche to heal itself by dismantling a false or faulty personality structure, so that something more genuine can grow in its place. The dissolving nature of the solutio is not meant to create wanton destruction. It is meant to renew life, through cleansing all that is false and poisoned in the prima materia. I would guess that, since Nick has already had one breakdown, his manner of adaptation to life is very fragile—what Winnicott called a "false self." He has tried to function through this false self without really dealing with the deep hurt that lies underneath, and the unconscious keeps tapping him because there is unfinished business that must be worked through before he can really move out into life.

Audience: Saturn is going to transit across those 12th house planets. Would you interpret that to mean something similar to the transit in Peter's chart? That there must be a confrontation of some kind?

Liz: Yes, I think so. But here the confrontation is with inherited family problems, because it is the 12th house which is involved, and not the 9th. All the muck from the family background will rise up to be faced, and that is bound to be terribly distressing. That is why I think he needs sympathetic containment. He will probably need to regress to a very young age, and go back through the very intense early feelings, but with a different and more positive kind of mothering. A good therapeutic community can provide that kind of mothering. Saturn will make a station right on his natal Saturn and Venus, so there is a very stressful period approaching. He could get a great deal of insight from this period, and break the power which this emotionally deprived childhood has had over his life. It is also of course his Saturn return, which is an opportunity to finally learn to stand on one's own feet. But he must have room to vent some very unhappy and very chaotic feelings in a place where he does not need to feel ashamed of them. A girlfriend is not the person to burden with such powerful infantile needs. It is not surprising that she would eventually leave him.

Audience: When he is more himself, does he have a very boyish and carefree manner? I am thinking of the Sagittarian Sun.

Alison: Yes, before this difficult period started, he seemed very casual and fun-loving.

Liz: He probably will be again, but with more authenticity. There is a burden of really desperate grief and loneliness behind that exterior. You can see what I mean by a "false self." The cheerful Sagittarian characteristics are not fake, but they have become split off from the emotions reflected by the conjunction in Scorpio. I have considerable faith in the transits of Saturn, if one is prepared to do the work and make efforts to be in the right place at the right time. I think this next year's transits could create something much more solid in Nick, and the passage of Saturn over the ascendant, as well as its return, suggests a consolidation of the whole personality. This is a potential coagulatio arising out of the state of disintegration. But he will need help in doing this. He would find it immensely difficult to do on his own, because his capacity for reflection and self-containment is weak to begin with. Not only is earth missing, but he isn't too hot on air either. Only Neptune is in an air sign, which is not especially helpful.

This is a particularly watery chart, both by signs and houses. The emphasis here is in the 8th and 12th, as well as in the watery trigon. There seems to be a tremendously imaginative and sensitive nature suggested by these placements. Nick needs to work to build more detachment, because it won't come his way naturally. Access to the inner world and to the artistic realm does come naturally, because of the Neptune sextiles to the Sun and Mercury as well as all the water and fire. But he badly needs containment. The transit of Saturn is likely to bring out all the demons, and Scorpionic demons, as we have seen from Peter's chart, are larger than others. He is in a state of dissolution, and there is nothing to hold back the flood. There is nobody—no *body*—home. But there is always a teleological dimension to these alchemical stages. Neptune is not an enemy, nor is Saturn. Neptune will ultimately release the Sun, the essence of individuality, by first disintegrating everything that comprises a false individuality. It would be much better for Nick to be in a therapeutic community than in a psychiatric hospital. There are enlightened psychiatrists who might be willing to work psychotherapeutically with him, but he may be unlucky and find one of the less enlightened ones. Also, I believe that, with the emphasis he has in Scorpio, he really needs to get to the bottom of his pain, not just have it temporarily alleviated. He will never be able to express his full potential until he scours the bottom of the psychic barrel. Also, I feel it would make a difference if he voluntarily applied to Arbors or someplace like it, because being forcibly taken into hospital under a section is humiliating on some level, even if he is in too distressed a state to recognise what is happening. Don't forget the famous Scorpionic pride. Perhaps you could suggest this to him, Alison, since you are his friend. He needs this solutio, but he also needs all the help he can get with it.

Audience: You mentioned artistic ability. Do you think this would be a good direction for him?

Liz: Probably, but he is not in a position to develop it at the moment. There is great strength in Scorpio, and it does contain the capacity to renew itself even in the midst of some pretty awful psychotic states. But he could not work at the creative side right now. There is no one home to do it. Nick is disappearing, and the unconscious is taking over.

Audience: What about a spiritual community?

Liz: I am not sure about that. In some ways there is considerable containment provided by such communities. There is an entire subculture of people like Nick who have been deeply wounded early in life and have never learned to cope with reality. They take care of each other in communities of this kind, and the protection is very helpful, a kind of surrogate family which is far more genuinely loving than the real family was. But it is also a very insulated existence, and the philosophical bent of such a community might be a negative rather than a positive contribution. Nick does not need to transcend life, nor be told that his retreat is a sign of spiritual evolution rather than psychological injury. He has the Sun in the 2nd house, along with the Moon's Node in Capricorn. That suggests to me that his path is down into the earth, and that he will eventually have to learn how to ground his imagination in the material world. I have mixed feelings about the helpfulness of a spiritual community. There can be great support for a person in a breakdown state, and in many ways it is perhaps preferable to spending time in hospital. But he will have to come out again, and such communities sometimes make it difficult for a person to leave. A need to enter life may be seen as rejecting the high teachings, and the person can be made to feel guilty about abandoning the leader or guru.

Alison: A lot of women are attracted to Nick. There always seem to be women around who want to take care of him, at least for a while.

Liz: I am sure there are. But that will not help him in the end. This is only a continuous chain of mother-surrogates, and I think he needs to find an internal father rather than yet another surrogate mother. There are strong sexual issues around the mother, because of the emphasis in Scorpio and the Moon-Venus conjunction. He is rather Oedipal. But mother is also the Great Mother, and he keeps getting swallowed up by her. That is the archetypal image of a breakdown. It may sound rather cynical, but I feel that any woman who needs to validate her sexual power by propping up a wounded boy such as Nick is somewhat suspect in her motives anyway. I am not referring to friendship, but to seduction. There is usually a large string attached to the love given by such a person, and considerable manipulation underneath the surface of the relationship. This is what Nick has already experienced in childhood, and he doesn't need another repeat performance. He would be much better off getting mothering from a community, and help from a male therapist. I am sure he has great charm and attractiveness, because of the rising Venus in Scorpio. He baits his hook with: "Maybe you're the woman who can finally understand and help me." Now what kind of fish do you suppose he will catch?

Alison: He is incredibly seductive.

Liz: To a certain aspect of a woman, yes. That is lovely, but it will not help him now.

Audience: You put a lot of importance on the 2nd house Sun.

Liz: I always do on the Sun. It is the centre of the individuality. Among other things, the Sun's house placement suggests that sphere of life where the person can really build a solid sense of himself or herself. In Nick's chart it is in the house which deals with the most basic earthy realities—the relationship with the body, money, security. This is why, for him, I am somewhat dubious about the idea of a spiritual community, which might be appropriate for someone else with, say, a 9th house Sun. Also, I associate the 2nd house with the development of self-sufficiency. The Moon's South Node is in Cancer in the 8th, and the line of least resistance for Nick is dependency upon others, materially and emotionally. The tough new work lies in the 2nd house, in Capricorn's realm. I don't think in the end that his salvation lies in the arms of a woman, although there is no reason why he can't eventually have a happy relationship. But his redemption does not lie outside. It is a 2nd house redemption, which means having to learn to cope and get on with it oneself.

The very thing that reflects the wound in Nick's chart is also the thing which can ultimately heal him. The depth and vulnerability of such a strongly Plutonian nature, which so easily carries the shadowy emotional undercurrents of the family, is also the depth and sensitivity which provides the insight that can heal. Nick also has a Sun-Pluto trine, which has a great capacity for self-regeneration from very dark places. On the one hand, so much Plutonian emphasis in the chart gives him great problems, because I think he is a kind of family scapegoat, at the mercy of his mother's unconscious ambivalence and feeling everything so terribly intensely and fixedly. But the fixity also gives considerable strength, and the vulnerability considerable insight and compassion. In Greek myth, the god Asklepios, who is the divine healer, first appears in the form of the disease which afflicts the person seeking healing. It is a deep paradox; the thing which is the healer is the thing which has made one sick. The Oedipal mess which I think Nick was caught by in childhood is also the source of a deep connection with the world of the imagination—another face of the Great Mother. That is why I think it is important to look at his incipient breakdown from an alchemical perspective, and see that it might be a necessary stage of a process which can ultimately result in his emerging as a strong creative individual. It seems to me that it would be better to put energy into making sure Nick is in the right place for a deep solutio, rather than putting energy into trying to think of ways in which he could avoid it. I am not suggesting that every psychotic state is necessary and wonderful. But the psyche is not stupid. It does not waste energy in random destruction. That is the most profound message of alchemy—that there is a natural process of development at work, which conscious participation can enhance. It is not a process of random destruction, but one which moves toward something of great value—the alchemical gold. This example is very sad, but it is no less a reflection of the wisdom inherent in that process.

SUGGESTED READING

THE ASTROLOGY AND PSYCHOLOGY OF AGGRESSION

Adler, Alfred. *Superiority and Social Interest*. New York: Norton, 1979; and London: Routledge & Kegan Paul, 1965.

Dickson, Anne. *A Woman in Your Own Right*. New York and London: Quartet Books, 1982.

Segal, Hanna. *Introduction to the Work of Melanie Klein*. New York: Basic Books, 1980; and London: Hogarth Press, 1973.

Storr, Anthony. *Human Aggression*. Harmondsworth, England: Penguin Books, 1982.

DEPRESSION

Klein, Melanie. *Envy and Gratitude*. New York: Free Press, 1984; and London: Hogarth Press, 1975.

——— . *Love, Guilt and Reparation*. New York: Free Press, 1984; and London: Hogarth Press, 1975.

Kernberg, Otto. *Borderline Conditions and Pathological Narcissism*. New York: Jason Aronson Inc, 1975.

Rossner, Judith. *August*. London: Jonathan Cape Ltd, 1983.

Yates, Frances A. *The Occult Philosophy in the Elizabethan Renaissance*. New York: Methuen, 1983; and London: Routledge & Kegan Paul, 1979.

THE QUEST FOR THE SUBLIME

Assagioli, Roberto. *Psychosynthesis*. New York: Penguin, 1971; and Wellingborough, England: The Thorsons Publishing Group, 1965.

Ferguson, Marilyn. *The Aquarian Conspiracy*. Los Angeles: Jeremy Tarcher, 1981; and London: Granada, 1980.

Ferrucci, Piero. *What We May Be*. Los Angeles: Jeremy Tarcher, 1981; and Wellingborough, England: The Thorsons Publishing Group, 1982.

Frankl, Viktor. *Man's Search for Meaning*. New York: Washington Square Press, 1984.

Maslow, Abraham. *The Farther Reaches of Human Nature*. New York: Penguin, 1985.

———. *Towards A Psychology of Being*. New York: Van Nostrand, 1968.

Rowan, John. *The Reality Game*. London: Routledge & Kegan Paul, 1983.

Russell, Peter. *The Awakening Earth*. London: Routledge & Kegan Paul, 1982.

Wilber, Ken. *No Boundary*. Boston: Shambhala, 1981.

———. *Up From Eden*. Boston: Shambhala, 1983; and London: Routledge & Kegan Paul, 1983.

ALCHEMICAL SYMBOLISM IN THE HOROSCOPE

Atwood, M.A. *Hermetic Philosophy and Alchemy*. New York: The Julian Press, 1960.

Jung, C.G. *Alchemical Studies*, Vol. 13. *The Collected Works*. Bollingen Series XX. Princeton, NJ: Princeton University Press, 19xx; and London: Routledge & Kegan Paul, 1967.

———. *Mysterium Coniunctionis*, Vol. 14. *The Collected Works*. The Bollingen Series No. 20. Princeton, NJ: Princeton University Press, 1963; and London: Routledge & Kegan Paul, 1963.

———. *Psychology and Alchemy*, Vol. 12. *The Collected Works*. The Bollingen Series XX. Princeton, NJ: Princeton University Press, 19xx; and London: Routledge & Kegan Paul, 1953.

_____ . "The Psychology of the Transference." In *The Practice of Psychotherapy*, Vol. 16. *The Collected Works*. Bollingen Series No. 20. Princeton, NJ: Princeton University Press, 1985; and London: Routledge & Kegan Paul, 1954.

Von Franz, Marie-Louise. *Alchemy*. Toronto: Inner City Books, 1980.

Wilhelm, Richard. *The Secret of the Golden Flower*. New York: Harvest Book, 1970; and London: Routledge & Kegan Paul, 1931.

Yates, Frances A. *The Art of Memory*. Chicago: University of Chicago Press, 1974; and London: Routledge & Kegan Paul, 1966.

_____ . *Giordano Bruno and the Hermetic Tradition*. Chicago: University of Chicago Press, 1979; and London: Routledge & Kegan Paul, 1964.

_____ . *The Rosicrucian Enlightenment*. New York: Methuen, 1986; and London: Routledge & Kegan Paul, 1972.

ABOUT THE CENTRE
FOR PSYCHOLOGICAL ASTROLOGY

The Centre for Psychological Astrology provides a unique workshop and professional training programme designed to foster the cross-fertilisation of the fields of astrology and depth, humanistic and transpersonal psychology. The programme includes two aspects. One is a series of seminars and classes, ranging from beginners' courses in astrology to advanced seminars in psychological interpretation of the horoscope. The seminars included in this volume are representative of the latter, although the same seminar is never given verbatim more than once because the content changes according to the nature of the participating group and the new research and development which is constantly occurring within the field of psychological astrology. All these seminars and classes, both beginners' and advanced, are open to the public. The second aspect of the programme is a structured, in-depth, three-year professional training which awards a Diploma in Psychological Astrology upon successful completion of the course. The main aims and objectives of the three-year professional training are:

- To provide students with a solid and broad base of knowledge both within the realm of traditional astrological symbolism and techniques, and also in the field of psychology, so that the astrological chart can be sensitively understood and interpreted in the light of modern psychological thought.

- To make available to students psychologically qualified case supervision along with training in counselling skills and techniques which would raise the standard and effectiveness of astrological consultation.

- To encourage investigation and research into the links between astrology, psychological models and therapeutic techniques, thereby contributing to and advancing the already existing body of astrological and psychological knowledge.

The in-depth professional training programme cannot be done by correspondence, as case supervision work is an integral part of the course. It will normally take three years to complete, although it is possible for the trainee to extend this period if necessary. The training includes approximately fifty seminars (either one-day or short, ongoing weekly evening classes) as well as fifty hours of case supervision groups. The classes and seminars fall broadly into two main categories: astrological symbolism and technique (history of astrology, psychological understanding of signs, planets, houses, aspects, transits, progressions, synastry, etc.), and psychological theory (history of psychology, psychological maps and pathology, mythological and archetypal symbolism, etc.). Case supervision groups meet on weekday evenings and consist of no more than twelve people in each group. All the supervisors are both trained psychotherapists and astrologers. Each student has the opportunity of presenting for discussion case material from the charts he or she is working on. At the end of the third year, a 15,000–20,000 word paper is required. This may be on any chosen subject—case material, research, etc.—under the general umbrella of psychological astrology. Many of these papers may be of publishable quality, and the Centre will undertake facilitating such material being disseminated in the astrological field.

Completion of the seminar and supervision requirements entitles the trainee to a certificate of completion. Acceptance of the thesis entitles the trainee to the Centre's Diploma in Psychological Astrology and the use of the letters D. Psych. Astrol. The successful graduate will be able to apply the principles and techniques learned during the course to his or her professional activities, either as a consultant astrologer or as a useful adjunct to other forms of psychological counselling. Career prospects are good as there is an ever-increasing demand for the services of capable astrologers and astrologically oriented therapists. In order to complete the professional training, the Centre asks that all students, for a minimum of one year, be involved in a recognized form of psychotherapy with a therapist, analyst or counsellor of his or her choice. The rationale behind this requirement is that we believe no responsible counsellor of any persuasion can hope to deal sensitively and wisely with another person's psyche unless one has some experience of his or her own.

The seminars in this book are just four of the fifty or so workshops offered by the Centre. The next volume in this series, *The Dynamics of the Unconscious*, will include a further four seminars. As stated earlier, these seminars are never repeated in precisely the same way, as the contributions and case material from each individual group vary and as there are constant new developments and insights occurring through the ongoing work of the seminar leaders and others in the field. If the reader is interested in finding out more about either the public seminars or the in-depth professional training offered by the Centre, please write to The Centre for Psychological Astrology, P.O. Box 890, London NW3 2JZ, England.

ARKANA – NEW-AGE BOOKS FOR MIND, BODY AND SPIRIT

With over 150 titles currently in print, Arkana is the leading name in quality new-age books for mind, body and spirit. Arkana encompasses the spirituality of both East and West, ancient and new, in fiction and non-fiction. A vast range of interests are covered, including Psychology and Transformation, Health, Science and Mysticism, Women's Spirituality and Astrology.

If you would like a catalogue of Arkana books, please write to:

Arkana Marketing Department
Penguin Books Ltd
27 Wright's Lane
London W8 5TZ

ARKANA – NEW-AGE BOOKS FOR MIND, BODY AND SPIRIT

A selection of titles already published or in preparation

Neal's Yard Natural Remedies Susan Curtis, Romy Fraser and Irene Kohler

Natural remedies for common ailments from the pioneering Neal's Yard Apothecary Shop. An invaluable resource for everyone wishing to take responsibility for their own health, enabling you to make your own choice from homeopathy, aromatherapy and herbalism.

The Arkana Dictionary of New Perspectives Stuart Holroyd

Clear, comprehensive and compact, this iconoclastic reference guide brings together the orthodox and the highly unorthodox, doing full justice to *every* facet of contemporary thought – psychology and parapsychology, culture and counter-culture, science and so-called pseudo-science.

The Absent Father: Crisis and Creativity Alix Pirani

Freud used Oedipus to explain human nature; but Alix Pirani believes that the myth of Danae and Perseus has most to teach an age which offers 'new responsibilities for women and challenging questions for men' – a myth which can help us face the darker side of our personalities and break the patterns inherited from our parents.

Woman Awake: A Celebration of Women's Wisdom Christina Feldman

In this inspiring book, Christina Feldman suggests that it *is* possible to break out of those negative patterns instilled into us by our social conditioning as women: confirmity, passivity and surrender of self. Through a growing awareness of the dignity of all life and its connection with us, we can regain our sense of power and worth.

Water and Sexuality Michel Odent

Taking as his starting point his world-famous work on underwater childbirth at Pithiviers, Michel Odent considers the meaning and importance of water as a symbol: in the past – expressed through myths and legends – and today, from an advertisers' tool to a metaphor for aspects of the psyche. Dr Odent also boldly suggests that the human species may have had an aquatic past.

ARKANA – NEW-AGE BOOKS FOR MIND, BODY AND SPIRIT

A selection of titles already published or in preparation

Head Off Stress: Beyond the Bottom Line D. E. Harding

Learning to head off stress takes no time at all and is impossible to forget – all it requires is that we dare take a fresh look at ourselves. This infallible and revolutionary guide from the author of *On Having No Head* – whose work C. S. Lewis described as 'highest genius' – shows how.

Shiatzu: Japanese Finger Pressure for Energy, Sexual Vitality and Relief from Tension and Pain
Yukiko Irwin with James Wagenvoord

The product of 4000 years of Oriental medicine and philosophy, Shiatzu is a Japanese variant of the Chinese practice of acupuncture. Fingers, thumbs and palms are applied to the 657 pressure points that the Chinese penetrate with gold and silver needles, aiming to maintain health, increase vitality and promote well-being.

The Magus of Strovolos: The Extraordinary World of a Spiritual Healer Kyriacos C. Markides

This vivid account introduces us to the rich and intricate world of Daskalos, the Magus of Strovolos – a true healer who draws upon a seemingly limitless mixture of esoteric teachings, psychology, reincarnation, demonology, cosmology and mysticism, from both East and West.

'This is a really marvellous book . . . one of the most extraordinary accounts of a "magical" personality since Ouspensky's account of Gurdjieff' – Colin Wilson

Meetings With Remarkable Men G. I. Gurdjieff

All that we know of the early life of Gurdjieff – one of the great spiritual masters of this century – is contained within these colourful and profound tales of adventure. The men who influenced his formative years had no claim to fame in the conventional sense; what made them remarkable was the consuming desire they all shared to understand the deepest mysteries of life.

ARKANA – NEW-AGE BOOKS FOR MIND, BODY AND SPIRIT

A selection of titles already published or in preparation

The TM Technique Peter Russell

Through a process precisely opposite to that by which the body accumulates stress and tension, transcendental meditation works to produce a state of profound rest, with positive benefits for health, clarity of mind, creativity and personal stability. Peter Russell's book has become the key work for everyone requiring a complete mastery of TM.

The Development of the Personality: Seminars in Psychological Astrology Volume I Liz Greene and Howard Sasportas

Taking as a starting point their groundbreaking work on the cross-fertilization between astrology and psychology, Liz Greene and Howard Sasportas show how depth psychology works with the natal chart to illuminate the experiences and problems all of us encounter throughout the development of our individual identity, from childhood onwards.

Homage to the Sun: The Wisdom of the Magus of Strovolos
Kyriacos C. Markides

Homage to the Sun continues the adventure into the mysterious and extraordinary world of the spiritual teacher and healer Daskalos, the 'Magus of Strovolos'. The logical foundations of Daskalos' world of other dimensions are revealed to us – invisible masters, past-life memories and guardian angels, all explained by the Magus with great lucidity and scientific precision.

The Year I: Global Process Work Arnold Mindell

As we approach the end of the 20th century, we are on the verge of planetary extinction. Solving the planet's problems is literally a matter of life and death. Arnold Mindell shows how his famous and groundbreaking process-orientated psychology can be extended so that our own sense of global awareness can be developed and we – the whole community of earth's inhabitants – can comprehend the problems and work together towards solving them.